The historical anthropology of early modern Italy

The historical anthropology of early modern Italy

Essays on perception and communication

PETER BURKE

Fellow of Emmanuel College
Cambridge

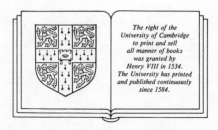

The right of the
University of Cambridge
to print and sell
all manner of books
was granted by
Henry VIII in 1534.
The University has printed
and published continuously
since 1584.

CAMBRIDGE UNIVERSITY PRESS

Cambridge
London   New York   New Rochelle
Melbourne   Sydney

Published by the Press Syndicate of the University of Cambridge
The Pitt Building, Trumpington Street, Cambridge, CB2 1RP
32 East 57th Street, New York, NY 10022, USA
10 Stamford Road, Oakleigh, Melbourne 3166, Australia

First published 1987

Printed in Great Britain by the University Press, Cambridge

British Library cataloguing in publication data
Burke, Peter.
The historical anthropology of early modern Italy:
essays on perception and communication.
1. Italy – Civilization – 1559–1789
I. Title
945'.07 DG445

Library of Congress cataloguing in publication data
Burke, Peter.
The historical anthropology of early modern Italy:
essays on perception and communication.
Bibliography.
1. Italy – Civilization – 1268–1559.
2. Italy – Civilization – 1559–1789.
I.   Title.

DG455.B84   1987   945   86-18830

ISBN 0 521 32041 0

UP

For Dora

Contents

Illustrations

Preface

The following sixteen essays deal with cultural history, mainly that of Italy in the sixteenth and seventeenth centuries. I have written them in the hope that some at least will be read not only by historians but by specialists in art and literature, sociology and anthropology, whether they have a special interest in Italy or not, and so I have tried to place Italy in a comparative framework and to refer to other parts of Europe. Reference is also frequently made to works on social theory, not so much to appeal to anthropologists and sociologists as because I believe that their concepts, models and theories can illuminate the past as well as the present. It is for this reason that the essays are described as contributions to 'historical anthropology', a term which is discussed in chapter 1 below. The research in Italy on which they are based was made possible by a five-year grant from the Social Science Research Council (as it then was), and by a grant from the Research Fund of Emmanuel College. I am extremely grateful for both.

A few of these essays have already appeared in print, though they have been revised to include new ideas and new information as well as to make the collection more unified. Chapter 4 appeared in Italian in *Quaderni storici* 41 (1979); chapter 5 in *Religion and Society*, ed. K. von Greyerz (London, Allen and Unwin, 1984); chapter 7 in *History Workshop Journal*, 1981; chapter 10 in *Kwartalnik Historyczny Kultury Materialniej* 1982; chapter 13, in French, in *Les jeux à la Renaissance*, ed. P. Ariès and J. C. Margolin (Paris, Vrin, 1982); chapter 14 in *Past and Present* 99 (1983). I should like to thank the respective publishers for permission to reprint. I am also grateful for constructive comments to the different audiences on which early versions of these papers were tried out, notably those at Amsterdam (ch. 8); Budapest (chs. 12, 16); Cambridge (chs. 6, 8, 10, 11, 13, 15, 16); Melbourne (chs. 11, 13); Oxford (chs. 8, 16); Paris (ch. 6); Princeton (ch. 8); Tours (ch. 13); Venice (ch. 3); Warsaw (ch. 10); Wellington (ch. 16); and York (ch. 11).

I am indebted to many predecessors in the various fields invaded here, and especially to a few individuals with whom I have regularly shared problems and discoveries, notably to Anton Blok, Natalie Davis, Carlo Ginzburg, Gábor Klaniczay, Roy Porter, Simon Price, Bob Scribner, and Keith Thomas (my mentor for more than twenty-five years.)

References

References to primary sources are given in the notes; secondary sources are referred to by the author–date system in the text, with full details in the bibliography. For the citation of manuscripts, the following abbreviations are employed:

ACG   Archivio del Comune, Genoa

ASF   Archivio di Stato, Florence

ASG   Archivio di Stato, Genoa

ASM   Archivio di Stato, Milan

ASR   Archivio di Stato, Rome

ASV   Archivio di Stato, Venice

BN   British Library

BN   Bibliothèque Nationale, Paris

BNF   Biblioteca Nazionale, Florence

TCG   Tribunale Criminale del Governatore

I
Introduction

I
The historical anthropology of early modern Italy

What is historical anthropology?

These essays on early modern Italy are offered as an example of 'historical anthropology'. The term has come into use in the last decade or so to refer to the work of Carlo Ginzburg, Emmanuel Le Roy Ladurie, Keith Thomas and a number of others. Is it anything more than a fashionable new term for social history? If so, what is distinctive about it?

I do not want to overemphasise the uniformity or the intellectual coherence of a movement which has appealed to different historians for different reasons. Some historical anthropologists are especially concerned with symbolism, others with material life; some with theory and comparison, others with local particulars. Despite the diversity of its practitioners, however, the term 'historical anthropology' does describe a distinctive approach to history. Five features in particular distinguish it from other kinds of social history.

1. Much recent work in social history has attempted to describe general trends on the basis of quantitative evidence; but historical anthropology is deliberately qualitative and concentrates on specific cases.

2. Many works of social history describe the lives of millions of people. Works of historical anthropology, however, are often deliberately microscopic and focus on small communities, such as Le Roy Ladurie's Montaillou, in order to achieve greater depth as well as more colour and life.

3. Many social historians offer causal explanations of trends over time, explanations which contemporaries would not have understood, concerned with trends of which they were often unaware. By contrast, historical anthropologists concentrate on what, following Clifford Geertz (1973) is often called 'thick description', in other words the interpretation of social interaction in a given society in terms of that society's own norms and categories.

4. The place of symbolism in everyday life has tended to be neglected

by both cultural historians (concerned with 'works of art') and social historians (concerned with social 'reality'). Historical anthropologists, on the other hand, make it one of their central concerns, and try to show, for example, how 'apparently trivial routines and rituals have an important role in maintaining or enforcing a certain world view' (Löfgren, 1981). Hence they have paid attention to the significance of the clothes people wear, the food they eat, the ways in which they address one another, and the manner in which they hold themselves, gesture, or walk.

5. Social history is informed – directly or indirectly – by the theories of Karl Marx and Max Weber. Historical anthropologists tend to be interested in theory, but their 'great tradition' runs from Emile Durkheim, through Arnold van Gennep (1908) on 'rites of passage' and Marcel Mauss (1923–4) on the meaning of gifts, to contemporary figures such as Geertz, Victor Turner and Pierre Bourdieu, and historical analysis would benefit if it drew more heavily on this tradition.

These contrasts should not be exaggerated. Quantitative and qualitative, microsocial and macrosocial approaches to the past are, or at any rate should be, complementary not contradictory, for case-studies are needed to show how major trends affected the lives of individuals, while statistical analysis is required to show that the cases discussed are really typical, and of what. Was Montaillou, for example, a typical medieval village? A typical Mediterranean village? A typical Languedoc village? Or was it not typical at all?

The contrast which has just been drawn between sociology and social anthropology was never all that clear and it has become increasingly blurred. Durkheim can be claimed for both disciplines. The Chicago school of symbolic interactionism was a movement within sociology which emphasised small groups, symbolism, and the importance of the participants' (or 'actors') own definitions of the situation. Erving Goffman, who owed a good deal to this tradition, is another figure who can equally well be claimed for anthropology or sociology. In any case, in calling this volume of essays a study in historical anthropology, I have no intention of rejecting either the global (macroscopic) view or quantitative methods (where these are appropriate). The point of the title is essentially that the historical problems discussed in the essays, on the border between traditional 'social' and traditional 'cultural' history, are ones which yield with least difficulty to a microscopic, qualitative approach.

As for perception and communication, these themes are central to any idea of culture, vague or precise, wide or narrow, high or low.

Structuralists regard culture as a communication system, a language (with its 'grammars' or rules for eating food, wearing clothes, and so on), or a 'system of signs', which can be 'read' like a text. As a cultural historian I have found some of these ideas stimulating and suggestive; the idea, for example that 'a sign or symbol only acquires meaning when it is discriminated from some other contrary sign or symbol' (Leach, 1976, p. 49), does help make sense of many phenomena in early modern Europe, from conspicuously splendid palaces to aggressively simple rituals.

The stumbling-block for historians who try to come to terms with the ideas of the structuralists is their wilful lack of concern with change, local context and individual intentions. To historians it seems obvious that the meaning of a sign changes in the course of time, varies with the situation in which it is used, and may be manipulated by the individual using it – which is not to deny the possibility of the sign in some sense manipulating the user. The essay on the art of insult (ch. 8 below) is an attempt to show both processes at work.

If they had not reacted against common-sense views, the structuralists would not have achieved their new insights. All the same, it is worth asking whether they may not have over-reacted, or, more constructively, whether it may be possible to domesticate the structuralist mind, to write the history of the 'grammar' of a culture and relate it to the messages emitted by individuals using this grammar, and the perception and interpretation of these messages by their recipients. This approach to culture as a communication system has the advantage of allowing historians to discuss the relation between specific texts or artifacts and the society in which they were produced without assuming that culture is some kind of 'superstructure', as the Marxists used to say, which simply reflects the 'real' changes taking place below.

Anthropologists have much to say about both perception and communication. On the perception side, they have suggested that what we rather too easily call 'social reality' should be regarded as no more than a shared image, what Durkheim used to call a 'collective representation'. Gender, for example, or illness – however natural they appear everywhere – are cultural 'constructions' in the sense that the characteristics attributed to sickness and health, males and females, vary from one culture to another. Hence 'man' and 'woman', 'healer' and 'sufferer' are social roles which have to be learned (Ortner and Whitehead, 1981; Kapferer, 1983). Again, it has been argued by a sociologist of the symbolic interaction school that 'social groups create deviance by making the rules whose infraction constitutes deviance and by applying those rules to particular people and labelling them as outsiders' (Becker, 1963). The outsiders may be madmen (Foucault, 1961), witches (Cohn, 1975) or beggars (below, ch. 6). The 'thick description' of the anthropologists may be redefined as a form of translation, a making explicit, for the benefit of non-members, of the rules implicit in a given culture.

These 'rules', it should be pointed out, do not determine behaviour. They may be broken (at the price of giving offence). In practice they are applied flexibly rather than mechanically. There may not be a complete consensus in a given society as to what these rules are. The idea of rules remains a useful one, and so does the attempt to tell the modern reader how he or she would have been expected to behave in another century; how to be polite, for example, or how to be insulting, how to be a thief, how to be a saint (below, chs. 5–8). This approach is not unlike a literary and art-historical tradition of studying the making, survival and breaking of stereotypes, a tradition associated with the Warburg Institute (Warburg, 1893; Gombrich, 1960; Baxandall, 1972). Perception has a history.

Forms of communication such as rituals are a long-standing interest of anthropologists, but communication became a centre of attention when they broke with the tradition of functionalism, in other words the study of the manner in which ideas and institutions are related to one another within a social (or cultural) system. This approach seemed to discourage any awareness of conflict or change, and it has been replaced by one which stresses process and views society in terms of interaction or 'transaction' (Barth, 1967, Kapferer, 1976). It was at the time of this debate, and in this context, that a group of American scholars established the discipline variously known as the sociology of language or the ethnography of communication, defined as the study of messages (or 'communicative events'), their channels and codes, senders and receivers, occasions and settings (Hymes 1964), or, more briefly, 'Who speaks what language to whom and when?' (Fishman, 1965). A classic example – of obvious relevance to historians of Italy – is an essay with the intriguing title, 'How to ask for a drink in Subanun', which is in fact a discussion of the whole complex of conventions surrounding drinking in that culture (Frake, 1964).

It is from this ethnographical perspective that I wish to look at various kinds of communicative event in early modern Italy, including speech and writing, politeness and insult, texts and images, official rituals and unofficial ones. My vocabulary of analysis will draw on this tradition as on that of symbolic interactionism, and terms such as 'transaction', 'negotiation', 'definition of the situation', 'presentation of self' and 'social drama' will recur in these pages. However, I shall try to integrate this approach with a cultural historian's concern with changes in symbolism over time, over some three or four hundred years (the essays focus on the sixteenth and seventeenth centuries, but move earlier or later as the subject requires).

The urban mosaic

These essays are not concerned with the whole of early modern Italy (ten million or more people at any one time, 90% of them living in the countryside), but with a few of the largest cities: with Milan, Genoa, Venice, Florence, Rome and Naples. A historical anthropology of Italian peasant society would be well worth attempting, but the attempt will not be made here (for further information, see Doria, 1968; McArdle, 1978). To study these cities, the concepts developed by urban sociologists and anthropologists have proved to be particularly useful.

In the 1920s, the leader of the so-called 'Chicago School' of urban sociology, Robert Park, recommended 'fieldwork' in the streets. 'The same patient methods of observation', he wrote,

> which anthropologists like Boas and Lowie have expended on the study of the life and manners of the American Indian might be even more fruitfully employed in the investigation of the customs, beliefs, social practices and general conceptions of life prevalent in Little Italy or the Lower North Side in Chicago, or in recording the more sophisticated folkways of the inhabitants of Greenwich Village and the neighbourhood of Washington Square, New York.
>
> (Park, 1916).

Over the last quarter-century or so, as the Third World has become hyper-urbanised, Park's advice has been taken more seriously. Social anthropologists have been turning their attention to the city, and a considerable body of work now exists dealing with the life of migrants and with their urban 'villages'. Some of it is of great interest to anyone concerned with perception and communication.

The crucial point was made by Park when he described the city, in a memorable phrase, as 'a mosaic of little worlds which touch but do not penetrate'. 'Space speaks' as one anthropologist puts it (Hall, 1959, ch. 10), and territoriality is particularly audible, or visible, in the city. All the Italian cities which will be discussed below were divided into social zones. In Florence, the parish of San Frediano was a low-rent area inhabited by the lowest-paid workers in the cloth industry (readers of the novels

of Vasco Pratolini will recall that the district was still a working-class one
after the Second World War). In Rome, Trastevere was a poor quarter
in early modern times as in classical antiquity; its very name reminds us
that it was on the wrong side of the Tiber. In Naples, Piazza Lavinaro,
Piazza Mercato, and Piazza Selleria formed a poor quarter which was the
main setting for the revolt of Masaniello (below, ch. 14). The upper
classes also had their zones. In Venice, for example, the patricians took
over the main square, Piazza San Marco, between five and eight in the
evening, thus giving a clear answer to the question, Whose City? Nobles
did not like commoners to come too close, and a Genoese patrician
records smugly in his diary that he told someone who did this 'you don't
see me' (*non mi vedi*), and then 'gave him a good slap' (*gli diedi un buon
schiaffo*), following it up with his dagger when the man resisted. He clearly
felt that what Goffman calls the 'territories of the self' had been invaded.[1]

The territorial imperative may have been particularly strong among
Genoese patricians, for some of them laid claim to particular squares,
which would have been public space in other cities. Piazza San Matteo,
for example, was Doria territory, while Piazza San Luca was in dispute
in 1565 between the Spinola and the Grimaldi, each clan claiming the
right to light a bonfire there to celebrate St John's Eve, and of course to
symbolise their possession (Grendi, 1975). This was an extreme case, but
territorial conflicts between nobles seem to have been commonplace in
the late Middle Ages, when the proliferation of noble towers gave most
Italian cities the appearance which only San Gimignano retains today,
and chains were regularly stretched across the streets to repel cavalry
(Heers, 1974, 146f).

Another point to make about the 'urban mosaic' is the coexistence of
what Park called 'contiguous but otherwise widely separated worlds', or
sub-cultures. In the city, the individual's status was (and is) largely
determined by what Park called 'front'; in other words by clothes,
gestures, expression, accent and other conventional signs. These signs are
described in detail in the literature of the picaresque, in which the rogue
hero learns to move quickly from one urban sub-culture to another and
so to 'pass' for what he is not. This literature was created and developed
in early modern Spain, but it was sometimes set in Italian cities and it
was in any case much appreciated in Italy, as the number of editions and
translations shows (below, p. 66). In our own day the outstanding observer
of this kind of 'impression management', as he called it, was Goffman,
and it has been suggested that the city was the natural stage for his
dramaturgical perspective (Hannerz, 1980).

Façades

If space speaks, and clothes communicate, it is obvious that different forms of speech, writing and ritual carry their own messages. The types of communication studied in this book could easily have been extended. It might, for example, have included tears, which may flow 'naturally' in most cases, but are governed by cultural conventions none the less. In early modern Italy, as in other parts of Europe at this time, it was neither unusual nor unseemly for men to weep in public, at least on certain kinds of occasion. An effective sermon on Christ's Passion, for example, was supposed to leave the congregation drying their eyes. In Florence at the end of the fifteenth century, the followers of fra Girolamo Savonarola, who was among other things an effective preacher, were nicknamed the 'snivellers' (*piagnoni*). Rage as well as piety could find expression in tears, as in the case of the quarrel between Nicholas of Cusa and pope Pius II recorded in the latter's autobiography (Book VII).

Joking is another form of communication, and the history of its conventions is only just beginning to be written (Thomas, 1977; Dekker and Roodenburg, 1984). They certainly differ a good deal from one period to another. If we were to visit early modern Italy, we might well find it difficult to adjust to a sense of humour which is now virtually confined to barracks (or its civilian equivalent, the college). Even at the court of Urbino, as described in Castiglione's *Courtier*, which is nothing if not idealised, pellets of bread were thrown at table. Practical jokes of different kinds were much enjoyed. Many sources confirm this propensity for *burle* or *beffe*, as these jokes were called. A comparison of the motifs of the Italian short story of the period, the *novella*, with those of folktales elsewhere suggests that the Italians were peculiarly fascinated by trickery and especially by the theme of the victim's humiliation (Rotunda, 1942). Practical jokes were literally built into Italian country houses such as the sixteenth-century Medici villa at Pratolino, where the host was able to drench his guests as they strolled in his garden, turning the spectators into the spectacle.[2]

The modern reader is likely to find both the joking and the weeping rather theatrical, at least if he or she belongs to a less demonstrative northern European culture. Goffman offered his analyses as if they were true of society in general, and he has a point; we all act in public, and perhaps in private as well. However, some societies, in some periods, seem to encourage this style of behaviour more than others, and the dramaturgical approach seems peculiarly appropriate to Italy in the early

modern period, the age of the Renaissance and the Baroque. Italy was
a 'theatre society' (*società spettacolo*; Titone, 1978, p. 116), where it was
necessary to play one's social role with style, *fare bella figura*, to work hard
at creating and maintaining as well as saving 'face'. There is of course
a danger for a northerner of seeing Italian society in stereotyped terms,
so it is worth pointing out that awareness of the theatre of everyday life
was expressed in the language of the time. In the autobiography, or better,
the memories and reflections of the seventeenth-century Neapolitan
lawyer Francesco D'Andrea, the author criticises a local noble who finds
nothing better to do than to show himself off on the piazza (*andar facendo
il bello in piazza*); on the other hand, he recommends a legal career to
his nephews because it offers an opportunity 'for showing off one's
talents' (*di far pompa del proprio talanto*).[3] In this respect, Italy was and
is part of the wider Mediterranean culture. 'Here, if you don't show off,
you are dead', as a Lebanese villager remarked to a visiting anthropologist
(Gilsenan, 1976, p. 198). The Mediterranean world is a world where life
(more exactly, male life) is lived in public, on the square, which is well
adapted to both performance and observation.

In sixteenth-century Italy, the café did not exist. It arrived, with coffee,
in the seventeenth century, and developed into a social institution – in
Venice and Milan, at least – in the course of the eighteenth century.
However, there were other forms of sociability. The nobles had their
loggias or 'porticos' to meet in (different porticos for different factions
in the case of Genoa and Naples), or they took over the public square
for part of the day, as at Venice, for what was called the *broglio*, a political
marketplace where deals were clinched to the accompaniment of many
compliments and much bowing and hand-kissing.[4] Merchants too, had
their public meeting-places, like the Rialto in Venice or the Mercato
Nuovo in Florence, and here too bargaining would take place in the open,
before the eyes of spectators. Respectable women were supposed to stay
indoors, but they could always observe public life from their balconies.

In such an urban setting, religion was virtually bound to take on a
particularly theatrical quality, whether in the Milan of San Carlo
Borromeo (1538–84), the Rome of Bernini, or the Naples of the Jesuit
missions of the middle of the seventeenth century. Solemn processions
wound through the streets and squares on important occasions, while city
centres were turned into sets for these performances by the erection of
statues or crosses; thirty-three in Borromeo's Milan, to allow the Stations
of the Cross to take place in the open (Buratti, 1982). Whole squares
might be reconstructed for liturgical reasons, as in the famous case of

Bernini's Piazza San Pietro (below, p. 180). The processions themselves were highly dramatic affairs, at least in some instances. In Naples, during the Jesuit missions of the 1650s, men walked hatless – unusual in those days – and barefoot, 'with crowns of thorns on their heads, ropes round their necks, and bones, skulls or small crucifixes in their hands'. They whipped themselves or beat their breasts with stones until the blood flowed. The hell-fire sermons preached during the missions were also dramatic performances, accompanied by shouts as well as by music.[5]

In this case violence was turned inward, against the self. Equally spectacular, however, were its secular, outward forms, whether duels (in the case of nobles) or brawls (in the case of the lower classes). The records of many quarrels suggest that they had a distinctly theatrical quality. For example, in the journal kept by a Genoese patrician between 1583 and 1589, references to disputes between his peers are not infrequent. *E seguito una costione*, 'there followed a quarrel', is a recurrent entry. The diarist obviously considered these events to be memorable. However, the participants rarely got beyond 'giving the lie' (*una mentita*, cf. p. 96 below), and its reply, a slap on the face, before they were parted and peace was made by a third party. As another patrician observed a few years later, the Genoese do not like to fight.[6] The quarrels of the Genoese patricians, like the fights observed not long ago by an anthropologist on Tory Island, were usually no more than a stereotyped, ritualised sequence of words and gestures which could be all the more violent because the participants could count on being separated by their friends before blood really flowed (Fox, 1977; cf. Bourdieu, 1965, p. 201).

It was not only among the merchant patricians of Genoa that violence was ritualised. The cases of 'excess' (*eccesso*) and 'insolence' (*insolenze*), which came before the tribunal of the Governor of Rome in the sixteenth and seventeenth centuries (below, ch. 8), also have a stereotyped quality as if the actors were following a script, had rehearsed their parts and had their eyes at least as much on the audience as on one another. A quarrel had to begin dramatically, to attract bystanders. You might knock loudly, for example, on the door of your enemy's house, shouting insults or singing verses in his contempt at the top of your voice; or you might strut up and down the street, sword under arm, looking into the other man's shop each time you passed, an action which would lead naturally to the stereotyped sequence, 'What are you looking at?' 'I look at whatever I like' (*Io guardo quello che mi pare*). There was a special word for this kind of behaviour, which came into use in the sixteenth century: *bravare*.[7]

I would not wish to suggest that threats of violence were always empty;

the judicial records are full of evidence to the contrary. But the fact that blood really flowed on occasion does not make the occasion less dramatic. The point I want to make here is one about the style of violence, the cultural rules of disorder or excess, and the need to act one's part well – to the death, if need be – before an audience of whose reactions the actors seem to have been acutely conscious. A case of 'insolence' to a judge, in Rome in 1617, began with the accused coming into the office in a rage. 'He began to raise his voice and shout...and throw his hat and his bundle to the ground, shouting...Justice, Justice.'[8]

Love had its rules as well as hate. As a student of eighteenth-century Venetian rape trials recently observed, as she described the way in which the preliminary period of courtship was managed, 'It is striking how well he [the accused] played the lover's part' (Gambier, 1980, p. 547). Politeness too had an element of theatre about it. At the papal court, the instructions for cardinals who were seeing distinguished visitors out instructed them not only to go to the top of the stairs but 'to pretend to want to descend' (*fingere di voler scendere*; below, p. 171).

It is difficult for northern Europeans to take this kind of behaviour quite seriously because to them it is likely to appear exaggerated. As Joseph Addison observed, 'The Italian epitaphs are often more extravagant than those of other countries, as the nation is more given to compliment and hyperbole.' Petitions to the courts tend to use flowery language with phrases like 'prostrate at the feet of your honour, with tears in my eyes...'[9] It seems to be laid on too thick, and the impression of artifice is increased because the petitions – as the elegance of the handwriting makes abundantly clear – were not the petitioner's own work but those of one of the public scribes. One could be reading fragments from the libretto of an Italian opera of the period. A similar impression is left by the discovery that a town house of moderate dimensions was known in Italy as a 'palace', and that the buildings which lie behind the grandiose marble façades of Renaissance and baroque churches are often relatively low-slung (below, ch. 15). Early modern Italy may well appear to have been a land of façades.

The judgement is too simple. We can learn from the anthropologists to beware of making crude contrasts between 'Them' and 'Us'. Goffman's metaphor of the theatre of everyday life was intended to refer to everyone, not just the Italians. And yet...there is a significant contrast to be made between the cultural styles of northern and southern Europe, if only it can be made with more finesse and formulated in a less ethnocentric way.

The sociologist Norbert Elias (1939, 114f) described what he called the 'threshold of embarrassment' in western civilisation and the way in which it was raised over the centuries. In a similar manner, it might be useful to speak of a 'sincerity threshold' which varies from one time and place to another (cf. Trilling, 1972). We might say that the sincerity threshold is higher in the West than (say) in China and Japan, and higher in northern Europe than in the south; and also that it has been raised at various times, notably the eighteenth century (below, p. 236). It might be added that a kind of sliding scale operates, so that a stress on sincerity in a given culture tends to be associated with a lack of emphasis on other qualities, such as courtesy.

Some contemporaries (such as D'Andrea, who has already been quoted), were well aware of the theatrical quality of Italian social life. This is scarcely surprising. Paradoxical as it may seem on the surface, sincerity cultures need a greater measure of self-deception than the rest, – since we are all actors – while 'theatre cultures', as we may call them, are able to cultivate the self-awareness they value less. In his famous treatise on the courtier, Baldassare Castiglione does not so much anticipate as out-Goffman Goffman in his discussion of the quality he called 'negligence' (*sprezzatura*), a graceful and apparently natural style of behaviour which requires considerable attention (and doubtless repeated rehearsals), to produce the illusion of effortless spontaneity (Book 1, ch. 26). The literature of the early modern period is full of references to the 'masks' and 'cloaks' which cover mens' true motives. There were many discussions of the art of dissimulation in early modern Italy; the art of painting façades, one might say. One of the most thorough discussions of the subject, Torquato Accetto's essay *Della disimulazione onesta* (1641), deals with the pleasure given by dissimulation, the practice necessary to perfect it, and so on. Not that Accetto recommends all forms of deceit. As the title of his treatise indicates, his concern is with *honourable* dissimulation. The qualification *onesta* is crucial.

It is crucial because it introduces the idea of honour, an idea which is central to theatre cultures, past and present; indeed, 'honour cultures' is a better term for them, and will be used henceforward. Honour was a much-debated subject in early modern Italy. The debaters were concerned with the problems of defining it (in terms of public 'reputation', and so on); winning it (whether by valour or 'magnificence', in other words conspicuous consumption; maintaining it (by being 'jealous' of it); losing it (by lack of virtue, accepting an insult, or by the adultery of one's wife); and regaining it (by violence or litigation).[10] The converse of honour was 'shame', *vergogna*. Honourable men would speak of 'dying' of shame (hyperbole again), and the so-called 'shamefaced poor' (*poveri vergognosi*) were impoverished nobles who were almost as ashamed to beg as they would have been to work. They not infrequently escaped from their dilemma by a form of dissimulation, begging in masks.

Such was the code for honourable men. For women, *vergogna* was a term of praise, their form of honour, since it implied a sensitivity to shame which kept them from 'shameless' behaviour, or more exactly from the appearances of such behaviour, which were what really mattered. Even the law recognised this; in Venice in 1697, a case brought against a prostitute was dismissed because she had avoided 'scandal' by keeping up appearances (Derosas, 1980, p. 460). One might say that what appearances required was low visibility in the case of women, high visibility in that of men. In this culture great importance was given to what Goffman (1955) has called 'face-work' defined as 'the actions taken by a person to make whatever he is doing consistent with face'. There was a sense in which one was not supposed to look behind façades, although it is clear that this kind of prying was taking place all the time. Witnesses under interrogation often begin their testimony with the stereotyped phrase 'I mind my own business' (*non tengo conto dei fatti d'altri*), in homage to this cult of appearances; and then they go on to reveal the most intimate details of the private lives of their neighbours.

This code of honour, which extended to craftsmen and shopkeepers (as ch. 8 will attempt to show), was part of a more general system of values. My aim, in the essays collected here, which might have been entitled 'Scenes from the Drama of Everyday Life', is to present this cultural code in action by analysing a small selection of different kinds of message.

2
The sources:
outsiders and insiders

Appropriating some of the concepts of social anthropologists is one thing; adopting their methods quite another. How can historians do 'fieldwork' among the dead? What substitute can they find for direct observation or for questioning informants? Historical sources can usefully be divided not only into 'primary' and 'secondary' but also into documents produced by insiders and outsiders respectively. The historian's instinct is to prefer the insiders, the indigenous inhabitants, the people who lived in the period under study. After all, it was *their* culture. There is, however, a problem. It is a common enough problem for historians, but it is particularly acute in the case of the history of communication and perception. It is that insiders are rarely conscious of their own cultural codes. They take for granted much of what the historian most wants to discover. The historian of the Venetian carnival or papal ritual who turns to a sixteenth-century diarist for details, for example, may find no more than a curt, cryptic, tantalising reference to 'the usual festivities' (below, pp. 177, 184).

The alien eye: the testimonies of travellers

In this situation, there would seem to be a case for inverting the normal order of things and beginning with the testimony of the outsiders, in other words foreign travellers to Italy. In the age of the Renaissance and the Grand Tour, these travellers were numerous, despite the discomfort felt by good Protestants in a Catholic country. Scores of their impressions have survived, whether in print or manuscript, noted on the spot or written up afterwards.[1] The concerns of these travellers were, naturally enough, extremely diverse, but a substantial minority were either interested at the start, or became interested in the course of their visit, in the very topics which now fascinate some cultural historians. Their testimonies are highly explicit, with all the freshness of a first impression. Some of them were highly intelligent and observant, and a few wrote well into the bargain. Montaigne, Montesquieu and Goethe remain the most

famous of these travellers, but the British contingent alone included men
of the calibre of John Evelyn, Gilbert Burnet, and Joseph Addison, as
well as two men who owe their reputation to their travel diaries, Thomas
Coryate and Fynes Moryson. These witnesses deserve to be taken
seriously.

Taking it seriously does not of course mean believing every word they
wrote. Like other types of historical document, the accounts of travellers
abroad need to undergo critical examination to reveal both specific
inaccuracies and general bias. They sometimes received an examination
of this kind in their own day, like Samuel Sharp's *Letters from Italy in
the Years 1765 and 66*, which irritated Giuseppe Baretti, a Piedmontese
who had settled in England in 1751, into publishing his own account of
Italian manners and customs. It begins with the heading 'Accounts of
travellers not much to be credited, and why Mr Sharp is not fit to describe
the Italians', and it goes on to make some severe but acute remarks about
people who 'inspect countries from their post-chaises' and are ignorant
of the local language but still prepared to generalise with confidence about
their inhabitants.[2] The breed is far from extinct today.

There was justice in Baretti's criticisms. The travellers do not only
describe what they see, but report a good deal of hearsay. Even when they
are describing what they observed directly, they may misinterpret its
meaning out of unfamiliarity with the cultural context. Coryate, for
example, describes a funeral attended by people he calls 'monks', the
details of which suggest that the participants were in fact members of a
lay confraternity, an institution with which Protestants were not
acquainted.[3] The contradictory accounts given by travellers of the
freedom – or lack of freedom – of Italian women may well have resulted
from the difficulty, for newly arrived visitors, of distinguishing courtesans
from respectable ladies. Perception, we have learned, involves interpretation in terms of the perceiver's mental schemata (Gombrich, 1960).
There is no innocent eye.

Even when the accounts confirm one another, suspicion cannot be
relaxed because, as Baretti pointed out, one traveller may be copying
another, or at least learning from literature how to perceive life. The
British in Italy, for example, were fascinated by the same features of that
alien society, such as the ex-votos in the churches and the flagellants in
procession in the streets. Their accounts are full of topoi or commonplaces
(cf. Canepa, 1971). One eighteenth-century visitor to Naples after another
remarks on the idleness of the 'lower class of people', the so-called
lazzari, whose 'great pleasure is to bask in the sun and do nothing'

(below, ch. 6). They found what they expected to find. Again, we find three British visitors to the Ambrosiana Library in Milan, in three successive generations, all commenting that money was spent on the building rather than the books. It is the perennial problem of façades. The first visitor, Richard Lassels, observed that 'Over the heads of the highest shelves are set up the pictures of learned men, a thing of more cost than profit; seeing with that cost many more books might have been bought'. The second, the Scots divine Gilbert Burnet, generalised and moralised from the example. 'Their libraries...all Italy over are scandalous things, the room is often fine and richly adorned, but the books are few, ill bound and worse chosen'. Addison displayed a similar reaction.

> I saw the Ambrosian Library, where, to show the Italian genius, they have spent more money on pictures than on books...Books are indeed the least part of the furniture that one ordinarily goes to see in an Italian library, which they generally set off with pictures, statues and other ornaments.[4]

More recent visitors to Italian libraries may feel some sympathy with these strictures. All the same, whatever the Ambrosiana was like at the time, it is clear that the comments of these visitors revealed a good deal about their stereotypes of Italy and indeed about themselves. A detailed analysis of the descriptions by Burnet and Addison in particular would show how these accounts are organised around a set of binary oppositions. Catholic Italy is presented as a land of superstition, tyranny and idleness, in other words as an inversion of the enlightenment, freedom and industry of Protestant Britain. This pattern looks like a typical case of a recurrent traveller's syndrome, which can be documented from the time of Herodotus (on Egypt) onwards; and that is the perception of an alien culture in terms of an upside-down version of one's own (cf. Hartog, 1980).

The foreign travellers, then, were not cameras. They were not neutral observers, and foreign historians of Italy run a risk of identifying with the prejudices of their fellow-countrymen and so of serving up stereotypes as good history. All the same, many of the day-to-day observations of these visitors retain the immediacy of an anthropologist's field-notes, while a few of them had what might be called an 'ethnographic eye', and were sensitive to cultural patterns, in general or in particular. The philosopher George Berkeley, who spent considerable time in southern Italy as tutor to a nobleman on the Grand Tour, devoted particular attention to healing rituals (below, ch. 14). Some travellers collected information systematically with a view to later publication. Coryate even claimed to have visited the courtesans of Venice only 'to see the manner of their life, and observe their behaviour'. He also made notes on gestures, such as the 'extraordinary custom', as he found it, 'that when two acquaintances meet...they give a mutual kiss when they depart from each other, by kissing one another's cheek'. John Moore, an eighteenth-century visitor with a medical man's attentiveness to body language, commented that 'in their external deportment, the Italians have a grave solemnity of manner' and not 'the brisk look, and elastic trips which is universal in France; they move rather with a slow composed pace'.[5] It takes an outsider to notice and record behaviour of this kind.

Two travellers with particularly sharp ethnographic eyes were Michel de Montaigne and Philip Skippon. Montaigne, who visited Italy in 1580, kept a journal of what he saw and heard. When he went to Mass in Verona cathedral, for example, he recorded his surprise at finding the men standing and talking, their backs to the altar and their hats on their heads, taking no notice of the service until the elevation of the host. In Rome, he watched a procession of more than five hundred flagellants, and was once again surprised by Italian behaviour, recording that although they were bleeding they did not seem to feel any pain but laughed and chatted as they walked along. Examining their footwear with attention, he concluded that they must be poor people who had hired themselves out for the occasion.[6]

Philip Skippon, the son of one of Oliver Cromwell's major-generals, was a young man just down from Cambridge when he went to Italy with his tutor, John Ray, in 1663. Skippon's perceptions may have been sharpened by his association with this famous botanist, as well as by the culture shock of contact with the Catholic South. At all events, he kept his eyes and ears open and filled his journal with fascinating descriptions of everyday behaviour. Like Montaigne, he was somewhat disconcerted by Italian behaviour in church. 'The Padua gentlemen seem not very devout at the mass or other service,' he wrote, 'discoursing and laughing with one another.' He watched a procession of flagellants, at Genoa this time, and his reaction was again much like Montaigne's. 'Many of the whippers that went in this procession seem'd to make but a sport of it. And we were inform'd that they are porters, and mean persons hired by the rich to undergo this penance enjoin'd by the priests.' Yet another example of Italian façades.[7]

It is of course possible that Skippon had been reading Montaigne, and that he had learned what to expect, but he makes equally interesting observations which have no such parallel. He described a funeral in detail, for example. When he went to the theatre he seems to have spent his time watching the audience rather than the play, noting that the occupants of boxes spat into the pit, and also that 'Some of the noblemen that stood near the stage would often interrupt the actors and discourse with them.' He made notes on the way in which Italians walked in the street, and he even included a diagram:

> When three persons walk together, that every one may have the middle by turns, they walk thus, ABC, from one end of the walk to the other. B steps back to the left before A who coming behind, steps into the middle; then A steps back to the right before C, who coming behind, steps into the middle.

In an old regime society where precedence was taken very seriously and was expressed in so many details of gesture and posture, a group of equals would take turns to be senior rather than abandon the principle of seniority altogether. Again, Skippon noted that 'It is a custom here, that those who have the wall on their right hands in the streets may keep it, unless they will pass a compliment on any they meet.' Or again, 'The ladies are not led, as in England, by the hand or arm, but a servant holds up his arm, and the gentlewoman supports herself by laying her hand upon him.' This will not be the last time that Skippon's journal will be laid under contribution in these essays.

Inside stories: the evidence of personal documents

Early modern Italy was not only described repeatedly by foreign travellers; it is also unusually rich in personal documents. Particularly famous are the memoirs of pope Pius II (on which Jacob Burckhardt drew heavily in his essay on the Italian Renaissance); and the autobiographies of Benvenuto Cellini and of the Milanese physician Girolamo Cardano. To these may be added several hundred journals and diaries of various kinds, which are especially numerous in Florence and are probably best described by their contemporary Florentine name of 'memoranda' (*ricordanze*). These documents, which are described on p. 118 below, complement the descriptions of travellers with views from inside the culture; but it is no less necessary to approach them in a critical manner. They are not innocent or neutral or transparent, but more or less sophisticated presentations of the self and its extensions, such as the family and the city. Whether they are well- or ill-written, they belong to a literary genre, which had its own models, conventions and common-places. Pius II, for example, wrote 'commentaries' on his life in the third person in the manner of Julius Caesar; no false modesty for him. Cardano, by contrast, took as his model the loosely-constructed medita-tions of the stoic emperor Marcus Aurelius. Cellini does not seem to have had a single model in mind when writing – or dictating – the story of his life, but he was very much concerned to impress readers with his exploits (sexual and military as well as artistic), and to justify himself against the calumnies of his many enemies.[8]

The stylisation of life in these texts is probably best approached through an example. Travelling through the Sienese countryside, Pius II was offered milk by a cowherd, so he tells us, and

> remembering the man who offered water in his two hands to Artaxerxes as he passed by, smiled and did not disdain to touch the black and greasy bowl with his lips, pretending to drink [*tanquam biberet osculari catinum*]...for he would not appear to scorn the attention and reverence of a poor peasant.

whether the incident took place or not, the point is to present a classical commonplace, taken as it happens from Plutarch's *Lives*, in order to make a particular impression on the reader. The pantomime of drinking makes a good example of the theatre of everyday life, with the pope in the role of the good prince.[9]

Even if an autobiographer is not deliberately attempting to impress the reader, he (it is almost invariably a male in early modern Italy), will still perceive his life according to the schemata current in the culture. Even the dreams he records are stereotyped. As anthropologists such as Dorothy Eggan and Irving Hallowell (1966) have pointed out, people dream the myths of their culture, and Renaissance Italians were no exception. When Cellini was ill, for example, he dreamed (or more exactly remembered himself dreaming) that 'a terrifying old man appeared at my bedside and tried to drag me by force into his enormous boat'. As a friend of his was acute enough to remark, Cellini 'must have been reading Dante', a poet who was important in sixteenth-century Florentine culture, for the artist had obviously perceived death in the form of Charon the ferryman, as described in Dante's *Inferno*.[10]

To read these personal documents, particularly the more self-conscious autobiographies, between the lines, a cultural historian needs to acquire the skills of a literary critic, more especially the kind of critic who has a sense of history, an interest in anthropology, and a concern with

'Renaissance self-fashioning' (Greenblatt, 1980). As in the case of the painted portrait, however (below, ch. 10), it turns out that the common-places and stereotypes so frequent in autobiographies and memorials are not so much hindrances to the historian as aids in the reconstruction of the rules or norms of the culture. On a first acquaintance, Cellini may well appear to the twentieth-century reader as a pathological boaster and indeed a paranoid personality altogether. However, when one sees similar references to calumny and treachery, honour and fame in Cardano, Pius II, and other sources, it becomes clear that the artist was playing his part – rather bombastically, perhaps – in accordance with a script furnished by his culture. Indeed, it may be useful to think of all social roles as scripts, or better, since they are flexible rather than fixed, as cores around which to improvise, like the characters in the *commedia dell'arte*.

There was of course a literary genre produced by insiders for insiders, which made these scripts or scenarios explicit in the course of teaching readers how to behave in public places, and that was the courtesy book, of which the sixteenth-century treatises by the courtier Baldassare Castiglione and the archbishop Giovanni Della Casa were and are the most famous examples. As Elias (1939), has pointed out, treatises of this kind reveal a good deal about what might be called the 'deep structures' of their culture; the norms for speech, for example, and also for such forms of non-verbal communication as gesture, laughter, table manners and body language generally, topics which have attracted the attention of anthropologists (Hall 1959, Polhemus 1978), and are beginning to interest historians.

These texts, however, are no more neutral descriptions of behaviour or underlying attitudes than the accounts of memorialists and travellers are. Castiglione's sense of the dramaturgy of everyday life has been noted already. His discussion of the place of laughter in polite society, including his definition of the comic in terms of 'a certain deformity' (*una certa deformità*), is a famous one. It is well known, however, that in this passage Castiglione is following Cicero, and that his main concern is not so much to interpret the manners of his world but to change them; not to make old rules explicit, but to formulate new ones. All the same, Castiglione remains a key witness to the kind of behaviour he rejects.[11] So does Della Casa, who recommends his readers, among other things, 'not to offer anyone else a glass of wine which you have tasted and touched with your lips, unless he is a very close intimate of yours. Still less should you offer him a pear or any other fruit from which you have already taken a bite'.[12]

He thus testifies to the lack of a sense of personal distance which Pius II's cowherd illustrates. 'Space speaks'.

It is not unlikely that these two treatises, which went through many editions, had considerable influence over the long term in moulding Italian upper-class behaviour in their image. All the same, historians need more direct evidence of the manner in which early modern Italians perceived the rules of their culture. The judicial records offer some valuable evidence of this kind. Breaches of the rules forced individuals on occasion to make explicit their view of a good wife, for example, or a good son, as in the following two cases, remarkable only for the precision with which expectations were formulated.

In 1612 the thirty-one-year-old Genoese patrician Marcello Doria committed to paper an account of what he called the 'correction' of his wife Barbara Spinola, in fact a list of his grievances – fourteen pages worth of them. He objected, for example, to her books, such as 'Tasso, and other similar books' because they dealt with love. He objected to her sleeves, or the lack of them; 'I did not care for her to go about with her forearms bare.' He objected to her language saying 'I don't want to', for example, rather than 'I can't.' He accused her of refusing to look up when he entered the room or to go to meet him when he returned to the house. In short, Barbara lacked the humility which he felt he had the right to expect from his wife. Her reaction to these criticisms, still according to him, was to say 'I didn't come here to learn manners' (*io non son venuta ad imparar creanza in casa vostra*). The evidence has an immediacy lacking in such how-to-do-it books as the rather bland *Education of a Wife* published in 1587 by a certain Pietro Belmonte.[13]

In a similar way, the historian is offered a glimpse of cultural norms in a family dispute recorded in a document drawn up before a notary in a Roman prison in 1597. The accountant Alessandro Ruggia solemnly gave his word before witnesses 'to be a loving and obedient son to Messer Fidele Ruggia my father and Madonna Prudentia my mother and to my elders'. What his father, a timber merchant, considered to be the role of a good son was made explicit in the course of the document, in which Alessandro promised not only 'to leave women alone, whether they be married or unmarried, public or private', but also 'to dress as Messer Fidele my father wishes', and to turn up for morning and evening meals. Alessandro did not keep his word, however, and a still more vivid account of how not to be a good son emerges from the testimonies to his breach of faith nine years later. He was still said to do nothing else but pursue women. 'He wanted to spend money on dressing as he pleased.' He

insulted and threatened his father, drawing a dagger on him, calling him
'old fool', and wondering aloud when he was going to die ('this old traitor
has died twice already but he always rises again').[14] Whether or not
Alessandro did, or even said all that was attributed to him does not
concern us here. The value of this example, like the previous one, to the
cultural historian is the light it sheds on normal expectations, showing,
for example, that a Roman father might have strong views about his son's
clothes, as a Genoese husband had about his wife's.

There is much else for cultural historians to glean from judicial
records. Insult cases, for example, reveal the importance of honour and
shame in Italian culture and show that insult was a form of communication
which followed strict rules (below, ch. 8). These cases, which exposed a
good deal of dirty linen and made private lives public, may be seen, in
the phrase of the anthropologist Victor Turner (1974), as a form of 'social
drama'.

Drama in the literal sense also has its value as a source. The sixteenth
century in particular was a golden age of Italian comedy, the age not only
of Ariosto and Aretino but of gifted minor figures such as the Paduan
'Ruzzante', while eighteenth-century Venice had Goldoni. These plays
did not reflect social reality directly; literature never does. The characters
of comedy are obvious stereotypes; clownish peasants, cunning servants,
heavy fathers, deceitful friars and so on. Yet stereotypes reveal a good deal
of the concerns and values of the culture in which they are current. In
a sense it is their very distortion of social reality which makes the plays
good sources for social history, revealing how contemporaries perceived
one another (or at least how some groups perceived others). Cultural
historians would be well advised not only to treat official statements of
fact, like the census, as in some sense fiction, but also to regard works
of fiction, such as plays and stories, as in some sense fact.

Another type of evidence which must not be neglected is that of
material culture; paintings, furniture, houses, clothes and so on. Although
the translation of such mute evidence into verbal statements about the
past raises acute problems of its own, which the fashionable metaphor of
culture as a 'text' glosses over, material objects must be regarded as a
mode or modes of communication. Chapters 10 and 15 attempt to analyse
portraits and other items of conspicuous consumption in these terms, as
a counter-weight to the volume's emphasis on rituals and words. The
reconstruction of a culture which has disappeared is an enterprise as
presumptuous as it is fascinating, and historians need all the help they
can get. They tread on safe ground only when they can support a

particular interpretation with evidence of different types; when the testimony of material culture confirms that of written sources, fiction tells the same story as 'fact' and insiders agree with outsiders. Although individual chapters often draw heavily on a single type of source, the fitting together of fragments of evidence of very different kinds has been a conscious aim pursued throughout this book.

II
Modes of perception

3
Classifying the people: the census as collective representation[1]

Historians of the Middle Ages are somewhat ambivalent about chronicles. The so-called 'Copernican Revolution' in history associated with Leopold von Ranke involved a shift in emphasis from literary sources to the more objective evidence of official records. It was soon realised, however – if it had ever been forgotten – that chronicles too had their value as testimony, not so much in spite of their subjectivity as because of it. They were witnesses to the attitudes and values of the chronicler, his social group, and his age (Galbraith, 1948, ch. 1).

A similar point might be made about official records, for they are not as pure a source as it was once assumed. Censuses, for example, do not reflect the societies they survey with the objectivity of a mirror. They are not only subject to human error, the information they contain is also filtered through a particular classification system. On the positive side, however, this classification system is itself evidence of the way in which a society perceives itself (or more exactly, of the way in which one group perceives the rest). It reveals the categories and the schemata current in that particular culture. In other words, the census is what the French sociologist Emile Durkheim (1912) called a 'collective representation' (above, p. 5). It is from this point of view that I shall be studying the censuses of early modern Italy, particularly those of Florence and Venice. My concern will be with social stereotypes as well as occupational structure, and more especially with the grey area between the two.

By the sixteenth century the census (known locally by such names as *anagrafo, catasto, estimo,* and so on) had become an institution in much of Italy. In Venice, where the ruling class were aware of Byzantine bureaucratic precedent, partial lists of inhabitants had been kept as early as the tenth century, while a count of adult males was made in 1338. In Tuscany in 1427, the government carried out an unusually ambitious survey of all the households in Florentine territory, some 60,000 of them, or more than a quarter of a million people. The number of such surveys seems to have increased sharply in the sixteenth century; there were censuses of Rome in 1526; of Florence in 1527, 1552 and 1562; of Venice in 1509, 1540, and 1581; of Naples in 1547 and in the 1590s; and so on. These surveys became increasingly detailed in the course of the early modern period. The Florentine census of 1632, for example, is more thorough than those of the sixteenth century, while the Venetian survey of the 1760s, with its many tables, was the most detailed of all.[2]

Modern historians have made considerable use of these sources to study changes in the Italian population and social structure. Before this can be done with safety, however, it is necessary to investigate for what purposes these 'sources' were made.

In the case of the catasto of 1427, the Florentine Domesday Book – as in the case of Domesday Book itself – the investigation has already been carried out in an exemplary manner. We now know that the Domesday survey of 1086 was the work of commissioners who went on circuit in different parts of England, interviewing the priest, the reeve and six villages in each community, asking them some twenty-odd questions, and compiling returns which were then copied into a register. The survey, which may have been inspired by that of Sicily ordered by the Norman Count Roger I (which itself, like the Venetian lists, followed a Byzantine model), has been described as 'the greatest administrative achievement of medieval kingship' (Galbraith, 1961).

In similar fashion we might describe the 1427 *catasto* as the greatest administrative achievement of medieval republics. How great an achievement becomes apparent if one reads the meticulous recent account of the different kinds of official (valuers, clerks, and so on), involved in making the census; the cost of making it; and the process by which it was made, with written returns for each household being read aloud in the neighbourhood for checking before they were transcribed into the sixty-six volumes of registers (Herlihy-Klapisch, 1978).

In the case of later Italian surveys, however, serious problems remain. Take, for example, the Florence census of 1552 ordered by Duke Cosimo de'Medici. A brief description of the fortresses of the state and the population of the countryside is followed by a detailed survey of the inhabitants of the city. For what purpose was it made?

As in the case of Domesday Book, the form in which the manuscripts of the census survive allows us to frame a hypothesis about the way in which the survey was made, and to move from this to the intentions of the makers. The 1552 census survives in two versions, both registers. One, now in the Archivio di Stato in Florence, will be described henceforward as the 'A-text'. It is written on paper in a handwriting showing signs of haste, but it is bound in blue velvet and decorated with illuminations on vellum. The pictures and the inclusion of an introduction addressed to the Duke suggests that this was his presentation copy, despite the handwriting (for which the introduction offers profuse apologies). The other copy is now in the Biblioteca Nazionale in Florence; let us call it the 'B-text'. It lacks decorations, but it is written on vellum throughout and in a neat hand. It would therefore seem to be the office copy, designed for hard wear and constant reference.[3]

The two texts do not agree in every way. The A-text gives the population of Florence as 59,557 (not counting the ducal household, which appears only in this version, as if Cosimo's household was his business alone). The B-text gives the population of Florence as 59,179, a loss of 378 people. How are these discrepancies to be explained? Could omissions have occurred in the process of copying the second version form the first? However, a collation of sample entries shows that neither text could have been copied entirely from the other, since each contains some information which the other lacks.[4] It is an axiom of textual criticism that if there are two manuscripts of a given text, then it has three possible 'stemmata' or genealogies. If A does not depend (or depend entirely) on B, while B is independent of A (at least in part), then they must both draw on a lost 'archetype'. If this archetype was a collection of loose sheets, like the 'original returns' for Domesday Book and their equivalents in 1427, we may well imagine that they were copied into the two registers by two clerks (since the handwriting differs), each of whom forgot to pick up some of the sheets, thus producing the discrepancies. Since each register contains households omitted by the other, the total population of Florence must be higher than is normally assumed, and a thorough collation of the two manuscripts is needed.

How, and by whom, was the census made? The preface to the A-text is the work of a certain Antonio Gianetti (alias de Mucione), who says that it is he who has arranged the data into its five columns (hearths, males, females, manservants and maidservants). He does not explain how the information was collected, but the fact that it is not organised by parishes but by streets suggests that on this occasion the basic leg-work was not done by that handy substitute for officials, the parish priest. In Venice, in the seventeenth century at least, it was the parish priests who conducted the census, helped out by a nobleman and a citizen for each parish, presumably to collect information from their social equals on the assumption that people of high status would not bother to answer the questions of an ordinary cleric. In the eighteenth century, however, the priest was expected to make the survey on his own.

Why were these censuses made? In early modern Italy, and indeed elsewhere in Europe, they had a number of different purposes, of which four stand out as particularly important. In the first place, there were censuses for tax purposes, as in the case of Florence in 1427. In the second place, there were censuses for welfare purposes. It might be the case that the price of bread was high, and that the government wanted to ensure that supplies went to local people and not to outsiders, as in the case of Naples in 1591, when tickets were issued to everyone entitled to rations.[5] Or it might be that the city was under siege, like Florence in 1527, or that there was a danger of plague, which was a kind of siege in that it cut the area affected off from the outside world. In Venice in 1586, the Health Board took over the administration of the census. In Florence during the plague of 1630, a survey was made of part of the Santa Croce district, which had to be quarantined, and a similar survey was carried out by the Health Board of Rome during the plague of 1656.[6] The census was part of the arsenal of plague-fighting techniques, of which early modern Italy was the pioneer (Cipolla, 1976). Other surveys were made soon after visitations of plague in order to count the losses, as in the cases of Florence in 1632, Venice of 1633, and Naples in 1656.

In the third place, there were the censuses made by the Church, the better to locate failures in the performance of the so-called 'Easter duties' of confession and communion. These ecclesiastical censuses were made on a regular basis following the Council of Trent; an early example is that of Bologna in 1568, ordered by the reforming archbishop Gabriele Paleotti (Prodi, 1967, p. 182). They were part of the growing concern of the clergy with the state of the laity, to be discussed in the next chapter. Finally, there were the censuses of able-bodied men able to defend the city (the Genoese census of 1531 notes which households possessed arquebuses), or, in the case of Venice, to row in its galleys.[7]

The reason it is so important to know the purpose of the census before using it as a source is that the purpose affected what was recorded and what omitted. Censuses for tax purposes generally count 'hearths' (*fuoche*), omitting those which are exempt from taxation (the households of the clergy, for example). Censuses for the sake of bread distribution count 'mouths', omitting unweaned babies, who have their own food supplies. Ecclesiastical censuses count 'souls', omitting non-Catholics, notably the Jews, and possibly children who have not made their first communion. These exclusions, however exasperating for modern demographers, made sense within the local system of categories. In some cases technical terms were used loosely; one of the problems with the

Florentine census of 1552 is that it oscillates between 'hearths', 'souls' and 'mouths'. In all cases, however, we need to keep early modern category systems in mind, because the categories, together with the princes, the priests, the clerks, and the ordinary inhabitants who just answered questions, are all mediators between ourselves and the social structures we are studying.

These category systems are the main focus of the present essay; but before examining them in detail, something needs to be said about attitudes to the census. As many early modern Italians knew, the census was an ancient Roman institution, taken every five years for military, financial and political reasons (Nicolet, 1976, 52f). The survey of Pistoia taken in 1569, for example, invokes Rome to show that censuses are a good thing, while the Venetian survey of 1761 opens with a reference to Servius Tullius king of the Romans.[8] It also referred to Moses; for the census was mentioned in the Bible, from Numbers 1.2 (the Lord's command to Moses to number the people), to Luke 2.1 (the journey to Bethlehem in response to the 'decree from Caesar Augustus, that all the world should be taxed'). At the top of a page of figures referring to Florence in 1661 we find the proud inscription, *in multitudine populi dignitas regis*, a quotation from Proverbs 14.28, 'In the multitude of people is the king's honour', going on to say that 'in the want of people is the destruction of the prince'.[9]

Of course there are many texts in the Bible which seem to contradict other texts, and we read that 'David's heart smote him after he had numbered the people. And David said unto the Lord, I have sinned greatly' (2 Samuel 24.10). This text was used by the Dominican friar and philosopher Tommaso Campanella as a criticism of the Neapolitan census of the 1590s, and it was still being used for similar purposes in England in the eighteenth century.[10] We know from the Anglo-Saxon Chronicle that Domesday book too was unpopular, as one might have guessed from its unofficial name. It involved counting the animals in everyone's possession. 'There was not even – it is shameful to record it, but it did not seem shameful to him to do – not even one ox, nor one cow, nor one pig which escaped notice in his survey'. Some sixteenth-century Italians reacted in the same way. When the Duke of Parma had a census of animals carried out in his dominions in 1550, some of the census-takers were murdered by the peasants.[11] A census is not politically neutral. Knowledge means power.

With these points in mind we may return to the census as collective representation; a representation of a collectivity, and at the same time a representation by means of certain collective categories and stereotypes. Not only 'numbering the people' was the aim, but classifying the people as well.

In fact the people were not the sole object of enquiry. It has already been pointed out that animals might appear in the census, divided, of course, into classes. The Tuscan survey of 1632 had five categories; pigs, goats, sheep, 'beasts of burden', such as mules, and 'yoke-animals', such as oxen. The Venetian survey of 1761, which omitted pigs, also separated the sheep from the goats and made an additional distinction between the oxen employed to pull ploughs and the bullocks raised for butchering.[12] There was even a place in the census for inanimate objects such as arquebuses (Genoa 1531, whether for reasons of defence or public order); gondolas (seventeenth-century Venice, reflecting a concern with conspicuous consumption); and coaches, a more spectacular item of conspicuous consumption which had its own census in Rome in 1594.

In the case of the people, a few binary oppositions were central to the classification system. Males and females, adults and children, family and servants were distinguished with varying degrees of precision. Where the Florentine census of 1552, for example, divided the population into four (males, females, manservants and maidservants), that of 1632 had six divisions, splitting both males and females into 'under 15' and 'over 15'. In Venice, the censuses of the seventeenth century distinguished 'boys' and 'girls' from 'males' and 'females'; the eighteenth-century census, on the other hand, grouped all females together, while distinguishing 'men' (between 14 and 60) from both 'boys' and 'the old'. Secular censuses tended to treat 14 or 15 as the entry to adulthood, whether for economic or military reasons. Ecclesiastical censuses, on the other hand, stressed the age of the first communion, which was considerably lower.

Ecclesiastical or soul-censuses had their own categories. In these records it was important to distinguish not only clergy from laity, but monks and friars from secular priests. The Church was concerned with the numbers of nuns; of the poor (at least the institutionalised poor, the so-called *poveri de spedali*); of the Jews and Muslims ('Turks' or 'Moors'), because they would not appear at the communion rails; and finally of prostitutes, whether because they were a source of temptation which needed to be controlled, or simply a group unable to take communion because they were in a state of mortal sin.[13]

Lay censuses might also list priests friars and nuns separately (as in the case of Florence in 1632), but they were much more concerned to classify the laity by status and occupation. The concern with status was particularly acute in aristocratic Venice, where the census-takers were issued with three kinds of sheet, on which to record the households of 'Nobles', 'Citizens', and 'Craftsmen'. Some individuals did not fit any of these categories easily, but the officals did their best to squeeze them in. Legally speaking, 'citizen' was a restricted category in Venice; a minority of much the same size as the patriciate which ranked immediately below it. However, the health commissioners told the priests to include under this heading 'advocates, physicians, notaries and other professional men and also priests who are not nobles in the cases in which they were heads of households'. As for 'craftsmen', they were treated as something of a residual category which was stretched to include gondoliers, school-masters, widows and so on.[14]

This ternary system reveals something of the assumptions of the Venetian ruling class about the natural order of things. Nothing odd about that; census classes have reflected and reinforced social classes from the days of ancient Rome onwards. Other surveys tell us more about the preoccupations of the organisers of the census, including their interest in foreigners and the unemployed.

'Foreigners' (*forestieri*), is a term which generally refers to anyone born outside the boundaries of the state conducting the census. The Florentine *catasto* of 1427 already records their numbers. In the case of Florence in 1552, there is no category for foreigners among the totals, but places of origin are frequently recorded in the register, most obviously in the case of prostitutes, who have little else to identify them because they are cut off from their families; *La Francesca spagnola*, *La Margherita francese*, *Daria Bolognese meretrice*, *Dianora pisana meretrice*, and so on. However, we also find men identified as '*Giovanni di Brizio da Pisa*, for example, or *Giorgino d'Arezzo pittore* (in other words, Vasari). Like nicknames, which are not uncommon in the census, the geographical description helps with identification, but it would not have been too difficult to retrieve all the foreigners from the register, and one wonders whether this was the intention of the Duke or his officials. In Venice too one finds a few such descriptions, such as *Zuane Greco mariner*, or, in the notorious parish of San Zuan Bragola (below, p. 45), *Barbara Todescha*, *Stella Greca*, *Elena Turca*, and *Nicoleta Schiaona* (who probably came from Dalmatia). Yet the impression remains that the Florentine census was more concerned with the numbers of foreigners, the Venetian with the distinctions between nobles, citizens and the rest.

Another preoccupation of the organisers of censuses was work – or the lack of it. It is sometimes suggested that the concept of 'unemployment', all too familiar today, was lacking in Europe before the early nineteenth century. The abstract noun may have been lacking, but the early modern censuses are part of the evidence that the idea was not, although contemporary attitudes to those who could not or would not work differed in important ways from ours. In Italy and elsewhere, nobility was often defined in terms of non-work. Machiavelli defined as 'gentlemen' (*gentilhuomini*), only those who 'live idly'. Nobles were not infrequently described as *scioperati* (literally 'workless'), which did not mean that they were looking for a job but that they were rentiers.[15]

The idleness of ordinary people was another matter, whether it was voluntary or involuntary. It was a matter of considerable interest to the organisers of censuses, together with its converse, the kind of work people did. The Venetian health commissioners, for example, told the parish priests who collected the information for the census to record the occupation (*esercizio*) of all householders who were neither nobles nor citizens. This may have been done to solve the problem of what is now called 'record linkage'; many seventeenth-century Venetians did not have surnames, so that occupations made identification simpler. Occupations are also recorded in the Florentine censuses of the sixteenth and seventeenth centuries, possibly for the same reason, and in some tax documents, like the Venetian *decime* of 1581 and 1711.[16] However, there is other evidence of official concern with work. In Florence during the plague of 1630, for example, a thorough survey was made of both the actual and potential occupations of the inhabitants of the quarantined area of Santa Croce. The economic recession of the seventeenth century seems to have prompted the surveys of workshops and trades which survive for some cities, such as Rome in 1622 (Delumeau, 1957, 371f), and Siena in 1640.

What particularly, and increasingly, preoccupied the organisers of censuses was the problem, as they saw it, of the idle poor. They did not of course take account of the many poor people who went from city to city seeking work or charity. Nor did they record individual details about the institutionalised poor. Their concern was with poor people with fixed addresses in the city. In the case of Florence and Venice, the censuses reveal significant changes in the manner in which these poor people were perceived.

In the Florentine census of 1552, the poor are almost invisible. One finds no more than the odd reference to someone who begs (*accatta*) or is crippled (*storpiato*). In the 1562 census, the impression is much the same. I found only one reference to a beggar, while three householders were described as 'blind', three as 'poor' and two as 'lame', like *Bartolomeo povero zoppo* from S. Maria Novella. In the 1632 census, however, there was a dramatic increase in the number of householders described in these terms, so that one wonders whether the problem had become more acute in these years of recession, or whether the 1630 plague had sharpened official perceptions of the poor. About fifty people were described as 'blind'; about thirty as 'beggars'; about a dozen as 'poor'; and half a dozen as 'crippled' or 'lame', making around a hundred householders altogether. It should perhaps be added that 'blind' should be interpreted as an occupational description, referring only to those people who made a living (however poor), from their disability, in other words begged. Occasionally the census specifies that the beggars begged for others; 'for nuns', for example, or 'for the prisons', while in one case, that of Dianora the blind widow, we learn that she 'begs and keeps what she gets' (*accatta e non rende*).

A similar trend towards the increasing visibility of the poor may be observed in the Venetian censuses from the mid seventeenth century (a curious time-lag, since the 1630 plague struck Venice as hard as Florence). The 1633 census describes very few householders as blind or crippled or as beggars apart from the area around San Marco, where the best pitches were. The 1642 census notes the existence of forty-one beggar households in the Dorsoduro area. In the case of the 1670 census, for which returns from only two quarters survive, twelve women in Cannareggio and thirty householders of both sexes in Santa Croce are described as blind, beggars or both. Finally in the eighteenth century, the language of classification is modified as offical consciousness of the problem of the poor becomes more acute. Instead of the quasi-professional description 'beggar', 'blind women', or whatever, we now find a special category for the unemployed (*senza impiego* or *senza mestiere*), which the census-takers have to fill up in the case of householders without means of support (rentiers were another matter). No fewer than 866 unemployed heads of household were recorded in 1768, and this total was regarded at the time as unrealistically small.[17]

The unemployed, once 'God's poor' and then 'a burden on society' (below, p. 72f) make a kind of sociological litmus paper for revealing the relationship between perceptions of the social structure and wider collective representations. They became more and more visible in the course of the early modern period. A second litmus test is provided by working women, another subordinate group which has tended to be perceived, officially at least, in terms of the dominant male's interests and stereotypes (cf. Ardener, 1975).

At any one time in the seventeenth century there were usually about

60,000 women living in Venice. Only a minority were heads of households, and only a minority of that minority were identified by any 'occupation' other than 'widow' (which was the way in which the parish priest generally filled in the category *esercizio*). One might say therefore that women's work had a low visibility, at least in the eyes of men, who of course made the records. Yet this visibility may have been increasing in seventeenth-century Italy, for a new kind of poem made its appearance, the work of Gianbattista Marino and his followers, describing beautiful girls at work sewing spinning and embroidering and also as laundresses, poultry-sellers, tailors, quacks, fortune-tellers, and even as bookbinders.[18] In any case, excluding maidservants (*massere*), and nuns, there remain over 900 women identified by occupation in the incomplete surviving records of the Venetian censuses of 1633, 1642 and 1670.

What is particularly striking is that these women were described by no fewer than 112 occupational adjectives, which, allowing for synonyms, suggests about 100 occupational categories (much the same as in seventeenth-century Amsterdam; Tas, 1938). The occupations may be divided into three groups. There were about 100 retailers; about 400 craftswomen; and over 400 women providing services of various kinds.

It was only to be expected, following research on other early modern cities, from Tas (1938) to Wood (1981), that women would be important in the retailing trades. The most numerous group was that of the dealers in second-hand clothes (*revedina*, *strazzaruola*, or *venderigole* are the different names for this occupation), who can also be documented from the records of the mercer's guild. There were also dealers in fruit, cheese, herbs, almonds, flowers, pearls, wine, water and aquavita.

The craftswomen were, again as one might have expected, concentrated in the textile sector. The most numerous were the spinners of silk and wool but there are not infrequent references to weavers, trimmers (*passamanere*), tailors, hat-makers, ribbon-makers, fringe-makers, and of course the sail-makers who worked in or for the Venetian Arsenal. There were also a few women described in the census as boat-maker, for example, button-maker, carpenter (*marangona*), cooper, glass-maker, mirror-maker, shoe-maker, and soap-maker.

In all these cases the census may look objective enough, but we may be seriously misled if we remain unaware of the mediators. Social historians of Venice have good cause to be grateful to the parish priests who went from house to house collecting data which can still be used, but they have also to recognise that what the priests recorded was filtered through their own conceptual categories. In some parishes, notably in the quarter of Santa Croce, in 1670, the census-takers seem to have been particularly conscious of women's work, and they recorded the occupations not only of female heads of household, as required, but of wives and daughters as well. In other parishes, however, the priest wrote down nothing but 'widow'. It is scarcely plausible that no female head of household in these parishes was doing any kind of work, so the priest must have failed to associate the terms 'women' and 'occupation'. It is therefore impossible to make meaningful comparisons between parishes or to calculate the total number of working women who headed households in Venice. The Florentine census of 1632, which is also full of details about women's work (about forty occupations all together), exhibits similar variations between districts, suggesting that any statistical conclusions based on this document should be treated with reserve (cf. Brown and Goodman, 1980).

The presence of the mediator is most obvious, however, in the case of our third main category, that of women providing services. Thirty-two landladies are recorded, for example, including one who specialised in actors (*Isabella tiene comedianti*), but this group is still curiously small for a city such as Venice, full of visitors, and prompts the suspicion that the priests may not always have considered landlady to be an occupation. Only eighteen women are described as midwives (*comare, allevatrice*), which is even more suspicious. The priest, who had been issued with a blank form headed *artefici*, may not have thought that midwives really qualified, particularly if they also happened to be widows. There are no healers or wise women either, unless we count two fortune-tellers, although the Inquisition records of the period do reveal Greek women working as healers in the Castello quarter. Their brush with the authorities may have discouraged them and others like them from declaring this particular occupation in the census.[19]

Still more palpable is the presence of the mediator in the case of another service occupation; prostitution. Nearly 200 heads of household in these Venetian censuses may be identified with some plausibility as prostitutes, but the priest rarely describes them as such in so many words. The presence of a taboo makes itself known by omission, euphemism, or the introduction of moralising comment. In the parish of San Zuan Bragola in 1633, for example, besides the four exotic figures already mentioned (p. 33), we find thirty-eight women living alone, identified by nothing but their first names. In the parish of San Marcilian in 1642, we find seventeen more; but in this case someone (whether the priest, or the clerk in the office of the Health Commission), has written a large M against each name and explained below that this stands for *Meretrici Publici*, Public Prostitutes. At San Paternian the same year, thirteen women are singled out and described in the margin as 'whores' (using the more colloquial term *puttane*). In the quarter of San Marco, a special list was drawn up of ninety-six 'single women from different countries', as the document rather coyly puts it, *donne sole e di diversi paesi*. In all these cases the language signals either indignation or embarrassment.

In Florence, on the other hand, where the census-takers were probably laymen, *meretrice* is generally treated as an occupation like any other, to be registered without comment in the normal way; 106 heads of household in 1562, 95 in 1632. The exceptions, in 1632, are of a rather different kind. The clerk must have known Via del Pino, in the quarter of San Giovanni, quite intimately, for he registers three of its inhabitants as follows (the capitals are his own); MARGHERITA PISANA PUTTANA SCORTESE ('boorish whore'); MARGHERA PUTTANA A FIORI L'ANNO 90 ('at her best in 1590'); and finally, and somewhat mysteriously, LA BELLUCCIA PUTTANA RIFATTA LIQUIDA E STREGA ('recycled, liquid and a witch'). We have moved from euphemism to slander. So much for the objectivity of a census of females carried out and recorded by males.

All the same, the veil of prejudice was not inpenetrable, and a few unexpected female occupations appear in the census. In Florence in 1632 we find one pawnbroker. In Venice, thirteen schoolmistresses (below, p. 129) and eleven barbers (it is not known whether they specialised in women's hair or whether – since barbers doubled as surgeons – they were more in demand for medical services). Among the more exotic female occupations was *ballottina* (counting the votes of the patricians in the Doge's Palace); fortune-teller; tooth-drawer; chimney-sweep; stevedore (*formentina*); porter (*fachina*); musician (*sonadora*); boatwoman (*barcaiola*); and, to my greatest surprise, sailor (*marinera*). There were ten such sailors heading households in the appropriate parish, that of San Piero in Castello; *Isabella marinera, Lucietta marinera*, and so on. Did they really go to sea?[20]

What is important here, though, is the fact that some census-takers were prepared to accept this identification. Perhaps the women insisted on it. At any rate it might be wise to view the occupational listings of the census, impersonal as they may look, as the outcome of a process of what might be called 'negotiation' between the officials who devised the census and its categories; the clerks who kept the registers; the priests and others who went from house to house asking questions; and, not least, the householders themselves. 'Negotiation' will be discussed further below (ch. 5).

The census, then, is evidence of early modern mentalities no less than – indeed, rather more than – it is evidence of social structure. The precocity and elaboration of the Florentine and Venetian censuses in particular suggests the early rise in those cities of what might be called 'the numerate mentality' (below, p. 131). In fifteenth-century Florence it had already been calculated that mean household size was five, leaving only the decimal point to be added by Peter Laslett 400 years later.[21] The printed forms (*facciate*) of seventeenth-century Venice, divided into columns and rows, are an impressive sign of an orderly, bureaucratic approach to the problems of numbering and classifying the people. In the course of the period, the census became more sophisticated. More questions were asked; categories were sub-divided; tables became more elaborate; and comparisons with earlier years began to be included, as can be seen from Roman soul-censuses as well as from the monumental mid eighteenth-century survey of Venice and her dominions.

The findings recorded in the census – the main ones at least – seem to have become common knowledge. Sansovino's sixteenth-century guide to Venice quotes some of the statistics, while a seventeenth-century Florentine patrician evidentally had access to Roman census data.[22] The availability of this information will have encouraged people to think in more quantitative terms. Indeed, the need to fill in all the boxes on the forms must have been a kind of apprenticeship in statistics for the parish priests of Venice. Thus the census not only records early modern mentalities or collective representations; it also played some small part in the process of changing them.

4

The bishop's questions
and the
people's religion

Since the pioneering studies of Gabriel Le Bras (1955–6), many historians of popular religion have seen themselves as retrospective sociologists. They would, if they could, conduct public opinion polls of the dead. They have naturally fastened with eagerness on documents recording situations where contemporaries – notably inquisitors (Dedieu, 1979) and bishops – conducted some sort of interview, collected some form of figures, or administered some kind of questionnaire.

Meanwhile, as so often happens when practitioners of one discipline borrow from another, sociology has changed. In the 1980s, sociologists are no longer as confident as they were in the 1950s about the reliability of their methods or the objectivity of their results. They are now less concerned with measurement and more with meaning. They have become aware that the way in which a given question is asked may have considerable influence on the answers received (Payne, 1951). Like social anthropologists, they have become conscious of the social construction of reality, and of the importance of stereotypes and labels in social life. Social historians too need this kind of awareness. If they are concerned with popular religion, they would be well advised to take as their starting-point the idea that visitation records, inquisitor's interrogations, and other ecclesiastical documents are not thermometers, objective measurements of the religious fervour of a given community. What they reveal are clerical images of the behaviour and beliefs of the laity. The inquisitors, missionaries and diocesan visitors who interrogated the laity about their religion may, like sociologists and anthropologists since, have been given the answers they expected, or the answers they were expected to expect.

This contamination of the ecclesiastical evidence for popular religious beliefs is most obvious in the case of inquisitorial records, where the stereotype of the heretic dictated both the questions asked and the interpretation of the answers. Contemporary accounts of seventeenth-century missions to remote parts of Europe are less obviously contaminated, but they too reveal stereotypes and leading questions. In the middle of the seventeenth century, some Jesuits recorded their amazed reactions to the beliefs of a group of shepherds they encountered near Eboli, in southern Italy, (where the north Italian writer Primo Levi would record an almost equal amazement 300 years later). 'Asked how many gods there were, one replied "a hundred", another "a thousand", another a still higher number.'[1] Perhaps Jesuit missionaries were instructed to ask this particular question, for a few years later another Jesuit, Julien Maunoir, found that the inhabitants of the island of Ushant off Brittany 'were unable to answer the question, how many gods there were.'[2] Perhaps the people of Eboli and Ushant really were as ignorant of the basic doctrines of Christianity as the Jesuits thought they were. However, if they were better informed, they would have been as surprised by the question as the missionaries claimed to have been by their answers, and in that case too they would not have known how to reply. One should not of course take too seriously the amazement of the missionaries; it is a rhetorical amazement, for the edification of the reader. Missionaries to remote parts of Europe expected such difficulties. The comparison of southern Italy and southern Spain to Europe's 'Indies', full of 'heathen', was a commonplace of the age (Prosperi, 1981). The expectations of the missionaries, their stereotypes of the dark corners of the land, determined their questions and also their interpretation of the answers – or the silence.

In the case of episcopal visitations it is also worth paying close attention to categories and stereotypes, notably the clerical stereotype of the 'the laity', and the learned stereotype of 'the people'. It is worth asking what the 'visitors' were looking for, what they expected to find, and how their aims and expectations changed over time. Le Bras did not do this, perhaps because he was a Catholic priest who identified with the clergy who carried out the visitations and accepted their assumption that attendance at Mass and the performance of the 'Easter duties' of confession and communion were reliable indicators of religious fervour.

More recently, however, Dominique Julia (1973) has focussed attention on the visitors themselves and has suggested the need to study the history of their questions. It is a long history, for Regino of Prum drew up a ninety-six point questionnaire for visitations as early as the tenth century.[3] In the centuries which followed, the questions changed only slowly, so that each generation of visitors was encouraged to perceive the diocese through the eyes of their predecessors. However, changes there were. Their history needs to be written in order for us to interpret the visitation records. It is also a subject of interest in its own right, one strand in the history of what we now call 'social surveys', the history of curiosity about collective beliefs and behaviour.

This chapter offers some notes towards such a history, some reflections on Italian visitations in the early modern period (or more exactly, between 1437 and 1865), studied with special reference to the clerical image of popular religion. The fourteen visitations discussed are simply those which happen to have been printed, whether in full or in part. They are no more than the tip of an ecclesiastical iceberg, but if they are examined in chronological order, they may be sufficient at least to reveal certain long-term trends and so to suggest some directions for future research.[4]

Before the Council of Trent, the visitors appear to have taken little interest in popular religion. They were more concerned with the state of the church buildings than the state of the people, and gave more attention to the shepherd than to his flock. During Ludovico Barbo's visitation of the diocese of Treviso in 1437, the only questions asked about the laity – to judge by the answers – must have been whether they went to church and whether they had made their Easter duties. The answer that this was the case, without any mention of numbers, appears to have been satisfactory (Pesce, 1969, Vol. 1, p. 30). At Pisa in 1463, the parish priests were also asked about the numbers of the laity. A typical reply runs as follows: 'he says that he has 200 souls and all of the appropriate age go to confession and communion' (Caturegli, 1950, p. 118). At Mantua, during cardinal Ercole Gonzaga's visitation in the 1540s, priests were asked to give the names of non-communicants together with the reasons for their failure to fulfill their duties and they were also asked to comment on the sexual morality of their parishioners (adultery, the keeping of concubines, marriage within the prohibited degrees, and so on). There were no questions about the beliefs of the laity.[5] Gian Matteo Giberti of Verona is often described, and with reason, as a model bishop, and he was much concerned with heresy, blasphemy and magic in his diocese. However, the twenty sections of his visitations questionnaire mention the laity only under the following three heads; 'On those who keep concubines and others who live in a scandalous manner'; 'On quarrels and conflicts'; 'On those who remain outside the church during Mass' (Prosperi, 1969, pp. 206, 267).

The Council of Trent took considerable interest in visitations (how often they should be made, and by whom), so it is scarcely surprising to find that in 1566, in the diocese of Brescia, the bishop, the Venetian partrician Domenico Bollani, should have employed a questionnaire about the laity which – again, to judge by the answers – was more elaborate than any we have seen so far. The parish priests had to respond to a whole series of demands for information about the morals of their parishioners, as this specimen answer reveals: 'he says he has 3000 or more souls, of whom 1800 eligible to take communion; there is no one who keeps a concubine, no one who fails to go to confession, and there are no usurers, no public blasphemers, and no public gamblers'. There must also have been a question, for the first time in this series of texts, about the beliefs of the laity, revealing anxiety about the possible spread of heresy, for there are answers like 'in this parish there is no one who criticises the faith and the dogmas of the Church'. My impression, however, is not one of a really searching enquiry. Figures for communicants are suspiciously round; more than one priest simply confesses to 'not knowing the total number'; and although a finger is often put on the men who lived with concubines, no one admits to knowing any heretics.[6] Archbishop Altoviti's visitation of the diocese of Florence two years later, in 1568, also included a question about the faith as well as the morals of the laity, as is shown by replies like the following: 'All the people live in a religious manner and no one is excommunicate, a public criminal or suspect of heresy.'[7] During the reign of Gregory XIII, a number of so-called 'apostolic' visitations were made by outsiders to a given diocese. One well-known example is the visitation of Bergamo by Carlo Borromeo in 1575. The printed records of this visitation certainly give an impression of great thoroughness. However, there was less emphasis on the laity than there had been in the Bollani and Altoviti cases. A typical answer runs as follows: '500 souls eligible for communion...two who live with concubines (see the book of trials)'.[8]

In the 1580s, three treatises on visitations devote considerable space to enquiries into the religion of the laity. Fuschus devotes fifty-four sections to the subject; Timotheus lists thirty-one articles of enquiry into the laity; while Ninguarda lists forty-five points, including heresy, reverence in church, and dancing at festivals.[9] Ninguarda, a Dominican, was bishop of Como and visited his diocese between 1589 and 1593. However, in his own visitation he employed a much more limited questionnaire as far as the laity was concerned asking only about their assiduity at communion and about the presence of 'scandalous' people, including heretics, blasphemers, usurers and keepers of concubines. In other words, he does not go beyond Bollani.[10]

Whether anyone did so in the first half of the seventeenth century is difficult to say, since no visitations of this period have yet found their way into print. In the later seventeenth century, however, it is possible to find a questionnaire which goes well beyond Bollani and Ninguarda in its details about the laity. It was the work of Vincenzo Maria Orsini, who was cardinal archbishop of Siponto from 1675 to 1680, and later pope Benedict XIII. Orsini's instructions for visitors ask for statistics not only of families, souls and communicants, but also of schoolmasters, doctors, surgeons, midwives, notaries, booksellers, innkeepers and artists, in order to check as closely as possible on the education of the laity, the books they read, the images they looked at, and to see whether they came into the world and left it in a proper christian manner. His questions about the morals of the laity mention adulterers, usurers and gamblers. Their beliefs were also subject to investigation, the visitors being required to ask 'whether there is anyone suspect of heresy. Whether there is anyone who owns or reads prohibited books. Whether there are any blasphemers or witches (*malefici*)'.[11] Giuseppe Crispino, an admirer of Orsini who was bishop of Amelia from 1690 to 1721, went still further in his own enquiries into the life of the laity, and into popular customs in particular. His fifty-one questions on the subject are concerned not only with heresy and witchcraft but also enquire, for example, whether widows, 'to show their sorrow, absent themselves from Mass, and for how long'; whether fiancées do the same 'to show modesty'; and 'what abuses there are' when women mourn the deaths of relatives (a reference to the wailing rituals to be found in southern Italy to this day, or at any rate until quite recently.[12] In this tradition we should also place Giovanni Angelo Anzani, who was bishop of Campagna and Satriano from 1736 to 1770, and made regular enquiries into witchcraft and magic in particular.[13]

In the nineteenth century, the picture changes again. The recently published records of four visitations of dioceses in the Veneto between 1803 and 1865 suggest an increasing interest in the beliefs of ordinary people and in the process of social change.

Ludovico Flangini's visitation of Venice in 1803 asked only two formal questions about the laity (their numbers and the means of instruction), but these were supplemented by more open-ended 'observations on the people'. The standard response was that 'there are no public sinners' or 'no one who has failed to go to confession', but, as in the case of the Venetian censuses of the seventeenth century (above, p. 37), the document reflects variations of concern at parish level, and some priests took the opportunity to make comments of an untraditional kind. Some gave a social dimension to their answers, saying that it was the soldiers or the 'lower orders' (*gente bassa*), who failed to go to confession or whatever. Or they gave a temporal dimension to their answers. 'In these times people don't listen to us'; 'we live in bad times'; 'we live in critical times'. Here at last we can hear the parish priests speaking.[14]

When Giovanni Ladislao Pyrker visited the same diocese in 1821, he was more concerned with the laity than his predecessor had been. Parish priests were interrogated about people who blasphemed, lived with concubines or failed to go to confession, while the laity were asked whether they knew anyone who spoke against the Catholic faith. The answers too reveal a more acute social consciousness than before. The priests often take care to describe the social composition of the parish; 'mainly poor people', 'the majority merchant families', and so on. Some of them use the language of class. The parish of S. Maria Formosa is described as 'of all classes', while S. Stefano is a parish 'of the upper classes' (*le classi più distinte*). As for S. Giovanni in Bragora, of which we have heard before (p. 33), it is described as 'a den of iniquity...everyone knows what the Bragora is like'. Apart from this social topography of Venice, the priests also make observations on particular social groups. Blasphemy, for example, is associated with 'plebeians', boatmen in particular, as a result of their lack of education'. Finally, in the space reserved for miscellaneous observations, the rector of S. Marcuola, who classified a quarter of his parish as poor, denounced the lack of concern which had left them ignorant of religion for so long, treating them as 'the dregs of the parish' rather than 'an important part of the Church's flock'[15] It should be clear how far changes in what is recorded in visitations are related to the changing attitudes of priests as well as bishops.

Giuseppe Grasser's visitation of Treviso in 1826–7 is less informative, perhaps because the town was relatively small. The language of class is absent, and social consciousness much less than in Venice.[16] In Padua, however, visited by Federico Manfredini between 1859 and 1865, both questions and answers depart from tradition in significant ways. The priests were asked about the relative numbers of men and women in the parish and also among the communicants. They were expected to reply in writing, and their observations on the morals of their parishoners were classified as 'secret' and filed separately. As for the answers, what is most remarkable is the attempt of a number of priests to explain as well as describe the situation in their parish. Since a substantial minority in some parishes did not make their Easter duties, there was clearly some explaining to do, whether in traditional terms like 'sloth and coldness', or new ones like 'the social chaos which began in 1848 and is getting worse and worse'. One priest distinguishes popular from official religion in order to denounce the former. 'For the solidity of christian works the plebs substitutes a religious practice according to its own caprice.'[17]

To sum up so far: visitation records suggest that the clergy were becoming more and more concerned with the religious practice and beliefs of the laity, and with popular attitudes in particular; and, more precisely, that there were three turning-points in clerical attitudes to the laity; in the late sixteenth century, the late seventeenth century, and the early nineteenth century. To explain these changes it may be useful to place them in comparative as well as local context.

In the years after the Council of Trent, the increasing interest in the laity shown by the visitors has an obvious enough explanation; the fear of heresy. If this explanation is correct, one would expect to find still greater interest in the beliefs of the laity in dioceses closer to the Protestants than Verona or Florence. This was in fact the case. Johann Hoya, for example, visited the diocese of Münster in 1571–3. He issued an 84-point questionnaire about the faith, including the enquiry whether any parishioners had impious or irreverent or even 'scurrilous' attitudes towards the Mass. An unusual question, but the diocese was an unusual one. It was less than forty years since the Anabaptists had taken Münster over, and another question does in fact ask whether there are any Anabaptists in the parish.[18]

In the seventeenth and eighteenth centuries, the presence of heretics in a given diocese seems to have continued to encourage the bishop to investigate the laity more carefully than elsewhere. One thinks, for example, of the diocese of La Rochelle with its Huguenot minority, or – to take an Anglican example – of the eighteenth-century bishop of Oxford who asked his clergy: 'Are there any Papists in your parish?...Are there in your parish any Presbyterians, Independents or Anabaptists?...Are there any Quakers in your parish?'[19]

The visitations reflect not only with heresy but also, from the later seventeenth century on, an increasing interest in popular customs which is also visible in other sources of the period, such as travel journals (above, p. 15f). One might call this interest 'ethnographical', not to make the bishops seem modern but to identify one strand in the cultural heritage of ethnography. It is worth pointing out that some of the missionaries active in seventeenth-century Italy had personal experience of other continents, like the Jesuit Francesco Bressari (who had worked among the Iroquois) and the Capuchin Giovanni Francesco Romano (who had worked in the Congo). The concern with customs is still more obvious in France. In Normandy in 1687, for example, the bishop, a true member of the Colbert family in this respect, produced a particularly elaborate 140-point questionnaire which included enquiries about charivaris and popular festivals: 'Does anything indecorous happen at Christmas, Hallowe'en, or other times?...Are second marriages dishonoured by tumults, noise and ridiculous mobs?' (Join-Lambert, 1953). It will be clear from the tone of the questions that in France as in Italy the concern for information about unofficial religious practice was part of a movement to root them out which I have described elsewhere as 'the reform of popular culture' (Burke, 1978, ch. 8). The movement was not new in the seventeenth and eighteenth centuries but it seems to have become more intense in Catholic Europe at this time. In Italy, Ludovico Muratori is a good example of a priest who combined a scholarly interest in old customs with a desire to purge devotion from 'superstition'. He is known to have had an influence on one of the bishops already discussed, Giovanni Angelo Anzani (Bertelli, 1960; De Rosa, 1971, pp. 71f).

In the nineteenth century, the clergy's increasing awareness of differences in religious practice within the laity and their increasing interest in explaining these differences seems to owe something to secular social surveys, which were proliferating at the time. One episcopal visitation which smells of sociology is that conducted by Mgr Dupanloup in his diocese of Orléans in 1850, which devotes forty questions out of fifty-eight to the laity, an unprecedented proportion, and asks about the occupations of parishioners as well as their 'superstitions', and also about the social environment of the parish, the state of the roads, factories and so on (Marcilhacy, 1962, ch.1; Marcilhacy, 1964, pp. 38–41). It would be good to know whether the nineteenth-century Italian bishops, such as Pyrker and Manfredini, shared his sociological interests. As in the case of the soul-censuses (above, p. 30) we see the Church appropriating the methods of lay social surveys. However, the traffic may have gone in both directions. The concern with identifying people who failed to perform their Easter duties made the clergy pioneers of quantitative methods, such as issuing tickets (*schedae* or *cedole*) which had to be handed back at confession and communion. Secular surveys of popular customs at the turn of the eighteenth and nineteenth centuries take over the questionnaire form from episcopal visitations, and a few of the actual questions as well.[20] In any history of social thought, the bishops deserve a place.

5
How to be
a Counter-Reformation saint

Saints are well worth the attention of cultural historians not only because many of them are interesting as individuals, but also because, like other heroes, they reflect the values of the culture in which they are perceived in a heroic light. As western culture has changed over time, so have the kinds of people honoured as saints; martyrs, ascetics, bishops and so on. To complicate the story, however, the way in which saints are created has itself changed over the long term. It has always been the outcome of some sort of interaction between clergy and laity, centre and periphery, learned culture and popular culture, but at various times the balance of forces has shifted towards the centre. One of the periods in which this happened was the Counter-Reformation.

In the early church, sanctity was essentially an unofficial phenomenon, as it still is in Islam (Gellner, 1969; Gaborieau, 1978). Some people became the object of cults after they were dead, and some of these cults spread outside their original locations. However, the process of saint-making gradually became more formal and more centralised. In the late fourth-century, it was appropriated by the bishops (Brown, 1981). At the end of the eleventh-century, pope Urban II emphasised the need for witnesses to the virtues and miracles of candidates for sanctity. In the thirteenth-century, Gregory IX further formalised the rules of procedure in cases of canonisation. It was the same Gregory IX who set up the tribunal of the Inquisition, and this was no coincidence. Like a good lawyer, Gregory was concerned to define both saints and heretics, the opposite ends of the Christian scale. He used similar legal methods in both instances: trials. The trial for sanctity required witnesses; it required judges; and it required the notorious devil's advocate, the equivalent of counsel for the prosecution (Toynbee, 1929; Kemp, 1948; Vauchez, 1981). A British visitor to Rome in the late eighteenth-century has left us a vivid account of the pleading by the devil's advocate, before an audience in St Peter's, in the beatification suit on behalf of Bonaventura of Naples.[1]

Side by side with these formally canonised saints, defined by the centre of religious authority, Rome, there survived informally chosen holy people, whose cult was local, not universal and permitted, not obligatory. It was a two-tier system analogous to the dual structure of local and international trade. It has been argued that medieval legends of the saints reveal the conflict and also the reconciliation of central and local factors (Klaniczay, 1983).

Holy people are not unique to Christianity. What does appear to be uniquely Christian, though, is the idea that saints are not only extremely virtuous people, but also efficacious mediators with God on behalf of the living. In other words, they are more useful and more powerful dead than alive. This was of course an idea which came under heavy fire at the Reformation. Erasmus, for example, pointed out that the veneration of the saints was 'not a great deal different from the superstitions of the ancients', such as sacrificing to Hercules and Neptune.[2] Specific saints were identified by humanists and reformers with the heroes of classical myth; St George, for example, with Perseus, another monster-slayer.

These criticisms worried the authorities, as can be seen from the discussion of the question of the saints at one of the last sessions of the Council of Trent. The fathers assembled at Trent admitted that there had been abuses. However, the decree which emerged from their deliberations simply reaffirmed the desirability of venerating the images and relics of the saints and of going on pilgrimage to their shrines. St George survived the criticisms and he was not removed from the calendar until our own day. Changes were made, but they were limited ones. One concerned the past, and the other the future.

In the first place, an attempt was made to emend the accepted accounts of the lives of the saints and to replace these accounts with something more reliable, according to the criteria of humanist historical criticism. The most elaborate and systematic attempt at criticism and emendation was the work of the Bollandists in the seventeenth-century, but the way had been shown by Erasmus himself in a biography of Jerome.[3]

In the second placed, the procedure for admitting new saints was tightened up. The last canonisations under the old regime were those of St Bruno (1514), St Francis de Paul (1519), St Benno and St Antonino of Florence (both 1523). There followed a hiatus of sixty-five years during which no more saints were canonised. It does not seem unreasonable to explain this hiatus by a failure of papal nerve and to speak of a 'crisis of canonisations' at a time when, as we have seen, the very idea of a saint was under fire. In Lutheran Saxony, for example, the canonisation of St Benno, a local worthy, was mockingly celebrated with a procession in which horse's bones figured as relics. On the other hand, the Protestants developed cults of their own holy people, notably the martyrs to Catholic persecution. Thus the church authorities were placed in a dilemma. To refrain from creating saints was to yield the initiative in propaganda to the Protestants, but to create saints was to invite mockery. The church first tried one solution to their problem, and then the other. It was not till 1588, twenty-five years after the close of the Council of Trent, that saints began to be made again, starting with St Didacus, otherwise known as Diego of Alcalà. There was time for only one more canonisation (St Hyacinth), in what remained of the sixteenth-century, but there were twenty-four in the seventeenth-century and twenty-nine in the eighteenth.[4]

The revival of saint-making was accompanied by an increase in the central control of the sacred, or the right to define the sacred. 1588 was not only the year of the elevation of St Didacus but also that of the institution of the Congregation of Sacred Rites and Ceremonies, a standing committee of cardinals whose responsibilities included canonisations. A treatise of 1610 reaffirmed that 'the authority to canonise saints belongs to the Roman pontiff alone'.[5] Procedures were made increasingly strict and formal by pope Urban VIII in 1625 and 1634. The distinction between full saints and second-class *beati*, or 'blessed', was made sharper with the introduction of formal beatification. A fifty-year rule was brought in: in other words, a suit for canonisation could not begin until fifty years after the death of the candidate for sanctity. This was a notable break with tradition. Carlo Borromeo, for example, and Filippo Neri had been canonised twenty-six and twenty-seven years after their respective deaths. The fifty-year rule was followed by a second hiatus, lasting thirty years this time; there were no canonisations between 1629 and 1658. The final touches to the new system were added in 1734 by the canon lawyer Prospero Lambertini, later pope Benedict XIV.[6]

According to the new system, sanctity was explicitly defined in terms of the Aristotelian–Thomist concept of a 'heroic' degree of virtue (Hofmann, 1933; De Maio, 1972). As for the procedures by which the possessors of this heroic virtue were recognised, they had become more 'bureaucratic', in Max Weber's sense of the term. The distinction between sacred and profane was made sharper than it had been, while recruitment procedures for the saints were made uniform and formal. In the trials for sanctity, the supernatural was defined, graded and labelled with increasing care. There was also an increase in the central control of the sacred, at the expense of local, unofficial and – one might say – 'wild cat' devotions. A papal monopoly of saint-making had effectively been declared. At a time of centralising monarchies, which included the papacy, the next world was being remade in the image of this one (on the Roman bureaucracy, see p. 180).

These changes did not mean that unofficial saints disappeared altogether, for the new rules were not made retroactive, and the status of some individuals remained ambiguous. That of the plague saint Roche or Rocco, for example. His cult had spread widely in the later fifteenth-century, and popes had authorised confraternities and masses in his name. The Venetians made his cult official at the time of the great plague of 1576, during the hiatus in canonisations which has already been mentioned. However, this cult could hardly be said to have existed from time immemorial, since Roche had lived in the fourteenth century. He was an awkward case, as the popes recognised. According to the Venetian ambassador to Rome, Sixtus V meant 'either to canonise him or to obliterate him' (*o di cannonizzarlo o di cancellarlo*), but in fact the pope died without having had time to make his choice. Urban VIII authorised a special mass of St Roche, but even he, who defined so much, did not clear up the ambiguity of this saint's status.[7]

Local cults not only continued, they also sprang up. Some were simply premature honours paid to those whose elevation might reasonably be expected. In Milan, Carlo Borromeo was venerated before his canonisation in 1610, and scenes from his life were displayed in the cathedral. (Wittkower, 1958, p. 61). In similar fashion, at Antwerp, Rubens painted the miracles of Ignatius Loyola and Francis Xavier about 1617, although the two men would not become official saints until 1622 (Martin, 1968, pp. 29f). In 1631 the Venetians instituted an official cult of their former patriarch, Lorenzo Giustinian, who was not canonised until 1690 (Niero, 1965).

Other unofficial saints were rather less conventional. In Castille, Luisa de Carrion, who died in 1636, was treated as a saint and as a miracle worker in court as well as in popular circles, although the Inquisition accused her of imposture and even witchcraft (Christian, 1981, p. 133). In Naples, the fisherman turned rebel, Masaniello, was widely regarded as a saint after his murder in the summer of 1647 (see below, p. 203). In seventeenth-century France, the Jansenists had their own unofficial saints, complete with miracles, despite the fact that some Jansenists were uneasy about the idea of venerating men and women in this way. Even in Rome itself, unofficial cults could grow up. In 1648, for example, 'in the monastery of the Quattro Coronati, a nun called Sister Anna Maria died with the reputation of a saint, and her body was exposed to public view for three days'.[8] The Franciscan Carlo da Sezze, who died in 1670, was regarded as a saint in Rome, where he lived, and was consulted on occasion by Pope Clement IX.

However, people like this who died in the odour of sanctity could not be tried for fifty years, and if they failed, the cult would be suppressed. Many were examined, but few passed; in the Kingdom of Naples alone, there were about 100 unsuccessful candidates between 1550 and 1800 (Sallmann, 1979a). There have been few studies of the failure, despite the potential interest and importance of this approach for an understanding of the saint system; among them are the recent articles on four Neapolitan women of the sixteenth and seventeenth centuries (Sallmann, 1984), and on the Florentine nun Suor Domenica, who was perceived as a healer who could help the city at the time of the plague of 1630 (Calvi, 1984). The remainder of this chapter will therefore be concerned with the successful, the happy few, the fifty-five individuals formally canonised between 1588, when the practice was revived, and 1767, which was followed by another hiatus, this time of forty years.

That the collective biography of the saints might be of value for an understanding of Catholic culture is no new idea. A number of historians and sociologists, from Coulton (1925), and Mecklin (1941) onwards, have studied the changing social origins and career patterns of the saints as indicators of social and cultural trends (Sorokin, 1950; George and George, 153–4; Delooz, 1969; Vauchez, 1981; Weinstein and Bell, 1982; etc). They have discussed such topics as the rise of martyrs in the sixteenth century and the rise of the middle class into sanctity in the eighteenth and nineteenth centuries.

However, these historians and sociologists have not always been conscious of a central problem of method, and that is the need to decide whether to treat the saints as witnesses to the values of the age in which they lived or the age in which they were canonised. In some cases, like those of Carlo Borromeo and Filippo Neri, already mentioned, the problem is not acute, because they were canonised so quickly. On the other hand, several Counter-Reformation figures, now venerated as saints, received this title long after their deaths. John Berchmans, for example, died in 1621 but was not canonised till 1888, while the Jesuit missionary Peter Canisius, who died in 1597, had to wait until 1925. It is true that biographies of Canisius were published in 1614 and 1616 and that his beatification suit lasted over 250 years, but if he is to be included as a Counter-Reformation saint, so should everyone whose suit began in this period. They may, after all, be canonised one day. Conversely, among the saints canonised between 1588 and 1767 were eight who had died in the fifteenth-century, six in the fourteenth, four in the thirteenth, and one, Isidore, who had died as far back as the twelfth-century. Most students of the saints have assumed that they are witnesses to the age in which they lived. As individuals they obviously are. However, anyone interested in the history of perception has to treat them as witnesses above all to the age in which they were canonised; there is no other justification for selecting this formally-defined group. It would also be worth looking at saints who were, one might say, 're-activated' in this period, (as Sallmann, 1982, has done for Naples, noting the importance there of St Anthony of Padua). However, since the criteria for re-activation are unlikely to be precise, it may be more useful, in this brief sketch, to concentrate on the newly-canonised alone. It might have been worth adding the formally beatified, of whom there were forty-three between 1662 and 1767 (Twenty-four individuals and the collective beatification of the nineteen martyrs of Gorkum). But to do this would mean changing the criteria of selection in the middle of the period studied (since formal beatification was only introduced in the seventeenth-century). In any case, sixteen of the individual *Beati* were canonised later in our period, so the addition of this group would not affect the conclusions very much.

Since the total 'population' of the saints is well below 100, precise statistics will be of little use, let alone percentages. In any case, too much emphasis, relatively speaking, has been placed in the past on 'objective' factors such as social origins and career patterns. 'Sanctity', as one social anthropologist has put it, 'more perhaps than anything else in social life, is in the eye of the beholder' (Gilsenan, 1976, p. 210). As the Belgian sociologist Pierre Delooz (1962, 1969) has remarked, the saints need to be studied as an example of the social history of perception. The objective factors will therefore be discussed only briefly.

What kind of person had the best chance, during the Counter-Reformation, of achieving this particular form of upward mobility? As in the Middle Ages (Schulenburg, 1978), men had better chances than women; the group contains forty-three males to twelve females. In this sphere as in others already discussed (above, p. 35), women lacked visibility. Geography as well as gender affected the results: Italians, with twenty-six members of the group, stood much better chances than others of achieving sanctity. Spaniards came next, with seventeen saints, leaving only twelve places for everyone else (four Frenchmen and women, three Poles, two Portuguese, one German, one Czech, Jan Nepomuk, and one

Peruvian, Rose of Lima). Nobles had better chances of becoming saints than commoners. At least twenty-six of the fifty-five saints were of nobel origin, including some from leading families like the Borjas and the Gonzagas, the Corsini and the Pazzi, while Isabel of Portugal was of royal blood. There is little or no precise information about the social origins of a number of the saints, but at least five were of peasant stock, while two more worked for a time as shepherds (Pascual Baylón and John of God), and one as a ploughman (Isidore). As for the 'middle classes', we know at least that John of the Cross was the son of a silk-weaver, Jean François Régis the son of a merchant, and Filippo Neri the son of a lawyer.

To stand a good chance of becoming a saint, it was better to be clerical than lay, and much better to be a member of a religious order than one of the secular clergy. Of our fifty-five individuals, only six came from the laity, and of these, Margherita of Cortona was a member of the 'third order' of Franciscans, while John of God was associated with the Hospitallers and Francesca Ponziani with the Benedictines. Three of the fifty-five were lay brothers, on the margin between the lay and clerical worlds (Pascual Baylón, Felice of Cantalice, and Serafino of Monte-granaro). The secular clergy account for eight more of the fifty-five.

That leaves thirty-eight full members of religious orders. The Fran-ciscans had the largest share of these, with one nun (Caterina of Bologna) and seven friars, but the Dominicans and Jesuits were close behind. The Dominicans had four friars and three nuns, while there were six Jesuits canonised in the period. The Carmelites had two nuns and two friars; the Servites, a nun and two friars; the Capuchins two friars (not counting their two lay brothers, already mentioned). The Theatines had two saints, the Benedictines one, the Augustinians one, and there were four saints who founded their own orders. It is obvious enough that these fifty-five men and women were not a random sample of the Catholic population at large. The question remains, why these particular individuals achieved recognition rather than the many people with similar social backgrounds. It is not sufficient to say that they possessed 'heroic virtue'; a social historian will also want to know who saw them as virtuous. There are two places to look for an answer to this question; at the grass roots, where particular cults grew up, and at the centre, where they were made official.

To begin with the periphery. Delooz was surely right to see the problem of the saints as a problem in the history of perception, or, to use the Durkheimian phrase, 'collective representations' (above, p. 27). 'One is never a saint except for other people'. Some societies are, as he puts it, 'programmed' to perceive sanctity, while others are not. Italy in particular was clearly programmed in this way. Saints were also perceived in a stereotyped manner, or manners; there is a relatively small number of saintly roles, or routes to holiness. It may be useful to distinguish five of them.

The first is that of the founder of a religious order. No fewer than twelve out of our fifty-five fall into this category. Francesca Ponziani founded the Benedictine Oblates; Teresa of Avila, the strict ('discalced') Carmelites; Ignatius Loyala, the Jesuits. François de Sales and Jeanne de Chantal between them founded the Visitation nuns. Gaetano of Thiene was one of the founders of the Theatines. Vincent de Paul founded both the Congregation of the Mission and the Daughters of Charity. Camillo de Lelis founded the Camilliani, Girolamo Miani the Somaschi, and José de Calasanz the Piarists. Filippo Neri is now regarded as the founder of the Oratorians, although he did not have a formal institution in mind; he disliked formality. In a similar manner, the manner of 'whig' or future-oriented history, John of God may be described as the posthumous founder of the Brothers Hospitallers.

A second important road to sanctity was that of the missionary. Nine of our fifty-five fall into this class, if we include Tomaso of Villanueva, who organised missions without leaving Spain. Diego of Alcalá, with whom the revival of canonisations began in 1588, was a missionary in the Canaries; Raimondo Peñaforte, in North Africa; Francis Xavier, in the Far East. Luis Bertrán and Francisco Solano both worked in Spanish America (in modern Colombia and Peru). Jean-François Régis tried to convert the Huguenots of the Cévennes, while Fidelis of Sigmaringen met his death on a mission to the Swiss Calvinists. Giuseppe of Leonessa worked in the mission field in his native Italy as well as outside Europe.

A third route to sanctity was that of the pastor, the good shepherd, with seven cases in the group, of which the most famous is surely that of the model bishop of the Counter-Reformation, Carlo Borromeo, with François de Sales, bishop of 'Geneva' (actually based at Annecy) not far behind. The others are pope Pius V; Turibio, archbishop of Lima; Lorenzo Giustinian, Patriarch of Venice; Tomaso of Villanueva, who overlaps with the missionary group; and Jan Nepomuk of Prague, said to have been murdered for refusing to divulge the secrets of confession.

The second and third routes were for men only. The fourth and fifth were open to women, like the first. The fourth category is that of charitable activity. There are seven obvious examples in the group, three women (Isabel of Portugal, Margherita of Cortona, Caterina of Genoa), and four men. Vincent de Paul's work among the galley-slaves is famous. John of God worked among the sick in Granada, while José de Calasanz set up schools for the poor in Rome.

The fifth and last main route to sanctity was that of the mystic or ecstatic, subject to trances, levitation and so on. Again there are seven obvious cases, four women and three men. The women were Teresa of Avila (who is also to be found in the first category); Rose of Lima; Maria Maddalena de'Pazzi, and Caterina de'Ricci, while the men were John of the Cross, Pedro Regalado, and Giuseppe of Copertino.

There were of course saints who did not fit any of these categories very well. Luigi (Aloysius) Gonzaga and Stanislas Kostka, for example, both of them Jesuit novices who lived ascetic lives and died young. However, the five roles which have just been described seem by far the most important.

Some omissions may well be found surprising. These Counter-Reformation saints include no theologians, no equivalent of Thomas Aquinas, unless one counts a minor figure, Jan Kanty, who had been a professor at Cracow. Nicholas of Cusa was proposed for canonisation, but without success. Equally surprising is the relative lack of martyr-saints, in a period in which many Catholics, some of whom have been canonised subsequently, did die for their faith, and in which the cult of the martyrs of the early Church was reactivated, encouraged by the discovery, late in the sixteenth-century, of the Roman catacombs. However, of our fifty-five saints, only Jan Nepomuk and Fidelis of Sigmaringen fall into the martyr category. Of course the nineteen martyrs of Gorkum, executed by the Calvinists, were beatified in 1675, and it is likely that other martyrs were regarded as unofficial saints. An early eighteenth-century historian of the mission to Japan described the martyred missionaries as saints, but added in his preface, 'to obey the decree of pope Urban VIII'; that he did not use this term in the strict sense.[9] Was this a case of reluctant obedience?

The clustering of our fifty-five saints around five roles suggests that a key factor in the attribution or 'imputation' of sanctity to an individual is the correspondence or 'fit' between his or her career and the best-known stereotypes of the saint. The process is of course circular or self-confirming. There are few lay saints, for example, because the stereotypes favour the clergy, and the stereotypes are biassed in this way partly because the clergy form the majority of past saints. New individuals have to be matched with old roles. They are perceived as similar to individuals who have already been recognised as saints.

In some cases, we know that the later saint consciously modelled himself or herself on an earlier prototype. It is yet another example of the presentation of self (above, p. 19). In saying this I do not mean to suggest that the individuals involved were insincere; like the rest of us (and more successfully than most of us), they were following cultural models. Maria Maddalena de'Pazzi and Rose of Lima were both said by their contemporaries to have imitated Catherine of Siena, who had been canonised in the fifteenth century. Caterina de'Ricci was described as receiving the stigmata, like St Francis, and as having a vision of a mystic marriage with Christ, like Catherine of Siena.[10] Carlo Borromeo modelled himself on St Ambrose, his great predecessor as archbishop of Milan.[11] One may also suspect that Filippo Neri, who was renowned for both his gaiety and his humility, was perceived as a second St Francis; Francisco Borja, general of the Jesuits, as a second St Ignatius; Ignatius himself, as a second St Dominic (another Spaniard who founded an order); and Aloysius Gonzaga, famed for his heroic degree of chastity, as a second St Alexis, who was celebrated for the same quality in poetry and drama in the Middle Ages. There were of course many lesser imitators of the saints. One of the main reasons for having saints, as the Church officially saw it, was to provide the faithful with models with which to identify themselves.

In the imputation of sanctity, contiguity was important as well as similarity – or to use the terms made famous by Roman Jakobson (1971), metonymy was important as well as metaphor. The sacred seems to be contagious, as Durkheim (1912, p. 457) has pointed out. At any rate we find clusters of saints around important figures. Thus Francis Xavier, Filippo Neri, Pius V, and Felice of Cantalice were all associated personally with Ignatius Loyola; Felice again, Camillo de Lelis, Maria Maddalena de'Pazzi and Caterina de'Ricci, with Filippo Neri; Francisco Borja, Pedro of Alcantara and John of the Cross, with Teresa of Avila; and Andrea Avellino and Aloysius Gonzaga with Carlo Borromeo.

So much for the growth of cults at the periphery. It remains to try to explain how and why certain cults were adopted by the centre of religious power and made official, while others were not. The heroic virtue of the candidates had to satisfy the examiners. To understand what happened it is necessary, but not sufficient, to study the trials themselves. One also needs to remember, for example, that particular popes took a special interest in saint-making: Sixtus V, for example, whose recovery of nerve put the whole process back into motion in 1588; Paul V, who only canonised two saints himself, but left five more cases pending, to be completed by his successor; Clement X and Alexander VIII, who canonised five saints apiece; Benedict XIII, who canonised eight in one year; and Benedict XIV, who had written a treatise on the subject in the days when he was still Prospero Lambertini.

Papal interests also help explain specific choices. Only one pope, Clement XI, canonised another, Pius V; but regional loyalties were extremely strong. In the fifteenth century, the Catalan Calixtus III had canonised the Catalan Vicent Ferrer, and the Sienese Pius II, Catherine of Siena. In a similar manner the Roman Paul V canonised the Roman Francesca Ponziani. The Florentine Urban VIII canonised one Florentine, Andrea Corsini, and beatified another, Maria Maddalena de'Pazzi. The Venetian Lorenzo Giustinian was canonised by the Venetian Alexander VIII. Another Venetian pope, Clement XIII, canonised one fellow-citizen, Girolamo Miani, and beatified another, Gregorio Barbarigo (who, like the pope, had been bishop of Padua). In one case we find loyalty of the 'old school tie' variety; Benedict XIV, an old pupil of the Somaschi, beatified the order's founder (Miani); while Alexander VII, in spite of the fifty-year rule, canonised his old friend François de Sales.

The centre did not simply make a selection from candidates presented by the periphery; it sometimes yielded to pressure from outside. The religious orders were particularly powerful pressure-groups and the high proportion of saints from their ranks has surely to be explained, partially at least, in these terms (Delooz, 1962; Vauchez, 1981, pp. 131f). Robert Bellarmine, for example, a Jesuit who was strategically placed at Rome, is said to have been largely responsible for the beatification of the founder of his order. There were also pressures from rulers. If there was a 'Spanish preponderance' (second only to the Italian) in the field of sanctity, it may be connected with a similar preponderance (unqualified this time) in the field of international relations. The first Counter-Reformation saint, Diego of Alcalá, was canonised following pressure from Philip II, while the bull canonising Ignatius Loyola refers to requests from both Philip II and Philip III. Philip III also pressed for Raimundo Peñaforte, Isidore the Spanish ploughman, and Carlo Borromeo, whose diocese of Milan was part of the king's empire. Sigismund of Poland pressed successfully for the canonisation of the Polish cleric Hyacinth (Jacek), and Louis XIII for Caterina of Genoa. François I, Henri IV, Ferdinand II, and Maximilian of Bavaria were other rulers who tried to exert pressure on behalf of particular candidates. As for Andrea Corsini, his case was urged by an alliance of his order, the Carmelites; the ruler of the region he came from, Tuscany; and his own family, patricians of Florence.[12] Family pressure must not be forgotten; it was to the advantage of Carlo Borromeo that he had his nephew and successor Federigo to plead for him (whereas Federigo himself had no equivalent support). As Addison put it, 'the interests of particular families, religious orders, convents or churches, have too great a sway in their canonisations.[13] Foreign visitors to Italy, Catholic and Protestant, were doubtless too cynical and too prone to repeat gossip about payments for canonisation, but Burnet claimed that Borromeo's 'cost the Town a hundred thousand Crowns', making them unwilling to press for the nephew as well, while Montesquieu quoted 180,000 in the case of Andrea Corsini.[14]

Such stories do not have to be taken too literally. Suffice it to say that it is impossible to explain the achievement of sanctity entirely in terms of the qualities of the individual, or even by the qualities which witnesses saw in that individual. The imputation of sanctity, like its converse, the imputation of heresy (and more particularly of witchcraft), should be seen, like other forms of labelling, as a process of interaction or 'negotiation' between centre and periphery, each with its own definition of the situation (above, p. 38). The process involved the official management of unofficial cults, which were, like the religious visions of the period, sometimes confirmed and sometimes rejected.

The process of interaction also involved the implantation of official cults in parts of the periphery other than the region where they first sprang up, a subject which deserves a good deal more attention on the part of historians of religion than it has achieved so far. The cult of St Isidore, for example, was spread in France by his biographer Richard Dognon, who was a friend of St Vincent de Paul. It was also important in Poland (Tazbir, 1969). By the end of the seventeenth-century, the cults of Counter-Reformation saints such as Filippo Neri, Francis Xavier, and Ignatius Loyola – in that order – had taken root in the Kingdom of Naples (Sallmann, 1982). The cults of Loyola and Xavier also seem to have become part of German Catholic popular culture in the course of the seventeenth and eighteenth centuries, a process which involved their assimilation to earlier local cults, their 'folklorisation'. Curative properties were now assigned to 'Ignatius water', for example. The argument of this essay has been that the whole body of saints may be regarded as a system of signs (a system which was, and is, neither static nor closed). In other words, the saints may be studied as a kind of litmus paper sensitive to the changing relationship between the church and the rest of society.

APPENDIX

New saints, 1588–1767

Note that Gregory VII (no. 4) is not included in the analysis in the main body of this chapter.

1 Diego of Alcala (died 1463). Spanish Franciscan missionary. Canonised [hereafter 'C.'] by Sixtus V (1588).

2 Hyacinth Odrovaz (d. 1257). Noble Polish Dominican. C. by Clement VIII (1594).

3 Raimundo Peñaforte (d. 1275). Spanish Dominican missionary. C. by Clement VIII (1600).

[4 Gregory VII (d. 1085). German pope. C. by Paul V (1606).]

5 Francesca Ponziani (d. 1440). Roman noblewoman. C. by Paul V (1608).

6 Carlo Borromeo (d. 1584). Noble Milanese archbishop. C. by Paul V (1610).

7 Teresa of Avila (d. 1582). Spanish Carmelite. C. by Gregory XV (1622).

8 Ignatius Loyola (d. 1556). Noble Spanish Jesuit. C. by Gregory XV (1622).

9 Filippo Neri (d. 1595). Florentine. C. by Gregory XV (1622).

10 Francis Xavier (d. 1552). Noble Spanish Jesuit missionary. C. by Gregory XV (1622).

11 Isidore (d. 1130). Spanish peasant. C. by Gregory XV (1622).

12 Isabel (d. 1336). Portuguese princess. C. by Urban VIII (1625).

13 Andrea Corsini (d. 1373). Noble Florentine Carmelite bishop. C. by Urban VIII (1629).

14 Tomaso of Villanueva (d. 1555). Spanish Augustinian archbishop. C. by Alexander VII (1658).

15 François de Sales (d. 1622). Noble French bishop. C. by Alexander VII (1665).

16 Pedro of Alcántara (d. 1562). Spanish Franciscan. C. by Clement IX (1669).

17 Maria Maddalena de'Pazzi (d. 1604). Noble Florentine Carmelite. C. by Clement IX (1669).

18 Rose of Lima (d. 1617). Peruvian Dominican. C. by Clement X (1671).

19 Luis Bertrán (d. 1581). Spanish Dominican missionary. C. by Clement X (1671).

20 Gaetano da Thiene (d. 1547). Noble from Vicenza. C. by Clement X (1671).

21 Francisco Borja (d. 1572). Noble Spanish Jesuit. C. by Clement X (1671).

22 Filippo Benizzi (d. 1285). Florentine Servite. C. by Clement X (1671).

23 Lorenzo Giustinian (d. 1455). Noble Venetian bishop. C. by Alexander VIII (1690).

24 Juan de Sahagún (d. 1479). Spanish Benedictine. C. by Alexander VIII (1690).

25 Pascual Baylón (d. 1592). Spanish shepherd and Franciscan lay brother. C. by Alexander VIII (1690).

26 John of God (d. 1550). Portuguese shepherd. C. by Alexander VIII (1690).
27 Giovanni Capistrano (d. 1476). Noble Italian Franciscan. C. by Alexander VIII (1690).
28 Pius V. (d. 1572). Italian Dominican pope. C. by Clement XI (1712).
29 Andrea Avellino (d. 1608). Noble Italian Theatine. C. by Clement XI (1712).
30 Felice da Cantalice (d. 1587). Italian peasant and Capuchin lay brother. C. by Clement XI (1712).
31 Caterina of Bologna (d. 1463). Italian poor Clare. C. by Clement XI (1712).
32 Turibio Alfonso (d. 1606). Noble Spanish archbishop. C. by Benedict XIII (1726).
33 Giacomo della Marca (d. 1476). Italian Franciscan. C. by Benedict XIII (1726).
34 Agnese Segni (d. 1317). Noble Tuscan Dominican. C. by Benedict XIII (1726).
35 Pellegrino Laziosi (d. 1345). Noble Italian Servite. C. by Benedict XIII (1726).
36 John of the Cross (d. 1591). Spanish Carmelite. C. by Benedict XIII (1726).
37 Francisco Solano (d. 1610). Spanish Franciscan missionary. C. by Benedict XIII (1726).
38 Aloysius Gonzaga (d. 1591). Noble Italian Jesuit. C. by Benedict XIII (1726).
39 Stanislaus Kostka (d. 1568). Noble Polish Jesuit. C. by Benedict XIII (1726).
40 Margherita of Cortona (d. 1297). Italian peasant, in third order of Franciscans. C. by Benedict XIII (1728).
41 Jan Nepomuk (d. 1393). Czech priest. C. by Benedict XIII (1729).
42 Vincent de Paul (d. 1660). French priest. C. by Clement XII (1736).
43 Jean-François Régis (d. 1640). French Jesuit missionary. C. by Clement XII (1736).
44 Caterina of Genoa (d. 1510). Noble Genoese. C. by Clement XII (1736).
45 Giuliana Falconieri (d. 1340). Noble Florentine Servite. C. by Clement XII (1736).
46 Fidelis of Sigmaringen (d. 1622). Suabian Capuchin missionary. C. by Benedict XIV (1746).
47 Camillo de Lelis (d. 1614). Italian. C. by Benedict XIV (1746).
48 Pedro Regalado (d. 1456). Noble Spanish Franciscan. C. by Benedict XIV (1746).
49 Giuseppe da Leonessa (d. 1612). Noble Italian Capuchin missionary. C. by Benedict XIV (1746).
50 Caterina de'Ricci (d. 1590). Noble Florentine Dominican. C. by Benedict XIV (1746).
51 Jan Kanty (d. 1473). Polish professor. C. by Clement XIII (1767).
52 Giuseppe da Copertino (d. 1663). Italian Franciscan. C. by Clement XIII (1767).

53 José de Calasanz (d. 1648). Spanish Piarist. C. by Clement XIII (1767).

54 Girolamo Miani (d. 1537). Noble Venetian, founder of Somaschi. C. by Clement XIII (1767).

55 Serafino da Montegranaro (d. 1604). Italian Capuchin lay-brother. C. by Clement XIII (1767).

56 Jeanne de Chantal (d. 1641). French noble. C. by Clement XIII (1767).

6

Perceiving a counter-culture

In the prison on the Sistine Bridge, in Rome, in February 1595, a young man was interrogated before a notary, and answered as follows:

> I am called Pompeo, I was born in Trevi near Spoleto, I am about 16 years old, I have no occupation, I was arrested by your men in the church of S. Giacomo degli Spagnoli, because I was begging for alms during Mass.
>
> Asked whether he knew of other poor beggars in Rome and whether they formed one organisation or many [*an omnes sint sub una tantum secta an vero sub diversis sectis*]...He replied: Sir, among us poor beggars there are different fraternities [*compagnie*]...the first is called the Fraternity of the Grencetti, those who, while they are begging for alms in the churches in a crowd, cut purses...The second is called the Fraternity of the Sbasiti, and includes those who pretend to be ill and lie on the ground as if they were dying and keep groaning and demanding alms. The third is called the Fraternity of the Baroni, who are healthy and upright [*stanno in piedi*], and they are sturdy beggars who do not want to work.

Pompeo went on to list nineteen groups in all, including the Rabrunati, who pretended to be epileptic or possessed and – thanks to a piece of soap – foamed appropriately at the mouth; the Dabbelolmi, who claimed to have escaped from Turkish captivity, had iron chains around their necks, and muttered 'Bran Bran Bran Bre Bre Bre'; the Formigotti, who passed as discharged soldiers; the Pistolfi, who pretended to be priests; the Burchiaroli, who stole bread from carts; and the Biganti, children who stood on street corners singing hymns such as 'O Maria Stella'. Pompeo himself admitted to being one of the Sbasiti, and he named his boss (*capo*), and their meeting-places on Piazza Navona, Ponte S. Angelo, Campo di Fiore, and the 'Rotonda', (in other words the Pantheon.)[1]

About six weeks later, a certain Girolamo was examined in the same prison:

> I was born in Rome, the son of the late Antonio Fornaro of rione Colonna near the Trevi fountain. My name is Girolamo, I am 22 years old, I have no job [*non ho esercitio alcuno*], except that I work four months a year digging salt.

63

1. G. Ceruti, *Beggar* (Göteborg)

He was interrogated about Pompeo's list and its accuracy: 'Sir, whoever gave you that list is not thoroughly informed, because they are not all there...', and he went on to add seventeen more groups, some of which overlap with Pompeo's while others are quite new, including the Marmotti, who pretended to be mute, and the Spillatori, who made a living in inns cheating at cards and dice. He added details about the bosses (*capi et maggiorenghi*), who stayed in Rome while the others moved about, their secret information service, and about their jargon (discussed below, ch. 7).[2]

These two documents, whether genuine or not – a question to which we must return – make a good introduction to the complex relation between the stereotypes of beggars and thieves and the social reality underlying them. (It should be clear that the link between beggars and thieves, or at least between some kinds of beggar and some kinds of thief, was taken very seriously by contemporaries.) It is with the history of the perception of beggars and thieves that this essay will be concerned, rather than with the structure and organisation of the 'craft', as Girolamo called it; 'they are not fraternities [*compagnie*], but crafts [*arti*], like shoemakers, tailors, goldsmiths and so on'. The beggars and thieves of early modern Italy – 'rogues', as we may call them for convenience – were often perceived as what we have learned to call a distinct 'sub-culture', recognisable by its jargon (*gergo*), a word which was first used in this context. They were sometimes viewed as what we might call a 'counter-culture', in conflict with society at large (Yinger, 1960), or in the early modern phrase, a 'world upside-down' (*mondo alla rovescia*), from which the modern term 'underworld' is doubtless derived. This topsy-turvy world might be seen as comic, a carnivalesque reversal of the natural social order; or it might be seen as diabolical, as in the case of witchcraft. Rogues were perceived in both ways.

Whose perceptions are we talking about? Was it the ruling class who saw rogues in this way, or ordinary people, or did the rogues themselves regard their culture in this light? To help answer this question in the case of early modern Italy there are a fair number of surviving images and texts, both 'literary' and 'documentary', a classic distinction which is difficult to sustain in this case. The evidence is not easy to interpret, and in some respects the 'conclusion' must remain inconclusive. The point which needs to be stressed here is the necessity of looking at texts and images as evidence of culturally stereotyped perceptions, rather than trying to force them into the opposed categories of 'fact' and 'fiction'.

In the late sixteenth and early seventeenth centuries, in particular, there was produced a whole series of texts and images representing the culture of rogues, or to use the contemporary terms – less specialised than those of Pompeo and Girolamo – *bari, bianti, calchi, furbi, furfanti, guidoni, pitocchi, scrocchi, sgherri*, and so on. Modern English seems to lack the necessary richness of vocabulary in this area, but 'cheats, knaves, rascals, scroungers and tramps' may serve as an approximation.

Among the best-known texts – which include prose and verse, formal treatises and scenes from plays – are the discourse on rogues in Tommaso Garzoni's *Universal Marketplace of all the Professions in the World* (*La piazza universale di tutte le professioni del mondo*, 1585), and a book called *The Vagabond* (*Il Vagabondo*), published in 1621 by a certain 'Raffaele Frianoro', a pseudonym for a Dominican friar by the name of Giaccinto de Nobili. His book went through at least fourteen editions, in Italian or French, before the end of the seventeenth century.[3] As for the images, the most famous are Caravaggio's paintings of cheating cardplayers which come like Girolamo's *spillatori*, from Rome in the 1590s, and Callot's twenty-five etchings of beggars, made about 1622–3. When he made these etchings, Callot, a Lorrainer, had just returned from a few years in Italy, and an Italian inscription on one of them, *Capitano dei baroni* betrays its provenance. These 'sturdy beggars' were one of Pompeo's categories. Callot is not illustrating Frianoro, but the book may have been his inspiration.[4]

These examples – and a number of lesser-known ones – allow us to speak of a vogue for representations of rogues in this period. This is not to say that interest in roguery was confined to Italy or to the years around 1600; it went back a long way (rogues, like the genuine poor, are always with us), and it could be found all over Europe.

In Spain, for example, this was the time of the rise of the 'picaresque', in other words the literature of the rogue (*picaro*), notably the anonymous *Lazarillo de Tormes* (1554) and Mateo Alemán's *Guzmán de Alfarache* (1599–1604), both of which were translated into Italian in this period, the latter as soon as 1606. The hero, Guzmán, who serves his apprenticeship in roguery at Madrid, still has a good deal to learn when he arrives in Rome, is taken aside by the 'Boss' (*protopobre*), and is informed about the different kinds of begging, which are described in the same general manner as by Garzoni and the rest. Cervantes tells a similar story, in his *Rinconete y Cortadillo* about the organisation of the underworld of Seville.[5] In France, *La vie généreuse des gueux* (1596) by 'Pechon de Ruby', which went through at least six editions by 1627, also distinguished different types of beggar (only six this time) and described their hierarchical organisation.[6] In England, there was Thomas Harman's *Caveat for Common Cursitors* (1566), and Robert Greene's 'Cony-Catching' pamphlets of the 1590s. These do not refer to Italy and they were not translated into Italian, but the London underworld they describe is organised on very similar lines to that of Rome and Madrid, similar enough to give us idiomatic translations for a number of expressions in Italian rogues' jargon. The *baroni*, for example, are 'upright men', the *marmotti* (mutes) are 'dummerers', the *formigotti* (discharged soldiers) are 'rufflers', while the beggars who feign sickness are called 'counterfeit cranks'. The main differences between London and Rome are the absence, in the former city, of nine 'Catholic' categories of rogue (fake priests, fake pilgrims, beggars carrying the images of saints, and so on), and in the latter city, of the many categories of female rogue described as practising in Elizabethan London; dells, doxies, walking morts, bawdy baskets and so on. The reference by Pompeo and Girolamo to *landre* (young women) and *cagnarde* (old women) is jejune by comparison.[7]

Descriptive works of this kind were also produced in Switzerland, Germany, the Netherlands, Poland and elsewhere. They cluster in the sixteenth and seventeenth centuries, but the theme or stereotype of the rogue in general and the cunning beggar in particular can be traced back through comic scenes in medieval religious plays, including Castellani's *San Tommaso* (1509), to classical antiquity, notably to the protagonist of Lucian's dialogue *The Parasite*, who calls sponging an 'art' (*tekhne*) (Kraemer, 1944).

We seem to have moved a long way from the interrogation of two prisoners in Rome in 1595. But appearances are deceptive. Garzoni's 'Universal Marketplace', published ten years earlier, distinguishes (without naming them) at least seventeen kinds of fraudulent beggar, including six of Pompeo's and five of Girolamo's, among them the fake epileptics, fake pilgrims, fake soldiers, and the fake prisoners of the Turks, who cry out *Illalla, Illalla, Maumeth rissollala*, which sounds a little closer to Arabic than Pompeo's *Bran Bran Bran*, and is in fact part of the Muslim profession of faith ('except God, except God; Muhammad is the messenger of God'). He also mentions the hierarchical organisation.[8] Then come our two prisoners, and the paintings of Caravaggio, and Alemán's account, written in Spanish but set in Rome and soon available in Italian in a rather free translation, which refers to the *baroni* of Campo di Fiore, and to begging as a 'craft' (*l'arte guidantesca*). Finally we have Callot's etchings and Frianoro's book, which describes thirty-four main types of beggar, many of whom we have met before, including the priests, the pilgrims, the epileptics, and the prisoners escaped from the Turks, whose muttering comes out this time as *Allah allah allah elhemdu lillahi la illah* ('God God God; praise be to God; there is no God...', which is the first half of the procession of faith quoted by Garzoni, the pieces together making up the famous 'There is no God but God, and

Muhammad is his prophet.'⁹ One wonders what the almsgivers would
have done had they known what the words meant. The two phrases,
fitting together like an indenture, show that Frianoro cannot have merely
borrowed from Garzoni in this instance, similar as the passages are. It
was recently discovered, however, that his book is itself an example of
theft, since with the exception of a few details, like the one just quoted,
it is an unacknowledged and somewhat free translation of a late fifteenth-
century Latin text, by a certain Teseo Pini.¹⁰ Even in their details, the
descriptions of rogues have a long history.

What are we to make of all this? There are two major problems. The
most obvious one is to decide whether the testimonies are fact or fiction.
In the second place, there is the problem of change. Do the images of
rogues illustrate nothing but the persistence of tradition, or can the
historian identify changes over time? Let us take the problems in order.

To begin with what might be called the 'realist' or 'common-sense'
hypothesis, which is that Italy, like other parts of Europe in early modern
times, swarmed with rogues who specialised in the roles of different kinds
of deserving case in order to attract the charity of the public, and that
texts and images are accurate reflections of social reality, honest accounts
of deceit (the study of Callot by Sadoul (1969) describes him in the
subtitle as the 'mirror of his age'). In this view, Pini and Frianoro were
respectable clergymen who wanted to warn rather than to entertain their
public. In its favour are the judicial and other records which confirm the
literary sources in a number of respects.

The most spectacular of these records are the testimonies of Pompeo
and Girolamo with which this essay began, but in sixteenth-century
Venice, too, the magistrates made discoveries not unlike those of the
English gentleman Thomas Harman, who claims to have interviewed a
'counterfeit crank'.¹¹ In the mid sixteenth century the health officials of
Venice found, for example, that blind Vettore had 325 ducats invested
in the public debt, although he still went begging; that lame Tommaso
kept old clothes to beg in, but dressed well at other times; that one man
had 'made himself yellow in order to go begging', another pretended to
tremble (the *accadenti* again), and others trained children to beg (just as
in Elizabethan London the Recorder discovered a training centre for
cut-purses).¹² If the authorities were shocked by these revelations, it was
not because the tricks were new to them, but because they were practised
by the local poor, with fixed addresses in Venice, and not by foreigners
and vagabonds. If there is a long literary tradition of descriptions of the
tricks of the trade, this might be because the tricks themselves are

traditional, passed on within the rogue counter-culture by the training institutions just mentioned. The tradition, incidentally, had persisted into our own day, as two vivid accounts from the 1950s will show. In Naples, an American writer, Morris West (1957, pp. 16f), claims to have seen a boy (who had swallowed citrate of magnesium, rather than the traditional soap), fall to the ground foaming at the mouth, while his companions took up a collection for him. (This 'soap trick', as we may call it, is described in texts from fifteenth-century France and Switzerland as well as from Italy). In Palermo, a pickpocket called Gino described the schools and hiring markets in his profession.

> When a kid had mastered his trade, his problem was to convince people he could be trusted and get someone to take him on...almost every family in the street I lived in had a youngster like myself who was learning to be a pickpocket. (Dolci, 1966, p. 26).

So much for the defence of the authenticity of the literary evidence. What about the case for the prosecution? The first and most obvious point is that the descriptions of rogues follow one another too closely to have been taken directly from observation. They copy one another reproducing traditional commonplaces or topoi. The fact that the different witnesses confirm one another in detail is precisely why we should suspect their testimony. It is hard to guess, when one is reading a particular text, whether or not it comes from a work of fiction, such as a picaresque 'romance' or 'novel'. Before historians use these texts for their own purposes, they would be well advised to ask 'literary' questions about what they meant to their original writers and readers.

It seems fairly clear that, like comedy, the picaresque novel was written in the 'low style' and dealt with 'low life', in order to point a moral as well as to entertain. The audience, which was assumed to be respectable, was supposed to find low life delightfully odd in itself, and also to derive both moral and practical instruction from books which blew the gaff and exposed the tricks of the underworld. 'It shows the skills, deceits, craft and trickery in order for you to avoid them, not imitate them' goes a prologue to one of the texts, the Italian translation of the adventures of the picaro Lazzarillo.[13] Texts and images alike appear to have appealed to an aristocratic audience. Caravaggio painted card-sharps for a cardinal. Barezzi, the main translator of the Spanish picaresque tales, dedicated them to Venetian patricians, while a rival translation of *Lazzarillo*, never published, was dedicated to cardinal Scipione Borghese. There was a *Masque of the Gypsies* at the court of Grand Duke Cosimo II of

Tuscany for the Carnival of 1614 (Callot was at court at the time, and his etchings have reminiscences of the sets for this occasion). Carnival was of course a traditional time for playing at the world turned upside-down (below, ch. 12).[14]

To present the world of rogues as a topsy-turvy world – yet one with its own laws, organisation, training and rulers – could at once provoke laughter and point a moral of a somewhat ambiguous and perhaps ambivalent kind. The audience was invited to laugh at the hypocrisy of the criminals, unsuccessfully aping normal society; or alternatively, at the bad faith of the straight world, no better than the rogues it despised. The classic cases of this strategy are the description by Cervantes of the underworld of Seville and its boss Monipodio, and Gay's *Beggar's Opera*, but the account by Alemán of the 'Generalissimo' of the Roman underworld, and of the 'regulations' (or better, 'anti-regulations'), dealing with the professional conduct of beggars, also follows this pattern. We learn, for example, that no beggar is to appear in the street dressed in new clothes, in order not to give a 'bad example' to the others.

The moral for the readers of the time is clear enough; but what about the moral for the historian? According to Roger Chartier (1974), in his penetrating essay on Pechon de Ruby and the other French descriptions of beggars, it is that these accounts tell us only about the attitudes of the gentlemen, clerics and other members of the elite who wrote them, more especially that they saw the world of rogues as a 'counter-culture' organised on the model of a kingdom or a guild. What about the documents with which this chapter began? They fit rather well – indeed, all too well – into this literary context, since they too make use of the guild model and differ only in degree of elaboration from the accounts of Pini and the recently published Garzoni. It should be added that these documents cannot now be found in the Roman archives, and are best known through a copy made a few years later, which used to be in the former Imperial Library in Berlin. This copy has the rather literary title of the 'delightful examination' of rogues, 'il dilettevole essamine de'guidoni, furfanti o calchi' (the three terms used by Garzoni in his chapter-heading, and in the same order). When and why the copy was made remains obscure, but we have at least to entertain the possibility that the documents are not genuine interrogations at all. Like theft, deceit seems to be exemplified by the sources as well as revealed by them.[15] My own suspicions about the literary quality of the accounts given by Pompeo and Girolamo became much stronger after reading a series of interrogations of thieves by the tribunal of the Governor of Rome two years earlier, in 1593. About thirty people were interrogated and it took over a month and nearly 130 pages to record their testimonies, some voluntary and others following torture. One man, asked whether he stole cloaks by night (a crime which seems to have been as common in Rome in the 1590s as handbag-snatching in the 1980s), replied that he had never practised that 'trade' (*arte*). In other respects, however, the witnesses presented a much less colourful picture than Pompeo and Girolamo. They worked in small groups, frequenting bridges and churches and other places where there would be crowds, taking bundles from peasants sleeping out in the piazza, or using a ladder or a pole to take cloaks or tablecloths hanging from windows, and selling the goods immediately to the Jews and eating and drinking the proceeds in the nearest hostelry. There is no specialisation, no leadership, but just a pool of men who know one another from which the day's gangs are formed. Thieves are not the same thing as beggars, but some of these men are described in the document as 'vagabonds' and in any case Pompeo's *Burchiaroli* and *Grancetti* and Girolamo's *Strascinatori* combined begging with theft.[16]

The important question, however, is the one which concerns not these two texts alone but the whole genre; and for my own part I am as unhappy with the answer of the total sceptics, like Chartier, as with that of the realists. On one side, it is obviously naive to treat each text, each link in the chain of testimonies, as if it was totally independent, uncontaminated by the stories about rogues which had been circulating for hundreds of years in different parts of Europe and reveal nothing so much as the hostility of have-nots towards 'haves', and sedentary groups towards nomads. On the other side, if we are not prepared to dismiss all the documents found in European archives as forgeries, we have to admit not only that beggars had their own jargon to communicate within their sub-culture but also that they had a number of strategies for presenting themselves in a sympathetic light, some kind of division of labour and – in some cases at least – a repertoire of deceits, such as the 'soap trick', which were passed on from one generation to another. In other words, we are dealing neither with pure fact nor with pure fiction, but, here as elsewhere in this book, with stereotyped perceptions of social reality. The stereotyped views of beggars and thieves were communicated orally as well as in writing and in print, and it may be useful to think of them as a kind of rumour, subject to the usual processes of distortion which rumours undergo. In a famous article published over forty years ago (Allport and Postman, 1945), two social psychologists distinguished three such processes of distortion, which they described as 'levelling' (the simplification of a complex story), 'sharpening' (in other words, selective emphasis), and finally the 'assimilation' of the story to the interests of the listener. Thus we see different kinds of beggar, more or less honest or dishonest, simplified into a single image of the rogue; and what may well have been a fairly informal organisation perceived as an extremely formal one, with a precise hierarchy, a sharp division of labour, and so on. It is not easy to catch observers in the act of stereotyping the behaviour they perceived, but all the same there is something to be gained by looking for changes in the image of rogues and vagabonds in the course of the period.

In the Middle Ages, the traditional attitude to the poor, in Italy as in other parts of Europe, was a positive one. They were 'God's poor'. Poverty was holy. In the thirteenth century, St Francis declared that he was 'married' to 'Lady Poverty' and he founded a begging order. Similarly, a century later, in 1360, Giovanni Colombi, having given away his goods, founded the order of the Gesuati to beg for the poor. Religious confraternities were active in poor relief as in the other corporal works of mercy. In Tuscany in the fourteenth and fifteenth centuries, it was not uncommon for beggars to be chosen as godparents to newly-born children (Klapisch, 1985b, p. 72). These attitudes persisted into our period. In a book published in 1549 the Lombard nobleman Saba da Castiglione could describe the poor as 'the true image of Our Lord Jesus Christ'.[17] However, from about 1350 on, and more rapidly after 1500, one sees the rise of a much more negative attitude to the poor, again in Italy as elsewhere, the result of what seems to have been an increasing polarisation of society into rich and poor (Geremek, 1980, ch. 3), and, from about the 1520s on, a kind of Malthusian crisis, with population pressing hard on the means of subsistence. This crisis was a stimulus to the municipal reorganisation of charity, producing a system of poor relief which was more efficient and more discriminating but also less humane than the system it was coming to replace. Serious attempts were made to separate the 'foreign' from the local poor and of course the genuine from the fakes, and also to shut up the able-bodied poor and compel them to work (Geremek, 1973).

In Venice, for example, new poor laws followed the famine of 1528–9, forbidding unlicensed begging, ordering parishes to look after their own poor, expelling the 'foreign' and the sturdy beggars and placing the sick in institutions. In 1545, a naval officer drew the attention of the authorities to the possible use of vagabonds in the galleys of the republic, and in the next few years the health officials made unusual efforts to track beggars down. In the 1590s, another famine led to the establishment in Venice of a special hospital or workhouse for beggars, the *Mendicanti* (Pullan, 1963–4, and 1971, part 2).

Similar attempts to control begging were made in other Italian states in the course of the sixteenth century. In Florence, for example, a decree of 1576 gave all vagabonds ten days to leave; if any were found after that time, they would be sent to the galleys.[18] In Genoa, a Poor Office was founded in 1539, and in 1582 it was ordered that vagabonds should be confined in the old leper house, and the officers of the law received a head fee for every beggar they captured (Grendi, 1975). In Palermo, action against vagabonds was taken in 1590. As for Rome, which might be described as the Mecca of early modern beggars (precisely because it attracted genuine pilgrims), a whole series of measures was taken in the later sixteenth century. In 1561, for example, Pius V forbade begging in churches and in the streets (making special reference to the *baroni* of Campo de Fiori), while his successors Gregory XIII and Sixtus V both had beggars locked up in workhouses (Delumeau, 1957–9, part 2, section 2).

The problem of beggars did not go away and the authorities remained concerned with it throughout the early modern period. Their concern is reflected, for example, in the collection of information about the poor and unemployed in Italian censuses (above, ch. 3); it may well be significant that in Venice the health officials were concerned with both beggars and the census. The growing fascination with the classification of rogues and vagabonds which our texts reveal may be an indirect result of the rise of the bureaucratic state. Some of the fullest accounts of the subculture of beggars and 'rogues' follow drives against begging, in Venice in 1545, for example (above, p. 68) or in Rome in the 1590s, the time of the interrogations of Pompeo and Girolamo. This kind of suggestion can never be proved, but it seems plausible to suggest that the new emphasis, in art and literature as well as official documents, on the idle and deceitful vagabond, the 'myth of the rogue', as it might be called, was a means of legitimating the repressive measures against people who had been regarded as 'God's poor' but were increasingly seen as useless members of the commonwealth. As in the case of the witch-trials of the period, we are confronted with an over-reaction to a perceived threat to society which may be described, like more recent reactions to 'hooligans', as a 'moral panic' which reveals more about the fantasies of respectable people than about the object of their fears (Cohen, 1972).

In using the phrase the 'myth of the rogue' I do not mean to imply that deceitful beggars, thieves, confidence tricksters and other miscreants were absent from the early modern Italian scene; what I am suggesting is that the poor were coming to be perceived by the non-poor almost exclusively in these terms. To make the point dramatically, one might say that society was becoming increasingly preoccupied, if not obsessed, with work and its converse (which was perceived as 'idleness' rather than 'unemployment'. One interesting indicator of these changing perceptions is the case of the so-called *lazzaroni* of Naples. The term *lazzaroni* or *lazzari* was coined around the middle of the seventeenth century, the time of the famous revolt of Masaniello (below, ch. 14), when upper- and middle-class fear of what their English counterparts called the 'mob' had some reason to be particularly strong (cf. Croce, 1985). The term has associations with the famous literary rogue, Lazzarillo de Tormes; with the *lazzaretti*, the old leper-houses, now being used to confine beggars; and of course ultimately with the poor man Lazarus, rejected by Dives. These *lazzari* appear in some Neapolitan paintings of the mid to late seventeenth century. They impressed foreign visitors to Naples, especially in the eighteenth century. Montesquieu, for example, who was in Naples in 1728, wrote in his journal that there were fifty to 60,000 men in Naples who had nothing, not even work, and lived solely on vegetables. An English visitor wrote that there were 6,000 of them, that they slept in the streets and 'are suffered to sun themselves, a great part of the day, under the palace walls', surviving on the charity of convents and by 'pilfering and begging'. Another Englishman's impression of Naples was that 'the wants of nature are so easily satisfied here that the lower class of people work but little; their great pleasure is, to bask in the sun and do nothing'.[19] It is easy to see a myth taking shape. The travellers read one another, as well as talking to respectable Neapolitans, so they knew what to expect. When they saw men lying in the sun they recognised them as 'lazzari', thus fitting them into a preconceived category much like that of the 'lazy native' for Europeans in the Far East (Alatas, 1977). In this piazza culture, idleness was extremely conspicuous. But how was an outsider to distinguish one of the *lazzari* from a man enjoying a brief and well-earned rest between bouts of work? Like the image of working women (above, p. 35), that of non-working men is dependent on the interests and prejudices of the beholder.

The point is not merely applicable to foreign visitors; insiders have their prejudices too (or more exactly, insiders to the culture at large may be outsiders to a particular sub-culture). The interrogation of Pompeo and Girolamo, supposing it is genuine, reveals the place of prejudice or stereotype very clearly. Among the first questions asked was whether beggars belonged to one 'sect' or many, a leading question implying a degree of formal organisation (even if the overtones of heresy in the term 'sect' may be anachronistic). As in other cases, notably witch-trials, the beggars told the interrogators what they thought these interrogators wanted to hear. They must have been well aware of the stereotypes by which the straight world perceived the upside-down world of rogues.

It is unlikely that we shall ever know very much for certain about the degree of internal organisation among the beggars and thieves of early modern Italy; like the paintings and the literary texts, the official documents are contaminated by prejudice, stereotype, and myth. However, these very prejudices stereotypes and myths have a great deal to teach cultural and social historians if they do not swallow them whole and reproduce them in their own work but ask instead who is labelling whom in these ways, and why. They should not believe everything they read in 'the documents', but they should not reject all that they find in works of fiction.

III

Modes of communication

7
Languages and
anti-languages
in early modern Italy

Unlike the pieces which follow it, this essay is essentially concerned with the spoken language. Its aim is to reconstruct a retrospective ethnography of speaking; to describe the oral culture of early modern Italy, or more exactly, to map the contours of the main oral sub-cultures and counter-cultures of the period. The subject is not only fascinating in its own right, it is an essential part of social and cultural history, because language is a sensitive indicator of social relationships such as deference, familiarity, solidarity and so on, and also an active force in society, a vehicle for social mobility, for the assimilation of new recruits to a group, and so on.[1] Despite its importance, the social history of speech has been somewhat neglected by historians.

There is of course one good reason for this neglect. The enterprise is obviously rather presumptuous, to say the least. How does one study speech acts some two to four hundred years after the event? It is clear that historians with this kind of interest must resign themselves not only to studying the oral through the written, but also to investigating the language of ordinary people via records made, for the most part, by members of the cultural elite. In the case of early modern Italy, however, the amount and the variety of the written evidence for the history of speech does deserve some emphasis.

Since the time of Dante, at least, educated Italians have been interested in what they call the 'language question', the best form to use for both writing and speaking (Hall, 1942; Vitale, 1960). Controversy naturally engendered both self-consciousness and awareness of the linguistic usage of other people. In addition to the literature of controversy, there are some rich sources which came into existence for quite different reasons. For example, the sermons of San Bernardino of Siena were taken down in shorthand when he preached them, in the early fifteenth century, so that the preacher's message would not be lost; the result is precious evidence of his speech 'code' as well, for the text has a really colloquial sound to it.[2] Court records in which witnesses testify to quarrels often have a similar oral flavour. Interrogations by the Inquisition, in their

79

concern for accuracy, often catch the spoken word with apparent precision. The intructions to interrogators were quite specific on this point, telling them to 'ensure that the notary writes not only all the answers of the accused but also all his comments and gestures and everything that he says under torture, including all his sighs, cries, laments and tears.³ A similar procedure was in use in the Tribunal of the Governor of Rome, and the files are full of exclamations like 'poor me' (*poveraccio me*), or 'mercy' (*misericordia*), or 'holy Mary of Loreto help me' or 'let me down let me down and I will tell the whole truth' (*calatemegiù calatemegiù che dirò tutta la verità*). Plays are another good source of evidence for speech conventions, despite the difficulty of distinguishing direct transcription from stylisation or parody. They suggest, for example, that in the sixteenth century, the language of Tuscan peasants was more archaic than that of townsmen (Brunet, 1976). Most precious of all, perhaps, because of their concern with change, are the comments by elderly people recalling their youth, such as the Florentine patrician Tommaso Rinuccini, writing in the later seventeenth century, and noting with regret the rise of ceremony in speech and writing in his milieu.⁴

This large subject deserves an equally large book, along the lines of the well-known linguistic history of Italy since 1860 (De Mauro, 1976). In a brief chapter, all I can do is to suggest the importance of oral culture in early modern Italy; to describe the variety of languages, codes and registers employed by different kinds of people for different purposes; and finally to comment on some of the more obvious and important changes over time. Let us begin with oral culture. How important it was, relative to writing, painting, printing and other media is of course impossible to calculate, but a historian from late twentieth-century Britain cannot but be struck by its centrality in early modern Italy. Speaking was an art, a kind of performance which mattered even more, one suspects, in the sixteenth and seventeenth centuries than in Italy today. The classical art of rhetoric was far from neglected in medieval Italy, but even greater importance was given to it from the Renaissance onwards. One way of showing its importance in elite culture, at least, is to note the amount of space devoted to speech in the two most famous sixteeth-century manuals of good behaviour, Castiglione and Della Casa (above, p. 21). Ten chapters out of thirty in Della Casa are devoted to the subject, while Castiglione's courtiers spend much of book one discussing how the perfect courtier should speak, returning to this topic in the forty chapters on jokes in book two, and once again when concerned, in book three, with the language of love. What I find particularly striking in these two treatises is the richness of vocabulary for discussing speech acts; the variety of adjectives, nouns and even verbs. Della Casa is concerned to instruct his readers to speak in a manner which is pleasing (*piacevole*), honourable (*onesta*), and elegant (*leggiadra*), avoiding tedium, frivolity, and boorishness. Castiglione, for his part, stresses grace and the avoidance of affectation, 'above all in speech', he also appreciates facility, 'abundance' or 'copiousness' (in which Italian speakers still excel), variety, wit, and a tongue which is both ready (*pronta*) and sharp (*mordace*). A similar picture of the importance of wit and repartee (*detti* or *motti*) emerges from the stories of Matteo Bandello and other writers of the period, who not infrequently describe the ready wit of their characters and sometimes tell a story simply to lead up to a particularly biting or amusing retort.[5] To make a good impression in society it was obviously necessary to be a good speaker. A father might be complimented on his newborn baby by being told he would grow up to be a *bel parlatore*, or he might advise his sons to read history, short stories and jest books to find epigrams which 'may bring you honour in a conversation'.[6] In this culture speech – and its accompanying gestures – were of crucial importance in the presentation of self, and every word was part of a performance, not least when insults were exchanged (below, ch. 8). People were often identified by oral nicknames, some of them wittily cruel, even in official documents such as the Florentine census of 1562, which includes *Francesco detto il Grillo* (the cricket); *Francesco detto guerriere* (warrior); *Domenico decto mezzo prete* (half priest); *Simone detto il lupo* (the wolf); *Bartolommeo detto Naso* (the nose); *Antonia decto mal occhio* (evil eye); *Betta detta la Pazzuccia* (the madwoman); *Cammilla detta la spiritata* (the possessed); *Domenica detta la giraffe* (the giraffe).

Formal oral performances were frequent, and excited much interest, both appreciative and critical. Most of these performances – songs, stories, plays, sermons, speeches, the sales-talk of charlatans, and so on – were improvised, or more exactly, semi-improvised. Speakers rehearsed what they had to say, making use of the classical art of memory, which had a 'place' for everything in some imaginary building, a church or theatre of the mind, but, unlike us, they made a bad impression if they read a written text aloud or learned it completely by heart. Improvisation was highly prized, in the famous *commedia dell'arte*, (an Italian speciality), and off-stage as well. Poets were rewarded for it, and *cantatore improviso* was a profession; a leading practitioner, in early sixteenth-century Florence, was a certain Cristoforo nicknamed *Altissimo*, 'highest', perhaps because the adjective was a favourite of his. It would be good to know more about what constituted effective 'live' eloquence, as opposed to that of published sermons and speeches, but genuine 'oral texts', like the transcription of San Bernardino's sermons, are hard to find.

What of the reactions of the audience? Not a few such reactions are recorded, by insiders and outsiders. A number of foreign visitors to Italy were sufficiently impressed by oral performances in public to record them in some detail, In the early seventeenth century, for example, an English visitor to Venice recorded a charlatan in full spate (below, p. 216). Goethe, in Venice in 1786, described the performance of a public story-teller. Five years earlier, a British visitor had made similar observations in Naples.

> As I sauntered along the Strada Nuova lately, I perceived a group of people, listening, with much attention, to a person who harangued them in a raised solemn voice, and with great gesticulation...men, women and children bringing seats from the neighbouring houses, on which they placed themselves around the orator. He repeated stanzas from Ariosto, in a pompous recitativo cadence, peculiar to the natives of Italy; and he had a book in his hand, to assist his memory when it failed...when he came to describe the exploits of Orlando...he assumed the warlike attitude and stern countenance of that hero; representing, by the most animated action how he drove his spear through the bodies of six of his enemies at once.[7]

That local audiences might be extremely conscious of the style and the limitations of a particular oral performance is a point which, given the evidence already cited, might almost be taken for granted, but it emerges in an amusing way in one of the notebooks of the diarist Marin Sanudo early in the sixteenth century. Sanudo went regularly to meetings of the Senate, and had the opportunity of listening to many speeches—indeed, he had no way of avoiding them. At one point he diverted himself by making a list of the favourite clichés of thirty-four senators; 'Let me speak' (*Lasséme favolar*). 'What cruelty is this' (*Che crudeltà è questa*). 'There is no obedience' (*Non è obedientia*). 'This is what I want to say' (*Voio dir cussi*), and so on. Nor can he have been the only senator to notice this, for eight of his specimens are described as 'before my time', so they must have been quoted, maliciously, on the piazza.[8] Variety, not repetition was the sign of the skilled orator.

After all this testimony to speech it might be thought that there could be nothing to say about silence, which is in any case an even more elusive subject. To understand an oral culture, however, one needs to study its silences; as one sixteenth-century courtesy-book put it, 'He who does not know how to be silent does not know how to speak' (*chi non sa tacere non sa parlare*).[9] Fortunately, the sources do allow at least a brief outline of the social history of silence–by which I mean who was supposed to be silent, when, where, and on what topics. Children were not supposed to speak very much in the presence of adults.[10] Women were recommended to speak little, especially in public; it was a sign of modesty or *vergogna* (above, p. 14).[11] A talkative woman might be described as *sfrenata di lingua* ('with her tongue unbridled') as if men thought she needed a bit in her mouth. The Roman courtesans are said to have mocked the ladies of Rome because they lacked skill in repartee and were 'as silent as stones' (*quiete della bocca come sassi*).[12] The ladies were more particularly recommended not to chatter in church, though as we have already heard, the noise levels in Italian churches during Mass surprised at least some foreign visitors. Keeping silence under interrogation was a major preoccupation for some, and there was a magical aid available for the purpose, *il maleficio della taciturnitá*, as some clerics called it, a piece of paper bearing words like the following:

O santa corda che legasti Cristo	O holy cord which bound thee, Christ
lega la lingua mia	Bind my tongue
che non dica nè bono nè tristo.	So that I say nothing, good or evil
Sator Aror Doroi	
Alor Arafa Aramor.[13]	

Most surprising, however, in view of what has gone before, is the suggestion in some courtesy-books–though not in Castiglione–that the gentleman should be sparing of speech. Chattering was for charlatans (which is how they got their name, for 'chatter' in Italian is *ciarlare*).[14]

So far, speaking in early modern Italy has been discussed at a rather general level. It is time to discuss the varieties of speech, the main codes and registers, as the sociolinguists call them; a 'code' being a variety of given language spoken by a particular social group while a 'register' is a variety spoken in a particular kind of situation (Halliday, 1978, 31f, 65f).

In early modern Italy there coexisted not only a large number of codes and registers but also a number of different languages in the strict sense of the term. In the north, there were groups whose native language was German or Dalmatian ('Serbo-Croat' had not yet been codified in our period); in the south, there were speakers of Greek and Albanian. To these settlers should be added the nomads, in particular the mercenary soldiers; German-speaking lanzknechts, and Greek- or Albanian-speaking stradiotti. More important, in terms of the numbers of people involved, were the second languages, notably Latin but also French and Occitan. The latter two languages had been important in both their written and their spoken forms in northern Italy in particular in the later Middle Ages. Indeed, in the thirteenth and fourteenth centuries, some of the most important works of Italian literature were in French, including the 'Trésor' of Dante's teacher, Brunetto Latini; Martin da Canal's 'Cronique des Veniciens'; and Marco Polo's account of his travels, 'Le divisament dou monde', which presumably follows the forms of the spoken language since he did not write but dictated it. French, or 'Franco–Italian', as this form is often called, seems to have been used in the speech domain of chivalry in particular, not only by knights but also by street singers when they were telling the story of Charlemagne or Roland (who was not yet 'Orlando'). The language of love, on the other hand, was Occitan, the language of the troubadours, and many Italian poets besides Sordello (Browning's hero, who lived in Mantua in the thirteenth century) wrote in it (Larner, 1980, ch. 5). With French and Occitan should be mentioned the original 'lingua franca', the language of Mediterranean trade, in which French was combined with Venetian, Greek, Arabic and so on (Folena, 1968; Whinnom, 1977). In the early modern period little of this seems to have been left, but Latin, on the other hand, was extending its empire.

The place of Latin in early modern European culture is too well known to need much comment here, though it should be pointed out that it was a spoken language as well as a written one, in three different social contexts or 'speech domains' (Fishman, 1965). In the first place, it was spoken in the ecclesiastical domain. It was not only the lingua franca of the Catholic clergy–a point of great practical importance, in Rome in particular, but the language of the liturgy, and as such familiar to a greater or lesser extent to many of the laity, even if they had not studied the language formally. In the second place, it seems to have been spoken as well as written in the legal domain, at least in some courts, notably church courts. It is of course hard to discover the nature of oral proceedings in courts which kept their records in Latin, but in this context it is worth recalling the complaint of Menocchio Scandella, the miller of Friuli recently brought back to life by Carlo Ginzburg: 'I think speaking Latin is a betrayal of the poor because in lawsuits the poor do not know what is being said and are crushed; and if they want to say four words they need a lawyer' (Ginzburg, 1975, p. 9). In England, a similar function was performed by what was known as 'law French'. Finally, Latin was widely used in the academic domain. University lectures were in Latin, and so were the 'disputations' in which students learned to argue and by means of which they were examined, and also the 'declamations' which gave them practice in rhetoric as disputations did in logic. In grammar schools, Latin was not only the main subject of instruction but the medium of instruction. Latin grammars were written in Latin; the pupils spoke Latin in class, whether they were acting out scenes from plays or simply asking to be excused; and finally, they were expected to speak Latin even at playtime, and a spy (*lupus*, in other words 'wolf') was appointed to report anyone who lapsed into the vernacular. Apart from this, it seems to have been quite frequent, especially in the earlier part of the period, for educated men to interlard their Italian, or even their dialect, in speech as well as writing, with Latin phrases such as *per viscera misericordiae Dei* ('by the bowels of the mercy of God'), *Est non dubito* ('There is, I have no doubt'), et cetera.[15] However, the most obvious point to make about the sociolinguistics of early modern Italy is about the variety of regional codes or dialects, from Piedmontese and Lombard (in its various forms) to Neapolitan and Sicilian. Other points about the use of dialect are much less obvious, indeed still unsettled and very much in need of research. It is likely, for example, that throughout our period most educated people knew at least one dialect and spoke it on occasion. The problem is to discover what these occasions were, in other words to learn the rules for switching codes between dialect and a higher-status Tuscan which was gradually turning into standard Italian. Presumably an urban patrician who owned country estates would speak dialect to his peasants. Would he speak dialect to his servants in his palace in the city? Would he speak dialect to his wife? Too little is known about the education of women in this period (cf. Masetto Zannini, 1980, and below, p. 129), but it is hard to see how many women could have been fluent speakers of anything but their local dialect. Speaking a particular dialect might serve as a marker or symbol of a particular kind of social occasion. In Milan about the year 1600, for example, a festive society to which the painter Lomazzo, as well as some noblemen belonged, chose to speak in the dialect of the Val di Bregno, the area of origin of the wine porters of the city of Milan, as if this dialect was for them a sign of wine and festivity.[16]

However, in early modern Italy dialect can hardly have been the symbol of informality it later became, because it was spoken on a number of formal occasions. To take Venice as a relatively well-studied example (whether typical or not in its use of dialect it is too early to say). In Venice, patricians spoke Venetian to one another not only in private but also, for example, at meetings of the Great Council and the Senate (Georgelin, 1978, p. 977, note 230; Finlay, 1980, p. 229). Advocates spoke Venetian in court, a contrast with the Latin usage of the ecclesiastical courts already mentioned (Vianello, 1957). It is not difficult to understand this choice; the use of dialect symbolised Venetian autonomy. On the other hand, dialect was associated, or became associated, with ordinary people and popular culture. In the plays of Ruzzante, in the early sixteenth century, Paduan patricians such as Sier Tomao speak dialect; in the plays of Goldoni, in the mid eighteenth, the patricians speak Italian and leave dialect to their servants, or to boatmen or peasants. Dialect was losing status; it was coming to be considered a non-language or anti-language (so that the word *lingua* could refer either to language in general or to standard Italian). There is other evidence for this retreat from dialect, which has its parallels in France and elsewhere; which is just as well, because plays are ambiguous witnesses. The printed texts are more or less reliable evidence of this important kind of oral performance, but to jump to conclusions about linguistic usage in ordinary life is much more dangerous, because the codes as well as the messages of the plays may have more than one level of meaning. Ruzzante, for example, whose real name was Angelo Beolco, wrote his plays in the dialect of the countryside round Padua, in order to amuse the urban patricians of Padua and Venice. He was writing in the 1520s, at time when a high style of literary Italian was being codified (as it happens by a Venetian patrician, Pietro Bembo), and his use of dialect may follow Bembo's recommendation to write about 'low' subjects in a 'low' style; or it may, on the contrary, express a critique of his high style. As Ruzzante the peasant (played by Ruzzante the dramatist) says at one point, 'Isn't it nicer to say "me" [the dialect form] than "I"?' (*no è pì belo a dire mi ca io?*).

A map of the varieties of language spoken in early modern Italy would not be confined to dialects. There were also languages associated with particular occupations; forms of slang, jargon or cant. One of the best-known and the most highly developed was the language of rogues mentioned in chapter six, a true 'anti-language' for a counter-culture. It is relatively well-recorded because it attracted the interest of a number of writers during the Renaissance. The fifteenth-century Florentine comic poet, Luigi Pulci, for example, left a little manuscript vocabulary of fifty-one words and phrases from the jargon (*gergo*) of beggars and thieves. Window, for instance, was 'the windy one' (*ventosa*); road 'the dusty one' (*polverosa*); money 'little brown ones' (*brunetti*), and so on. An anonymously compiled manuscript vocabulary of *c.* 1500 includes nearly two hundred and fifty terms of this *lingua furbesca*, one of the most intriguing of which is *Turcare* for 'to go'. The first published vocabulary of this kind was the 'New Method of understanding Jargon' (*Nuovo modo di intendere la lingua zerga*) of 1545, which combines verses with a vocabulary of more than 600 terms, including vivid phrases for stealing ('to lift', *alzare*; 'to fish', *pescare*; 'to weed', *gramignare*, and so on); talking ('singing', *canzonamento* or *contrapunto*); and being hanged ('to go to Picardy', a pun on the normal word, *impiccare* and on the *picardi* or Bohemians).[17] A number of terms from the last collection reappear in the discourse of Pompeo and Girolamo (above, p. 63), together with the account of a general assembly of rogues who planned to change their slang (*mutare il gergo di parlare*) because outsiders had discovered it.

There are a number of other occupational jargons, or speech domains, though none of them as richly documented as the anti-language of the underworld. Pride of place should probably go to 'court language' (*la cortigiana lingua*), a variety of speech used by certain kinds of people, in certain places, for certain kinds of topic. The best guide to it remains Castiglione's famous *Courtier*, the work of a participant observer who knew this speech domain from inside but was sufficiently detached from it to be able to analyse its principles. The main difficulty in studying the court as a sub-culture (language included) is that it was a cultural model, making it hard to distinguish its jargon from what had already passed into polite usage. A number of other occupational varieties of language are discernible in early modern Italy, most obviously the language of lawyers, 'a barbarous jargon which they call the language of the law', as Giuseppe Baretti once put it.[18] Lawyers were notorious for speaking and writing in a mixture of Latin and the vernacular, *macaronica verba* as one writer described it, a phrase which could perhaps be translated as 'linguistic stew'. The writer in question was Teofilo Folengo (1496–1544), who went on to make his reputation as a writer of comic verse in macaronic Latin; that is, Latin treated as if it were Italian. It is more than likely that he was exploiting for literary purposes a spoken language, or anti-language, with which students mocked the academic culture, with its compulsory Latin, to which they were subjected (cf. Paoli, 1959). Soldiers were another sub-culture with their own language, or set of languages, including the Germanic Italian of the *lanzknechts*, (the *lanzichenecchi* as the Italians called them), a variety of speech which according to one linguist displays the typical features of a pidgin (Coates, 1969).[19]

No linguistic map of early modern Italy can afford to confine itself to regional and occupational varieties of speech. It is also necessary to discuss how different social groups communicated with one another. To a modern reader, one of the most striking, and indeed alien features of the texts of this period is the language of hierarchy, the formality of modes of address, the elaborate vocabulary of deference, all of which were to be found in speech as well as writing. A classic case of a mode of address which at once expressed and reinforced the social hierarchy is that of non-reciprocal 'tu', which was not of course confined to Italy (Brown and Gilman, 1960). When, in Florence in 1378, a shoemaker used *tu* to the patrician Carlo degli Strozzi, the incident was considered worthy of note in a chronicle, as a sign that the revolt of the unskilled cloth workers, the Ciompi, was turning the world upside down.[20]

Some of the most important points to listen for in the language of hierarchy were conveniently recorded for us by a Genoese patrician of the early seventeenth century, Andrea Spinola, a critic of the inegalitarianism of his age. He warned young men of his class not to play the grandee by saying 'tu' to the watchmen. He described how his fellow-citizens, 'better furnished with money and imagination than with wisdom', distinguished between greetings between equals, such as 'I recommend myself' (*mi ricommando*) or 'I am all yours' (*son tutto suo*), and greetings to superiors, such as 'I kiss your hands' (*bacio le mani*), or 'your slave' (*vostro schiavo*), showing a deference to the great which Spinola himself regarded as 'unworthy of a free city'.[21] Genoa, like Venice and Florence, had a long republican tradition.

These forms of politeness and deference need to be placed in their social context, that of a society where it was natural to perceive others as one's superiors or inferiors and behave accordingly; where deference was expressed not only by saying 'I kiss your hands' but actually kissing them; by tone of voice; by avoiding disagreement with a superior, or at least wrapping it up in several layers of circumlocution, and so on, as Della Casa recommends (chs. 22–3).

After encountering many examples of the language of superiority and inferiority it is striking to discover than in the Jesuit college at Bologna, in the seventeenth century, the masters called everyone by the polite 'voi' (it must have been striking then too, for someone takes the trouble to record it). Were the Jesuits pioneers of egalitarianism? It is more likely that they were trying to deal with the contradiction between their superior status as masters, and the superior status of their pupils, as nobles. In a similar way, they would address pupils by name as *Conte Pepoli*, for instance, rather than as *Pepoli* or *Signor Conte* (Christian names were not used, and if two brothers were in the same class, one spoke, as in English public schools, of *Gonzaga Minor*, or more exactly, *Marchese Gonzaga Minore*).[22]

After this sketch-map of varieties of speech in early modern Italy, it is time to outline what appear to be the most important changes within the period. It may be useful to distinguish four points within a complex of interrelated changes.

1. The decline of spoken French and Latin. In the case of French, the decline had largely taken place by 1500; in that of Latin, it is considerably harder to date. The suggestion made by a group of church reformers in 1513, that the vernacular should be used in the liturgy – and by notaries – had no effect (Prosperi, 1981, p. 206). The suggestion soon came to smack of Protestantism. However, Italian began to infiltrate the academic domain. Although the Jesuits insisted on the use of Latin in their schools, other orders, such as the Piarists, founded by Calasanz (above, p. 55) and concentrating on poor children, introduced the vernacular (Brizzi, 1976, pp. 23, 225). By the middle of the eighteenth century, even the universities were beginning to change. At the university of Naples, for example, the great political economist Antonio Genovesi was the first professor to give his lectures in Italian. The vernacular was gradually adding to its functions.

2. With the changes in the functions of the vernacular went changes in its forms. Around 1300, the time of Dante, and again around 1500, the time of Bembo, a stronger need seems to have been felt than before for a vernacular, spoken as well as written, which would be 'standard' or 'correct'. There was a long debate about the form of this purified vernacular; the *questione della lingua*. In practice, the job came to be done by Tuscan, which spread among high-status males, at least, in other regions, though it is obviously hard to be sure when the change occurred and how far Tuscan was modified in the course of its reception.

As Tuscan spread, some intellectuals tried to codify it, in the sense of enunciating rules for speech and writing based on the usage of the great writers of the past, notably Dante, Petrarch and Boccaccio. This was what was advocated by Bembo, for example, while the Florentine Academy set up a committee in 1550 to prepare a grammar. The great linguistic arbiter of the later sixteenth century, Leonardo Salviati, founded another academy, the Crusca, to separate the wheat from the 'chaff' after which it is named, and this Academy produced its dictionary in 1612.

From a comparative point of view, the relative autonomy of the rise of Tuscan deserves emphasis. The linguistic hegemonies of southeastern English, northeastern French, Castillian and Mandarin, for example, all seem to follow and derive from the political dominance of these regions over their neighbours. In Italy, however, the story seems to be rather different. The hegemony of the speech of Florence over other forms of Tuscan, such as Sienese, might reasonably be explained in political terms, but the hegemony of Tuscan over other regional dialects cannot. This is not to say that the language question was completely dissociated from politics in the early modern period. On the contrary, Cosimo de 'Medici, the first Grand Duke of Tuscany, took a strong interest in the promotion of Tuscan, which he seems to have regarded as a source of prestige for his regime, and founded the Florentine Academy partly for this purpose (Bertelli, 1976). His absolute monarchy, or mini-monarchy, is not unlike the one developed in the France of Richelieu and Louis XIV (and the Académie Française, founded by Richelieu, owes something to Cosimo's example). However, the Grand Dukes of Tuscany did not exercise hegemony over Italy, so the spread of what might be called the 'Tuscan standard' cannot be explained in political terms. The obvious explanation for Tuscanisation is a cultural one. Dante, Petrarch and Boccaccio were all Tuscans, and it was their literary achievement which spread their language. Tuscanisation is the triumph of a cultural, not a political centre over its periphery. The most that a political historian might reasonably argue is that this freedom from political pressures has a political explanation; that it was the Italian political balance – or vacuum – of the period, which allowed cultural factors free play. The spread of printing is another factor to be taken into account in any discussion of Tuscanisation, but as in the case of politics, its place is a subordinate one. In early modern Europe, the spread of printing encouraged the standardisation first of the written language and ultimately that of the spoken language as well; but what it explains is how the winner in this race between dialects increased its lead over its competitors, not how it came to win in the first place.

3. Another linguistic trend of the sixteenth and seventeenth centuries is the increasing elaboration and formality of modes of address. A famous example is the rise of a new polite pronoun, 'lei', regretted by a number of sixteenth-century traditionalists such as Annibale Caro, Girolamo Muzio, Girolamo Ruscelli and Claudio Tolomei (Croce, 1917; Weise, 1961, ch. 3; Brunet, 1978). Another was the spread of titles. If we are to

believe contemporary complaints, *Messer* and *Signore* or *Signora*, and even *Vostra Signoria* had descended so low in the social scale that even porters and prostitutes expected to be addressed in this way, driving people of higher status to increase the linguistic inflation by appropriating the formerly aristocratic 'Eccellenza', 'Magnificenza' and so on. As one satirist complained, 'From now on, to speak correctly you will need a reference book' (*bisognerà tenerne un calendario*). One does not have to take such remarks literally to recognise that there was a real trend towards the inflation of titles, a linguistic equivalent of the increasingly conspicuous consumption of the early modern period (below, ch. 15), together with a trend towards codification. It was in 1631, for example, that cardinals were formally granted the title by which they have been addressed ever since, that of 'Your Eminence' (*Eminenza*; Pastor, vol. 29, p. 161). In the later seventeenth century, a Florentine patrician, Tommaso Rinuccini, looking back on his youth, noted that in those days in his circle, men used 'Vostra Signoria' to one another, but that it had been replaced by 'most illustrious' (*illustrissimo*) in speech as well as writing, and that this term too had become debased in its turn, so that 'even ordinary people use it to gentleman, even the poor when they beg for alms'. Allowing for his nostalgia for the world he had lost, we should still take Rinuccini's testimony seriously. It suggests that the remarks of foreign travellers, Englishmen in particular, about the flowery forms of address in Italy need to be placed in chronological context. Fynes Morison, for example, who was in Italy in the 1590s, noted that the term 'Signore' was so 'cheapened' that it was used to everyone. Coryate, in 1608, observed that an Italian would use a similar 'circumlocution' when speaking Latin: 'As for example he will not say, *Placet ne tibi* [may it please you] but *Placet ne dominationi tuae* or *vestrae* [may it please Your Worship]. So that they doe most commonly use that circumlocution, even to the meanest person that is.' John Ray, in Italy in the 1660s, made a similar point about the vernacular. 'Methinks the Epithets they bestow upon mean persons are somewhat extravagant, not to say ridiculous, as when they style a mechanic or common tradesman "Signor molto magnifico" and the like'.[23]

Why the change took place is a question which has intrigued historians as it did contemporaries. The traditional explanation, which goes back to the period itself – to Traiano Boccalini, for example – ans was adopted by later historians, such as Benedetto Croce, is in terms of the influence of Spain, which ruled Milan, Naples and Sicily from the mid sixteenth century onwards and was a culture already famed for formality and ceremoniousness.[24] However, the inflation of polite and deferential forms of address had already been noted in the 1540s and 1550s, so that Spanish influence (which is noticeable elsewhere, in costume, for example, and possibly in ritual) can have done no more than accelerate a trend which had already begun (Brunet, 1978, p. 308). Why did it begin? An important clue in the search for an explanation is provided by what might be called the political geography of deference. Opposition to the trend was greatest in the surviving republics; in Venice, where Boccalini lived and wrote, and in 1632 one patrician denounced another for using the term 'Excellency' (*Eccellenza*); and in Genoa, where Andrea Spinola, who has been cited already, made a number of remarks in similar vein. It is plausible to suggest that the fundamental reason for the change in modes of address in Italy was a political one, the decline of the republican city-state and its ideology of equality, and the rise of the mini-monarchy with its ideology of deference. Turning the point around, it may be argued that apparently trivial changes in language, like the rise of *illustrissimo*, are indicators of changes in social relations; and, more speculatively, that the inflation or democratisation of honorific terms was a means by which craftsmen and shopkeepers resisted the imposition of a stricter social hierarchy and affirmed their own sense of honour. Some historians would describe the change as part of the 'refeudalisation' of Italian society in the sixteenth and seventeenth centuries. I would rather not use this formerly precise technical term, which is itself in danger of inflation or debasement by indiscriminate use, and am far from happy with attempts to explain the rise of deference in fundamentally economic, rather than political and social terms, but I would certainly agree with supporters of the refeudalisation thesis (discussed again below, ch. 10) that cultural changes of this kind are unintelligible unless they are placed in their social and political context.

4. These trends towards formality, rules, and Tuscanisation did not take place uncontested. As we have just seen, a number of writers, republican patricians and others, protested against the growing vocabulary of deference. By the middle of the eighteenth century, if not before, these protests had reached the dimensions of a trend. In Venice, for example, Gasparo Gozzi founded the Accademia Granellesca in 1747 to encourage simplicity in language, and his article in the 'Venetian Gazzette' of 1760 raised the question of modes of address, arguing that it was best to greet equals and inferiors by *signor* or surname alone, as this was more cordial and more sincere. In Milan, the patrician Pietro Verri, an admirer of

Rousseau, made a similar point in his article on 'Tu, Voi and Lei'. He mocked his fellow-Italians for wanting to be addressed as *Signoria*, like 'so many Sultans'; praised the Quakers for their simplicity of language, and suggested following their example. F. S. Quadrio also attacked what he called the 'tyranny' of titles of honour.[25] In Rome, pope Benedict XIV, a former Bolognese patrician, was known for his liking for plain, informal speech (Pastor, vol. 35, pp. 40-1).

Others reacted no less strongly to the attempt to impose rules of correct speech by Pietro Bembo and others. For example, Pietro Aretino was almost certainly answering Bembo in his dialogues, letters and plays of the 1520s and 1530s. The colloquialisms, oaths and obscenities he scatters so liberally in his writings are a deliberate use of what Bembo would have regarded as 'anti-language'. The reference to Bembo is most transparent when Aretino makes reference to a woman who – 400 years before the English debate about 'U' and 'non-U' – declared that a window had to be called a *balcone*, not a common *finestra*, that a face should be described as a *viso*, rather than the vulgar *faccia* and so on.[26] It is not irrelevant to add that Aretino was the son of a craftsman who obviously regarded academic rules as unnecessary. In this he was supported by the Florentine shoemaker, Gianbattista Gelli, whose reaction to the appointment of a committee of the Florentine Academy to prepare a grammar of the vernacular (still an unusual enterprise) was to ask 'Which comes first? Do rules create languages, or languages rules?[27] As for resistance to Tuscanisation, it is most obvious in the case of Paolo Beni. Beni, who taught at the University of Padua, published in 1612 a book called 'Anticrusca', in other words an attack on the authority of the recently published dictionary of the Accademia della Crusca (above, p. 89), and a defence of what the Crusca considered 'anti-language' against the Tuscan standard. The Archduke of Tuscany wrote immediately to the Venetian Senate asking them to have Beni's book suppressed; a demand which reveals the importance of the politics of language, for some rulers at least, in the seventeenth century. These cases of resistance to the new orthodoxies are obvious enough; others are more problematic. Should we include the plays of Ruzzante, for example, with their Paduan dialect? What should we make of the Venetian patricians who continued to write poetry in dialect in the seventeenth and eighteenth centuries? The dialect may be an unselfconscious expression of regional conservatism; but it may be used deliberately, for comic effect on an audience which is now attuned to Tuscan; or again, it may be a protest against Tuscan linguistic hegemony. Each case has of course to be considered individually and in its own context, but a general conclusion would seem to follow from the profusion of these ambiguous instances. It is that standardisation did not so much drive out the alternatives to correct speech as transform their meaning. Classicism and anti-classicism, language and anti-language developed together and fed off one another (cf. Segre, 1953, and Borsellino, 1973).

Not the least important result of the controversies about correct language in early modern Italy was to make people linguistically self-conscious to a degree unparallelled earlier, and also interested in the history of their language. In the fifteenth century, two Italian humanists debated the question of what the Romans had spoken (as opposed to writing), Latin or Italian? (Grayson, 1960). In the sixteenth century, scholars such as Vincenzo Borghini did serious research into the origins and varieties of Tuscan.[28] As in the case of so many other institutions, interest in the history of language was the by-product of debates about its reform.

8

Insult and blasphemy
in early modern Italy

'Meglio è morir che viver con vergogna'

One day in 1620, Ferdinando Fredini got a nasty shock. This Milanese embroiderer, living in Rome, woke up one morning to discover that during the night, an unknown hand had stuck to his door a paper reflecting in no uncertain terms on his honour and that of his wife. Written in clumsy capital letters, it went as follows:

> QUI STAN LI GRAN[DISSI]MI BECCO
> FERDINANDO .RACAMATOR
> E PUTANISSIMA SUA MOGLIE
> RIFIUTO DE' GIUDEI
> CHE SOL IL BOIA RESTA
> CHI NE VOL DE INFAMI
> VENGA CON POCHI QUATRIN
> DAMI LA QUERELA BECCONE
> CHE TE HO IN CULO
> OVE SOLETE TENERE IL CAZZO
> CHE VE SE TAGLIARA LI MOSTICCI[1]

In the neighbourhood the incident was doubtless worthy of gossip for a time, encouraged by the official investigation which followed. However, in the long term, at least, it was far from isolated. From the point of view of the Tribunal of the Governor of Rome, which conducted the investigation, this *cartello infamante* (or, as the Englishmen of the time would have called it, this defamatory 'libel'), was only one in a series. Eighty-nine such cases are recorded in just over a hundred years, 1565–1666. The 'dark figure' of uninvestigated libels is of course impossible to calculate. In addition to these written examples, spoken insults are also recorded by witnesses before the Tribunal in many cases of assault.[2] Like the Tribunal, I too am concerned with the Fredini incident as an item in a series, though from a rather different perspective, that of the ethnography of communication (described above, p. 6). This chapter is concerned to place insults in their social and cultural context, and show how these acts, a breach of the rules in one sense (leading to the intervention of the Tribunal), in another sense followed rules or conventions as closely as a sonnet. They were stereotyped, or as the linguist William Labov puts it in a study of insult in the United States, 'ritualised' (Labov, 1972). As in the case of the sonnet, however, these rules allowed considerable scope for creativity and invention.

Let us define insult as an act of communication directed against another individual, group or institution. Some modern linguists (Brown and Levinson, 1978), speak of 'Face Threatening Acts' (abbreviated to FTAs), an appropriate term to apply to a culture so much concerned with 'face' as early modern Italy. As for contemporaries, they referred variously to *affronto, calunnia, parole contumeliose, diffamazione, deturpazione* (a technical term, to which we must return), *infamia, ingiuria* (meaning insult, not injury), *insolenza, maldicenza, mentita, vilipendio, vituperazione*, and so on. The richness of this vocabulary of vilification, the existence of all these distinctions and fine shades of meaning itself tells one something important about the culture in which it was employed. One writer of the period devoted a treatise to the *mentita* (in other words, 'giving the lie') alone, and its sixty-eight chapters give a good impression not only of the complexity of the subject but also of contemporary sensitivity to these FTAs. Can it be done in fun, and how in that case should the victim respond? Is it possible for the aggressor to apologise without compromising his own honour? What difference does it make if the insult is uttered by a man in a mask? How long does a provocation last? And so on.[3] A subject which will probably seem trivial to most readers now was taken very seriously indeed by contemporaries; honour depended on it (cf. Berger, 1970). Insults thus offer us a key to the history of mentalities or value-systems.

So far as I know, contemporaries did not discuss what might be called the 'insult system' as a whole; the vocabulary, the media, and the kind of people who participated, whether actively or passively. However, the system needs to be reconstructed – at least in outline – before specific cases, like Fredini's, can be interpreted.

To begin with the vocabulary, which was stereotyped. In the Roman records, the terms most commonly used of men were 'thief' (*ladro*), 'rogue' (*furfante*), 'traitor' (*traditore*), 'coward' (*poltrone*), 'spy' (*spia*), 'bugger' (*bugiarone*), 'pimp' (*ruffiano*), and, above all, 'cuckold' (*becco, beccone, beccaccia* – the Italians are masters of the contemptuous ending – *becco contento, becco cornuto, becco fottuto, grandissimo becco* (as in Fredini's case), etc). Literally, *becco* means 'goat'. This animal metaphor was popular in verbal abuse because the goat allows his mate to be mounted by other animals. Studying the collective representatives of the Mediterranean world today, the anthropologist Anton Blok has pointed out the complementary opposition between rams (symbols of virility) and silly billy-goats, an opposition which he describes as 'a key to the Mediterranean code of honour' and possibly as a survival from pastoral times (Blok, 1981). On the evidence produced before the Tribunal of the Governor, the code, or at any rate the goat half of it, was still very much in vigour in one of Europe's capital cities in the seventeenth (only in one cartello did I find the neighbours warned to lock up their wives because the local 'ram' was about). In accordance with this virility-centred code, men were insulted by being placed symbolically in the position of the female in phrases such as *becco fottuto*, *te ho in culo*, etc., phrases which still have their equivalents in the Mediterranean today (Dundes, Leach and Ozkök (1972); Dundes and Falassi (1975); Brandes, 1981; Driessen, 1983). The vocabulary of insults directed against women was also stereotyped. *Bugiarona* and *poltrona* occur in the documents, together with *vigliaccha* (another term for coward), but the most popular terms are 'witch' (*strega*, *fattucchiaria*). 'procuress' (*ruffiana*), and, above all, 'whore' (*puttana*, *bagascia*, etc.), with various unpleasant adjectives such as 'dirty' or 'poxy' (*scrofolosa*) tacked on. If a man is insultingly compared to a goat, or sometimes to a dog, the animal category most commonly used in the verbal abuse of women is 'sow' (*porca*; cf. Leach, 1964).

As the trials for assault make abundantly clear, ordinary speech was rich in insults of this kind, as one might have expected in a culture in which great value was and is placed on oral skills (above, p. 80), including the art of repartee, which must be both quick and biting. 'A biting tongue' (*lingua mordace*) was a not infrequent description for an individual in this period, and it is generally hard to decide whether the overtones are of disapproval or admiration, or both. Even spontaneous quarrels could easily take on the quality of performances. A somewhat more formal use of the oral medium was the practice of singing obscene songs in front of the house of one's enemy.[4] In addition, Italians had – and have – a rich repertoire of insulting gesture, well illustrated in Morris (1979, nos. 10–12), although he pays too little attention to context and cannot decide how seriously to take the different cultures of naked apes, as opposed to their biological drives (cf. Cocchiara 1932, pp. 77f). An early seventeenth-century treatise on gesture listed in its section on insults not only sticking out one's tongue at one's enemy, pulling his beard and spitting in his face, but the more distinctively Mediterranean 'making horns' (*fare le corne*), and 'making figs' (*fare le fiche*), defined in an old-fashioned Italian–English dictionary as 'a gesture of insolent contempt made by extending the hands with the thumbs clasped between the first and second fingers'.[5] The fig, incidentally, is supposed to symbolise a woman's genitals. Bonifacio's treatise, which seems to have been more concerned with literature than with life, by no means exhausted the contemporary repertoire of insulting gestures, which courts, travellers and other sources have preserved for us. In sixteenth-century Rome, the celebrated courtesan Isabella de Luna, faced with an unwelcome official document, a summons for debt, sketched the gesture of wiping her bottom with it; an action which was considered a grave insult to the Governor of Rome, from whom the document ultimately emanated.[6] In seventeenth-century Genoa, an English visitor with an interest in man-watching, John Evelyn, saw one boatman push in front of another. The offended party 'put his finger in his mouth and almost bit if off by the joynt, shewing it to his antagonist as an assurance to him of some bloodie revenge'. One does not have to be an out-and-out Freudian to see this gesture as a castration symbol.[7]

Insults could be pictorial. In Florence, Venice and elsewhere the commune punished treacherous or cowardly condottieri, rebels, bankrupts and other criminals by painting them in some conspicuous place, from the Palazzo del podestà to the public brothel at the Rialto, not infrequently hanging upside down. The meaning of these pictures has been debated by historians, and hypotheses range from the utilitarian (the equivalent of a 'wanted' poster, which would have been more useful the right way up), to the magical (on the analogy of sticking pins into the image of one's enemy), but the most plausible suggestion is that this form of symbolic destruction was aimed at the honour of the individuals concerned (Ortalli, 1979; Edgerton, 1985). Similar methods were adopted by private individuals for unofficial vengeance. In Verona in 1475, for instance, two noblemen were accused of going at night with torches and an armed guard to the house of another noble, with whom they had a vendetta (not the Montagus and Capulets, as it happens), and of ordering two painters to cover the facade with obscene figures in order to shame the victim and his family (Simeoni, 1903). Iconoclasm had a similar function. On the deaths of certain popes, such as Julius II, and Sixtus V, there were attacks on their statues. In Rome, in 1610, a case came before the Tribunal of the Governor in which ink had been thrown at the coat of arms of the Grand Duke of Tuscany, displayed over a shop; while the cartelli with which this paper is principally concerned were not infrequently illustrated with obscene drawings of a rather stereotyped kind. The insulting misuse of corpses may be seen as a kind of iconoclasm; dragging them by the feet, cutting off their genitals, covering a decapitated head with orange peel (below, p. 202), and so on.

Finally we come to insults in writing, of which there was a long tradition in Rome. Graffiti in Latin have survived from classical times; and as for Italian, a graffito in what is recognisably that language was inscribed in the eleventh century on the wall of a church in Rome. It consists of three words, *fili dele pute* (sons of whores).[8] The cases which came before the Tribunal of the Governor in the sixteenth and seventeenth centuries involves sheets of paper stuck or pasted to the victim's door in a symbolic violation of his or her domestic space. These cases appear to have been taken much more seriously by the courts than their oral equivalents (recorded only because an assault followed). The permanence and publicity of writing, in this semi-literate culture, made it a powerful weapon against an individual's honour.

Who insulted whom? It may be useful to follow a leading medieval canon lawyer, known as 'Hostiensis' because he was bishop of Ostia, in his chapter on curses (*de maledicis*), and to distinguish insults to one's equals, superiors and inferiors. Abuse traded between equals might be punishable for all that. The constitutions of the cathedral chapter of Montepulciano included the rule that if one canon insulted another, he had to pay twenty lire, while if the insult was to a chaplain, the fine was halved (the annual income of a labourer or chaplain in 1500 was about fifty lire a year; canons did rather better).

Generally speaking, insults by inferiors to superiors were taken very seriously. In fourteenth-century Venice, 'verbal violence' against the doge or lesser officials of the commune was severely punished (sometimes by cutting of the offender's tongue). In the sixteenth century, Isabella de Luna paid dearly for her 'extremely grave disrespect' towards the Governor of Rome (she was whipped). In Milan in 1629, a merchant was fined for contempt of court simply for saying, when an emissary from a particular tribunal arrived, 'You prick, you must have come from the judge' (*Cazzo, sete stato dal sindicatore*). The mere association of the two nouns *cazzo* and *sindicatore* was considered to reflect on the court.[9]

Insults to the authorities generally took the safer form of anonymous inscriptions. In 1500, for example, papers (*bolettini*) were placed over the door of a Venetian nobleman who held the office of state attorney (*avogador del comun*), calling him a thief and a traitor: 'Paulo Pisano ladro et traditor del stato de Venetiani'. Five years later, a libel was posted at the Rialto with a cartoon of the doge (Leonardo Loredan, best known, in England at least, from his dignified portrait by Bellini, now in the National Gallery), complete with a speech balloon saying 'I don't care as long as I get fat, me and my son Lorenzo'.[10] In the case of Rome, insulting the authorities in this way was institutionalised around the year 1500 as a tradition grew up of attaching pungent verses in the vernacular to the mutilated classical statue known as 'Pasquino', who gave his name to the *pasquinade*[11]. Insult shades into political protest by means of graffiti, of which there is a long tradition in Italy (below, ch. 9).

The extreme case of insults by inferiors to superiors is of course blasphemy against God and his saints, but it seems to have been common enough, at the end of a colourful spectrum of oaths. If we can trust the evidence of sixteenth-century Venetian comedies, different social groups swore in recognisably different ways. In the anonymous play 'The Venetian Woman' (*La Venexiana*), for example, the high-status widow Angela tends to say 'for the love of God' (*per l'amor di Dio*); the servant-girl Oria, 'by this cross' (*per questa Crose*), while the male servant Bernardo ranges between 'the devil' (*diavol*), 'canker' (*cancar*), and 'shit blood' (*chigasang*). In the plays of Ruzzante, already discussed (above, p. 23), we can distinguish at least three groups of more or less hard swearers. There are girls like Dina, who confine themselves to 'on my faith' (*sora questa fe*); professional men and patricians like Messer Andronico and Sier Tomao, who say 'the devil', or 'by my body' (*al corpo di mi*), or 'by the body of Saint Kate' (*al corpo di Santa Cataruza*) or 'by the body I won't name' (*al corpo che no digo*); and the servants or peasants, rough types who prefer 'blood of the canker' (*al sangue del cancaro*), 'blood of the wolf's sickness' (*sangue del mal della loa*), or simply 'cunt' (*pota*). This variation seems to illustrate the tension between two principles. Leaving on one side the degree of irritation shown on a particular occasion, it is clear that hard swearing is an affirmation of masculinity, while mild swearing is an affirmation of gentility.[12]

At the hard-swearing end of the spectrum, at least, we can augment this evidence from other sources. Benvenuto Cellini, for example, records what he identifies as a specifically Perugian mode of blasphemy, though he, or his amanuensis, or his editor, had scruples about setting it down in full, leaving 'per lo...di Dio' to stimulate the imagination.[13] At least one outsider is more forthcoming. Philip Skippon, whose observations of Italians have been cited already (pp. 18–19), kept his ears open as well as his eyes. 'The Venetians (as all Italians do) swear frequently', he remarked, and went on to record twelve oaths, most of them blasphemous: 'per Dio, per Dio santo, per Diana, Corpo di Christo, per Christo, Cospetto di Dio, Cospetto di Diana, etc. Some will make a cross and then say, per questa Croce. Others will say, per Catzo di Dio, per Puttano di Dio. When they scornfully admire any thing, they say Catzo, Heibo'.[14]

Other evidence comes from the courts, for both church and state in early modern Italy were concerned with the prevalence of blasphemy. Bishops on diocesan visitations frequently asked parish priests about 'public and habitual blasphemers' in the locality. Governments often issued decrees against blasphemy, and in Venice there was a special committee called the 'Executors against Blasphemy' – though their responsibilities were in fact considerably wider. The cases from the end of the seventeenth century which survive in the files of this body suggest that individuals were generally arrested because their neighbours had informed on them, using the famous 'mouths of truth', the letter-boxes in the shape of lion's mouths, for their secret denunciations. The court took the cases very seriously and expended a good deal of effort on what we might call 'mere words', inviting witnesses to describe in detail the various occasions on which the accused had uttered such well-worn phrases as *corpenazo de Dio, cospetazzo di Dio, pota di Dio, puttana* or *puttanazza di Dio, sanguenazzo de Dio, puttana di Maria Vergine*, or, on one occasion, rather more imaginatively, *putana di San Piero con tutte le sue chiave* ('whore of St Peter with all his keys').[15]

Two points about the attitudes of the authorities deserve to be mentioned, at least in passing. The first is that they must have turned a blind eye, or more exactly a deaf ear, most of the time. A few unfortunate individuals ended up in court for saying, on particular occasions what they and many of their fellow-citizens had otherwise said with impunity. One has the sense (as so often in reading judicial records of the early modern period), that someone (perhaps the denouncers), was out to get these individuals by appealing to laws which were only occasionally enforced. The second point is that when the affair came to court, the authorities treated these verbal acts (to my mind, rather implausibly), as if they were deliberate acts of aggression against God rather than as symptoms of chronic badmouth. This is not to deny the existence of a few deliberate acts of blasphemy, some of a paralinguistic kind; it is hard to find another interpretation for the action of the sixteenth-century Florentine who threw dung at a holy image and was executed for it (Edgerton, 1985), or the seventeenth-century Roman who showed his private parts at a window, in the classic gesture of contempt, just when the Blessed Sacrament was passing in procession in the street below.[16] Individuals, then, insulted the authorities; but to complete this outline of the insult system we have to include the cases where the authorities insulted individuals. The official public shaming of traitors, cowards, bankrupts etc. followed similar lines to the shaming by private initiative which is the central theme of this chapter (whichever practice was modelled on the other). The portrayal of criminals on the walls of public buildings has already been mentioned. In Naples following the revolt of 1585, the viceroy had a kind of anti-monument constructed with the heads of twenty-four rebels and an inscription. In Milan, following the plague of 1630, a 'pillar of infamy' (*colonna infame*) was erected to the eternal infamy of the barber who was believed to have spread the disease. It was described by Addison in his journal and made famous by Manzoni in his great novel 'The Betrothed' (*I Promessi Sposi*), which is set in this period. On the façade of the cathedral at Genoa it is still possible to make out some seventeenth-century anti-epitaphs, in other words public inscriptions recording the names of traitors to the commune in order to keep their dishonour fresh for posterity. Such cases need to be borne in mind as part of the system of signs which expressed the value system of early modern Italy, in which honour and shame were paramount.

This system was not static, but there are not many signs of change. In the case of politeness (discussed above, p. 90), trends over time, notably the debasement of the verbal currency, seem relatively easy to discern, but there seems to have been no symmetrical development of impoliteness. Perhaps insult is too basic, too close to the unchanging id, while politeness belongs to the sphere of the superego and the civilising process. The only assertion about change within the early modern period which I can made with any confidence concerns the punishment of blasphemy. The authorities of church and state alike came to take it more seriously from the middle of the sixteenth century onwards, perhaps associating it with heresy. In Verona, that model bishop of the Catholic reformation, Gian Maria Giberti, showed himself particularly concerned with this sin. In Venice, the 'Executors' against blasphemy were set up in 1537, as part of a more general attempt at the moral reform of the city (Derosas, 1980). In 1559, the senate of Milan issued an edict against blasphemy, and a little later the Grand Duke of Tuscany did the same. So did pope Pius V in 1564. The authorities had become extremely sensitive to the honour of God, and blasphemers now risked not merely being ducked in a basket to wash their mouths out (a traditional medieval remedy), or paying a small fine (twenty soldi at the Scuola di San Rocco in Venice in 1493; Pullan, 1971, p. 50), but of having their tongues bored through or removed altogether or of serving a term slaving in the galleys, like one peasant from the Cremona area, condemned to two years in the galleys for uttering two words: 'Dio becco' (Politi, 1976, p. 374).

In the case of insults to mere mortals, however, it is difficult to discern a trend. In Rome, for example, the Governor, monsignor Ferdinando Taverna, issued an edict against defamatory libels in 1599, but it seems to have had little effect. The eighty-nine surviving cases referring to the city (omitting the other towns which came under the Tribunal's jurisdiction, such as Narni), are spread fairly evenly over the period 1565–1666, before and after which few of its records have survived. It would have been particularly interesting to see whether libels declined in the eighteenth century, a time when there was a reaction against duelling and hypersensitivity to honour generally in at least one section of the Italian upper classes.[17] The Tribunal itself has not yet received the study it deserves. It seems to have worked along the lines of the Inquisition, with interrogations of suspects in private rather than trials in open court. However, the fact that investigations usually began when the victim appeared at the Tribunal to make a complaint suggests a certain degree of confidence on the part of the laity in the justice it administered.

Looking at the history of insult over the long term, one hypothesis about change over time springs to mind. It is that a traditional system, in which shaming was an important means of controlling behaviour which broke the rules of the community, was giving way to a more modern one, in which the repression of deviant behaviour was increasingly taken over by the state. The result of this political centralisation was, ironically enough, that traditional control devices, such as the *cartello infamante*, came to be seen as a form of deviance to be suppressed, leading to the trials before the Tribunal of the Governor. Both systems, needless to say, were open to manipulation by interested parties, but in different ways. The trial records are not inconsistent with this hypothesis about change over time, but breaking off abruptly as they do, they are insufficient to confirm it.

To return to microhistory, eighty-nine cases out of something like 16,000 is not very much (though the cases involving insult by speech and gesture, and the subsequent violence, amount to about 1,400, about an eleventh of the total); but at least it is sufficient to reveal a pattern.

To these cases of defamatory libel we should perhaps add a handful of non-verbal insults in which the victim's door was the target. They fall into two groups. The first group of cases (thirteen of them altogether) is described in the records as *deturpazione*, or more rarely, as *lordatura*; the plaintiff's door, or occasionally shutters, are smeared with ink, or excrement, or the blood of an animal. This rather vague if unpleasant expression of hostility would seem to be an urban adaptation of a traditional rural ritual. In Cremona in 1599, for example, the clergy denounced the local custom of dirtying the door of unmarried girls on the eve of St Blaise's day (3 February).[18] The medium permits only the simplest message. A somewhat more precise example of a non-verbal face-threatening act is known in the Roman records as *apposizione di corna*, of which seven cases are recorded. The victim's door was decorated with horns, bringing us back to the central theme of the libels, which were posted in the same place, usually at night (on one occasion during Mass, as if it were safe to assume that everyone would be in church at the time). When the injured party had recourse to the tribunal, to restore his or her lost honour by legal action against the unknown aggressor, the offending libel was carefully detached by the officers of the court and preserved to become exhibit A in the file of the case, where it may still be read by the historian, in many cases with the sealing-wax or flour paste with which it was originally attached still adhering to the back of the document.

What the Tribunal called *libelli famosi* was a category covering a considerable range of variation. In one case they simply misinterpreted an adolescent's love letter, illustrated with obscene drawings, as an insult; in another case a love letter was accompanied by a threat. The eighty-nine cases also include one elegantly written sonnet, which reflected on the honour of the fair recipient, and one pasquinade (in the most literal sense; it was attached not to the victim's door but to the statue of Pasquino, and the case was abandoned when the question, 'Who did you see reading it?', was answered by 'I don't know everyone in Rome').[19] However, this periphery of exceptions surrounds a hard core of stereotyped cases. The libels do not in most cases reveal great skill either in calligraphy or in composition. They are clumsy productions for the most part, written in crude capital letters, no doubt to disguise the author's handwritings as well as to increase legibility (in one case the letters were cut out of print). The style and the physical appearance of the majority of libels is so similar that one might almost think, were they not spread over more than a century, that they were written by the same person, to such an extent did the genre follow rules.

The basic message is brutally simple, and not so different from *apposizione di corna*. Male victims are described as cuckolds and female victims as whores. An exception has to be made for a convent of friars, who were the collective victims of another libel in sonnet form, but in this case too the reference was to their sexual behaviour.

As for the rhetoric of these libels, it is perhaps best seen as a combination of two very different styles. In the first place, there is the oral style of insulting or threatening colloquial speech, inattentive to the rules of grammar, making great use of the impolite 'tu', and of contemptuous suffixes (*beccone* and so on), and often ending in a threat; 'you will see what will happen to you', or 'your head will be cut from your shoulders' or 'if you don't keep your tongue between your teeth you will be bumped off' (*serai ammazzato*). In the second place, there is a literary style, sometimes poetic (as in the case of the two sonnets), but more often bureaucratic in form, a style based on public notices, doubtless to give authority to the text by making the description seem official. In one particularly elaborate case the libel imitates an edict of the governer of Rome. Another contains the sentence, 'I cite you before the Tribunal of the Capitol as a most solemn bugger' (*solennissima buggiarone*). In another case, it is an excommunication which is copied or parodied. More common are stereotyped phrases like 'house to let' (*est locanda*, an interesting use of Latin), in one case expanded into 'to let for half a grosso, night and day'; or 'here lives' (*qui sta*), a variant on 'here lies'. In one case the mock-tombstone theme is worked out more fully: 'the sodomite Broccholo lies here/Reader, flee, his spirit has the same tastes' (*Il sottomitta Broccholo qui giace/Fuggi lettor al spirito anco 'l cul piace*). It is worth noting the names by which the witnesses described these libels. One recurrent term is *pasquinade*; another is *epitaph*, a term which suggests a reference to the quasi-official style. In any case, that is exactly what the libels were; epitaphs on dead reputations.

The libel addressed to Ferdinando Fredini, with which the chapter began, is, as will now be obvious, a fairly typical production of its place and time. The official-sounding 'Here lives' and the colloquial *becco* are juxtaposed in the first line. His wife is not merely described as a whore, but as superlatively whorish (*putanissima*), and to blacken the remains of her reputation still further, she is associated with two infamous groups. She is 'the Jews' leavings'; there is considerable evidence of popular antisemitism in Rome, ritualised in the Jews' race every Carnival, when old men had to run through the streets naked while the crowd pelted them. 'Only the hangman remains'. To this day Italian graffiti not infrequently refer to the hangman (*boia*). In early modern Italy, as elsewhere in Europe, executioner was what was known as an 'infamous' occupation. Those who practised it often had to live at the edge of town (thus symbolising their marginal, indeed liminal position between the law and the criminal, life and death), and they were unable to marry their children to respectable people. There was a proverb, current in the sixteenth century, 'as lonely as a hangman'.

Following this description of Fredini's wife, the libel now takes a dramatic turn, with a challenge, a triumph and a threat. DAMI LA QUERELA BECCONE. The anonymous writer assumes that the victim knows his identity, and he plays on this by challenging him to do something about this, implying that he will not and that the cuckold is also a coward. TE HO IN CULO: an assertion that 'I've got you where I want you', but also that the victim is in the passive, female position, a common Spanish insult to this day (Brandes, 1981, etc). The libel ends with a threat, CHE VE SE TAGLIARA LI MOSTICCI, 'you'll have your moustaches cut off', a reference to a classic virility symbol, especially in the Mediterranean world.

As in the majority of cases, the libel is concerned almost exclusively with the sexual behaviour of the victim and his wife. However, it would not be wise to be too literal-minded in interpreting the allegations. In this particular culture, this was how one destroyed reputations. I doubt whether the libels tell us anything at all about the sexual activities of the recipients, though it might be safe to apply the 'no smoke without fire' principle to the comparatively rare non-sexual allegations, like the suggestion that the treasurer of a confraternity had his hand in the till.

One of the most obvious and important questions to ask about these libels is Lenin's; who whom? The second half of the question is naturally the easier to answer, as most plaintiffs identify themselves by occupations before the Governor's Tribunal. A small minority are of high or fairly high status; a cardinal the Commendatore of the Arch-Hospital of Santo Spirito, the wife of a notable, a widow who seems to be well off, and a Jesuit teacher. The rest are mainly from the craftsmen-shopkeeper class, including three innkeepers, two apothecaries, two courtesans, a painter, a miniaturist, an embroiderer, a tailor, a barber, a butcher, a coppersmith and a letter-carrier. According to the treatises on honour, it was confined to the upper classes (Bryson, 1935); but the fact that some craftsmen and shopkeepers – what proportion of the victims we shall never know – complained to the Tribunal of the Governor about libels suggests that they too felt that they had honour to lose and cared about it enough to have recourse to law to defend or regain it. Occasionally this point is made explicitly; the coppersmith exhibits a painting which caricatures his twisted foot and describes it as made 'to my dishonour' (*in mio gran dishonore*). It confirms the observation made by the Piedmontese writer Guiseppe Baretti a century later, in the course of explaining Italy to the English, when he remarked on the 'touchy temper in our low people'.[20] On the other hand, the absence of the sword-wearing classes is perhaps to be explained by the fact that for them it would have been dishonourable to take insults to the Tribunal. Insults from equals had to be wiped out in duels, while insults from inferiors would have been dealt with out of court.

Who were the aggressors? As the Tribunal had good reason to know, the identity of the insulters was not easy to discover. The technique was to interrogate the neighbours, asking them whether they knew of anyone with a grudge against the victim, and bringing the suspects in for questioning. In more than one case professional scribes were called in as expert witnesses to identify the handwriting of the libel, sometimes by comparing it with a document written by the suspect; but as one might have expected from people with their livings to gain in the neighbourhood, their testimony was generally inconclusive.[21] Despite the problems of identifying any one individual with certainty, the reader is left with an impression that the aggressors were either the social equals of their victims, or somewhat lower in status. They include a physician, a solicitor, a goldsmith, a sculptor, two painters (one of whom was Caravaggio, whose brushes with the law are notorious); a sword-maker, a corn-measurer, a rosary-seller, two courtesans, some friars and some students. The cardinal was insulted by a cleric of lower status; the letter-carrier, by someone he employed; a master, by a journeyman; the teacher, by his students. The obvious exception here, in reality if not in form, is the widow in whose case the accused were the servants of a marquis, presumably carrying out the orders of their master. Generally speaking, men insulted men through women. I have only found one female suspect who was not a courtesan, a quarryman's wife who was also a school mistress and was accused of defaming an innkeeper. Women were of course less likely to be literate than men, but illiteracy was no obstacle to libel; the rosary-seller, a local eccentric nicknamed 'Cecco matto' claimed to be unable to read and write but explained, under threat of torture, that he had the libel written for him by someone else.[22]

The function of these libels is obvious enough, but their strategy deserves a comment. They present themselves as the voice of public opinion, 'fama commune', or at least as the voice of the neighbourhood, to which one of the texts makes explicit reference, while in others witnesses testify to what was commonly said about the victim. In this way the libels resemble charivaris, as also in the fact that they were a festive form with a nasty sting in the tail. In fact, one of the libels, the earliest surviving, was not affixed at night in secret but by 'many men' who made a great noise, and shouted insults, in an incident which reminded the plaintiff of 'a bacchanal'.[23] The rhetoric of the libels, their adoption of fragments of offical language from the courts, the Church and so on, was a means of reinforcing the impression that they expressed the judgement of the whole community. However, the investigations conducted by the Tribunal offer an opposite perspective. The investigators unmask the claim of the libel to represent public opinion by showing that the libeller was a particular individual, and, what is more, an individual with a grudge against the victim. It was of course the court's job to do this, and the questions the neighbours were asked were loaded ones, but it is worth at least entertaining the possibility that they were right and that – if evidence permitted – a similar analysis might be made of charivaris. The genre represents the anonymity of public opinion, the voice of the pueblo, as one student of Andalusia puts it (Pitt-Rivers, 1954, ch. 11), but it is open to manipulation by an indiviual or a small group (cf. Ingram, 1985). The libel posted on the door was the equivalent of the anonymous letter of denunciation to a newspaper today, in which public spirit may also mask the private grudge (Boltanski, 1984). It would be good to know more about attitudes to libels, whether they were regarded favourably or unfavourably by the neighbours, but the interrogations tell us little of this and that little is untrustworthy, given that the witnesses are reacting to the expectations of the officials who interrogate them.

The libels are, among other things, vivid testimony to the quality of life at street level in a large early modern city, encouraging the view that it was in many ways a confederation of villages. However, this intensely local evidence ought also to be seen in comparative perspective. Even the differences between the names people called one another when quarrelling can tell one something about other cultural differences. In Amsterdam, for example, according to the notarial archives of the early eighteenth century, the names included not only *pokkige hoer*, *schelm* and *dief*, all of which can be parallelled in Rome, but also *bankroerier* (bankrupt) and *rasphuishoer* (referring to the notorious workhouse-prison).[24] Defamatory libels and the reactions to them should tell us still more. They were no Roman or even Italian monopoly in this period. They can be found in England, horns and all, in Essex, for example, in Wiltshire, and in Somerset (Ingram, 1985; Quaife, 1979, pp. 158–63; Underdown, 1985, p. 128). Similar points might be made about France.[25] In England as in

Italy defamation cases reveal 'plebeian notions of honour', and a trust in the process of law (Sharpe, 1980, though the author is unaware that the Romans too resorted to the courts as well as to violence).

So much for parallels; it would be easy to extend them, but it is perhaps more interesting to emphasise what is unusual about the Roman cases of defamatory libel; their number. This may of course be nothing more than the accident of survival, but the genre might be described as peculiarly appropriate to Rome for two reasons. The first, on which I would not care to lay too much stress, is the continuity of seventeenth-century practice with certain standard forms of defamation in ancient Rome, from singing loudly in front of one's enemy's house to writing, or more exactly carving the insult on stone (Veyne, 1982). The second, which has been mentioned already, is the institution known as Pasquino. Pasquino is a classical statue; the custom of attaching verses to a statue has classical precedents, such as the *priapeia* (Richlin, 1983). The verses were originally classical. However, this learned custom was vulgarised in more than one sense (popularised; vernacularised; etc.), giving us mordant comments on the authorities by a statue which (whether or not manipulated by private individuals on occasion) became the mouthpiece of Roman public opinion, and has remained so down to our own day. One might regard the defamatory libel as a kind of private pasquinade, drawing on the language of Pasquino as well as on public notices. More than one of the libels appeal to this patron, signing 'io Pasquino' or asking rhetorically, 'What are you doing, Pasquino?' (*Pasquino, che fai?*), while the witnesses before the Tribunal sometimes call the libels *pasquinate*. Alternatively, one might reverse this interpretation and see Pasquino as an example of the transference of a traditional private practice to the public domain, like the politicisation of the charivari in nineteenth-century France. Whichever view one takes, the interaction which these texts reveal between public and private domains, oral and written media, and learned and popular traditions is one of the most interesting features of this remarkable corpus of documents.

9
The uses of literacy
in early modern Italy

In the middle of the twentieth century, when many new nations were embarking on massive literacy campaigns, scholars in several disciplines began to take the subject of reading and writing more seriously than before. Sociologists argued, for instance, that 'Literacy is the basic personal skill which underlies the whole modernising sequence' because it gives people access to the world of vicarious experience' (Lerner, 1958). Anthropologists suggested that the traditional distinction between 'logical' and 'prelogical' thought should rather have been framed in terms of 'literate' and 'preliterate', because what made abstract thinking possible was literacy (Goody, 1977; but cf. Goody and Watt, 1962–3). Historians too began to concern themselves with this topic, to measure the extent of the diffusion of literacy in different periods and to discuss the economic, social and political consequences of these techniques (Cipolla, 1969).

Less than a generation later, a reaction against this approach has set in, marked by a critique of its assumptions. Scholars who have written about the literacy revolution are accused of exaggerating the distance between oral and literate cultures; of underestimating the achievements and resources of societies without literacy; and, most serious of all, of treating literacy as a uniform neutral technology which can be studied in detachment from its social context, as if the meaning, uses and conventions of literacy did not vary from one society to another (Street, 1984).

This reaction against an older approach is itself part of the context of what is now called the 'ethnography of writing', an approach which has grown out of the ethnography of communication (above, p. 6) and emphasises the settings in which literacy is learned and the purposes for which it is used, whether in the United States (Basso, 1974; Szwed, 1981), or in Liberia (Scribner and Cole, 1981). The dust has not yet settled on this debate, and it is doubtless too early to say whether or not there are common features underlying the different literacies, their settings and conventions. What has become clear is the need to occupy the middle ground between the grand theories of literacy and its consequences on the one hand, and the empirical but limited research on literacy 'rates' and 'levels' on the other. This essay will therefore focus, like some other recent historical studies, on what Richard Hoggart (1957) called 'the uses of literacy' (Wormald, 1977, Hyde, 1979; Clanchy, 1979).

To work on Italian literacy in the early modern period is in some ways frustrating. The preliminary work of more-or-less approximate measurement is much more difficult to carry out than it has been in the case of Britain, let alone Sweden. Despite the growing interest of the bishops in the attitudes of the laity (above, ch. 4), there was nothing in Italy like the Swedish church-inspired house-to-house investigations (*husverhör*; Johansson, 1973). Nor was there anything like the British Protestation Oath of 1642, the signatures to which have been used as an indicator of male literacy (Schofield, 1968). Even a tradition of signing marriage registers was lacking and there was of course no unified Italy till 1860. Before the coming of national surveys, like the one carried out in 1911, there is little historians can do but collect fragmentary information from fragmentary sources (Petrucci, 1978).

One famous fragment which is often used as a baseline is the testimony of the Florentine merchant chronicler Giovanni Villani, to the effect that, in 1338, between 10,000 and 12,000 Florentine children were going to school. This figure, if accurate (as many historians believe it to be), is quite extraordinary for a fourteenth-century city with a population of under 100,000. It is likely that most if not all the schoolchildren were male, and on this assumption it would follow that from 45% to 60% of Florentine boys of school age were actually attending a school of some kind (Klapisch, 1984, p. 775).[1] This figure makes a remarkable contrast with the statistics from the 1911 survey, which found the national average literacy rate to be only 38% of the population over the age of six, even if we allow for the fact that the 38% is an aggregate which is pulled down by the figures for women, for the countryside, and for the south.

For Venice too in the late Middle Ages – or early Renaissance – there are figures which suggest a population which was relatively highly-schooled. In the early fifteenth century, when the city contained about 85,000 people, there were fifty or sixty teachers, in other words one to every 350 males under twenty. By the late sixteenth century the ratio had improved to one to 135, for more than 250 practising schoolmasters are recorded in a population which had risen to about 135,000 (Cipolla, 1969, p. 59n; Baldo, 1977). In Milan at the end of the sixteenth century, there were said to be 120 schools of christian doctrine, combining religious instruction with elementary literacy.[2] Rome seems to have lagged behind till the end of the seventeenth century but in 1703, 126 schoolmasters are recorded in a population of about 150,000 (Giuntella, 1961; for the seventeenth century, Petrucci, 1982, nos. 42, 199).

Although systematic comparisons have not been made, it seems likely that literacy in northern Italy, at least, was high relative to other parts of Europe (with the possible exception of the Netherlands) from the year 1000, if not before, till about 1600, and that the Italian lead was only challenged in the seventeenth century, with the rise of the Dutch Republic and of the great literacy campaign in Sweden. Yet this conclusion, however, plausible, cannot be established; that is what is so frustrating. Prospects improve if we turn from the literacy rate to the true subject of this chapter, the question of the ways in which this hard-won and highly-prized skill was used. This is of course not so much one question as a whole cluster. The ethnographers of writing (notably Basso, 1974, and Szwed, 1981), have emphasised the need for studying a whole range of problems who; in a given culture, writes to whom, in what social settings, and also on what subjects for not all information is necessarily considered to be appropriate for transmission by written channels. It is on these problems that I shall concentrate.

A similar set of questions could be asked about reading, which should ideally be discussed separately from writing because of the likelihood that many people who could not write were able to read. Villani describes children in elementary schools who 'stick to reading' (*stanno a leggere*), while writing was taught to fewer pupils elsewhere. We need to ask who read what, indeed who read what to whom (since there was much reading aloud), and in what settings. To learn, for example, that in the early fifteenth century pope Eugenius IV used to read in bed is to have acquired more than a piece of picturesque trivia, for the example helps to document the slow but significant shift from public to private reading (cf. Chaytor, 1945).[3] To discover that the legend of St Margaret was read aloud to women in childbirth in sixteenth-century Italy (below, p. 211) tells one something about contemporary attitudes to the power of the word. However, it is with the manifold uses of writing, or active literacy, that this chapter is principally concerned, whether the writing was in Latin, or in what was becoming standard Italian (above, p. 89), or in dialect; whether the handwriting was gothic, or the elegant Italic script which was spreading in humanist circles, whether the message was written on parchment or paper, or carved in stone, or indeed scribbled on walls (Petrucci, 1980).

So far as these questions are concerned, there is certainly no shortage of evidence. On the contrary, it is copious; so copious as to create serious problems for historians who want to use it. From the eleventh century, if not before, Italy – or at least, the many towns of the north and centre – was becoming what might reasonably be called a 'notarial culture', with a high proportion of notaries in the population (eight per 1,000 in Florence in 1427), thanks to the high demand for the registration of wills, contracts of marriage, apprenticeship and partnership, and other legal 'acts' and 'instruments' (Cipolla, 1973). Italy was not alone in this respect. The notarial culture seems to have extended over much of the Mediterranean christian world in the later Middle Ages. Yet a contrast with England, which might be extended to other parts of northern Europe, is suggested by the remark of an Italian notary who visited this country in the thirteenth century. 'Italians,' he wrote, 'like cautious men, want to have a public instrument for practically every contract they enter into; but the English are just the opposite, and an instrument is very rarely asked for unless it is essential' (Clanchy, 1979 p. 37, though he believes that the writer, Giovanni da Bologna, exaggerated the contrast).

The remains of this notarial activity are massive. The idea of writing on this subject came to me while waiting for documents in an Italian archive (a process which not infrequently affords leisure for contemplation), together with the realisation, at once intoxicating and sobering, that every document in that vast repository would be of relevance to the research. One would in a sense be interrogating the documents about themselves, rather than, as usual, about something else; asking for what purposes they were originally made, and dividing them into genres – notarial acts, bills, certificates, licences, passes, denunciations, petitions and so on.

The uses of literacy obviously include what we call 'literature' and what the humanists knew as 'bonae litterae' (categories which overlap to a considerable extent but do not coincide). This function will not be discussed here, not because it is unimportant (the period under consideration runs, after all, from Petrarch to Goldoni), but because it has attracted so much scholarly attention, while practical or 'pragmatic' literacy, as it is now called, has not. Sociolinguists distinguish what they call 'domains of language behaviour', different styles of speech which are to be found in different settings (Fishman, 1965). In a similar way I should like to distinguish four principal domains of practical literacy and discuss them in turn; business, the family, the church and the state. Although it is impossible to distinguish four styles of writing, one to each domain, there is evidence of variation in style as one moves from one 'use' to another. In three of the domains, distinct types of handwriting were customarily employed. Merchants used 'business hand' (*lettera mercantescha*) in its regional varieties (*mercantile fiorentina, venetiana*, etc.). Administrative documents were generally produced in 'chancery hand' (*lettera cancellarescha*), while clerks in the service of the church used 'ecclesiastical hand' (*lettera ecclesiastica*), together with special styles for papal bulls and briefs.[4] Latin was the language not only of the church but of the law and of much public administration. The alternative to it was not Italian but dialect. Although Tuscan was gaining ground in the early modern period in the domain of literature, it had not yet invaded the public domains of business, politics and the church, let alone the privacy of the family.

Literacy and business

The uses of literacy in business are relatively well known. In the fourteenth and fifteenth centuries, writers of advice to merchants – a genre which itself illustrates one of the practical uses of literacy – counselled them not to spare their pens and told them that the good merchant had inky fingers.[5] In the early seventeenth century, the Genoese patrician Andrea Spinola was still giving similar advice to anyone who wanted to succeed in business. Even nobles ought to know how to write a good hand and to keep accounts; 'it is really shameful' that some of them rely on other people to do this for them.[6]

The numbers of surviving bills, receipts, contracts and so on suggests that the advice was often taken. The business papers of one fourteenth-century merchant, Francesco Datini of Prato, near Florence, are so vast as to daunt historians who wish to study them and make them wonder how Datini and his agents found the time to do anything besides produce this mass of documentation, which includes some 500 account-books and ledgers, piously inscribed 'in the name of God and of profit' (Origo, 1957; Melis, 1962). In Datini's time it was in fact normal for nine different ledgers to be kept in a single firm, dealing respectively with income, expenditure, wages, petty cash and so on, not forgetting the master ledger or 'secret book' (*libro segreto*). The ledgers were kept in Roman numerals but they employed the method of double entry which the Italian businessmen pioneered (Bec, 1967, p. 49–50).

Keeping accounts in this way was a skill which had of course to be learned, and numeracy was taught to a relatively high level in what were known as 'abacus schools' (such as the six in Florence mentioned by

Villani). The abacus was a board with counters on the ancient Roman model, not the system of beads on wires used in the Far East. The curriculum of these abacus schools seems to have been a practical, business-oriented one (Goldthwaite, 1972; Murray, 1978). The evidence comes from surviving schoolbooks, which include questions about buying and selling wool and converting different weights, measures and currencies. The existence of schoolbooks such as these from the fourteenth century – in other words, well before the invention of printing – deserves emphasis, even if the books were intended for the teachers rather than the students.[7] So does the abacus. It is mind-boggling to imagine Italian merchants adding up long columns of Roman numerals but in fact there was no need to do so, thanks to the abacus, which also allowed the otherwise illiterate to calculate at speed.

It is the numeracy of the Florentines in the fourteenth and fifteenth centuries which has attracted most attention from historians, but the same skills can be documented for a later period and other cities. The *Summa of Arithmetic* published in 1521 discussed rates of interest and exchange. The *Universal Treasure* published in Venice about 1530, claimed to teach book-keeping and 'all business methods' (*ogni ragione di mercantia*), and it gave examples with a distinctly Venetian flavour, such as the buying and selling of sugarloaves and spices and the journey time of a galley going to Crete.[8] In 1587, again in Venice, there were 143 pupils at one school who were learning arithmetic and double-entry bookkeeping (Baldo, p. 29). One begins to wonder whether there were enough businesses to employ all these pupils after they had finished the course, and to understand why the 'Universal Treasure' was directed to 'friars, priests, students, doctors, gentlemen, craftsmen and especially to the sons of every father who desires his son's welfare'.

Business affairs depended on other kinds of document besides account; on letters, for example. Over 125,000 letters survive in the Datini archive in Prato. Letters brought news and news was a matter of life and death – economic life and death at least – for the business community. Priority was crucial. 'If you are in business', goes one famous piece of advice, 'and your letters come in the same packet as other letters, you must always think of reading your own letters before passing the others on'.[9]

Letters did not merely give news of supply, demand, and prices elsewhere. Payments could be made by particular forms of letter. The Medici bank in Bruges, for example, sold what were called 'letters of credit' to travellers to Italy, the letters being addressed to its Milan branch; the travellers bought the letters in one local currency and redeemed them for the other on arrival. Also in general use in the fifteenth century were bills of exchange, again in the form of a letter, which allowed the advance of funds in one place and repayment in another (de Roover, 1966, p. 125).

With all these letters to write and accounts to keep, not to mention the bills and receipts which had to be made out, it is no wonder that the fingers of the good merchant were so inky. And not his fingers alone; for running a family, as well as running a business, could generate a good deal of paper.

Literacy and the family

The second domain of practical literacy to be discussed here is that of family, more especially the urban patrician family (although its dominance of the written record may be in part the result of a higher documentary survival rate). For what purposes, in early modern Italy, were family papers written and preserved? At this point we need to distinguish three kinds of family document. In the first place, 'carte di notaio', as they were called, in other words notarial papers such as wills, marriage contracts, inventories *post mortem* and so on, documents which were supposed to be preserved with care in chests in case disputes about the inheritance should arise, as they often did.

In the second place, family letters. What the Paston letters are to the historian of fifteenth-century England, the letters of Alessandra Macinghi Strozzi are to the historian of Florence in the same period. The Strozzi letters were printed in the nineteenth century, but the letters of a number of families of the period remain unpublished; those of the Donà, for example. The Donà were a Venetian patrician family whose letters survive in considerable numbers from the middle of the sixteenth century onwards. As in the case of the Strozzi, the letters were written because of the absence of the adult males of the family. Alessandra's sons Filippo and Lorenzo were in exile, living in Bruges and in Naples. 'If I were with you,' she wrote in her vivid, colloquial way, 'I shouldn't be writing these old letters' (*queste letteracce*).[10]

She wrote about the possible marriages of the daughters of her household as well as letting off steam about her servant problems, more exactly slave problems (since Florentines bought Circassian and other slaves at this period). Similarly, when the head of the Donà household, Gianbattista, was away in Cyprus on business, his wife Paolo wrote to

him with news of the children (one of them, as it happens, a future doge):
'Lundardo is learning very well and I believe that we can expect well of
him...Antonio...is beginning to speak and is my solace.'[11] It should be
clear that the 'sense of childhood' as the late Philippe Ariès (1960) called
it, was not a discovery of the seventeenth and eighteenth centuries, at least
not in Italy. For Paola Donà's interest in her children has a number of
parallels in the family papers of the time. In 1501, for example, Isabella
d'Este, Marchioness of Mantua, wrote to her husband (another ab-
sentee from home) about their little son;

> Our little boy began to walk today, and went four steps, to his great
> pleasure and ours, with no one holding him (though he was watched
> carefully)...he staggered a little, so that it seemed as if he was
> imitating a drunkard. Asking him if he wanted to send his regards
> to Your Lordship, he replied Ti Pa.

The next year, she again reported her son's progress to her absent
husband:

> Yesterday I was saying my prayers when he came in and said he
> wanted to look for Daddy [*il Pa*], and he went through the
> prayer-book himself and found a bearded face, which delighted him,
> and kissing it more than six times he said 'fine Daddy' [*papà bello*],
> with the greatest joy in the world.[12]

The Medici papers tell a similar story of the sense of childhood and the
uses of letters. In the fifteenth century Clarice, wife of Lorenzo the
Magnificent, wrote to him about their three-year-old son Giovanni
(better known as pope Leo X), that 'he keeps saying, when will Loencio
come?' Giovanni's younger brother Giuliano at the age of six was
described in a letter by a gentleman in Medici service as 'as fresh as a
rose', and as saying 'with a long O: O, O, O, O, where is Lorenzo?' (it is
interesting to find that these children called their father by his first
name).[13]

With the exception of the last example, all these domestic details come
from letters from wives to husbands. On the other hand, G. B. Donà
wrote no surviving letter to his wife asking for news of the children; he
wrote to his grown-up son about the arrival of ships and other business,
adding various messages to be passed on to different individuals. The
letters were clearly family rather than individual affairs, which helps
explain their preservation. Politics, however, was a taboo subject, at least
for Gianbattista Donà, who once reprimanded his son for having referred

to it in a letter. 'Never write about the concerns of the authorities [*cose di signori*, a remarkable phrase from the pen of a patrician], neither to approve nor to disapprove, because it can get you into trouble.'[14] The problem was that one could never be certain who would see one's letters, since they circulated in bundles, as was implied by the advice to merchants quoted above. A Florentine apothecary of the late fifteenth century records receiving a letter from his godfather 'though it was addressed to other citizens'.[15]

A third use of literacy within the family was to compile what the Florentines called *ricordanze*, a term which might perhaps be translated as 'memoranda'. From Florence alone, about a 100 such memoranda survive from the fourteenth, fifteenth and sixteenth centuries, generally from patrician families such as the Guicciardini, Medici, Pitti and Rucellai, but also from craftsmen and shopkeepers such as Landucci the apothecary and Arditi the tailor.[16] They are rarer elsewhere but patricians in Venice and Genoa also kept memoranda, and so did a few ordinary citizens, including a builder from Bologna and a carpenter from Milan.[17]

Memoranda of this kind overlap with urban chronicles, but their emphasis is on private rather than public life. They are sometimes called 'diaries' by their editors and others, but this term is rather misleading, for they were not, for the most part, records of the individual deeds and thoughts of the writer. Like the letters we have just discussed, and like many portraits of the Renaissance (below, ch. 11), these memoranda are concerned not so much with the individual as with the family, as is shown by the fact that in some cases, such as Landuci's and that of the Vellutis, they were continued by another member of the family after the first 'remembrancer' had died.[18] The prologues to particular texts tell the same story, explaining that the purpose of the record – which was presumably read out on occasion – was to remind the family (the *nazione*, as it is sometimes called), of its past.[19] They deal there with the origin of the family or branch, with the births, marriages and deaths of its members, and with the acquisition of property.

Beyond that, the memoranda have a somewhat miscellaneous character. They are a 'mixed salad' (*una insalata di più erbe*), as one remembrancer rather charmingly put it.[20] Some of them, like the journal kept by the Genoese patrician Pallavicino, lean towards local history. Others concentrate on the family finances, so that it would not be too unfair to describe them as glorified account-books. Even the memoranda of the great sixteenth-century historian Francesco Guicciardini, which are one of the most self-consciously literary examples of the genre, bear the marks of their origins. Like some diaries in early modern England, Guicciardini's manuscript was bound up with his book of debtors and creditors.

The assumptions behind these records are made explicit in a fourteenth-century text, itself on the margins of the genre, the collection of proverbs and other pieces of advice compiled by the Tuscan merchant Paolo da Certaldo for his son, brother and others. 'Foresight is an excellent thing', he wrote, 'so you should always plan all your affairs ahead'. Among other things he recommended keeping a record of all the occasions when a notary has drawn a document up, together with the date and the names of the witnesses; and also carrying in one's purse a paper listing everything that has to be done, so as to catch the eye whenever the purse is opened.[21]

These documents bear witness not only to the habit of active literacy but also to a particular mentality, prudent and calculating (it is tempting to add, 'bourgeois'). The statistics of school attendance in the Villani chronicle, with which this chapter began, are of interest not only for what they tell us about education but as evidence of the mentality of the chronicler, a 'numerate mentality' for which there is considerable supporting evidence from later medieval Italy (Murray, 1978, ch. 7). Whether the memoranda also bears witness to what Burckhardt (1860) called 'the development of the individual' is more doubtful, not least because of the concern with the family which they reveal – not only the nuclear family but also, on occasion, a wider group of kin. Burckhardt's view must be described as anachronistic, or at the very least as somewhat premature, in the sense that what a later age would call 'autobiography' does seem to have developed out of this habit of keeping memoranda, which were made for the whole family but were necessarily made by one individual at a time, encouraging him (for the individual is male in the vast majority of these cases), to express his own opinions.

Studies of literacy in our own century often suggest that it encourages self-consciousness. At all events it was Italy, and more especially Tuscany, the heartland of memoranda, which produced the best-known and the most numerous personal documents in early modern Europe (at least in the period 1350–1600), from Petrarch's *Private Book* (*Secretum*) to the autobiography of Benvenuto Cellini (above, ch. 2). Cellini's self-celebration is linked to the tradition of the memoranda by his concern for his family. Of course the autobiography had religious roots as well. The tradition of Augustine's *Confessions* was well known to Petrarch. All the same, even the spiritual autobiography was perceived in this culture as a kind of accounting. Petrarch's disciple Giovanni da Ravenna called his the *Account-Book of his Life* (*Rationarium Vitae*, Zimmermann, 1971; cf. Guglielminetti, 1977). Looking back, we can see how the spiritual autobiography gradually became secularised, and the family record individualised in the sense not only of dealing with a single individual but of being intended for that individual's eyes alone. A striking Florentine example, all the more striking because the individual concerned is not particularly interesting in other ways, is the journal (described by its author as 'Ephemerides seu Diarii') kept in the first years of the seventeenth century by the young patrician Girolamo da Sommaia when he was studying at the University of Salamanca. He protected himself against other readers, as Samuel Pepys was to do later in the century, by recording his frequent sexual encounters in a simple private code, the Greek alphabet. Transliterated, the entries take the form of *dolcetudine con Francisca, dolcetudine con Isabella*, and so on.[22]

Literacy and the church

In the two domains described so far, business and the family, there has been little to say about change. The arithmetic books of the sixteenth century are difficult to distinguish from those of the fourteenth century, while a guide to the notary's art written in the thirteenth century was considered relevant enough over 300 years later to be worth reprinting.[23] Family memoranda seem to have become more numerous (especially outside Florence) and more personal as time went by, but the shift was neither sudden nor sharp. The situation in the remaining two domains, religion and politics, makes a dramatic contrast. Here change positively forces itself on the historian's attention. It will also be necessary, in these cases, to say rather more about reading.

The clergy had of course long needed to be literate in order to 'say' Mass, since this oral performance was in fact a public reading from a service book, the *Missal*. Priests were also obliged to recite other prayers or 'offices' in private every day, reading them from a smaller book, the *Breviary*. It was of course useful for them to read other works too, whether they were theological, devotional, or practical; an obvious example of the third class is the *Mirror of Conscience*, a manual for confessors compiled in the mid fifteenth century by archbishop Antonino of Florence.

All the same, there is evidence from the records of episcopal visitations in rural Tuscany and Lombardy in the fifteenth and sixteenth centuries that occasional parish priests were 'illiterate' (*ignarus litterarum*), while otheres were reported as 'knowing nothing', whatever these phrases meant (unable to read? unable to write? ignorant of Latin?). Others lacked breviaries, and were given a month to acquire them, while one illiterate priest was told to learn these basic skills by Easter and was suspended from his functions until he had done so (Hay, 1977, p. 56; Cairns, 1976, pp. 176, 199).

Given the relatively high literacy of the laity in Florence and elsewhere, even a few cases of clerical illiteracy, if this is what it was, are striking, and one can see why the bishops were shocked. On the other hand, only a few cases are recorded. From the perspective of the uses of literacy, the existence of the sources from which this information is derived is what deserves emphasis; the existence of written records of official inspections of every parish in a given diocese. Records of this kind have survived in small numbers from the fifteenth century but they become increasingly common in the sixteenth, especially after 1560 or thereabouts, as the movement historians now call the 'Catholic Reformation' or 'Counter-Reformation' grew in strength (above, ch. 4). The systematic, separate, professional education of the clergy in seminaries was another part of this movement. Seminaries were founded in Italy from the 1560s onwards in Milan, Verona, Rome, Bologna, Padua and so on. As a result, priests became better-educated, and also more remote from ordinary people (Burke, 1978, p. 271; Allegra, 1981). What about the literacy of the laity? From the church's point of view, both the literate and the illiterate laity presented a problem The illiterate were a problem because they were what the clergy called 'superstitious', which meant, in the sixteenth century at least, that they were addicted to magic. At this time what might be called the magical uses of literacy were extremely important; the use of writing to communicate with supernatural forces unofficially, without going through proper ecclesiastical channels. These were what might be described as the uses of literacy for the illiterate, signs of the respect for the written word common in societies where literacy is restricted (Goody, 1968, p. 202).

Inquisition records and other sources of the sixteenth and seventeenth centuries reveal the importance of the written word in the equipment of Italian cunning men and wise women in town and country alike, and the belief in its power to cure the sick. A common amulet, which was supposed to cure fevers if worn round the neck of the sufferer, took the form of a triangle lettered abracadabra, thus:

A
AB
ABR
ABRA
ABRAC
ABRACA
ABRACAD
ABRACADA
ABRACADAB
ABRACADABR
ABRACADABRA

Again, words would be inscribed on 'papers of goodwill' (*carte del benevolere*), which by touching someone would prevent them bearing ill will towards the person carrying the paper. Diocesan synods not infrequently denounced the 'superstitious words' inscribed on sheets of paper (*bollettini, brevi, polizze* etc). To give them more power, words would be inscribed in the form of a cross, or a triangle (as above); or they would be written by a virgin on virgin paper; or on the leaf of a herb; on almonds; on bread; or on a host.[24]

Not only spells but whole books had their magic. At least one devotional book was popularly believed to possess healing powers, the legend of Santa Margherita. According to some sixteenth-century editions of this text, it should be recited to a woman who was having a difficult childbirth, or alternatively, placed on her stomach. Whether it was taken internally or externally, the book was medicine.[25] There were also books which gave instruction in magic and could be found in the possession of villagers as well as in the libraries of the learned. A man from Friuli, for example, who claimed, in 1630, to recognise the bewitched and to tell who had bewitched them, possessed 'a book in which he had learned all this' (Ginzburg, 1966, p. 91). Oral and literate cultures not only coexisted but interacted. If some ordinary people had not been able to read, the life of Santa Margherita would not have been recited from the book. If, on the other hand, literacy had not been restricted, books and papers would hardly have possessed such glamour. From the church's point of view, illiteracy encouraged superstition.

On the other hand, the literate laity were also a problem in the eyes of the church. There was a good deal of orthodox devotional literature in circulation in Italy from the introduction of printing onwards; at least 735 editions of 248 titles between 1465 and 1494 (Schutte, 1980). All the same, there was anxiety lest the laity fall into heresy as a result of reading the wrong books, a fear which became more acute from the 1520s onwards as protestant literature began to be available in Italy. Around the year 1530, one preacher went so far as to declare that 'all literate people [or intellectuals?] are heretics' (*tutti i literati siano heretici*, quoted in Prosperi, 1981, p. 195). Reading the Bible in the vernacular was thought by the clergy to lead the laity into unorthodox paths; they may well have been right. Thanks to Carlo Ginzburg (1975), we all know what Menocchio Scandella, the miller of Friuli, made of his reading; the Bible, the Golden legend, Mandeville's travels, and so on. To take a less extra-ordinary case, one among many, from the records of the Venetian Inqui-sition, we find a tailor from Burano accused of heresy in 1585. He was described as having 'no grammar' (as we would say, no secondary edu-cation), but all the same he owned a Bible in the vernacular and talked about it.[26]

The church was thus caught in a classic double bind, with a problem if it encouraged the spread of literacy and another problem if it did not. Its leaders seem on the whole to have opted for spreading literacy, but in a controlled way. Carlo Borromeo, archbishop of Milan in the later sixteenth century, was exemplary in this area as in other forms of pastoral activity (Casali, 1982, pp. 72f). He recommended fathers of families, to read aloud after dinner from a devotional book or the life of a saint ('if you can read'). He also promoted the 'schools of christian doctrine' which have been mentioned already (p. 111), requiring each parish to have such a school, which functioned on Sundays and feast days. In other words, a Catholic Sunday school movement was under way in northern Italy before the end of the sixteenth century. It is a pity that little is known about the working of these schools; whether, for example, they taught writing, reading, or only the elements of the faith. However, we do know that broadsheets printed with the Pater Noster, Ave Maria and Credo – in Latin and Italian – were distributed, and also that one layman who was associated with these schools in Milan taught writing gratis 'for the honour of God the salvation of souls, and the common good'. He was the carpenter already mentioned who kept a journal, thus illustrating the link, familiar to English historians, between piety and diary-keeping.

Having opted for the encouragement of literacy, the Church was aware of the need to control these dangerous media, notably by investigating schoolmasters and asking them to sign professions of religious orthodoxy, as at Venice in 1587 (Baldo, 1977, pp. 7f), and of course by the censorship of publications (Rotondò, 1973; Grendler, 1977). It was also aware of the ways in which the media could help them in their campaign to supervise and control the beliefs and behaviour of the laity. Visitation records have already been mentioned. There were also 'communion tickets' (*biglietti di communione*), used by the famous reforming bishop Matteo Giberti in his diocese of Verona (above, p. 42), an example which was imitated elsewhere. Annual confession and communion was a duty for the laity. At confession an individual would be given a ticket with his or her name on it, which had to be returned at communion. The names could be checked against a register of the inhabitants of the parish so as to identify the negligent and the heretical. Even travellers might find themselves in the net. Some Englishmen left Rome hurriedly at Easter 1593 because 'the priests came to take our names in our lodging' to check on the annual communions.[27] Another use of literacy for the purposes of control is revealed by the letters of denunciation of heretics, blasphemers and other sinners, still preserved in the files of the Inquisition in Venice and elsewhere. Literacy was not necessarily on the side of the unorthodox.

Literacy and the state

The obvious uses of literacy for 'social control', or more exactly, the control of the subordinate classes by the ruling class, were perceived not only by the church but also by the state. The connexion between literacy and bureaucracy (or, less precisely but more accurately, officialdom), goes back at least as far as the administrative lists of ancient Mesopotamia. The administrative uses of writing for storing and sorting information have been obvious for a very long time (Goody, 1977, pp. 8of.). However, there is evidence to suggest that the connexion between writing and administration became a closer one in Italy from the fourteenth century onwards, especially in the case of the larger states such as Milan, Venice, Florence, Rome and Naples.

Some kinds of official document were common enough all over Europe, most obviously the various kinds of letter going upwards with information or requests and going downwards with orders; each state had its own categories. In Rome and in Venice (until 1501 in the latter case), the man who sealed important documents was required to be illiterate, to ensure that the documents were not tampered with; illiteracy, like literacy, had its political uses (D'Amico, 1983, p. 36; Cipolla, 1969, p. 58). Literacy was a threat to secrecy. As a defence against the breaches of security which the spread of literacy made more likely, cipher was invented. A historian of diplomacy has pointed out that 'The first extant ciphered document in the archives of Venice dates from 1411, at Florence from 1414, at Milan from 1454 and at Genoa from 1481' (Queller, 1967, p. 140). In the sixteenth century, the post of cipher secretary came into existence. Giovanni Sora, for instance, exercised this function in the service of the Venetian state from 1502 onwards. Books were written explaining how different kinds of cipher worked, and the publicity made it necessary for yet more complex ciphers to be invented.[28]

Cipher was a field in which the Italians were pioneers. The same goes for a special kind of official report, the *relazione*. It was normal European practice for ambassadors to present written reports on their return from missions, but in Venice the custom went back earlier than elsewhere – to the thirteenth century – and by about 1500, if not before, this report was required to be particularly thorough and to follow a fixed form, dealing with the geography, history and political structure of the state visited, the personality of the ruler, his foreign policy, and so on. These reports were filed in the chancery and they could be consulted by newly-appointed ambassadors before they set out.[29]

Another important type of document developed by Italian states in this period is what (despite the variety of local names such as *anagrafo*, *catasto* and so on), it is convenient to call the 'census' (above, ch. 3). The precocity of the Italian censuses of the fourteenth and fifteenth centuries deserves particular emphasis. It was obviously easier to make a census of a small state like Florence, than of a large one like France; but only a state with a high literacy rate – and a high numeracy rate – could have carried out a project of this kind. A census was no small enterprise. In the case of the famous 'catasto' of 1427, which listed every household in Tuscany under Florentine rule – some 60,000 of them – the services of at least twenty-three clerks were required, not counting the specialists who estimated the value of each household's property. The declarations *portate*), had to be copied into registers (*campioni*), and summaries had to be made to facilitate reference to this huge document (the history of information retrieval is still to be written, but it is likely that the Italians of this period will have quite an important place in it). This was an expensive business; the bill for paper alone came to more than 250 florins, enough to keep twenty-five students at university for a year (Herlihy and Klapisch, 1978, ch. 3; the information is not available in the abridged English version of this study).

It is easy to see why a census was regarded in this period not as an ordinary part of the business of administration, but as an extraordinary or even an emergency measure. The 1427 *catasto*, for example, was part of the war effort. Famine lay behind the Neapolitan censuses of the 1590s, and plague behind those of Florence and Venice in the 1530s (above, p. 30).

In these cases, the government was concerned with organising the distribution of bread. Recipients might have to present tickets or cards (*cartelli* or *polizze*), to ensure that they did not claim twice. The procedure is not unlike that of communion tickets; did the church imitate the state, or the other way round? Yet another type of official document which the Italians seem to have pioneered, and of which they made increasing use in the period, was the pass (*bolletta, bollettino*). Passes or licenses were issued allowing certain people to carry arms in a certain city, or to be out in the streets after curfew. There were also 'health passes' (*bollette di sanità*), required from the later fifteenth century onwards for people and goods on the move in time of plague (Cipolla, 1976, p. 29). They spread widely in Italy but they seem to have been an Italian speciality, to judge by the comments of foreign travellers. Montaigne at Ferrara noted the inscription on all the doors of his inn, 'remember your pass' (*recordati della bolleta*), while Philip Skippon was so fascinated by these documents that he copied several of them into his journal, as well as recording the occasions on which they were issued and inspected.[30]

Reports, censuses and passes far from exhaust the administrative uses of literacy in early modern Italy. There were public notices, for example, more especially the proclamations or edicts of various sorts (called *bandi* in Rome, *parti* in Venice, *gride* in Milan, and so on). Armies were already producing a mass of paper including billetting regulations, paysheets, and muster rolls, which described the horses more carefully than the men because it was particularly important to ensure that they were not counted twice (Mallett and Hale, 1984, pp. 117, 123, 125, 127 etc.). In the navy, too, literacy and numeracy had its uses. Clerks sailed with Venetian galleys, and a writer on naval matters in the early seventeenth century argues that gunners needed to be numerate (*il bombardiero dovrebbe essere abachista*).[31] In republics, the selection of officials required many lists. In Florence, for example, the names of individuals qualified for office had to be written in registers and also on slips (*polizze*) which were placed in bags and – in theory at least – drawn out at random (Rubinstein, 1966, chs. 1–2). In Venice, the patricians, who were the only people eligible for most offices, had to be registered soon after birth in the so-called 'Golden Book', and a record was also kept of the numbers of votes cast for candidates for particular offices (Davis, 1962, p. 19).

Another political use of literacy, and not the least important, was secret delation. Visitors to Venice in particular often remarked on the stone letter-boxes, the slots in the shape of lion's mouths, which were used for denunciations of deviants. The inquisitive and precise Skippon noted fourteen of these mouths in the doge's palace alone.[32] That the mouths were in regular use is clear from the denunciations still preserved in the Venetian Archives; of blasphemers, for instance (above, p. 101).

How efficiently all this material was organised after it had been collected is hard to say. In Venice there were officials in the Doge's Chancery employed making indexes by name and subject (Queller, 1967, p. 4). In other parts of the Venetian administration, however, officials seem to have been overwhelmed by the task of organising the documents (Caro Lopez, 1980, pp. 291f). Elsewhere, in the sixteenth century in particular, we find archive-conscious rulers such as Grand Duke Cosimo of Tuscany and pope Gregory XIII; but the distinction between private and public was not drawn as sharply then as later, and it was quite normal for officials to treat official documents as their private property and pass them on to their heirs.

In many ways, literacy facilitated the state's control of its subjects, as it facilitated the church's control of its flock. However, the effects of technological change are rarely simple. Literacy could also serve the cause of heresy and political protest. The authorities were well aware of the danger and operated a political as well as a religious censorship of printed books. Much was published in Venice that could not be printed elsewhere, but in the early seventeenth century several important books were unable to appear in print for political reasons. One was the history of Venice by the late doge Nicolò Contarini; another was Paolo Sarpi's history of the Council of Trent; a third was the commentary on Tacitus by Traiano Boccalini. However, the number of surviving manuscript copies suggests that these works had considerable circulation in private in the seventeenth-century equivalent of samizdat.

More spectacular, however, and addressing a far wider audience, was the use of graffiti and placards ('cartelli') for the purpose of protest, or at least for candid unofficial commentary on politics. In Florence this tradition goes back at least as far as the fourteenth century, and by the sixteenth it can be found in Venice, Padua, Brescia and Naples. It was an institution in Rome, birthplace of the 'pasquinade' in the fifteenth century (above, p. 100). By the eighteenth century, the practice had spread to rural communes such as Altopascio in Tuscany (McArdle, 1978, pp. 205f.). It is a pity that, pasquinades apart, no anthologies have been made of these graffiti, which give a vivid view of politics from below, and were taken seriously, and with good reason, by the authorities. Placards inciting the population to rebel appeared in the streets of Naples in 1585 and 1647; in both cases the advice was taken (below, ch. 13). The comments were usually pithy and pungent. 'Nine fools are out' (*e usciti nove pazzi*) said a placard on the Palazzo della Signoria of Florence in 1466, referring to the outgoing administration.[33] 'House to let' (*Caxa d'afitar*) was the laconic message on the empty state granary in Venice in 1529.[34]

The demand for documents in these four domains was great enough to call into existence all sorts of specialist producers of the written word, the number and variety of whom will be obvious to anyone who cares to read through early modern censuses, those of Florence and Venice in particular. The best-known and most numerous of these groups was that of the notaries. There were eight notaries to every 1,000 people in Verona in 1605 as there had been in Florence in 1427 (Cipolla, 1973). Then there were the schoolmasters, more particularly the writing masters. Such was the prestige of calligraphy in early modern Italy, as in traditional China and Japan, that some of these writing-masters became famous, especially in the sixteenth century; notably Leonardo Arrighi, Gianantonio Tagliente, Giambattista Palatino and Gianfrancesco Cresci. There were the printers of course, to be found in many Italian towns, even small ones, especially numerous in Venice, where Aldo Manuzio among others settled. There were the booksellers and stationers, down the 'leggendaio', the humble itinerant hawker of the lives of saints, one of those who 'sell the stories of saints, and prayers to saints, and sing them and also ask for alms'.[35] There were private secretaries, an occupation which included a number of distinguished writers on their way to fame, a famous sixteenth-century example being Annibale Caro. There were clerks (*scrivani*), and freelance copyists (*copiascritture*). The numbers of clerks in the law courts of Naples in 1728 made a deep impression on one visitor, Montesquieu: 'les seuls scribes font une petite armée, rangée en bataille, le canif à la main'.[36] There were official couriers and more humble messengers (*portalettere*). There were also the specialists in numeracy, such as accountants, book-keepers, cashiers and valuers (terms which recur in the censuses are *cassier*, *computista*, *calcolatore*, and *stimatore*), as well as the teachers in abacus-schools.

The evidence is so abundant that the historian has to be careful not to exaggerate the importance of all these activities, which have left traces in the archives while oral transactions have not. We need to remind ourselves that the majority of Italians, throughout this period, must have been illiterate; some professional men, most peasants and almost all women.[37] Let us look at the relationship of women to literacy in a little more detail.

In the fourteenth and fifteenth centuries, some men argued that girls should have nothing to do with reading and writing, and suggested that they should stay at home and wait for a husband rather than go to school. Reading was dangerous because girls might read love-letters (Klapisch, 1984, p. 776). In fact illiteracy was not enough to stop girls receiving and sending love-letters through intermediaries, as a case which came before the Tribunal of the Governor of Rome in 1602 vividly illustrates. Margherita, the sixteen-year-old daughter of a notary, could not read or write but she corresponded with the boy next door via another friend, throwing the notes from the kitchen window into the courtyard. By the time her parents had discovered the correspondence, Margherita was no longer a virgin.[38]

It is easy enough to find exceptions to the rule of female illiteracy, but very hard to say how common these exceptions were. The wife of Francesco Datini, the superlatively inky-fingered merchant of Prato, did not learn to read till she was over thirty; her daughter, on the other hand, learned when still a child (Origo, 1957, p. 213). in any case we know that some girls went to school. Villani refers to 'boys and girls' learning to read in fourteenth-century Florence; it is too bad that this lover of statistics gives us no idea of the relative percentages. Again, we know that in sixteenth-century Milan, the Compagnia delli Servi, which was part of the Sunday-school system, taught girls as well as boys, but not the proportion of pupils of each sex. In Venice in 1587, the bishop's survey turned up 4,481 schoolchildren, of whom only twenty-eight were female, and 258 teachers, of whom only one was female, a certain Marieta (Baldo, 1977, p. 21). This may be an underestimate: at all events, the Venetian censuses of the seventeenth century refer to women teachers. Two are mentioned in 1633; six in 1642 (not counting the twelve teachers at the Zittelle, a home for the daughters of prostitutes, whose names are not given), six more in 1670, and this is an absolute minimum, since the records are incomplete and in any case list only heads of households. The laconic 'keeps a school' (*tien scola*) does not give very much away, but in two cases it is specified that the pupils are female, and in three cases that what is taught is reading.[39] In Rome in 1695, sixteen schoolmistresses are recorded, teaching reading and sewing (Giuntella, 1961, 555f).

References to writing are rather more rare. Letters in the name of women do not prove that those women could write, since professional scribes were available. However, Alessandra degli Strozzi announces on one occasion that her letter was 'written with my spectacles on' (*questa mia è scritta cogli occhiali*), suggesting that she wrote for herself, while in the early seventeenth century the Genoese patrician Andrea Spinola, suspicious of literacy as he is, does allow women to write down expenses and draw up inventories.[40]

Having taken account of evidence like this, as well as of the handful of women who studied the classics or published books in this period, it still seems reasonable to suggest that women had little more than a toehold on literate culture. For them and for the illiterate majority of males as well, culture was essentially oral. It had already been suggested (above, p. 80) what a rich oral culture there was in early modern Italy. Its existence needs to be borne in mind as a corrective to the over-emphasis on literacy encouraged by the survival of archives and libraries. All the same, I should like to suggest that writing was more important in daily life in Italy than in most parts of early modern Europe; that its importance was increasing steadily from the thirteenth century (if not before) to the seventeenth century (if not later); and that the uses of literacy diversified within each of the four domains discussed as new types of document proliferated. These suggestions cannot be proved but the evidence discussed so far should at least make them plausible.

To this evidence should be added the fact that print multiplied texts of every kind from the later fifteenth century onwards. The effects of the new medium have generally been discussed from a literary point of view or in relation to cultural movements such as the Renaissance. There is more than a little to say, however, about the practical uses of print in the three public domains discussed above. In the sphere of business, one finds not only printed manuals for beginners but also printed forms of leases and IOUs, flysheets to advertise the sale of property, and so on. In the religious sphere, not only devotional treatises and manuals for confessors, but catechisms and broadsheets with prayers printed on them, some produced by order of the local bishop, while others have a less official character. There were printed forms for the parish priest to certify the good religious behaviour of orphan girls before they were married.

However, it is in the domain of politics that one finds the real invasion of printed matter in the course of the sixteenth and seventeenth centuries. Printed proclamations multiplied. They were still read aloud in the traditional manner but they were also posted up in public places. Laws were printed. News-sheets were printed: from the *avvisi da Roma* in the sixteenth century, which took the form of letters (Delumeau, 1957–9), to the first *gazzette* in the seventeenth century, with a format more like that of a modern paper. There was also a growing use of printed forms. By the middle of the seventeenth century, one even finds cardinals in conclave making use of such forms to elect a new pope (below, p. 179). Forms were also employed in Venice by the census-takers to ensure that the information for each parish was organised in the same way (above, p. 33). These forms are striking evidence of the numerate mentality, and they doubtless helped to spread this mode of thought throughout society. Like the self-consciousness engendered, or at least encouraged by journal-keeping, the propensity to think in terms of precise figures should be reckoned as one of the most important consequences of literacy in early modern Italy; a consequence derived from its uses in practical contexts in this town-dominated society.

10

Conspicuous consumption in seventeenth-century Italy

The hope of distinguishing oneself by means of luxury is a very strong incentive for amassing riches.   (Pietro Verri).

The aim of this chapter is to study consumption as a form of communication. It centres on what sociologists, following Veblen (1899), call 'conspicuous consumption', a term which is both useful and potentially misleading. Veblen's aim was to show that the economic behaviour of what he called the 'leisure class' was irrational, indeed foolish. It was wasteful: he used the term conspicuous waste as an alternative to 'conspicuous consumption'. He was, however, aware that this waste had a purpose – competition, or as he would say, 'invidious distinction' or 'emulation'. His essay went into picturesque detail to describe how elites in both 'barbarian' and 'pecuniary' cultures have displayed their wealth and power in their houses, clothes, feasts and so on.

Veblen drew some of his most striking examples from the research of one of the leading anthropologists of his day, Franz Boas, who worked among the Kwakiutl of the Vancouver area. The Kwakiutl were an intensely competitive people; *homo agonistes* was not the creation of capitalism. Until the middle of the nineteenth century, they had competed for victory in war. After the coming of the whites they shifted to ritualised violence, to what they called 'fighting with property'. As Boas explained, 'The rivalry between chiefs and clans finds its strongest expression in the destruction of property.' The characteristic expression of Kwakiutl emulation was the now celebrated 'polatch', a meeting of rivals at which they destroyed their two main forms of wealth, blankets and copper plates, taunting their opponents to do the same. Participants thus showed their contempt for the property destroyed, humiliated competitors who were unable to follow suit, and so converted wealth into prestige (Boas, 1897; Codere, 1950).

Since Boas studied the Kwakiutl in the late nineteenth century, they have not ceased to fascinate anthropologists, sociologists and historians. Marcel Mauss (1923–4) treated them as an example of wealth without trade, while Ruth Benedict (1934) saw them as a dionysiac, megalomaniac culture. David Riesman (1950) asked himself and his students how far the competitive society of the United States resembled that of the Kwakiutl. Closest to Veblen, perhaps was Georges Bataille (1949), who was concerned to incorporate prodigality into a general theory of economic behaviour. However, Bataille was a Veblen with the plus and minus signs reversed. Veblen was a passionate egalitarian who thought waste immoral and condemned barbarian and pecuniary cultures alike; Bataille, on the other hand, despised commercial society but romanticised prodigality.

Some at least of these studies have made an impact on historians of early modern Europe. Lawrence Stone (1965) has confessed to Veblen's influence on his studies of conspicuous consumption by the English aristocracy between 1558 and 1641. Gérard Labrot (1977) quotes Bataille in his analysis of the behaviour of the aristocracy of Naples. This chapter will follow in their tracks, adopting an anthropological approach to the history of consumption. It will attempt to steer between Veblen and Bataille, emphasising the rationality of conspicuous consumption in the seventeenth century (given the social and political system in which the consumers lived), and supplementing these two theorists with the ideas of Norbert Elias (1969) on courtly society; Erving Goffman (1969) on the presentation of self in everyday life; Pierre Bourdieu (1979) on the strategies by which people distinguish themselves from others, and Mary Douglas (1978) on ways of 'reading' material culture as if it were a text. It is perhaps unnecessary to add that no reductionism is intended in this approach; that I do not assume that palace-building (and still less, art patronage in general), was no more than a continuation of the endemic conflict between Italian nobles by other means. What I want to do is simply to stress the importance of this form of conflict and competition, the informal rules of consumption which individuals and families ignored at their peril.

The Kwakiutl knew very well that they were 'fighting with property'. So did the burgomaster of Gdańsk who had 'in order to be envied' (*pro invidia*) inscribed on the façade of his house (Bogucka, 1978). What were the attitudes of seventeenth-century Italians to what we call conspicuous consumption?

The vocabulary available to describe this particular lifestyle was appropriately rich. Among the more common terms were *fasto, grandezza, larghezza, liberalità, lusso, magnificenza, ostentazione, pompa* and *splendore*. The words themselves explain in a nutshell why people engaged in the activities they describe. The overtones of status, power and generosity should be sufficiently audible to need no further emphasis, though it might be added that *lusso* and *ostentazione* seem to have lacked the pejorative associations of 'luxury' and 'ostentation' in modern English. Even *appariscente* in other words 'having a fine appearance', was an adjective of praise, reminding us of the importance in this culture of the façade, literal and metaphorical (above, p. 9). Despite the fact that ostentation was so normal as to be taken for granted, contemporaries do offer a little more in the way of clarification. Jacopo Soldani's eulogy of the late Grand Duke of Tuscany in 1609 made the common assumptions explicit when he described Ferdinando as surpassing other princes in 'magnanimity', as revealed by the 'splendour of his way of life, the magnificence of his buildings, his liberality to men of talent, and his beneficence to all'.[1] Magnificence was the outward sign of magnanimity, the greatness of spirit which is a central virtue in Aristotle's *Ethics*. There was a sufficiently close parallel between the value system of early modern Italy and that of Aristotle's Greece for his prestigious language to be utilisable – with some conscious or unconscious adaptations – to justify the economic behaviour of princes and patricians.

For families who had already arrived at the summit, conspicuous consumption was regarded as a duty, *l'obbligazione di viver con fasto*, as one leading Neapolitan lawyer, Franceso D'Andrea, described it.[2] It was necessary to avoid 'shame', in other words loss of face, and to 'sustain' a high position of the honour of the house (*sostentar la splendidezza della casa*).[3] The function of such consumption was to distinguish a given individual or family from others, whether equals (therefore rivals), or social inferiors. D'Andrea refers to 'the drive to outdo others which the nobles have in them from birth' (*l'appetito di soprafar gli altri che porta seco la nobiltà della nascita*).[4] Hence the indignation of the Decurions (or magistrates), of Milan when their archbishop, Carlo Borromeo, ordered uniformly plain hassocks to be used in church. They complained to the pope that 'in this as in other matters, there ought to be a distinction between ordinary people and the magistrates and others of high status' (Cattaneo, 1958, p. 70). The Florentine patricians built their magnificent and ornate palaces, so we are told by a writer of the late seventeenth century, 'to distinguish themselves from commoners' and 'in order to be respected'. There was also, he admitted, an element of gentlemanly competition involved (*la gara onoratissima nata fra Nobili et Nobili*).[5] The same point had been made with reference to Florentine villas earlier in the century, in more critical spirit, by Jacopo Soldani. 'What makes building so incredibly expensive is not custom but the attempt by the rich to distinguish themselves from others'.

> L'uso non dunque, ma la distinzione
> Che 'l ricco sopra gli altri oggi pretende,
> I fantastichi prezzi a 'sassi impone.[6]

Critical comments of this kind by contemporaries are far from uncommon. An anonymous dialogue on the affairs of Genoa, written about the year 1600, went so far as to suggest that magnificence was deliberately sadistic, and that the patricians – like the Kwakiutl – tended 'to spend more than they needed in order to give pain to those who were unable to do the same, and to make them sick at heart' (*spendere cose superflue per dar pena è dolore di cuore a chi non può fare il medesimo*)[7] From Naples there come stories of barons building palaces higher and higher to outdo one another and even to spoil a rival's view (Labrot, 1979, p. 61n.). In Venice, one of the most elaborately magnificent of seventeenth-century church façades was constructed at the expense of one patrician, Antonio Barbarigo, to spite another, Francesco Morosini, who lived close by and who had, when Captain-General of the Venetian forces in the Cretan war, dismissed Barbarigo for incompetence (Haskell, 1963, pp. 248–9). Cities, according to the late sixteenth-century political and social theorist Giovanni Botero, encourage this kind of behaviour. 'A baron spends much more in the city, out of rivalry and competition with others' (*per la concorrenza e per l'emulatione de gl'altri*).[8] Keeping up with the Medici, Corner (in Venice), Spinola (in Genoa), Caraffa (in Naples), and other great families was an extremely expensive business.

If established families had to engage in conspicuous consumption in order to maintain their position, new families had to do so in order to acquire one, to gain admittance to the upper circle. In Venice, for example, a cloth-merchant called Polinaro was admitted to the patriciate in 1662 after making a formal declaration that 'the supplicant lives in splendour with fine clothes and a gondola'.[9] In Vicenza, the Montanari family were admitted to the nobility in 1687 soon after building a magnificent palace (Haskell, 1963, p. 249n). There was a sort of double-bind in operation. Conspicuous consumption was formally forbidden to the new rich by the sumptuary laws which were a prominent part of the legislation of Italian states in this period. At the same time, this kind of behaviour was informally compulsory for any family which aspired to be accepted by and incorporated into the nobility. The house (in the sense of palace) was the outward sign of the splendour of the house (in the sense of family). In case the message carried by a particular building was not clear or specific enough, the point might be driven home by coats of arms or even names carved in huge Roman capitals across the façade. Thus cardinal Alessandro Farnese had FARNESIUS inscribed on the façade of the Gesù in Rome, and pope Paul V had his family name BORGHESIUS put in an equivalent position on St Peter's (although he did no more than pay for the completion of the church). Cardinal Pietro Aldobrandini had ALDOBRANDINIS inscribed on his villa at Frascati, together with the comment that 'he built it most magnificently' (SUMPTUOSIUS EXTRUXIT. Schwager, 1961–2, p. 371). When the newly-ennobled Vincenzo Fini had his name placed on the façade of S. Moisè at Venice, an action which Ruskin (1853, p. 124) described as an example of 'insolent atheism', he was not doing anything extraordinary by the standards of the seventeenth century.

Conspicuous consumption was of course public as well as private and it was sometimes justified in terms of reason of state. Republics and principalities which spent large sums on palaces (not to mention more evanescent forms of consumption, such as festivals) were acting in accordance with Machiavelli's advice to rulers who wanted to be respected. Andrea Spinola, a merciless critic of the extravagance of his contemporaries in Genoa, argued that the town hall or 'Palazzo Pubblico' should be ornamented with more 'magnificence' because such ornaments encouraged respect for the institution (*servono alla conservatione della maestà publica*).[10] There was also a growing awareness that magnificence in the form of elaborate public works was good for the economy, especially at times of unemployment (Cipolla, 1981). For example, Grand Duke Ferdinand II of Tuscany seems to have had the Palazzo Pitti enlarged as part of his attempt to remedy the economic depression of 1629–30 (Cochrane, 1973, pp. 195f). When pope Alexander VII considered cancelling the inauguration ritual of the *possesso* (below, p. 172), in order to give the money saved to the poor, he was told that spending money on the ritual was itself a 'pious work' because it went to pay tailors and other craftsmen.[11]

It is time to turn from seventeenth-century theory to seventeenth-century practice, and to look more closely at what exactly was consumed so conspicuously – where, by whom, and at what expense, and finally, over what period. Stone's main categories for the description of the consumption patterns of the English peerage in the late sixteenth and early seventeenth centuries were building, food, clothes, transport, funerals and tombs, in that order. In the case of the Italian ruling class it is equally obvious that one has to begin with building. It would be difficult to draw up a complete list of even the major palaces constructed in the seventeenth century, and a selection is likely to be biassed by two irrelevant factors, the distinction of the architect and the building's survival into later centuries. However, it is clear that the following were among the more important palaces constructed in the seventeenth century.

Bologna: Daria-Bargellini (1638–); Cloetta-Fantuzzi (1680).

Florence: Covoni (1623); Fenzi (1634); Corsini.

Genoa: Durazzo-Pallavicino (1619–); Balbi-Senarega (*c.* 1620); Rosso (1672–).

Milan: Visconti (1598–); Annoni (1631); Durini (1644).

Naples: Reale (1600–); Caivano (*c.* 1632); Donn'Anna (1642–); Sigliano (*c.* 1647).

Rome: Borghese (1590–); Barberini (1628–); Pamphilli (1644–); Falconieri (*c.* 1645); Altieri (1650–); Monte Citorio (1650–); Chigi (1664–).

Turin: Carignano (1679).

Venice: Pesaro (*c.* 1663); Flangini; Morosini; Pisani.

Some country houses of the period were also in the palace class. Villa Aldobrandini (1598–) at Frascati, for example; Villa Borghese (1613–) and Villa Ludovisi (1622–) outside Rome: Villa Da Lezze in the Trivigiano (Wittkower, 1958, remains the best general guide; on Rome, see Portoghesi, 1966).

All these houses must be imagined stuffed with expensive furnishings, such as tapestries, velvet curtains, four-poster beds, mirrors, inlaid tables and cabinets, vases and candlesticks, armour and weapons, statues, and so on. If we were to judge these interiors by the furniture which has survived, the effect would be magnificent enough, but it would fall far short of the reality, as the accounts left by amazed foreign visitors make clear. The best pieces must have been melted down. One English visitor to Mantua was informed that before it was sacked in 1630, the duke's palace

> had seven changes of hangings for every room in the house; besides a world of rare pictures, statues, plate, ornaments, cabinets, an organ of alabaster; six tables, each one three feet long, the first all emeralds, the second of Turkey stones [turquoises], the third of hyacinths, the fourth of saphyrs, the fifth of amber, the sixth of jasper stone.[12]

In the Palazzo Doria at Genoa, John Evelyn observed 'tables and bedsteads of massy silver', and 'many of them sett with Achates, Onyxes, Cornelians, Lazulis, Pearle, Turquizes and other precious stones'. At Padua, he saw in the Palazzo Ruzini a bedstead set with jewels in this manner which was 'esteemed worth 16,000 crounes', and in the Villa Ludovisi outside Rome, another 'esteemed to be worth 80, or 90,000 crownes'.[13] That foreign visitors were admitted to see these beds is a reminder of how conspicuous this kind of consumption was expected to be. Once again, however, the outsiders recorded impressions which the indigenous inhabitants rather took for granted.

If noblemen lived in such houses, the house of god had to be equally magnificent. Many churches were built in seventeenth-century Italy in towns which were filled with them already. Among the best-known were the following:

> Bologna: S. Salvatore (1605–).
> Florence: Ognissanti (1635–); S. Gaetano (1645–).
> Genoa: Sta Teresa (1616); S. Carlo (1629–).
> Milan: S. Alessandro (1602–); S. Giuseppe (1607–).
> Naples: S. Agostino (1603–); Ascensione (1622–); S. Carlo all'Arena (1631–); Sta Teresa (1650–); Sta Maria Maggiore (1653–).
> Palermo: S. Giuseppe dei Teatini (1612–).
> Rome: Sta Maria della Vittoria (1608–) S. Ignazio (1626–); Sta Agnese (1652–); S. Andrea al Quirinale (1658–); Sta Maria di Monte Santo and Sta Maria de'Miracoli (1662–); S. Carlo alle Quattro Fontane (1665–)
> Turin: Cappella della SS. Sindone (1667–); S. Lorenzo (1668–).
> Venice: Salute (1631); Sta Maria agli Scalzi (1656–).

Many other churches were provided with grand and expensive new façades, like S. Moisè (*c.* 1667) and Sta Maria Zobenigo (1675–) at Venice. Like palaces, churches were furnished in ever more splendid style, with interior decoration of marble, porphyry and serpentine, and 'those prodigious masses of Plate with which their altars are covered on holidays', as a Scottish Protestant, Gilbert Burnet, disapprovingly observed. The same visitor remarked that the Venetians were 'unconcerned' with religion, so that the wealth displayed in their churches was no more than 'a point of magnificence, or a matter of emulation among families'.[14] His first point is pure Protestant prejudice, but it is easy enough to see what he meant by the second when one is standing in front of Sta Maria Zobenigo, or in the many new family chapels, like the Cornaro chapel – designed by Bernini – in Sta Maria della Vittoria, or the Borghese chapel in St Maria Maggiore on which pope Paul V planned to spend 150,000 scudi in 1605, a chapel described in a German guidebook of the period as 'this wonderful example of the magnificence of the Borghese family' (*diser wunderbarlichen magnificentz Burghesiorum*).[15] One thinks too of funeral monuments so huge that they seem to take over the church, like the monument to doge Giovanni Pesaro in the Frari (1669), or the still bigger one to doge Silvestro Valier in SS. Giovanni e Paolo (1705–) in Venice.

Building has of course been a major item of conspicuous consumption in many societies. A rather more distinctive item in seventeenth-century Italy was the carriage or coach. In Rome in 1594, there were 883 carriages, according to a surviving list to which attention was recently drawn (Lotz, 1973). In Milan in 1666, there were 1586 of them.[16] An additional status symbol was the number of horses harnessed to the carriage. Six was thought the right number for Italian cardinals. It is an indication that magnificence was considered a duty as well as a pleasure that pope Paul V is said to have asked one cardinal to explain why he did not have six horses to his carriage (Orbaan, 1910, p. 14n). Another sign of magnificence was the number of carriages a given household kept. In Rome in 1594 (according to the list already cited), eleven households (eight of them the households of cardinals) kept four carriages or more. The appearances of the carriage, outside and inside, was also a sign of the owner's status, or at any rate his self-image. Gilded and painted carriages were commonplace, but in 1628 the Duke of Parma outdid any possible rival by coming to his wedding (to the daughter of the Grand Duke of Tuscany), in a coach said to have been made of solid silver. It was still to be seen by English visitors to Parma in the 1660s, though Philip Skippon, who was among them, was more deeply impressed by the coach of the Grand Duke of Tuscany, 'the coach-box, and behind, and wheels plated with silver and richly gilt; a thick embroidery of gold mix'd with some silver was the curtains, lining within, seats, coachman's cushion, and the furniture for six horses'.[17] More subtle and decorous was the impression management of Monsignor Fabio Chigi, later pope Alexander VII, whose carriage of black velvet, decorated with silver, was of a splendid modesty which revealed its owner to be at once unworldly in outlook and high in status (Ciampi, 1878, pp. 209f.)

In Venice, gondolas replaced carriages as status symbols, and in defiance of the sumptuary laws they were sometimes gilded or lined with

silk (Bistort, 1912, pp. 220f, 459f). In Genoa, where carriages were again
ruled out, in this case because the streets were so narrow, their place was
taken by sedan chairs and litters, a brutally eloquent sign of the dominance of some men over others. In Naples, both carriages and sedan chairs
were common sights. In 1615, an English visitor confessed to finding
'incredible' the number of carriages in Naples, 'as of the sedges not
unlike to horse-litters but carried by men'.[18] The town clerk of Naples
confirms this observation, replacing the Englishman's amazement by
malice masquerading as ethnography. 'These nobles', he wrote, 'live so
comfortably, that they cannot go a hundred paces without having
recourse to the convenience of horses, carrages or sedan chairs, like the
palanquins which the Portuguese use in India.'[19] One has to imagine
seventeenth-century Naples swarming with rickshaws.

Houses, carriages and furniture must be seen as 'properties' in the
theatrical sense of the term. So must clothes, whether the style was the
stiff, dark, rich, heavy Spanish fashion current at the beginning of the
century, or the lighter, softer, more colourful French fashion which was
coming in towards its end (Levi Pisetzky, 1966). The male of the species
was no less expensively dressed than the female. Noblemen as well as
women wore their estates on their backs; dressed in fine materials such
as damask, brocade, and cloth of gold; and loaded their bodies with
jewels, rings, and golden collars and chains. It is a pity that Veblen, who
devoted a celebrated passage to the social history of the corset, was not
inspired to say anything about the ruff, which swelled at the end of the
sixteenth century into an enormous cartwheel, so as to make conspicuous
not only the wealth of anyone who could affort to have such an object
laundered daily but also the wearer's sublime detachment from the
practical problems of everyday living on earth, a detachment which is part
of the ideology of many elites (Bourdieu, 1979, pp. 56f). Whoever was
inside the ruff obviously had no need to bend or even to turn his or her
head. Ruffs were for people with servants to look after them. The servants
were of course fitted out in splendid liveries for their walk-on parts in
the aristocratic social drama. Their function was not only to serve in the
literal sense, but also to accompany their masters and mistresses. They too
were properties, signs of wealth and power, and as such they appeared
in aristocratic portraits (below, p. 161).

Since everyday life was such a grand performance for the Italian
nobility, it is hard to find words appropriate to describe the theatricality
of festivals, whether 'ordinary' recurrent festivals like Carnival, or
extraordinary ones such as the reception of particularly distinguished

visitors or the celebration of marriages. The splendour of the show was not necessarily an expression of joy, for funerals were almost as elaborate as weddings. The point was rather to mark particular occasions as memorable; to celebrate the status, wealth and power of the hosts; and perhaps to make it manifest that, unlike individuals, institutions (including the Medici family as well as the Papacy), were immortal.

Different cities had their characteristic festivals. In Rome, they centred on the Church and the pope (below, ch. 12). Among extraordinary celebrations, pride of place went to the canonisations of saints, especially Carlo Borromeo (1610); the quadruple canonisation of Loyola, Xavier, Teresa, and Filippo Neri (1622); François de Sales (1665); and the quintuple canonisation, in 1671, of Rose of Lima, Luis Bertrán, Gaetano da Thiene, Francisco Borja, and Filippo Benizzi (above, p. 58). In Venice, on the other hand, the major festal events of the century, apart from the celebrations of victories over the Turks, were the receptions of distinguished visitors such as the Duke of Savoy (1608), the Duke of Mantua (1623), and the duke of Brunswick (1685), for whom a mock-battle was staged at Villa Contarini at Piazzola. In this way Venice was coming to discover its vocation as a tourist city (below, ch. 13). In Florence, the focus of the major festivals was on the domestic life of the Medici. In the first half of the century, there were four major Medici weddings, two male and two female. Marie was married to Henri IV of France (1600); Cosimo, to Maria Maddalena of Austria (1608); Caterina, to Ferdinando Gonzaga (1628); and Ferdinando to Vittoria della Rovere (1637). In the second half of the century, the emphasis fell on funerals, notably those of Ferdinando (1670), Leopoldo (1676), and Vittoria della Rovere (1694: see Gaeta Bertelà, 1969, and Riederer-Grohs, 1973).

It would be useful to know how much was spent on different forms of consumption relative to one another (and in Italy relative to other countries). Until systematic, quantitative, comparative studies force inventories to give up their secrets, the following figures, collected from scattered sources, and referring to particularly expensive enterprises, may still have their uses. The figures, rounded off, are in scudi. To give a very rough idea of their value in real terms it should be added that at this time, skilled building workers earned about fifty or sixty scudi in a year.

500,000 Pallazzo Pesaro, Venice (*c.* 1663–)
300,000 Palazzo Altieri, Rome (1650–)
250,000 Palazzo Monte Citorio, Rome (1650–)
200,000 Palazzo Pisani, Venice
200,000 Baldacchino, St Peter's, Rome (1624–)

200,000 altar at the Gesù, Rome (1697)
150,000 Borghese Chapel, St Maria Maggiore, Rome (1605–)
106,000 Cathedra Petri, St Peter's, Rome (1657–)
100,000 Medici wedding, Florence (1608)
90,000 Prince Ludovisi's bed, Rome (*c.* 1645)
90,000 façade of S. Moise, Venice (*c.* 1669)
60,000 Giostra del Saraceno, Rome (1634)
40,000 Palazzo Medici, Florence (1659; second-hand price)
30,000 façade of Sta Maria Zobenigo, Venice (1675–)
20,000 monument to Silvestro Valier, Venice (1705–)
14,000 diamond cross for Maria Cristina of Savoy (1646).

It may be useful at this point to look in a little more detail at the accounts of a particularly well-documented patrician family, (the ones who bought the Palazzo Medici), the Riccardi of Florence (Malanima, 1977). In the eight years 1677–84, their ordinary household expenses amounted to 13,000 scudi, of which 23% went on food, 16% on alms (a form of conspicuous consumption which for lack of evidence I have rather neglected here), 15% on clothes, 15% on wages and 9% on the stables. These ordinary expenses should be compared with their extraordinary ones, which include a funeral in 1675 (3,500); a three-month mission to Rome in 1670 (5,000); a longer embassy to Vienna in 1673 (11,500); a Grand Tour, spread over 1665–6 and 1668–9 (18,000); and extensions to the palace in 1672 (32,000) and 1684 (58,000), which cost well over double what they had paid for the building in the first place. In 1678 the family was estimated at 44,000 scudi, a sum which makes the silver beds which so amazed Evelyn somewhat less surprising, and confirms his guesses at their value. The Ricardo also handed over 40,000 ducats as dowries for two of their girls, Maddalena (married 1665), and Camilla (1673), However, these losses were more than compensated by incoming dowries, 25,000 ducats apiece with Cassandra Capponi (1669) and Giulia Spada (1692).

The Riccardi may not be altogether typical of florentine patricians in the seventeenth century, since they had only just reached the top of the tree. Cosimo and Gabriello were made marquesses in 1629, while Francesco became Master of the Horse (Cavallerizzo Maggiore) to the Grand Duke in 1677. The family may have displayed more wealth than was normal in order to gain status quickly, like the most notorious of the new men in Italy in this period, the financiers; Bartolomeo d'Aquino in Naples, for example (Musi, 1976). However, this possible untypicality should not be stressed. The conspicuous consumption of the seventeenth century derived from values which were widely shared. It was a normal feature of that society, not a pathological trait.

All the same, consensus on this matter was not complete, as it was among the Kwakiutl – if we are to believe their ethnographers. If there was no seventeenth-century debate on luxury as articulate and sophisticated as there would be during the Enlightenment, criticisms of conspicuous consumption were not lacking. The criticisms were expressed by different individuals and groups for different reasons, three in particular: moral, political, and social.

1. There were moral objections to worldly display as a manifestation of pride (not to mention other deadly sins), objections which had been formulated with vigour by such leading counter-Reformation figures as Carlo Borromeo (whose views on embroidered hassocks have already been mentioned), and were repeated in the seventeenth century. An attack on Carnival, for example, mentioned the 'superfluous banquets' and 'immoderate expenses' of that season in true Catholic puritan style.[20] Pope Innocent XI, unlike most of his immediate predecessors, was a stern opponent of unnecessary expenditure. As Burnet commented, he had 'no magnificence in his court'.[21] He reproved his cardinals for their extravagance on carriages, and when, in 1679, the Jesuits asked permission to use the papal foundries to cast decorations for the Gesù, he answered that 'this was not the time to indulge in useless luxuries' (Haskell, 1963, p. 163). Innocent XII, who issued a decree against luxury in 1694, was a man of the same stamp. Similar views were expressed by satirists, who liked to illustrate this traditional literary theme with up-to-date examples. The Florentine patrician Jacopo Soldani, for example, devoted one satire to coaches, claiming to have seem 'many estates dragged behind a carriage' (*molti poderi andar dietro una treggia*), and another to expensive villas which were no more comfortable than modest ones.[22]

2. Political objections, in the name of republican simplicity, with overtones of what has been called 'hard primitivism', in other words the idea that there used to be a golden age when men lived a noble, simpler and more 'Spartan' life (Lovejoy and boas, 1935). In Venice in 1606, for example, a senator, possiblty Angelo Badoer, denounced what he called 'our unbearable luxury, arrogance and ostentation, so remote from the customs of our ancestors'.[23] He should have been pleased by the election that year of doge Lunardo Donà, a famous example of a Venetian patrician of the old thrifty school who bought his carriage (for use on the

mainland) second-hand and made himself unpopular by cutting down on the largesse at his inauguration and on state banquets thereafter (Seneca, 1959)[24] In Genoa in the early seventeenth century, a spectacular example of private wealth combined with public poverty, the old republican virtues were defended by the patrician Andrea Spinola who made biting comments on 'the madness of our luxury', criticised spending on coaches, funerals and palaces as examples of politically dangerous vanity, and defended parsimony because it was associated with freedom, as the example of the Swiss, which he knew at first hand, demonstrated.[25]

3. Economic and social objections were voiced at opposite ends of the social scale. On the one hand, governments were worried that the older noble families might be ruined by trying to keep up with the new rich. If they were ruined, the social order was threatened. If, on the other hand, they failed to keep up with upstarts, the social order was also threatened. This worry seems to have been one of the main reasons for the sumptuary laws issued in the seventeenth century, to judge by the explanations given in the preambles of the laws themselves. Five sumptuary laws were issued in Rome in the seventeenth century, eleven in Milan, twenty-one in Florence, and more than eighty in Venice (Levi Pisetzky, 1966, pp. 462–7), a preponderance which underlines the importance of republican opposition to conspicuous consumption in the name of civic equality and 'modesty'.

On the other hand, ordinary people resented extravagance, money thrown away on luxuries while they went without necessities. The reaction of Pasquino (above, p. 100) to the tax levied in Rome in 1648 to pay for the famous Four Rivers Fountain in Piazza Navona, designed by Bernini, was that 'We don't want steeples and fountains but bread, bread, bread, bread':

Noi volemo alto che guglie e fontane:
Pane volemo, pane, pane, pane.[26]

In Naples the previous year, when Masaniello led the revolt against the fruit tax, discussed below (ch. 14), crowds attacked the palaces of the rich and burned their contents. One contemporary suggests that some of these attacks expressed resentment of the new rich in particular, such as Francesco Basile, who had once been a baker; whether the snobbery was that of the rioters or merely of the nobleman who reported the incident it is now impossible to say.[27] A clearer view of some reasons for popular dislike of luxury emerges from a diary kept in the late sixteenth century by a Florentine tailor. He was old enough to remember the republic, and he disliked the Medici anyway, but he objected in particular to their extravagance. On the occasion of a grand funeral he commented drily that 'They threw away a lot of wax this morning'. Elsewhere he expressed his indignation over the Grand Duke's entertainment of the Venetian envoys at great expense while people were dying of hunger in the city and the surrounding countryside.[28]

Behind most of these objections, moral, political, or social, one hears echoes of the traditional ethic of 'holy thrift' as the Florentines sometimes called it (*santa masserizia*). The virtues of the shopkeeper were not yet extinct in the seventeenth century. It may not be irrelevant to point out that Innocent XI, one of the few popes of the period not to engage in conspicuous consumption, came from a merchant family of Como.

Despite this chorus of protest, however, conspicuous consumption continued and perhaps even escalated in the course of the seventeenth century. It is tempting to describe it as 'baroque'. The theme of the contrast between appearance and reality (*parere* and *essere*) which runs through the literature of the seventeenth century, in Italy as elsewhere in Europe, together with the theme of the world as a stage, seem especially appropriate to an age when consumption took such spectacular forms. Façades magnified palaces, palaces their owners, and clothes their wearers – quite literally in some cases, for some male clothes were designed to make the wearer look bigger than he really was (Levi Pisetzky, 1966, p. 303).

It is time to focus more sharply on the process of change, and tempting to link the rise of conspicuous consumption with what Braudel (1949) called 'the bankruptcy of the bourgeoisie' in the Mediterranean world in the late sixteenth century, and in particular with the economic decline of Italy (Cipolla, 1952–3). It is not difficult to find contemporaries who declare that a fatal trend towards greater magnificence could be noticed around the year 1600.

Let us take the case of Florence, and call a few witnesses. It was in the year 1600 that the envoy from Lucca, Bartolomeo Cenami, reported that the Florentines had 'abandoned the traditional parsimony of their private life' and adopted 'the way of life of courtiers', and that they were now living 'with as much splendour in their houses and outside as any nobles in Italy'. In 1618, a committee was set up to investigate luxury because it was feared that 'expense, luxury and ostentation have increased so much' that the city faced ruin (quoted in Malanima, 1977, p. 125). An elderly patrician, looking back from the 1660s, recorded his belief that it was around the beginning of the century that extravagance set in, marked by the rise of carriages, increasing numbers of servants, more splendid interior decoration, and the use of silver plate at meals instead of earthenware, as well as by a number of verbal signs which have already been discussed (above, p. 91).[29]

Similar testimonies can be collected for Venice, Genoa, and Naples. Doge Nicolò Contarini, who was, like Donà, a patrician of the old school, began his history of Venice with the year 1597 and remarked that it was about this time that Venetian prosperity came to be accompanied by 'ease and its companions pleasure and luxury', while the British ambassador, Sir Dudley Carleton, reported about 1612 that the Venetian nobles now 'change their manners... buying house and lands, furnishing themselves with coach and horses, and giving themselves the good time with more show and gallantry than was wont' (Cozzi, 1958, pp. 311, 15n; cf. Burke, 1974, pp. 101f). A visitor to Genoa in 1601, Monsignor Agucchi, was impressed by the magnificence of the city and its leading inhabitants, despite his acquaintance with Bologna and Rome. That this magnificence was a new trend in Genoa was suggested the following year by a Veronese nobleman who had lived for some time in the city.[30] As for Naples, it was about 1600 that the philosopher Tommaso Campanella commented on the splendour and extravagance of the court and nobility; about 1607 that the town clerk remarked on the 'great splendour' with which the nobles lived; and about 1620 that a report declared that the nobles were dressing and living in a much grander style than they had done in the past.[31]

However, this chorus of agreement must not be allowed to create too much confidence. 'Hard primitivism' is a recurrent phenomenon, and people are always thinking themselves the last survivors of an earlier, simpler, superior way of life. It would not be difficult to find similar evidence pointing to earlier turning-points. Jumping on to what Raymond Williams (1973), discussing a similar problem in English history, calls the 'escalator', we find a Genoese patrician, writing in 1575, who placed the shift in the years following the constitutional changes of 1547. 'Splendour has increased, and a new level of expense on buildings, clothes and fine foods has been introduced into Genoa'.[32] Let us travel backwards a little further. A Venetian diarist of the early sixteenth century believed that it was in his day that the nobility were deserting work for pleasure and earning for spending.[33] There is no reason to stop the escalator in 1500. A fifteenth-century Florentine complained of the 'rich banquets and regal clothes' in which his contemporaries indulged.[34] Come to that, Dante has some sharp remarks, in his Inferno, Canto XXIX, about some extravagant young men of thirteenth-century Siena, known as the 'spendthrift brigade' (*brigata spendereccia*). It is clearly hazardous to base any account of social change on literary sources and reminiscences alone.

Until a comparative study of inventories has been carried out, we shall not be sure exactly when, where, and among whom the shift from 'masserizia' to 'magnificenza' took place. Given the politically and economically polycentric or fragmented nature of Italian society at this time, it is likely that the shift towards more conspicuous forms of consumption took place in different cities at different times and, even more important, for different reasons. At any rate, this is what is suggested by the examples of Naples and Genoa.

In Naples, there is a good case for regarding the years 1532–53 as a major turning-point. These were the years of power of the most famous of Neapolitan viceroys, Pedro de Toledo, whose policy it seems to have been to encourage the great nobility, who had previously lived on their estates, to come to court, in order to weaken them politically (by cutting them off from their local power bases) and economically (because the expense of urban life was sure to get them into debt). Louis XIV was not the inventor of this 'Versailles syndrome'. At all events, the great nobles did move into town and a fever of palace construction broke out in the later sixteenth century. In the seventeenth century, construction slackened, but the nobles continued to compete with one another in displaying their wealth (Labrot, 1979). 1,930 goldsmiths and jewellers are said to have died in the plague of 1656 (Romano, 1976, p. 19), a figure which would suggest that there was more than one goldsmith to every thousand inhabitants of the city.

In the case of Genoa, the shift from thrift to magnificence seems to have come at much the same time, in the years around 1550, or a little later. The most obvious piece of evidence is a street of splendid palaces which began to be built at this time, Strada Nuova. It does not look like coincidence that this street of palaces for the so-called 'old' noble families was built at a time when they were not only becoming richer than ever before by lending money at high rates of interest to Philip II of Spain, but also more anxious than before to distinguish themselves from the new families who had been allowed to adopt their names. As a somewhat hostile account of 1579 puts it, having made 'excessive profits...they became proud and ambitious and abandoned the republican way of life, buying titles and fiefs, building sumptuous palaces with regal ornaments, and living with unheard-of splendour and grandeur, far in excess of what republican modesty requires'.[35]

The cases of Florence, Rome and Venice seem rather more complicated or obscure. Florence was of course the home of the classic formulations of the ethic or thrift or 'inconspicuous consumption' early in the fifteenth century. 'Every unnecessary expense is madness' says one speaker in the dialogue on the family by the humanist Leonbattista Alberti. 'Never show off your wealth', Giovanni Morelli advised his sons, 'but keep it hidden, and always by words and acts make people believe that you possess one half as much as you have'.[36] Yet it was at just this time that private palaces with impressive façades began to be built in Florence. About a hundred of them were constructed in the course of the sixteenth century, culminating in the truly magnificent Palazzo Strozzi (Goldthwaite, 1980). Then there was a pause, but after 1550 came another wave of private building, whether encouraged by Grand Duke Cosimo de 'Medici (for the same reasons as Pedro de Toledo), or simply following the example of the ruler. There are some indexes of the spread of luxury in the early seventeenth century which fit in well with the more subjective impressions of the witnesses quoted earlier. Florence had forty-two goldsmith's shops in 1561, but forty-eight in 1642. There were no carriage-makers in 1561, when the fashion was only just beginning, but by 1642 they had thirteen shops (Brown and Goodman, 1980, pp. 90f).

The case of Rome is complicated by the fact of the relatively rapid succession of rulers with very different consumption patterns and attitudes. It is hard to imagine magnificence on a grander scale than what was planned by pope Julius II, even if his major projects remained unfinished at his death. Adrian of Utrecht, on the other hand, was the reverse of magnificent. Paul III was in favour of conspicuous consumption and the Palazzo Farnese, built for his family by Michaelangelo and others, must be one of the grandest private houses ever built. The popes of the later sixteenth century, following the Council of Trent, were less sympathetic to private display, but it began again in the seventeenth century. About the year 1670 a priest who had been living in Rome for forty years declared that 'luxury has increased visibly to a great extent' (*In quarant'anni ch'io sono in Roma, il lusso è cresciuto evidentemente a gran segno;* Pastor, 1886, vols. 32, p. 27n). The evidence of the palaces listed above and of their high cost (p. 141) would seem to bear him out.

The case of Venice too is complicated by the alternation of heads of state who might well be taken as a model by other patricians but varied extremely in their own patterns of consumption. Despite the grand scale of some sixteenth-century palaces (notably Palazzo Corner), and the testimony of the British ambassador in 1612, there is a case for saying that the most significant change occurred in the later seventeenth century.

There was no major piece of private building in the years before 1660 as there was in the years which followed. A detail from the wills of some of the procurators of St Mark's, the elite of the Venetian elite, may be revealing; the number of masses they required to be said for the repose of their souls increased in the course of the century from hundreds to thousands.[37]

The culture of seventeenth-century Europe has been illuminated by the bold comparisons and hypotheses of V. L. Tapié (1957), and J. V. Polišenský (1971). In their different ways both scholars have contrasted two cultures; on one side the Europe of the baroque, Catholicism, courts and aristocracies; on the other the Europe of classicism, Protestantism, republics and the bourgeoisie. Between magnificence as a symbol of status – we might add in this context – and modesty as a symbol of virtue. These grand generalisations have their limitations. They assume too much homogeneity in societies. The examples of Carlo Borromeo and pope Innocent XI, quoted earlier, should act as a reminder that there was a Catholic as well as a Protestant opposition to magnificence. All the same, Tapié and Polišenský are invaluable in helping us to place local trends in European perspective. The shocked comments of British Protestant visitors, notably Gilbert Burnet, who has been quoted more than once on the wasteful display of the Italians seem to confirm the hypothesis of two cultures (it may be worth adding that Thorstein Veblen, who was also obsessed with waste, came of Pietist stock). As for politics, is it an accident that conspicuous consumption increased in Italy as republics gave way to principalities?

II
The presentation of
self in the
Renaissance portrait[1]

The purpose of this chapter is to discuss Italian portraits, especially those of the Renaissance, not from the usual point of view – that of the painters and their individual achievements – but from the point of view of the sitters, not as individuals so much as social types. This does not entail the assumption that paintings mirror physical or even social reality; their relation to the outside world is much more indirect. Portraits need to be regarded as a form of communication, a silent language, a theatre of status, a system of signs representing attitudes and values, and as a means to 'the presentation of self'.

The last phrase is a quotation from the late Erving Goffman, part of the title of one of his books. The book is an analysis of everyday life in terms of performance; a study of the art of 'impression management', as he calls it; an investigation of the various means adopted for the saving, or maintenance or indeed the improvement of 'face'. To achieve these ends it is necessary, but not sufficient, to attend carefully to 'deportment, dress and bearing'. This social 'demeanour' is more effective if supported by what he calls 'front', in other words the definition of the situation for observers by means of what he calls 'setting', 'scenery', 'stage-props' or 'sign-equipment' (Goffman, 1959).

Goffman's views have strong affinities with those of Robert Park, W. I. Thomas, and more generally with the Chicago School of symbolic interactionism whose leading concepts have been employed in this book on a number of occasions (above, p. 7). My recourse to this particular group of sociologists and anthropologists may seem odd in that the symbolic interactionists, and Goffman in particular, were not particularly interested in what is specific to particular societies or periods. However, the extended theatrical metaphor informing their work would seem to be particularly appropriate to Italy, where it was and is important to cut a good figure in public (*fare bella figura*), and to the early modern period, when the old metaphor of the world as a stage seems to have had an even wider currency than usual. There is an obvious affinity between the Goffman view of social life and the one put forward in the many Italian treatises of manners, notably Castiglione's 'Courtier' with its detailed instructions for creating the illusion of spontaneity, if necessary by careful rehearsal.

Neither Castiglione nor Goffman discuss the painted portrait, but it is not difficult to see the relevance of their approaches to behaviour to the semiotics of this pictorial genre.

Before exploiting any historical source, it is a good methodological principle to put it in context, to ask how and why it came into existence. We have to imagine portraits not as they now hang, in museums and galleries, associated with other 'works of art', but in their original setting, the houses or 'palaces' of the upper classes in a period when 'conspicuous consumption', as it is now called, was not only a pleasure but a duty for families which enjoyed or aspired to high status (above, ch. 10). Palaces, furniture, clothes, and so on were props for the successful presentation of self.

One of these props to identity was the portrait, commissioned to hang in the family residence with the images of the ancestors, genuine and spurious. In early modern Italy, the portrait was associated with the upper classes (with some surviving exceptions, often relatives of the painter). These paintings were for the eyes of the family, their friends and their guests. They were themselves items of conspicuous consumption, increasingly magnificent as the period progressed. They were also a part of what Goffman calls 'personal front'. The painted face made its contribution to social 'face'. The portrait was, or became, a representation of conspicuous consumption (on clothes, curtains, clocks, etc.), and so a document of impression management, with the advantage to the sitter (and the disadvantage to the modern historian), that in this type of document it is possible to control the information available to the spectators with a fair amount of success. Take the case of Federigo da Montefeltro, for example. Seeing him portrayed in profile, notably by Piero della Francesca, one might not be aware that he had lost an eye. Or we can take the rather more complicated case of melancholy. The poetry of the Italian Renaissance suggests that it was fashionable to be melancholy, that the malady was not just an Elizabethan one. Individuals who did not have the fortune to be melancholy by nature might want to present themselves in this light. However, it was not done to appear melancholy in public;' there are no instructions for learning this particular kind of body language in Castiglione's *Courtier* or other courtesy-books. It was in private, or to use Goffman's term, 'backstage', that one was supposed to prop one's head on one's hand or stare vacantly into space.

2. G. Bellini, *Doge Leonardo Loredan* (London, National Gallery)

But then how would others know? Here the painted portrait had the advantage of making the private public.

In other words, the painter has the power to adjust the appearance of the sitter to his or her social role. This might seem to rule portraits out of court as a historical source. From the historian's point of view, however, all is not lost. This adjustment of actor to role, which makes portraits rather unreliable records of the mere external appearance of individuals, turns them at the same time into a faithful representation of the values of their age.

One should beware of course of assuming complete consensus between artist and sitter. The portrait was the outcome of a process of 'negotiation' between two parties; it was a 'transaction' in more than the simple financial sense of the term (above, p. 48). Sitters are more or less demanding, artists more or less accommodating. The process of negotiation is rarely documented; an exception is the case of Isabella d'Este complaining about the results, or on another occasion, in middle age, asking Titian to paint her as she had been as a young girl. What the artist thought we do not know. We have to bear in mind the possibility that a painter might take a dislike to a particular sitter; Titian is known to have disliked the art dealer Jacopo Strada, whom he once described as 'one of the most pompous idiots you will ever find', and it has been suggested that he injected into his portrait an element of caricature (as Goya is said to have done in the case of the Spanish royal family). Even Raphael has been described on occasion as the 'cruellest of portrait-painters', with 'his hog pope and fox-and-ferret cardinals'.[2] I would not care to dismiss these suggestions *a priori*. To avoid the obvious dangers of subjectivity and anachronism, however, interpretations of this kind need to be based on a thorough knowledge of the local conventions of portrayal, the current pictorial translations of the language, or rhetoric, of the body, including gesture, posture, and the expression of the face. Apparently trivial details turn out to be clues which help us decode portraits, and something of the wider culture in which they are embedded.

In China, as Goffman reminds us (1956), mandarins used to appear in public with a 'stern and forbidding aspect', whatever their private thoughts, feelings, or character, simply because this was required by their role of dispenser of justice. This stern aspect, on which western travellers remarked, is confirmed by Ming dynasty portraits of officals. Some Italian ruler-portraits are almost equally forbidding, or at least severe; Bellini's doge Leonardo Loredan, for example, or Bronzino's Cosimo de'Medici, which communicates a sense of the *terribilita* appropriate to a prince.

Cosimo looks like a lion, as a ruler should; a comparison which is even more explicit in his bust by Cellini, with lion's heads on his armour (Summers, 1981, ch. 15; Meller, 1963). The art theorist G. P. Lomazzo was quite frank about what was needed. A ruler needs to look grave and majestic in his portrait, 'even if he does not in practice' (ancora che naturalmente non fosse tale).[3] More of a problem is Cosimo's wife Eleonora, as presented by the same artist. In her case the severity cannot be explained in the same way. Perhaps she had to look like this to match her husband. Perhaps this is simply a Bronzino expression – but one should not underestimate his range. It may be relevant to add that Eleonora's father, Pedro de Toledo, the King of Spain's viceroy in Naples (above, p. 147), had surprised the high nobility there by his Spanish manners, and notably by the fact that when he gave audience he remained immobile and expressionless, or as one observer put it, like a 'marble statue'.[4] His successors seem to have followed this precedent; an Italian who saw the viceroy carried in a litter in 1591 commented that he was so grave and motionless 'that I should never have known whether he was a man or a figure of wood'.[5] Bronzino's frozen style was peculiarly appropriate for recording this equally frozen behaviour, a case of art imitating life imitating art.

The cultural historian has to learn to read not only changing expressions but also the furnishings of the face; beards, for example. The beards of the clergy are particularly interesting in this respect, since they were a subject of contemporary debate. Beards were a virility symbol in this culture in which – as chapter 8 tried to show – the values of virility were taken very seriously. 'The beard is a sign of manliness...beardlessness is for children, eunuchs, for women'.[6] The celibate clergy posed more of a problem, and we find some with beards, some without. Take the popes, for example. The famous portraits by Raphael and Sebastiano del Piombo shows Julius II and Clement VII with beards, while Leo X is clean-shaven. A contemporary chronicle suggests that the reason that Julius II let his beard grow at Bologna in 1510 was 'to avenge himself' and that 'he did not want to shave it again until he had driven King Louis of France from Italy' (Partridge and Starn, 1980, pp. 43f). Clement VII grew his beard, apparently as a sign of mourning, after the sack of Rome in 1527. Many of the clergy imitated him. The implications of these two stories is that in the West – unlike the Orthodox world – a clerical beard was a marker of a special occasion. This view was challenged by the treatise 'in defence of priest's beards' published by the humanist Giovanni Pietro Pierio Valeriano in 1531, arguing that beards were a sign of piety, gravity and dignity, while shaving showed effeminacy (Chastel, 1983, pp. 184f). The beards of Paul III and cardinal Bembo, as painted by Titian, are consistent with this view. On the other hand, in the later sixteenth century Carlo Borromeo, beardless himself (as his portrait by Crespi shows) ordered his clergy to shave, and his view seems to have prevailed generally, though not completely. Van Dyck's cardinal Bentivoglio and the Innocent X of Velázquez are obvious examples of seventeenth-century clergy who sport beards, even if they are less thick than those of their sixteenth-century predecessors and so reflect something of a compromise.

Unlike beards, postures do not seem to have been a matter of much controversy, apart from odd remarks on the need to aim at the golden mean between 'the restlessness of monkeys' and that 'statuesque immobility' which so surprised visitors to the viceroy of Naples.[7] Problems of interpretation remain, however, particularly for historians coming from a culture in which the seated position is no longer associated with high social rank, respect is no longer expressed by bowing, and the slouch has replaced the upright position as the norm – even in portraits. For an example of the problems we may take the Titian portrait of pope Paul III with his 'nipoti', one of whom, Ottavio Farnese, is bent almost double, 'cringing' one is tempted to say, in a caricature of obsequiousness. But were the Farnese family really so obtuse as not to notice the caricature? For Vasari, who moved in this circle, testifies in his life of Titian that they were well satisfied with this portrait. It is therefore worth entertaining the hypothesis that a posture which signifies obsequiousness in one period (or culture) may have quite a different significance in another. Like the 'threshold of embarrassment', that useful term coined by the sociologist Norbert Elias (1939, pp. 114f), there is a 'threshold of respect' which may be raised or lowered in the course of time. In the case of Paul III, it is worth bearing in mind the elaborate forms of deference built into papal ritual (below, ch. 12), and especially the fact that he was the one individual in Europe in a position to have his foot regularly kissed in public, even, on occasion, by the emperor. If Charles V could stoop to the pope without shame, Ottavio could perhaps bend without cringing.

In the case of gesture, which no historian of Italy, of all places, can afford to omit in a study of body language, the evidence is more explicit because contemporaries were aware of its significance and discuss the eloquence of the hands, in particular, in treatises on rhetoric, manners and so on. 'Among all nations', as Vico put it, 'the hand signified power'.[8] Art historians are surely on the right lines when they try to

3. Titian, *Paul III and his* nipoti (Naples, courtesy of Mansell)

match the gestures in early modern paintings to those described in the
eleventh book of Quintilian's famous 'Education of the Orator' (Baxandall, 1972; Heinz, 1972). One has of course to remember that Quintilian
came from another culture – he was a Spanish Roman of the first century
AD – but also that his recommendations were taken seriously in early
modern Italy.

Some gestures in portraits are not too difficult to read – the conven-

4. Titian, *Cardinal Pietro Bembo* (Washington, National Gallery)

tional blessing gesture in the portraits of popes, Pius V for example or the conventional gesture of penitence made by fra Gregorio in his portrait by Lotto. Quintilian thought it somewhat excessive, indeed theatrical, for an orator to strike his breast in this way, but by the sixteenth century it had of course become a standard liturgical gesture associated with the *confiteor* at Mass. The outstretched hand, palm upwards, of cardinal Bembo seems to reproduce the gesture recommended by Quintilian for the beginning of a speech. Bembo had of course written on rhetoric. What more appropriate example of the rhetoric of gesture than the gesture of a rhetorician? More problematic is the hand-on-hip gesture of a number of young noblemen. For us this smacks of swagger, but in sixteenth-century Italy it may have signified no more than a proper sense of superior status, or the 'sprezzatura' or aristocratic negligence recommended by Castiglione in his 'Courtier'.[9] The spreading of the fingers, with the two middle fingers close together (a gesture to be found in portraits by Lotto and Bronzino before it became a hallmark of El Greco) may well seem affected today, but its popularity suggests that this gesture was perceived as a sign of the sitter's elegance, like the crossed legs of young bucks painted by Reynolds and Gainsborough. We shall never know whether this body rhetoric was the painter's or the sitter's; but from the standpoint of this chapter, concerned with the reconstruction of a cultural code, this gap in our knowledge does not matter too much.

The elegantly posed self displayed in these portraits was supported by a number of properties of attributes which identified the sitter socially. The language of objects has to be decoded as well as the language of the body (Castelnuovo, 1973). The problem is that objects spoke more than one language. They were bilingual at the very least. Many of the properties represented in portraits were symbols of status; but some were emblematic, identifying the sitter individually by means of visual puns (laurel for Laura, for example), or pointing some moral. The recurrent motif of a lady with a dog, for example, apart from immortalising a favourite pet, imparts a moral lesson; dogs, as the emblem-books of the time make plain, were symbols of fidelity. The point might be spelled out in the form of the proposition that dog is to master as wife is to husband (or at any rate, should be). The clothes of some of the girls in fifteenth-century Florentine portraits should be read heraldically. The portraits are probably those of brides, who were 'marked' as members of their new family by dresses bearing that family's badge (Klapisch, 1985, pp. 225, 239n).

Here, however, we are more concerned with accessories designed to enhance the sitter in the portrait – as indeed in daily life; with symbols of wealth, status and power, whether actual or merely hoped-for. Rich clothes are obvious status symbols, together with rings and necklaces and gold chains, like the heavy chain around the neck of Titian's Aretino (commemorating a gift to the sitter). 'There is nothing that humbles men more than to be ill-dressed', as one political theorist put it.[10] Another added that 'The clothes of a prince should express majesty, those of an elderly gentleman gravity, those of a young one elegance, those of a cleric dignified modesty, those of a matron should be decorous, and those of a maiden should be comely and stylish '.[11] The colours of clothes are more problematic. A red gown often signifies that its wearer is a Florentine citizen. In fifteenth-century Italy, black seems to have become fashionable in aristocratic circles, perhaps as a means of distinction from 'the flashy new rich' (Baxandall, 1972, pp. 14f). In the sixteenth century, soldiers were advised never to wear black – and always to wear a plume – so that their identity would not be mistaken.[12] Around 1600, black might in some circles be associated with support for Spain, while Francophils wore a French style which was more colourful.

Turning to details, gloves held rather than worn by the sitter were a somewhat ambiguous symbol, at least in the case of ladies, where they might well evoke the much-imitated poems of Petrarch on the 'beautiful naked hand' of his beloved, a nice example of the part representing the whole. Veils, not infrequently worn by Italian ladies of the period, may be making a similar point (Mirollo, 1984, chs. 3 and 4). Clocks may be moral symbols, reminders to sitter and spectators alike that time flies and that life is short, but some of them, in their heavy gold casing, are status symbols as well.

The armour to be found in so many aristocratic male portraits of the period is obviously heavy with symbolic significance. It is a sign of valour, still the appropriate virtue for rulers and aristocrats, whether or not they actually fought; Cosimo de'Medici did not, but he allowed or encouraged artists to paint him in armour all the same. Cased in steel, the sitters took on a heroic, epic quality; 'Arma virumque pingo'. The symbolic importance of the armour is particularly obvious in a portrait of Federigo of Urbino, perhaps by the Spaniard Berruguete, perhaps by Justus of Ghent. A portrait of a man in armour reading a book obviously cannot be read literally, as the representation of a moment in the sitter's life, without absurdity, even though Federigo really did fight in battle. Yet the painted figure makes a neat, economical, effective symbol of the combination of arms and letters, the two domains in which the prince, like the courtier, should excel, as Castiglione, writing at the court of Federigo's son, makes abundantly clear. According to Lomazzo, it was only the nobles who had themselves portrayed in arms. It is 'truly ridiculous', he observed, that 'merchants and bankers who have never seen drawn swords' be painted armed and even 'with batons in their hands like generals', rather than with a pen behind their ear and an account-book beside them.[13]

5. [?]Berruguete, *Federigo of Urbino with his son* (Urbino, courtesy of Mansell)

The place of books in portraits deserves some amplification. Books symbolised the contemplative life, so they were appropriate furnishings for portraits of the clergy, and they were doubtless provided on occasion for clerics who never studied, like armour and weapons for nobles who never fought. In a society where literacy was more or less restricted to an elite they were also, perhaps, symbols of power, like the letters and papers in the hands or on the desks of some sitters, showing how important and how busy they were. Painters not infrequently identify these books precisely, and it might be of interest to compile a bibliography. Lotto's fra Gregorio, for example, holds a work by St Gregory, an appropriate volume of homilies as well as a pun on the sitter's name. Lawyers are shown with the Corpus of Roman Law, physicians with the works of Hippocrates and Galen, the tools of their high-status trades. Fashionable young men and women are often to be seen holding the love poems of Petrarch, as in the case of Bronzino's Laura Battiferri, a choice doubly appropriate in this case because her name was that of Petrarch's beloved and because she wrote poems herself. It is even possible, in here case and also in that of a young lady painted by Andrea del Sarto, to identify the poems on the open page, allowing allusions which a particular in-group would have appreciated. In the case of another Bronzino sitter, the scholar Ugolino Martelli, there are three books, identifiable as works by Homer, Virgil and Bembo, and the pointing gesture must be intended to remind the spectator that Martelli wrote a commentary on Homer. Similarly, other sitters, like Veronese's Daniele Barbaro, point to the titles of their own books, or hold them open, like Bugiardini's Francesco Guicciardini. If the gesture strikes some readers as immodest, they should remember the values of the *società spettacolo* (above, p. 10).

Together with books we often find signs of the sitter's artistic interests. Statues, busts, coins and medals are all common in portraits of the period, from Botticelli's Giuliano de'Medici and Lotto's Odoni to Bronzino's Martelli and Titian's Jacopo Strada (who appears to be trying to sell something to the spectator). There are also more general signs of wealth, status and power. One is the velvet curtain. Among its most skilled manipulators were Titian, Bronzino, and van Dyck (who painted a number of Italians in Genoa and elsewhere). There is also the classical column, bearing obvious associations with ancient Rome and also with splendid palaces, represented metonymically, a small part for a very large whole. Another dumb yet eloquent symbol of status was the servant, like the black boy in Van Dyck's portrait of Elena Grimaldi, a noblewoman of Genoa. It is not difficult to imagine what that severe republican Andrea

6. A. van Dyck, *Elena Grimaldi* (Washington, National Gallery)

Spinola would have thought of that portrait, since he was critical of the fashion for these little page boys or *menini*.[14] The umbrella in this portrait, incidentally, offers more than a splash of colour and protection for the sitter; it has associations with high status because of its use in rituals to cover the most important participant, whether pope, prince, or blessed sacrament (below, ch. 12).

Dogs, horses and birds may all be status symbols on occasion. The hound had obvious associations with the hunt, a sport which was at once manly and aristocratic. These associations are particularly obvious in another of the Genoese van Dycks, the portrait of Anton Giulio Brignole Sale. To look at this magnificent portrait, associating a man and his horse, hound and hawk, one might not think that one was faced with a patrician of recent merchant origins (best known today as writer), rather than a great nobleman of old family and extensive estates. It is one more reminder that the painter was not a camera but a dealer in more than one kind of illusion, social mystification as well as *trompe l'oeil*. One might even talk of the portrait as a piece of mythology in a metaphorical sense (cf. Barthes, 1957), as well as the obvious literal sense typified by Bronzino's representation of the Genoese admiral Andrea Doria as Neptune. One kind of myth served the other.

It might well be useful to draw up an inventory of all the properties represented in Italian portraits of the early modern period, to see how frequently they were associated with one another and with different types of sitter in what might be called pictorial 'formulae', and when and why the conventions were broken. Caravaggio's portrait – if it was his – of the young cardinal Maffeo Barberini, for example, provides the sitter with a vase of flowers. This is unusual, but we should beware of seeing it as effeminate. A generation earlier, an archbishop had inveighed against the representation of flowers (together with animals and birds), in the portraits of churchmen, but for a different reason. He saw these accessories as too worldly.[15]

This chapter has been concerned so far with the portrayal of a system of signs, and a portrait requires the sitter to keep still. It is of course as unrealistic as it is – temporarily – useful to try to halt the march of time in this way. That is the greatest weakness of the so-called 'structuralist' approach to culture, and the reason why it has been discussed relatively little in these pages. It is time to suggest how portraits changed between the fifteenth and eighteenth centuries, and to see whether or not these changes are associated with developments in other forms of conspicuous consumption or other sign-systems (notably language).

If one arranges dated Italian portraits in chronological order, certain changes spring to the eye. Fifteenth-century portraits are relatively plain and unimpressive (from the self-presentation point of view, at least; this is not a comment on the artistic achievements of Antonello da Messina, say, or Botticelli). It was possible to paint the sitter 'warts and all' (as Ghirlandaio painted the merchant Sassetti, although this identification is disputed). Few properties are visible, and only the head and shoulders or at most the top half of the sitter, who is almost seen in profile. Omitting the special case, already mentioned, of Federigo of Urbino, we should not assume too easily that profiles failed to impress fifteenth-century spectators, for the analogy between painted portraits and ancient Roman coins probably carried weight with them. In any case, the portrait was a novelty. In a poem by the fifteenth-century Venetian patrician Leonardo Giustinian, the lover tells his beloved that he has painted her image on a piece of paper 'as if you were one of God's saints'.

Io t'ho dipinta in su una carticella
Come se fussi una santa di Dio.

Even in the late sixteenth century, according to the archbishop of Bologna, Gabriele Paleotti, infamous people (among whom he included heretics, tyrants, courtesans and actors) should not be portrayed at all.[16]

All the same, looking at the portraits in series, one has a sense that people became blasé, that more elaborate means were soon necessary if the spectators were to be impressed by the sitter. Profiles gave way to three-quarter views or full-face. Half-lengths expanded to full-lengths, so that some portraits are considerably larger than the people looking at them. Props multiplied: chairs, tables, curtains, columns, books, papers, clocks, dogs, servants, and so on. By the turn of the sixteenth and seventeenth centuries, portraits had become very much more impressive and more elaborately formal than they had been in the fifteenth. Why? Explanations of artistic trends are never precisely verifiable, but it makes sense to begin by looking at changes which were taking place in the same milieu at more or less the same time. Buildings too were becoming grander, and consumption generally more conspicuous (above, ch. 11). There is also evidence that modes of address were becoming inflated (ch. 7), and politeness more elaborately ritualised. For some historians, these trends are merely symptoms of a much more massive change which can be summed up in one word; 'refeudalisation', in the sense of the recovery of dominance by the landed nobility, coupled with what might be called 'the fall of the middle class'. They may be right. There were changes in the balance of power between different social groups in early modern Italy. It is possible that these changes had cultural consequences, although the connexions cannot be demonstrated and I am not sure that merchants, for example, were cultural pace-setters even in fourteenth-century Florence.

There is, however, an alternative explanation of changes in the presentation of sitters in Italian portraits, an explanation which is microsocial rather than macrosocial, modest rather than ambitious, and a good deal easier to document than its rival, though the two theories are better seen as complementary than contradictory. According to the alternative theory, the grander manner in which noble sitters came to be portrayed in the sixteenth and seventeenth centuries was in part at least a response to the democratisation of the portrait. There is evidence that some ordinary people, craftsmen and shopkeepers, were beginning to have their portraits painted, to the extreme annoyance of observers higher in the social scale. 'It is the disgrace of our age', wrote Pietro Aretino – himself a shoemaker's son who had risen socially – 'that it tolerates the painted portraits even of tailors and butchers'.[17] The painting of a tailor by Morone, now in the National Gallery, London, suggests that Aretino was reacting against a real trend. Portraits of craftsmen and shopkeepers are rare now, but they had fewer chances of survival than portraits of aristocrats. A few years after Aretino, the artists and art theorist Lomazzo made a similar point. 'Whereas in the time of the Romans, only princes and victorious generals were portrayed, now the art of portraiture from life has become so vulgarised (*divulgata*), that virtually all its dignity is lost'.[18] When the very existence of a portrait was a sign of the high status of the sitter, the portrait itself could afford to be simple, but as soon as portraits became commonplace, a new means of differentiation had to be employed by those who wanted to stand out.

In the eighteenth century, on the other hand, what we see in the work of Ceruti, Longhi, fra Galgario, and others, is the reverse trend, a move towards increasing simplicity and informality. Expressions became less stiff, and it was at last possible to represent even a doge with human emotions. Smiles become more frequent in eighteenth-century portraits (they should probably be read as signs of affability rather than amusement). One eighteenth-century pope told the painter to make him look gentle, because he was the people's pastor (*Fa dolce: sono pastore dei popoli.* Quoted by Andrieux, 1962, preface). It became possible for painters to portray cardinals in undress uniform, and gentlemen taking snuff, or in the act of reading, spectacles on nose, rather than posing

7. Morone, *Tailor* (London, National Gallery)

elegantly beside a book, as had been the custom. The Longhis and others painted family groups. There was a rise of domestic props such as teacups, fans, screens, harpsichords and children, particularly in female portraits, which seem to have become more common (in the Dutch Republic in the seventeenth century, the numbers of male and female portraits seem to have been about equal; in Italy at the same time, the preponderance is overwhelmingly male). One might talk of the rise of 'naturalism', but it would be more accurate to speak in terms of an alternative convention, a rhetoric of the natural and the domestic. These changes coincide with an increasing informality of speech (ch. 7), an increasing distrust of ritual (ch. 16), and a trend towards more relaxed behaviour in upper-class society, a trend which is more obvious in the cases of France and England but is also noticeable in parts of Italy. Some anonymous Venetian verses of 1768 describe the unconventional habits of some noblewomen, including sitting 'a la sultana', in other words with one leg over the other (Molmenti, 1906–8, vol. 3, 331–2). In the case of this trend towards informality (unlike its converse), it is hard to offer anything but a macrosocial explanation.

The wheel seems to have come full circle, but the rise of informality, like that of formality, suggests that portraits can tell us something important about society in general as well as about a particular sitter. This is not to reaffirm the view, rejected earlier, that the painter is a mirror or camera. On the contrary, he (or occasionally she, as in the case of Sofonisba Anguisciola), is a rhetorician. The point is that the rules of rhetoric changed as the wider culture changed, so that they too must be studied as a historical source. Historians not only can but must use portraits and other paintings as part of their evidence, because images often communicate what is not put into words. Yet this evidence cannot be interpreted until the paintings are replaced in their frames, the frames of the culture and society of their time.

12
Sacred rulers, royal priests:
rituals of the
early modern popes

Like speech, writing and images, ritual is a form of communication, the one with which the remaining chapters in this volume will be mainly concerned. As in the case of other forms of communication, historians need to answer the question of who was saying what to whom through these rituals, a question which will involve some discussion of the relation between ritual and political power. This essay will attempt to respond to a recently formulated programme of research (Cannadine, 1983), in which historians are urged to relate royal rituals to the power of a given monarchy, the personal character of the monarch, the social structure, the state of the media, the level of technology, the condition of the capital city and the self-consciousness of the nation. It is obvious that this programme was formulated with secular rulers in the nineteenth and twentieth centuries in mind, and it will require some modification here, but a questionnaire of this kind does have the great advantage of forcing historians of festivals and other rituals to go beyond mere description (to which they have often confined themselves), and to reflect, as some anthropologists have done, on the relationship between symbols and power (Cohen, 1969; Geertz, 1980).

This relationship is unusually complex in the case of the popes because they were such ambiguous, amphibious creatures, not really flesh or fish, princes or priests, but on the border of some of the main categories of their culture. As temporal rulers they only controlled a mini-state, with about a million inhabitants, a twentieth of the size of Louis XIV's France. Stalin's brutal question, How many divisions has the pope? might have been asked in this period; indeed it was, in a sense, asked in a chapter of Machiavelli's 'Prince'.[1] The lack of a papal army, apart from mercenaries, was a serious weakness. Yet the spiritual domains of the popes remained vast, despite the inroads of the Reformation. They also united a local role, that of bishop of Rome, with a central, indeed a universal one, just as they united the dignified with the efficient and the charismatic with the bureaucratic (cf. Prodi, 1982).

This is not, or not simply, a case of modern scholars failing to catch this particular butterfly in their net of categories. Contemporaries were also aware of some at least of these problems, and the ambiguities were reflected, as I shall suggest, in the papal rituals themselves. This chapter, which offers no more than an outline of a large subject, will therefore be concerned to describe and analyse the repertoire of papal rituals, more especially the way in which this ritual system was used to present the pope to the public, to represent him or to 'construct' him (cf. Price, 1984). The period with which we shall be concerned is that between the fifteenth century and the eighteenth, more particularly the thirty papal reigns between the accession of Nicholas V (1447), and that of Clement XIII, 311 years later. The sources for the reconstruction of this ritual system are fortunately both rich and varied. The outsiders, the foreign visitors, include Michel de Montaigne and Philip Skippon, two men with unusually sharp ethnographic eyes. The insiders include the papal masters of ceremonies, who were responsible for the organisation of the events, and recorded them in their diaries at the time. In between the two come accounts left by citizens of Rome, from Infessura in the fifteenth century to Gigli in the seventeenth.

Papal rituals can be divided into two groups, ordinary and extraordinary (it is convenient to use the ethnographic present, and in any case, many of these performances still take place today). Some ordinary rituals take place almost every day, like the 'audience', in which visitors kiss the pope's foot. The procedure was actually rather more elaborate, as Montaigne, who took part in it in 1580, may remind us. He describes his entry into the room, marked by a genuflexion; his passage halfway across the room, marked by a second genuflexion; and finally his arrival at the feet of the pope, when he knelt on both knees and kissed the papal slipper.

> Là l'ambassadeur qui les presentoit se mit sur un genou à terre, et retrousse la robe du pape sur son pied droit, où il y a une pantoufle rouge, atout une croix blanche audessus. Ceux qui sont à genoux se tiennent en ceste assiete jusques à son pied, et se penchent à terre pour le baiser. M. de Montaigne disoit qu'il avoit haussé un peu le bout de son pied.[2]

More important is the annual cycle of the pope's major liturgical engagements, which is not spread evenly throughout the year but squeezed into the six months from midwinter to midsummer.[3] At Christmas, the pope says High Mass in St Peter's and blesses the people. He blesses a cloak and sword which he presents to a Catholic prince. He makes a visit to Santa Maria Maggiore, a visit which was witnessed, in 1662, by the invaluable Skippon.

when he [the pope] came to the church, he was carried in an
embroidered chair on a bier, supported by twelve men with red
habits; on each side of him was carried a great fan made of white
peacock's tails; he had his triple crown on...Trumpets sounded at
his entrance, and before him went a rich black cap wrought with
silver, and two maces went on each side of it; next followed two
mitres and the cross-bearers, and immediately before him came the
cardinals two and two together.[4]

On the feast of the Purification of the Virgin (Candlemas, 2 February),
the pope distributes candles to the cardinals. On the feast of the
Annunciation (Lady Day, 25 March), he gives dowries to poor girls. On
the fourth Sunday in Lent, Laetare Sunday, the pope blesses the golden
rose, which is sent to a layman or woman of high status in an elaborate
ritual of the gift. In 1451, for example, it was the doge of Genoa who
received the rose, in 1510, King Henry VIII, in 1600, Queen Marie
de'Medici.[5] On Palm Sunday, the pope blesses the palms and receives the
so-called 'obedience' of his cardinals, a triple kiss on his mouth, hand and
foot. On Maunday Thursday comes the 'mandato', the ritual foot-
washing of thirteen priests (called the 'apostles') in the Vatican. On
Easter Sunday, the high point of the ecclesiastical year, he says pontifical
High Mass, receives the obedience of the cardinals, and blesses the people,
who are shown the most precious relics in Rome, the holy lance and the
Veronica.[6] The Ascension (when the Veronica was again displayed),
Pentecost, Corpus Christi and the feast of St Peter are also important ritual
occasions. Then the pope and his court go on 'vacation' (an ecclesiastical
term before it became an academic one). When it returns from 'villegg-
iatura', there are no major feasts until Christmas.

All the same, there is good reason for the suggestion that in the
sixteenth century Rome 'may have offered more grand public entertainment than any other city of the Western world' (Mitchell, 1973, p. 59).
The annual cycle was particularly splendid in what was called a 'holy
year'. Originally there was only one a century, but in the early modern
period they came to take place every twenty-five years. To inaugurate the
year a new door, the 'porta santa', would be opened in St Peter's, by the
pope striking it with a ceremonial hammer (Prinzivalli, 1899; Thurston,
1900; Jung-Inglessis, 1975).[7] On these occasions, papal audiences multiplied and the ordinary flow of pilgrims swelled into a torrent (Delumeau,
1957–9, vol. 1, pp. 169f). It has been calculated that half a million visitors
came to Rome in the year 1600.

Besides this annual cycle, there are, however, many extraordinary or irregular rituals, such as the creation of a knight of St Peter, the presentation of his pallium to a new archbishop, or the welcoming of a distinguished visitor. Feasts ('banchetti') were an important part of the ritual; they are described in some detail in the guides to protocol or 'cerimoniali'.[8] When, for example, the Duke of Mantua visited Rome in 1618, the pope invited him to dinner. They ate at separate tables, the pope's under a 'baldacchino' or canopy, with the duke's table at his right. On arrival and departure the duke genuflected. When the pope washed his hands, the duke held the towel. Whenever the pope drank, the duke took his hat off.[9] Drinking rituals were formal and hierarchical. 'Cardinals', we learn, 'pull off their hats or caps only when they drink the pope's health, but ambassadors stand up'.[10] The more important the visitor, the more splendid the reception. One might have thought that the limit had been reached at the beginning of our period with the entry into Rome in 1452 of the emperor Frederick III, but the ritual employed ten years later shows that the entry of St Andrew's head was considered more important; the pope went out to meet it at Ponte Molle.[11] Other splendid occasions were papal 'entries' into other cities, such as those of Julius II into Bologna, Leo X into Florence (Shearman, 1975), Paul III into Piacenza, and so on, and their formal return to Rome afterwards.[12] The importance of these state entries can be gauged from the street widening programmes, including the demolition of buildings, which preceded the pope's arrival. Giving and receiving official visits was so important a part of a pope's life that his relatively rare unofficial visits provoked comment, whether it was Paul III going to see Michelangelo in his workshop in the meat market, or Paul V going to dine in his family home, the Palazzo Borghese. By the late seventeenth century, if not before, the procedure for receiving ambassadors had been standardised, with various grades of reception for ambassadors of the first class (Venice, for example), second class (Florence), and third class (Bologna), grades which affected the costume worn by the cardinal who formally 'received' and returned the visit, how far he went to meet the visitor, and how far he accompanied him on his way out (in the case of first-class ambassadors, the cardinal was instructed to 'pretend to wish to go downstairs').[13]

Other major ritual occasions include the canonisation of saints, more than sixty of them in the sixteenth, seventeenth and eighteenth centuries (above, p. 50). For canonisations, the cardinals wear white instead of their usual red, there are processions with lighted candles around St Peter's Square, and a special offering of live birds, including doves, to the pope with the bread and wine at Mass.[14] Rather more unusual ritual occasions are interdicts and absolutions – Sixtus IV absolved Florence, Julius II and Paul V both absolved Venice, and Clement VIII absolved Henri IV of France. Finally, there are the rites of passage, which, given the age of popes on election (in their mid-fifties, on average in this period), recurred rather frequently. Since they have much to tell us about contemporary conceptions of the role of pope and how it should be played, they are worth describing in some detail.

Before making his official declaration that 'the pope is dead', the cardinal chamberlain strikes the head of the corpse three times with a silver hammer, calling on the dead man by name. Then the master of ceremonies takes the fisherman's ring from the late pope's finger and gives it to the chamberlain to be broken. All the bells of Rome toll for the departed. Skippon adds the detail that 'When the pope dies, every house is obliged to set out a light every night; which custom is strictly observed all the time the sede vacante. The bells at the Campidoglio are never rung but at the pope's death'.[15] The corpse lies in state and first the cardinals, and then the general public, pay their respects to the pope by kissing his foot for the last time. Finally, there is a solemn funeral.[16]

The conclave which follows is, as everyone knows, an event which is at once highly politicised (the great powers of the early modern period, such as France, Spain and the Empire, frequently tried to influence papal elections via their cardinals), and highly ritualised. The cardinals enter singing the hymn 'Veni creator spiritus', asking the Holy Ghost to preside over their deliberations. They vote. They bargain. They make and break alliances. They vote again. Finally the successful candidate is asked whether he accepts office. He prays before replying. If he accepts, he is asked what name he will take. He prostrates himself before the altar, in order to be cleansed, purified, changed into a fit occupant of his high and responsible role (cf. Fortes, 1966). He is then dressed in the papal robes and enthroned, the fisherman's ring is placed on his finger, and the cardinals 'adore' him – that is the technical term for what is otherwise known as the 'obedience' – kissing his hand, foot, and mouth. The public are told that 'we have a pope' (*habemus papam*). Some days later comes the papal coronation, which takes place partly in St Peter's, and partly outside it, and is followed by a solemn procession to the church of St John Lateran.[17]

The coronation is doubled by another inauguration ceremony, the so-called 'possesso', the ritual by which the pope takes solemn possession of his city. He rides through it on a white mule blessing the people as he goes, preceded and followed by his light horsemen, pages, lawyers, cardinals and so on, a mixture of social types reflecting the mixture of papal roles. On the Capitol he receives, and returns, the keys of the city. Arches are erected through which the cavalcade passes in triumph, and the fountains run with wine. As in a number of other inauguration ceremonies (that of the doge of Venice, for example), money is thrown to the crowd (Cancellieri, 1802).[18] There follow the formal visits of congratulation by the ambassadors of different states.

All these rituals deserve analysis in detail, but in a brief sketch it is possible to draw attention to only a few of their salient features.

In the first place, this body of rituals appears to form a single system, in the sense that it is full of cross-references. There are a number of elements in these rituals which are at once distinctive and recurrent. The most obvious example is that of the 'osculum pedis', the kissing of the papal feet, which occurs at daily audiences, on Palm Sunday, at the death of a pope, at the accession of a new one, and so on (Wirth, 1963). Foot-kissing was not a uniquely papal privilege – it could happen to the emperor on occasion – but it was something of a papal speciality. Correspondents even ended letters to the pope with the respectful formula, 'I kiss your most holy feet'. Processions, blessings, genuflexions and other liturgical elements also recur frequently, so that different papal rituals may be regarded as permutations of what a structuralist might describe as the same basic *ceremoniemes* (cf. Lévi-Strauss, 1955).

A second general point which deserves emphasis is the importance of the properties used in these presentations of the pope, and of the stages on which the performances were played. The properties include the pope's litter (*Sedia* or *lectica*); the *baldacchino* or canopy held over him (the right to carry it was considered a great honour); the *flabella* or ostrich-feather fans (which Skippon described as 'made of white peacock's tails'), carried by his attendants; the pope's triple crown, his stole, his ring, his red slippers; and the chair or throne from which he blessed the people, seeming 'to sail forward...like a celestial being', as another British visitor put it.[19] In the background there were the rich robes of the cardinals, and the colourful costumes of the barons, the consistorial advocates, Swiss guards and other attendants. The major festivals of the church's year had been declared 'scarlet days' (another ecclesiastical term which became an academic one) in which the cardinals wore full dress, while the advocates wore purple (*paonazzo*) on the day of the *possesso*. The frequent changes of clothes prescribed in the books of ceremonies are a reminder of the amount of time which must have been spent by the papal court in the preparation for ritual activity.

The physical settings for these performances, the stages on which they are played at once enhance and constrain them. These settings include the Sistine Chapel, scene of many conclaves; the Cappella Paolina, where conclaves have also taken place; the Sala Regia, also within the Vatican, where formal audiences are held; the Sala Ducale, where the foot-washing ritual takes place; St Peter's; its portico (the old one, razed in 1609, and the new one), and its loggia, from which the pope blesses the people; the square beyond; St John Lateran, which also has a portico and a *loggia di benedizione*; Santa Maria Maggiore; certain processional routes across Rome, along which the ground would be covered and the houses hung with tapestries or crimson silk; and indeed the whole city, which might be regarded as a theatre city, the capital of a 'theatre state' not unlike traditional Bali (Geertz, 1980).

The visual impressions were of course enhanced by oral ones, such as the singing of the papal choir, not to mention the drums, trumpets and cannon at the *possesso*, the bell-ringing and cannon-firing when the pope blessed the people at Christmas and Easter, and so on. It is also necessary to imagine a great deal of audience participation – even more uninhibited than it is today, if we can trust the reports of visitors – with shouts of *Viva il santo padre*, or *Benedizione, santo padre* and people prostrating themselves on the ground before the pope's mule. John Evelyn, in Rome in 1644, watched the *possesso* and noted 'multitudes upon their knees, looking out of their windows and houses with loud vivas and acclamations of felicity to their new Prince'.[20] Formally unprescribed, and varying in intensity with the pope and with the occasion, this participation was an essential part of the ritual.

Who is saying what to whom through all this spectacle and sound? The speaker is elusive, as so often in the case of rituals, which is part of their force. It is not the pope speaking so much as tradition speaking through him, even if this tradition may be manipulated, consciously or unconsciously, from time to time. As for the audience, it is a multiple one. The traditional phrase for it is 'the city and the world'. The Christmas and Easter blessings are given 'urbi et orbi', in the first place to Rome, the pope's city and his diocese, and in the second place to everyone else. The special relationship between the pope and his city is revealed most clearly by the ritual of the *possesso*, in which he receives the keys, but representatives of the city also hold the *baldacchino* at the coronation. Yet the *urbi et orbi* formula is less inclusive than it may look. It omits God, to whom a number of the ritual messages are primarily addressed. Ritual is, among other things, a way of regulating relations between society and the supernatural. God plays an important if invisible role and inspires the choice of popes. The hymn *Veni Creator Spiritus* suggests that conclaves are re-enactments of Pentecost.

What is the essential message of papal rituals? We must not assume either that there is a single message or, even if there were one, that it is completely translatable into words, for rituals are designed not just to say something but to do something – to impress the bystanders, to reinforce (if not create) solidarity, and so on. A more fruitful question might be: what do these papal rituals tell us about their protagonist? Their message seems at least on the surface to be an ambiguous one, ambivalent, even contradictory, as is perhaps to be expected in the case of a ruler who is both temporal and spiritual, dignified and efficient. Let us examine in turn the two major components of that message.

It is clear enough that most rituals stress the majesty of the pope, his royalty, indeed his imperial nature, for 'the pope is the true emperor' as the saying went (*papa est verus imperator*: Wilks, 1963, pp. 254f). Kings and emperors kiss his feet, 'adoring' him in the way in which Roman emperors were once adored, in what has been called 'the western counter-part of the eastern proskynesis' (Ullmann, 1955, p. 315).[21] The *baldacchino*, which is reminiscent of an oriental ceremonial umbrella (used, for example, in Bali); the fans, which resemble oriental fly-whisks; and the litter, which resembles an oriental palanquin, all underline that part of the message. The pope is an absolute monarch. Indeed, the phrase 'absolute power' (*potentia absoluta*) was used of him before it was applied to the secular rulers of early modern Europe (Oakley, 1968). The term had originally been used of God, but then the pope is in the place of God. He is the Vicar of Christ. He has the power to open the gates of heaven, symbolised by the *porta santa* which is ritually opened every twenty-five years, in an enactment of Christ's words 'I am the gate' (John 10.7; cf. Jung-Inglessis, 1975). The pope is described as a second Melchisedech, a priest-king who is compared to Christ in the liturgy of the Mass. The pope is often referred to (by his masters of ceremonies, for example) as 'Our Lord' (*Dominus Noster*). Two canopies are carried in Roman processions, one over the Blessed Sacrament and the other over the pope. The major theme in papal ritual is majesty.

However, there is a minor theme, more unusual in the royal rituals of early modern Europe, and that is humility. At the pope's inauguration, the master of ceremonies burns a piece of cork in front of his nose to remind him of the transience of worldly glory.[22] The pope is not only the true emperor, he is also the servant of the servants of God, *servus servorum dei*. Cardinals are birds of colourful plumage, but the pope wears white. Perhaps white is a way of trumping colour, but it symbolises simplicity as well as establishing a distinction between the holy father and his multicoloured entourage. The pope is not always carried in a litter. He sometimes gets out and walks in procession, as Nicholas V, for example, insisted on doing. In 1517, Leo X walked barefoot from St Peter's to Santa Maria sopra Minerva to beg God for deliverance from the menace of the Turks. Alexander VII even planned to walk barefoot at his *possesso*. (Cancellieri, 1802, p. 257). When he rides, the pope sometimes mounts a white palfrey, but more often he chooses a more humble animal, a mule, which was also an appropriate mount for a celibate cleric because it is incapable of breeding. On Maundy Thursday he washes the feet of ordinary priests and serves a meal to beggars. In these respects he imitates Christ, who rode into Jerusalem on an ass and washed the feet of the apostles, but he is imitating Christ in his deliberately chosen humble role, as opposed to Christ the King. In a sense, then, the theme of humility subverts the imperial theme. In another sense it reinforces it, by giving the pope the spiritual power of the holy man as well as the power of the monarch. 'He who humbleth himself shall be exalted.' I would not care to argue that this ritual, like myths in the eyes of some theorists, resolved the conflict between the pope's temporal and spiritual roles, his two bodies, the two sides of his amphibious nature (Lévi-Strauss, 1958). But it did at least express this conflict.

How far these messages were received and understood it is obviously very difficult to say. Much of the audience must have been unable to see or hear very much of what was going on. Newcomers to Rome, or people who had not benefited from a classical education (in other words, the majority of people) must have missed many of the allusions. However, the existence of an important minority of connoisseurs of ritual must not be forgotten. Many people will have known what they were supposed to see, and some will have remembered it in terms of the explanatory booklets which were issued to commemorate the event. And to be impressed by the magnificence it was not necessary to know precisely what it all meant.

This brief outline of a general interpretation has stressed what is recurrent and repetitive. This is, of course, the essence of ritual, to abolish time, at least temporarily (below, ch. 13), but all the same, it is possible to identify quite significant changes over the long term, and in any case, no performance is exactly the same as any other.

To take the second point first. One reason that ethnographers like to spend more than a year in the field is to watch some annual rituals come round for a second time, to see whether the forms are relatively free or fixed. Historians can at least note the variations in the way the annual cycle of papal rituals is described in the diaries of the masters of ceremonies. Among the most important of these records are the diaries of Johannes Burchardus and Paris de Grassis.[23]

Grassis gives the impression of an ecclesiastical sergeant-major with a sharp eye for anyone late on parade or improperly dressed. The special value of his diary is its testimony – all too rare in the history of ritual – of the gap between plan and performance. Grassis is constantly grumbling about what went wrong; the mistakes made by his colleagues, the unseemly wrangles over precedence, and the need for the management of ancient cardinals who were none too steady on their legs and sometimes had to be excused walking in procession, standing or kneeling – gerontocracies have their problems, in the field of ritual as elsewhere.[24] From the modern historian's point of view, Grassis, like other insiders, has the disadvantage of taking too much for granted, and it is sometimes frustrating to learn no more than that 'the usual things' occurred, 'more solito' or, somewhat unclassically, 'omnia prout in ordinario'. All the same, Grassis shows himself to be well aware of the unprescribed. What emerges clearly from his account is the impact on the Roman ritual system of an individual with a strong personality who is impatient of formalities, the 'terrible' Julius II. Julius suffered from gout, so he could not always genuflect as required.[25] He had to be prompted: such an important actor as the Vicar of Christ could not be expected to know his lines. Julius preferred his ordinary clothes to the formal apparel of special occasions, and he might even leave off his stole when ritual required it to be worn.[26] The martinet Grassis had to put up with a commanding officer who often broke the rules.

Historians of ritual have recently been enjoined to investigate whether or not the performances that interest them were carried out in a 'slovenly' manner (Cannadine, 1983). Like disorder, slovenliness is a culture-bound concept, and it might be more useful to operate with a more neutral typology which contrasts the relatively 'taut' (not to say 'rigid') with the relatively 'relaxed'. However, I do not doubt that papal rituals of the early modern period would have appeared slovenly to observers from England in, say, the late nineteenth or early twentieth centuries. To quote a recent comment on the noise level during sermons in the papal chapel in Julius's time: 'A rigid code of protocol and convention often combined in public functions with an astonishing degree of spontaneity, even of coarseness' (O'Malley, 1979, p. 21). One is reminded of the surprise of foreigners like Montaigne when they first observed Italians in church (above, p. 18). However, there is no evidence that this 'spontaneity' disturbed Italians in the sixteenth century. I am not sure that it disturbs them now.

Apart from the inevitable gap between plan and performance, precept and practice, there were other reasons for variations in what was officially the same ritual programme. One suspects on occasion that a particular ritual of encounter, such as a papal entry, was deliberately manipulated by its protagonist in order to raise his status, or more exactly, to force others to recognise particular papal claims. In 1459, for example, the Florentine Signoria (the eight priors and the gonfaloniere who were officially the rulers of the republic, although Cosimo de'Medici was actually in control), were forced, despite their objections, to carry the pope's litter. In this case we can see Pius II using ritual in order to change the balance of power. In 1515, the Florentine Signoria did not object to carrying the papal litter, but on that occasion the pope was a Florentine, indeed a Medici, Leo X (Trexler, 1980, pp. 311–2; cf. Irvine, 1974 and Salmond, 1974). Leo X was fortunate. His coronation and *possesso* were marked by unusual popular enthusiasm, perhaps because his mother, Clarice Orsini, came from the Roman nobility. Paul III, who came from the noble Roman family of the Farnese, received a similarly warm welcome. Audience participation could modify the meaning of a ritual event.

In short, the same ritual was not the same on different occasions, because the protagonists were different. There were also changes in the system over time. Many of them look relatively insignificant, but over the long term they added up, despite the effort by the masters of ceremonies to keep everything the same, to follow precedent, to play it by the book, 'prout in libro meo', as Grassis put it.[27] Documents had their value for the organisers of papal rituals as well as for their historians. Julius II, for example, asked Grassis to do research into precedents when a rare ritual had to be performed, such as the absolution of the excommunicate Venetians. Did the high-status representatives of Venice have to strip in public? Did they have to be whipped with real force, or was it sufficient for the pope and cardinals to strike them light (or 'ritual') blows?[28] Again, Grassis organised the entry of Leo X into Florence on the model of the entry of Eugenius IV into the same city almost a century earlier. When Charles V was due to enter Rome in state in 1536, Paul III ordered a study to be undertaken of the obvious precedent, Frederick III's entry of 1469.

Despite the concern with precedent, changes did occur. They have not yet received the study that is needed to see whether an underlying pattern will emerge (cf. Prodi (1982), pp. 98f). In 1450, for example, Nicholas V decreed that holy years should occur at fifty-year intervals instead of once a century, while the interval was reduced to twenty-five years by Sixtus IV in 1475. The formal opening of the *porta santa* to inaugurate the holy year was introduced in the fifteenth century (Thurston, 1900, p. 39), while Clement VII established its formal closing in 1525. The Swiss guards were introduced by Julius II. Paul IV created the feast of St Peter's Chair. Sixtus V forbade the customary throwing of money to the crowd at the papal coronation (Pecchiai, 1970). There were also unsuccessful attempts to modify the system which help reveal the forces which maintained it as it was. Alexander VII, for example, tried to cancel the *possesso*, but he allowed himself to be persuaded not to do so. After all, although the pope was the protagonist in these performances, he was not the script-writer or even the producer. Even Julius II seems to have accepted that, as his research into precedents suggests.

Two kinds of change may reasonably be described as structural. The first concerns the relation of ritual to other media. In the very long term, ritual may well have lost some of its functions, notably that of publicity, as a result of the rise of literacy and the rise of print, but what is more obvious in the early modern period is its interaction with the new medium. Print both reinforced and explained the message of the ritual, thanks to the commemorative booklets which were on sale after the event (and perhaps before). Print also had a tendency to change what it recorded; for example, it encouraged a trend towards the increasing codification of ritual, playing it by the book, with the year 1488 marking what was at least a symbolic turning-point, the year when the two masters of ceremonies, Agostino Patrizi Piccolomini, bishop of Pienza, and Burchardus, presented a book of ceremonies to pope Innocent VIII. When in 1517 a certain Marcellus published a version of this book, the irascible Grassis was furious, presumably because this brought private knowledge, on which the status of master of ceremonies depended, into the public domain. However, Grassis was almost equally furious with his predecessor Burchardus for keeping his expertise secret.[29] After Marcellus came a steady flow of treatises on papal ritual, some of them cited in the notes to this chapter. Ultimately print became incorporated into the rituals themselves. Pietro Alaleone, master of ceremonies to Sixtus V, notes on more than one occasion that the pope was 'reading the prayer from our book', or 'reading everything from the book'.[30] By the middle of the seventeenth century, if not before, there were printed forms for cardinals to use when they voted in conclave (in Latin of course); *Ego...cardinalis...eligo in summum pontificem Reverendum Dominum meum Dominum cardinalem...*[31] Certain popes, notably Sixtus V, who set up the committee known as 'the Congregation of Sacred Rites and Ceremonies', and Urban VIII, were actively concerned with the codification of the ritual system.

A second major change over the long term is the trend towards increasing magnificence. Of course the popes started from a rather low baseline on their return from Avignon in the early fifteenth century, but they soon made up for what had been lost and went much further, restructuring the city so that it would enhance the rituals and make them more impressive. Nicholas V, for example, planned the complete rebuilding of St Peter's and also began a programme of road widening after some two hundred people had been crushed to death in the holy year crowds (Magnuson, 1958). Pius II built the 'loggia di benedizione' outside St Peter's. Sixtus IV was responsible for the Sistine Chapel. Julius II had Bramante redesign not only St Peter's but also much of the Vatican (adding, for example, a courtyard for tournaments). Sixtus V's road programme, which has gained him honourable mention in modern histories of 'urbanism' (notably Giedion, 1941), was motivated at least as much by considerations of ritual as by the desire to solve Rome's growing traffic problems. He also had the Vatican rebuilt, and it was in his time that the *possesso* became an elaborate ritual, a 'demonstration of power' (Labrot, 1978, p. 480). The new St Peter's, which was completed at last in the early seventeenth century, was designed on an open plan to make the pope visible to the maximum degree and to allow space for processions. The grand and expensive projects carried out by Bernini for popes Urban VIII and Alexander VII were also intimately related to ritual. The bronze baldacchino, a virtuoso imitation – on a gigantic scale – of the canopy held over the pope on ceremonial occasions, was erected over the altar used by the pope alone to celebrate Mass. The *cathedra Petri* was the throne on which he sat to bless the people after Mass and show himself the true successor of St Peter. The *scala regia* was the staircase which the pope descended on solemn occasions to pass from the Vatican to St Peter's. Piazza San Pietro was a great 'crowd container' for the people who flocked to be blessed at Christmas and Easter, and one function of the famous curving colonnades may have been to enable spectators to keep dry in bad weather (Rietbergen, 1983, ch. 7). Papal ritual came to centre more and more on the Vatican complex as the pope became – like other absolute monarchs, in Spain, France and the Empire – increasingly remote from the people. Where their predecessors had generally participated in Carnival, the popes of the Counter-Reformation (notably Paul IV, Pius V, Gregory XIII and Sixtus V) disapproved of it. Pius V moved Carnival to the Corso to keep it away from holy ground, thus illustrating the trend towards an increasingly sharp separation between sacred and profane. In the early seventeenth century, the private celebrations of cardinals competed for space with the popular Carnival so that a recent writer has referred to the 'annexation' of Carnival (Clemente, 1899; Boiteux, 1977). Changes in language are often good indicators of changes in social relationships. In the middle of the sixteenth century, the conventional mode of referring to the pope, 'most holy father' (*santissimo padre*), was replaced by references to 'his Holiness' (*sua Santità*) or even 'Our Lord' (*Nostro Signore*), a term the masters of ceremonies had used somewhat earlier. The history of papal numismatics suggests a similar change. From Martin V on, the popes came to present themselves and the major events of their reigns by means of medals, which were given away to impress influential contemporaries, or buried in the foundations of buildings to impress posterity.[32]

Ritual, it has been said, is a way of solving problems. The early modern popes were not short of problems. In the fifteenth century, they needed to rebuild their position after the Schism. In the sixteenth and seventeenth centuries, they needed, still more obviously, to respond to the challenge of Protestantism, to the denunciations of Rome as Babylon and the pope as Antichrist. Faced with this challenge, the church did not at first know how to respond. Cardinals gave conflicting advice, popes followed different policies, and the general impression is one of indecision. The hiatus in canonisations, for example, discussed above (p. 49) would seem to indicate a loss of papal nerve. All this changed, however, after the conclusion of the Council of Trent in 1563. After the Council, as a distinguished art historian has pointed out (Mâle, 1951), Catholic art came to emphasise the very themes which had originally provoked the protest of the Protestants. Papal ritual seems to have done the same; the creation, in the mid sixteenth century, of the feast of St Peter's chair, is an obvious example. Lutherans had attacked the arrogance of the pope for allowing his foot to be kissed by princes. The increasing magnificence of papal ritual was a deliberate means of persuasion, a 'polemical instrument' (Labrot, 1978), a visible demonstration of the pope's power and majesty and his link to St Peter and to Christ. There may also have been an element of competition with secular rulers at a time when their magnificence was also increasing. Perhaps we should talk of the 'escalation' of ritual. It was only in the eighteenth century that some popes made the attempt to cut it down (below, p. 237).

The papal monarchy has sometimes been compared to the rule of the Dalai Lama in Tibet. In the wake of Geertz's famous essay on Bali (1980), it is tempting to make this comparison too and to speak of the 'theatre state' of a ruler without the means of physical coercion and without much temporal territory. The phrase is a useful one in that it serves to make the point that, unlike most European rulers (or to a greater extent than they), the pope was efficient because he was dignified. For this reason it is not particularly helpful to ask whether the increasing magnificence of papal ritual in our period reflected an increase in papal power or compensated for a decrease in it. In temporal terms, the pope probably carried less and less weight after the death of the fiery Julius II. In spiritual terms, on the other hand, it may be argued that by the early seventeenth century, the pope had not only recovered the ground lost at the Reformation but actually strengthened his position as a spiritual leader. We have been concerned with the power of symbols as well as with the symbolism of power. Ritual did not so much reflect what was happening as help make it happen. Whether or not it was consciously manipulated to this end, it was politically efficacious.[33]

13
The carnival of Venice

Like the preceding chapter on the popes, this one studies a ritual as a form of communication and examines the way in which it was modified over the centuries. It has been suggested that the whole point of ritual is to abolish history, or to replace linear time, the time of change, by circular time, the time of repetition (Eliade, 1949). Whether or not this is the intention, rituals, including the Carnival of Venice, are not proof against history, as I hope to be able to show.

In order to do this it will be necessary to look at specific carnivals over the very long term, from the thirteenth century to the nineteenth, but the focus will be on the seventeenth and eighteenth centuries. At that time, Venice was as much associated, in foreign eyes, with Carnival as she was with Piazza San Marco, the mixed constitution, or gondolas. Operas on the theme of the Carnival at Venice were performed on French, German and English stages; at Drury Lane in 1781, for example.[1] Carnival was part of the so-called 'myth of Venice', the image of the republic as a uniquely harmonious social and political system (Gaeta, 1961; Logan, 1972, ch. 1). One cynical foreigner hinted that the festival was a trick to distract the people; 'Je pense donc que les Nobles, qui d'ailleurs ne sont pas fort aimez, sont bien aises de trouver quelques moyens adroits, de plaire au peuple et de l'amuser.'[2] One might add that there was also a myth of Carnival as something specially Venetian. This it was not, at least not until the seventeenth century. Before 1600, Carnival was no more characteristic of Venice than of Florence, Rome or Naples, or indeed of cities elsewhere in the Mediterranean region; Montpellier, for example, Barcelona, or Seville. On the periphery of proceedings, the less formally organised events were much the same everywhere. There was the massive eating and drinking, the licence to wear a mask, insult one's neighbour with impunity, pelt him (or her) with eggs, oranges or lemons, and sing songs with double meanings, sexual or political. Of course each city had its local variations on the universal themes of gluttony, sex and violence, and its characteristic central events. In Florence, there was the procession of floats through the streets. In Rome, the races along the Corso. In

Naples, the spoliation of the 'cuccagna', the mountain of food heaped up in front of the viceroy's palace.

As for Venice, here the central events took place in the natural open-air theatre of the Piazzetta, not on Shrove Tuesday, as was generally the case elsewhere, but on the Thursday before Lent, 'Fat Thursday' (*Zuoba Grassa*). The doge, accompanied by senators and foreign ambassadors, watched from the window of his palace as if from a royal box. What they saw has often been described (Muir, 1981, pp. 160f). As a thirteenth-century Venetian chronicler put it, in the earliest surviving account, 'There were pigs, and dogs hunted them...the pigs were captured and taken before the doge...a man came with a naked sword and cut off the pig's heads...the doge gave the carcasses to the noblemen and gentlemen of Venice.[3] In other words, the basic structure of the central ritual consisted of three main elements, a mock-hunt, a mock-execution, and a distribution of food. Nearly a hundred years later, there is a reference to the hunt in Boccaccio's *Decameron* (the second story of the fourth day). In the sixteenth century, there are more references to the hunt, execution, and distribution in the journal of the indefatigable chronicler Marin Sanudo.[4] Sanudo's journal has the great advantage for the historian of recording individual carnivals every year for more than three decades, even if this insider writing for himself may have no more to say than 'there were the usual festivities'. Minor details changed, but the central ritual of execution survived for hundreds of years...In the late seventeenth century, two foreign visitors commented admiringly on the way in which the head of each animal was struck off with a single blow.[5]

In the best tradition of ancient rituals, this one was provided with its etiological myth. For the earliest surviving version of it we are indebted to a foreigner who, like a good outsider, took nothing for granted. Arnold von Harff, a German nobleman who was passing through Venice in 1497 on his way to the holy land, records his question to a Venetian patrician about the execution of the twelve pigs and a bull, together with the reply. 'He told me that near Venice there was a country called Friuli, which was ruled by a patriarch...', and went on to explain that the patriarch had attacked Venice, that he had been defeated and captured, and that the animals, which were sent to Venice every year as tribute, represented him and his twelve canons. The standard sixteenth-century guide-book to Venice tells the same story with the addition of the patriarch's name, Ulrich, and the date, the middle of the twelfth century.[6] It is too bad that the pigs are not recorded before 1222, or the bull before 1312 (Kretschmayr, 1905, p. 251).

There was of course more to Carnival than this central ritual. By the sixteenth century, if not before, a number of less formal events had come to cluster around it. This 'semi-periphery', as it might be called, included chasing bulls through the streets, riding at the ring on Campo San Stefano (the biggest open space after Piazza San Marco), and the production of pageants on different themes. These 'triumphs' (*trionfi*) as Sanudo calls them included giants and nymphs (1527); a combat between four young men and four 'wild men' (1529); a devil tempting a pilgrim (1531); and a combat between Wisdom and Ignorance (1532), Ignorance being seated on an ass 'with its tail in his hand'. Among these traditional medieval themes the Renaissance pageant of 1528, featuring Neptune, Mars, Mercury and other gods, stands out as somewhat unusual. However, it was not to be the only one of this kind; in 1587, for example, there was a pageant, or masque, of Venus and the planets. As a background to these shows one needs to imagine singing, dancing (including sword-dances), plays, banquets and balls in the palaces of patricians, and the sound of fifes and trumpets by day and by night; all this is recorded in Sanudo. Further towards the periphery were a number of other events such as boat races along the Grand Canal and bull races across the bridge at the Rialto.

Still further towards the periphery, not to say on the fringe, were a number of less formal happenings both on and off Piazza San Marco, which were spread over the whole Carnival season, which went from the feast of St Stephen on 26 December till Shrove Tuesday. Participants generally wore masks (to which there is a reference as early as 1268), and they frequently wore fancy dress. A young Englishman who was in Venice in the 1660s noticed 'thousands of masquerades walking for the most part about the piazza of St Mark'.[7] The repertoire of costumes was a limited one, though it tended to grow over the centuries. Boccaccio refers to people dressing as bears or wild men. In the early sixteenth century, there are references to women dressing as men, and to people dressed as members of flagellant fraternities, or as doges and their attendants.[8] From the later sixteenth century on, it became increasingly fashionable to choose masks from the *commedia dell'arte* and the streets of Venice filled with varieties of the boastful soldier (Capitano), the heavy father (Magnifico), the pedant (Gratiano), and the various kinds of comic servant (Zanne, Harlequin, Pulcinella, and so on). Other common figures were kings, beggars, peasants, madmen, Turks, and Jews, portrayed with long noses and sometimes weeping.[9] Foreign visitors were impressed by the way in which the maskers, despite their numbers, not only dressed but also acted out their roles.[10]

What did it all mean? It is tempting to interpret not only the personification of Carnival but also the bear and the wild man as symbols of nature (as opposed to culture) or the id (as opposed to the ego), for in Venice, as elsewhere, this season was perceived as a time of 'universal liberty' or 'universal madness'.[11] It was, to quote the title of one of Goldoni's plays, 'the world turned upside down (*Il mondo allo roverso*). According to a seventeenth-century description, in verse, by a citizen of Venice, 'A porter dresses up as a knight, and a gentleman as a baker...a plebeian woman puts on the airs of a lady, while a countess turns herself into a peasant'.[12] This is of course an old literary commonplace which goes back to ancient Greece or even beyond, but it is or was more than that, at any rate during the Carnival. For example, the sumptuary laws were suspended, and the courtesans appeared 'decked with jewels as if they were queens'.[13] Gambling in public, normally forbidden, was now permissible. It was possible to dress up as the doge, or to mock the Venetian way of life, clothes, and frugality ('their customs, their habit, and misery') to their faces ('unto their very noses').[14] Pasquinades (*pasquils*, as John Evelyn calls them) were legitimate and a Venetian's house ceased to be his castle, 'all places being then accessible and free to enter'.[15] Carnival was a time of licence; licence not only to overeat and drink and indulge sexually before the abstinence of Lent, but also to engage in acts of ritualised aggression. One of the most attractive sources for the history of the Carnival of Venice, a collection of engravings with commentary, mentions and illustrates the 'scented eggs' (*ovi odoriferi*), that it was customary to throw at this time. One wonders whether personal experience lay behind John Evelyn's wry comment about 'flinging of eggs filled with sweet water, and sometimes not over sweet'. The invaluable Skippon also noticed that 'some had baskets of eggs attending on them, which they threw at those that looked out of their windows. Some of the egg shells are filled with rose-water to throw at their friends, and some are fill'd with ink.'[16] Violence could be real as well as symbolic. An English visitor of the late sixteenth century records seventeen deaths on one day.[17] In the eighteenth century there were night patrols in each parish during the carnival season, presumably to reduce disorder (Georgelin, 1978, p. 806, n. 10).

Of course historians must not allow themselves to be deceived into taking the myth of Carnival for the reality. It is unlikely that many porters could afford to dress as nobles; in any case the source for this piece of information is a poem about Carnival, which was part of the festivities, not a detached account of it. Foreign travellers may have tried to describe exactly what they saw, but every description is in part an interpretation, and outsiders were in no position to tell whether a particular woman was a respectable lady or a courtesan, let alone who exactly was inside a mask. No wonder they disagree. During Carnival, a French traveller claims, 'les gentilles Donnes rompent leurs fers, et ont la liberté de se faire voire en public, de masquer, et se recontrer aux Bals et aux Assemblées'.[18] An Englishman, on the other hand, assures us that 'Wives and daughters are seldom permitted to go in masquerade unless accompanied by their husbands and parents or other trusty person to watch over them'.[19] It is clear that there were considerable differences in carnival behaviour, which probably varied with the period and also with different social groups. One can only regret that the fragmentary sources do not allow a full historical ethnography of Carnival to be written. What the fragments do suggest, though, is that Carnival was a time of relative licence, a time of mounting excitement, a time which was perceived as one of 'universal liberty' by the participants, who seem to have had a sense of power, of impunity, of (almost) everything being permitted. As one sixteenth-century song put it, 'Carnival makes me potent' (*Carneval me fa possente*).[20]

Carnival did not please everyone. The devout, the prudish and those responsible for public order (including the famous Council of Ten), all had their reasons for discomfort on the arrival of the festive season. Many attempts were made to limit 'excesses' on particular occasions, or over the long term. Some of these attempts were associated with the Counter-Reformation. Carlo Borromeo, who did his best to reform Carnival in his diocese of Milan, had his followers in Venice. The Jesuit Robert Bellarmine, who preached in Venice during the festive season of 1567 or thereabouts, and denounced the dances and other 'follies', claims that his sermon was well received, indeed that a number of senators tried to kiss his hand afterwards.[21] In 1581 the Council of Ten voted by a narrow majority to prohibit plays altogether. The reformers were particularly opposed to clerical participation in the festivities; in 1616, for example, the prior of ca'di Dio was fined for holding the 'customary' masked ball (Howard, 1975, p. 118). However, the reformers were far from having everything their own way. As late as 1663, Skippon records seeing women dressed in priest's cassocks. More effective in the long run, although harder to characterise with any precision, was a change in the attitude of the ruling class. Sanudo, for example, expressed his disapproval of the maskers who dressed up as the doge and his attendants. At much the same time, a traditional carnival dance, the *tripudio*, was abolished because the government found it indecorous. In 1561, the author of a guide to Venice expressed a certain embarrassment over the execution of the pigs on the piazza.²² In 1594, they were replaced by bulls. Venetian patricians seem to have acquired a new or sharper sense of decorum. In the thirteenth century the doge could wear his crown and look with pleasure at people hunting pigs across the Piazzetta, but in the late sixteenth century he apparently could not. The bodies of the animals had formerly been given to the nobility, as one of the three annual redistributions of food by the doge; but in the early modern period, the carcasses were sent to the monasteries or to the prisons. The executioners, once esquires, were now blacksmiths or butchers. The patriciate seem to have been distancing themselves from certain carnival activities, abandoning them to 'the people'.

Conscious attempts to make Carnival more decorous had a mixed success. However, other important changes took place in the early modern period, changes which may be summed up in a single word; commercialisation. More and more tourists came to Venice to see the Carnival and the festival became more and more a spectacle for the tourists.

I use the word 'tourist' deliberately, although it is a modern term, because the influx of visitors into Venice was already a mass movement at the end of the Middle Ages, when Venice was a major port of embarkation for pilgrims to the Holy Land, who tended, like Arnold von Harff, to see the sights of Venice while waiting for a favourable wind. By the fifteenth century it is possible to find touts who pushed the unwary into particular inns; official guides on duty at the Rialto and Piazza San Marco to interpret for foreigners and help them change money; and conducted tours of the Arsenal, glass-making at Murano, and the Doge's Palace (if you were lucky, you could get a view of the doge's bed).²³ In the early sixteenth century, a Norfolk parson was recognised as an Englishman as soon as he arrived in Venice, and addressed in English.²⁴ By the seventeenth century there were professional guides or *ciceroni* who took foreigners round the picture collections of the city.

The tourists were naturally interested in the festivals and the Venetians made it easy for them to participate or at least to observe. In the late fifteenth century, for example, it was possible to hire a boat to follow the doge's barge and witness the ritual of the Wedding of the Sea.²⁵ In the middle of the sixteenth century, Sansovino's guide to Venice lists the main festivals. It is therefore hardly surprising to find foreigners coming to Venice for the Carnival. An engraving of 1610, showing charlatans plying their trade on Piazza San Marco, has inscriptions identifying the bystanders as 'Greek', 'Turkish', 'French', 'Spanish', and 'English'.[26] Skippon thought it worthy of comment that 'one day there were 5 or 6 French officers richly habited, who came to see Venice and the Carnival, but were more gazed at than any of the maskers'.[27] Evelyn, on the other hand, declared that 'all the world repairs to Venice' for the Carnival season, and other visitors of the late seventeenth century tell the same story. 'On y vient... de toutes parts; et les plus grandes villes d'Italie sont désertes et perdent leur plus beau monde pour s'y rendre.'[28] 'Les étrangers et les courtisannes accourent par milliers à Venise... On m'assure qu'au dernier Carnaval il y avait sept princes souverains et plus de 30,000 autres Etrangers.'[29] One does not have to take this figure, based on hearsay, too seriously, but the impression of large numbers of visitors should count for something. In 1740, Lady Mary Wortley Montagu complained of the 'inundations' of her fellow-countrymen who 'broke in upon us this carnival'.[30] Eighteen foreign princes are recorded to have visited Venice during the Carnival between 1686 and 1791 (Georgelin, 1978, p. 701).

The influx of visitors turned Venice into a city of leisure and pleasure (Gaeta, 1961). 'Venice is the place in the world where pleasure is most studied', wrote Gilbert Burnet in 1686; it was 'the center of Pleasure', according to Lady Mary Wortley Montagu, in 1760.[31] One indicator of the increasing importance of this function of the city is the number of people employed in catering for visitors. In 1642, 2,818 heads of household (19% of the working population) were employed in inns. In Verona, on the main road to Venice, there were only five innkeepers in 1502, but there were twenty-seven in 1616 (Beltrami, 1954, p. 209; Mączak, 1978, p. 72). Another indicator of the importance of the tourist trade is the multiplication of guidebooks.[32]

This influx of tourists altered the festival they had come to see, making it more professional and more commercial. In the early sixteenth century, professional entertainers – actors like Cherea, clowns like Zanpolo, acrobats like Battistin – were involved in the public festivities, subsidised by the Council of Ten, as well as putting on shows in private houses. In the seventeenth and eighteenth centuries, however, the evidence for the activities of a variety of professionals becomes overwhelming. There were the charlatans or mountebanks (below, ch. 15); the puppets; the rope-dancers and other acrobats; the fortune-tellers; and the fireworks. Public gambling became a business and took place in special *ridotti*, the Venetian ancestors of the modern casino. Animals were shown to the public for a fee; the rhinoceros of 1751 (painted by Longhi) was particularly famous. The theatre, private and largely amateur in the early sixteenth century, became public, professional, and commercial. By 1580 there were two permanent theatres in Venice, despite the opposition of the moralists. In the seventeenth century, the theatre was overtaken by the opera; the first opera house opened in 1637 and was a great success. By the end of the century, 358 operas are known to have been performed, while in the eighteenth century there were 1274 more (Wiel, 1897; cf. Worsthorne, 1954). Theatre made its comeback in the age of Goldoni. In the late eighteenth century, there were seven theatres in Venice: 'one for the serious opera, two for comic operas, and four play-houses...they are all full every night'.[33] The Carnival season was too short for the visitors and those who stood to profit from their visits; it had to be extended. So the theatres now opened in May for the festival of the Ascension, 'a kind of summer Carnival, which lasts for six weeks', and they had a third season in the autumn.[34] The real Carnival came to incorporate formerly independent events, notably the annual battle or 'fist war' (*guerra de'pugni*) between the rival parishes of the Castellani and Nicolotti which was now put on for important visitors, who might lay bets on the outcome.[35] It might even be exported, as it was to Parma for the wedding of the prince in 1690.[36] The 'staged authenticity', as one American sociologist calls it (McCannell, 1976), which is to be found in so many modern centres of tourism, goes back as far as the seventeenth century in Venice. Commercialisation was accompanied by homogenisation. The standardised side-shows multiplied at the expense of what was specially Venetian. A guide-book of 1740 mentions the mock-execution on Piazza San Marco only as an afterthought.[37] The periphery had invaded the centre, and the meaning of the festival had completely changed. When the traditional centrepiece disappeared in 1797, with the fall of the Republic, it made little real difference.

14
The virgin of the Carmine
and the
revolt of Masaniello

This chapter has two aims. The more specific one is to contribute to the understanding of one of the most spectacular of the 'revolutions' of seventeenth-century Europe. Despite the fundamental researches of Michelangelo Schipa (1913), for example, of Rosario Villari (1967), and others such as Comparato (1974), the last word on the revolt of 1647 is very far from being said. The more general purpose is to contribute to an understanding of that revolt by looking at the ritual elements in it and what they were supposed to communicate.

The traditional view of popular violence as 'blind fury', signifying nothing, a Pavlovian response to hunger or the expression of an urge towards disorder, is far from dead (Mousnier, 1967). However, it has been challenged a number of times in recent decades, and it is now commonplace to point out that this popular violence is often the organised – and ritualised – expression of particular aims, and also that it has a calendar of its own, and tends to occur at the time of major festivals, of which it is in some sense the extension (Thompson, 1971; Davis, 1973; Reddy, 1977). Beyond this point, consensus among the challengers begins to break down. The scholars who have revised traditional views of popular revolts have drawn their concepts from two rival sociological traditions, that of Emile Durkheim and that of Karl Marx. Some, like Thompson (1978), stress class conflict, others, like Bercé (1974) and Pillorget (1975), emphasise community cohesion. What is needed now is a synthesis, as opposed to an unstable compound, of these opposing elements. To this synthesis a study of Naples in 1647 may have something to offer.

It should be emphasised from the start that this 'ritualistic' interpretation of the revolt of Masaniello is not intended to sweep away but to complement the received account, lucidly summarised by Elliott (1970). It would be difficult to deny that the 'precipitants' or 'triggers' of the Naples revolt were, as he put it, 'rising food prices, dearth and taxes', notably the taxes on flour, fruit and vegetables levied to pay for the Spanish military contribution to the Thirty Years War, then in its final phase. It would be equally hard to deny that the 'preconditions' of the revolt included social and economic grievances, such as the increasing demands which aristocratic landlords were making on their peasants so as to pay for their increasingly conspicuous consumption in the city of Naples (above, p. 146). Many of these peasants themselves fled to Naples to escape the demands, and will be found among the followers of Masaniello.

Although the distinction between 'preconditions' and 'precipitants', in other words long-term and short-term factors, is a useful one, the 'behavioural science' language of 'precipitants' and 'triggers' (characteristic of American political science in the 1950s), is both inhuman and deterministic. It too smacks of the Pavlovian response. It does, not, in the specific case of Naples, come to terms with the charisma of the young fisherman who began the revolt, his mythic quality, his appeal both to the people of Naples and the intellectuals of a number of European countries, including England, France and the Netherlands.[1] Hence the behavioural approach needs to be complemented, if at all possible, by some discussion of what might be called the culture of the crowd, in other words the hopes and fears, feelings and thoughts of the rebels, who seem to have included many of the ordinary people of Naples.

But is such a discussion possible? Is the evidence full or reliable enough? If the feelings and thoughts of ordinary Neapolitans of this period can be reconstructed at all, it can only be by a process of 'reading' collective actions, and showing that what appeared to others as a blind fury, signifying nothing, really did have a meaning for the participants. Such a process of reading is what will be attempted here. The actions to be studied are those of the first ten days of the revolt, 7–16 July 1647, when Masaniello was the leader; and, to a lesser degree, the second revolt, from 21 August onwards. The later stages, after the French intervened in December, melt into the international power struggle between Habsburgs and Bourbons, and reveal much less about popular attitudes. Hence the so-called 'royal republic' of 1648, despite its great historical interest, will not be discussed.

More than twenty contemporary narratives of the 1647 revolt have survived. So far as the sequence of events is concerned, the most reliable accounts are the reports of three diplomats (the representatives of Florence, Venice and Genoa), who wrote home while the rising was in progress, before they knew what the outcome would be.[2] The letters from the archbishop of Naples to the pope have the same advantages of being uncontaminated by hindsight.[3] Of the remaining narratives, the best known is that of Alessandro Giraffi, published in 1647, and translated into

English – political conditions being favourable to an account of a popular revolution – three years later.[4] Of the remainder, the pro-Spanish accounts by De Sanctis, Nicolai and Tontoli all contain material relevant to my purpose, like the more neutral 'Liponari' (an obvious pseudonym).[5] However, the accounts which are richest in what might be called 'ethnographic detail' are two anti-Spanish accounts, both, as it happens, by physicians; one by Giuseppe Donzelli, which was published in 1647, but suppressed by the authorities when they regained control of the city; and another by Angelo Della Porta, which has never been published at all.[6]

The limitations of these narrative sources for our purpose need emphasis. Some of the authors wrote to rehabilitate the authorities and so to disparage or 'delegitimate' the revolt. All of the authors belonged to dominant groups, noble or professional, and they perceived these 'tumults' (to use one of their favourite words), like Professor Mousnier, more or less in terms of blind fury. It must also be remembered that these writers worked within the conventions of a Renaissance–baroque historiographical tradition which, like the classical tradition from which it largely derived, was organised around the idea of the 'dignity of history'. Like epic and tragedy, history was a literary genre of high status, a genre which required its practitioners to choose a noble subject and to write about it in the high style, omitting vulgar words and things. As the literary critic Erich Auerbach pointed out in a famous study of Tacitus and Ammianus Marcellinus (1947), these classical conventions did not allow historians to find sense in, or make sense of, the actions of 'low' people. The patrician conspiracy of Catiline found a historian, but the slave revolt of Spartacus did not. There were similar rules for painters of 'histories', who were also supposed to choose noble subjects and present them in a dignified manner.

These conventions were still very much alive in 1647. Indeed, they had recently been reiterated, in an Italian context, by Agostino Mascardi, professor of rhetoric at the Jesuit Collegio Romano, and Mascardi had already practised what he was preaching in an account of the Fieschi conspiracy at Genoa which was modelled on Sallust's account of Catiline.[7] The very existence of Masaniello was a challenge to these conventions, a challenge to which some contemporary painters responded (Saxl, 1939–40; Haskell, 1963, p. 139). The historians, on the whole, did not. The Genoese patrician Raffaello Della Torre, for example, wrote a Latin history of the revolt of Naples in which he did his best to assimilate it to Catiline's conspiracy.[8] As for the writers already mentioned, they give an

impression of not knowing quite what to do with their subject. They were
unsure whether to treat the revolt as a 'tragedy' or a 'tragicomedy' (the
latter term being used not because the story ended well but because its
protagonist was of low status).[9] They could not make up their minds
whether Masaniello was the real leader, or merely a puppet manipulated
by the lawyer Genoino; and whether the people played an active or a
passive role. Some of the metaphors used to describe the actions of the
people are revealing. For archbishop Filomarino, the people 'boiled' like
some liquid. For Giraffi, they resembled a thoroughbred horse which
resisted saddle and bridle.[10] Donzelli presented the revolt as 'the heroic
decision of the people of Naples to free themselves from the unbearable
yoke of the Spaniards', but the equally anti-Spanish Della Porta stressed
the inconstancy of the people, their passivity until worked on by 'those
who fomented the tumult', and finally their 'strange madness' when
aroused. Although he approved of the aims of the rebels, he perceived
their actions as 'stravaganze', in other words as irrational.[11]

Despite their dependence on these traditional schemata, some of the
contemporary accounts of the revolt are so detailed in their descriptions
of popular action as to make possible an alternative interpretation of the
same events, against the grain of the texts. This alternative interpretation
will be couched in terms of 'social drama'. The anthropologist Victor
Turner, who launched the phrase, distinguished (1957) four phases in
such dramas; breach, crisis, redressive action and reintegration. The
history of Naples in the mid seventeenth century could no doubt be
discussed in terms of all four phases, but this chapter is concerned only
with the phase of redressive action. My division of the revolt into four
acts does not correspond to Turner's. The theatrical metaphor,
incidentally, would not have displeased the Neapolitans, who lived in a
society where it was necessary 'fare bella figura' (above, p. 10). Contemporary references to the 'tragedy' of Masaniello have been quoted
already, while a seventeenth-century history of the viceroys of Naples was
entitled, in best baroque style, the 'theatre' of their actions.[12]

Before the curtain goes up on this play, it may be useful to say a few
words about the setting. Naples in 1647 was one of the largest cities in
Europe, with some 300,000 inhabitants. It was a busy port with a
considerable population of fishermen, sailors and stevedores. There was
also a substantial silk-weaving industry, and a university with perhaps as
many as 5,000 students. Naples was also the seat of the viceregal court
and so a city where the upper nobility congregated, living in huge palaces
and surrounded by swarms of servants. As the administrative and legal

capital of a kingdom of 3,000,000 people, the city also contained many lawyers and officials. However, there was not sufficient employment in the city for all the immigrants who came to it from the surrounding countryside, 'pushed' by the need to escape the demands of landlords and tax-collectors, and 'pulled' by the twin attractions of cheap food and fiscal privilege (Petraccone, 1974; Romano, 1976).

Tommaso Campanella, a Calabrian who had lived in Naples and perceived it as the disorderly converse of his orderly utopia the *City of the Sun* suggested, earlier in the seventeenth century, that of the city's 300,000 inhabitants, no more than 50,000 worked.[13] He probably exaggerated, but there is little doubt that by the middle of the century the upper classes were becoming increasingly aware of the problem of the so-called *lazzari*, able-bodied but idle men who could be seen sleeping in the streets by day as well as by night (above, p. 16); it was at this time that the term *lazzari* was coined (Migliorini, 1960, p. 492).[14] What gave these people a particularly high profile was the fact that some zones of the city, around Piazza del Mercato, Piazzo del Lavinaro and Piazzo della Sellaria, were essentially popular quarters, overcrowded by the middle of the century, with 'high rise' developments not far away and shacks and huts erected on Piazza del Mercato itself (de'Seta, 1973, p. 268).[15]

'The People is a huge and inconstant animal which does not know its own strength', wrote Campanella, who had himself tried to mobilise it against Spain in 1599 – without success.[16] The implication, that ordinary people, in Naples and elsewhere, lacked a common consciousness, is of course highly relevant to the central theme of this chapter. Campanella's point was not often made in this period, and it is probably no accident that it came from a friar of peasant stock. Upper-class observers generally found the people of Naples all too prone to rebel. 'The populace (*plebe*) is like Cerberus', wrote one (as Pavlovian as it was possible to be in the seventeenth century), 'and to stop it barking it is necessary to fill it with bread' (quoted in Comparato, 1974, p. 418). In similar vein the town clerk, writing early in the century, declared that 'Every popular tumult and every rising in this city is the work of this canaille [*questa canaglia*], for whom there is no cure but the gallows.'[17] By distinguishing respectable *popolo* from seditious *plebe*, he was offering a kind of class interpretation of the many rebellions in Neapolitan history. He was thinking, no doubt, of the 1510 rising against the Inquisition; of the second rising against the Inquisition, in 1547, led by a certain Masaniello, and, above all, of the events of 1585.

The year 1585 was one of famine. At this time, Naples was administered by six *eletti*, in other words elected officials, five representing the nobility and one the people. The representative of the people, Giovanni Vicenzo Starace (or Storace) by name, was made the scapegoat for the famine and the policies of the government, and following a public meeting he was lynched. The victim was carried to the place of 'execution' hatless and facing backwards as though undergoing a *charivari*, and his corpse was later dragged through the streets in the ritual of 'drawing' a dead criminal. The meaning of these rituals of popular justice will be obvious enough (Villari, 1967, pp. 42–6; cf. Muir, 1984).[18]

Notorious for disorder since Roman times, Naples was also celebrated for its religious devotion, especially popular devotion. There would be abundant evidence of this popular devotion during the Jesuit mission of 1651, and still more during the plague of 1656 (above, p. 11; below, p. 206). Devotion focused on San Gennaro, the most important of the city's eight patron saints, whose blood liquefied regularly on his feast-day as a sign of his concern for his people, and it also focused on the Virgin Mary, especially the Virgin of the Carmine, in other words the church of the Carmelite friars on the corner of Piazza del Mercato. This church contained a miracle-working image of the Virgin which was dark in colour and was at some point given the affectionate nicknames of 'Maria la Bruna' (Brown Mary) and 'Mamma Schiavona', a reference to the Slavs, especially the Dalmatians (Doria, 1971, pp. 104–5).[19]

Naples in 1647 experienced a long hot summer of tension. Palermo had risen against Spanish rule on 20 May, and the *gabelle* (fruit tax) was abolished there the next day. By June news of this event had reached Naples, and on the 6th, the feast of the Ascension, there was an attack on the tax office on Piazza del Mercato. Several sources refer to the effect on the Neapolitans of the Sicilian example and of remarks like 'Aren't we as good as Palermo?' (*Siamo noi da meno da Palermo?*).[20] A number of placards (*cartelli*) offering 'extremely pungent' criticisms of the government appeared on walls, alarming the viceroy, the Duke of Arcos. Here as elsewhere in Europe the authorities viewed festivals as occasions of potential disorder, and in late June the cavalcade customary on the feast of St John the Baptist (which was usually celebrated in the popular quarter of the Sellaria) was called off by the archbishop, Cardinal Ascanio Filomarino, for fear of riots.[21]

However, in July two major feasts of the Virgin Mary were due to be celebrated, Sta Maria della Grazia on the 7th and Sta Maria del Carmine on the 16th. At this dangerous time, the Carmine area was a particularly dangerous place, for religious, economic and political fields of force (emanating from the miraculous image, the fruit market and the tax office), happened to intersect on Piazza del Mercato. At a highly charged moment such as a festival, a festival moreover, following the imposition of an unpopular tax on food, these three elements formed a potentially explosive combination – and an explosion there certainly was.

For the feast of the Virgin of the Carmine it was the custom to erect a castle of wood covered with painted paper in the middle of Piazza del Mercato and to besiege it in a mock battle, or ritual battle, between young men armed with fruit and sticks, watched by a crowd. Such battles and sieges were common items in Italian festivals at this time, and indeed as late as the nineteenth century. The mock-battle was organised in this case, as in so many others, by a festive society composed of young men from the quarter. Some of them dressed 'like Moors' (*alla moresca*) and blackened their faces, thus gaining the group the nickname of the 'Arabs' (*la compagnia degli Alarbi*). Some sources suggest that 400 young men were involved and that the leaders met in the hostelry of the Buffalo.[22] Prominent in the group was a fisherman in his twenties, who lived on Piazza del Mercato and had recently had a brush with the tax authorities, who had imprisoned his wife for attempting to smuggle flour. He had only a few days to live, but his name, and indeed his appearance as well, was soon to be known all over Europe: Masaniello. It was the same name as that of the leader of the 1547 revolt, a coincidence which may have given him ideas.

Whether Masaniello, or anyone else, planned revolt before 7 July, as some sources assert, we shall probably never know for certain. Perhaps he created his opportunity; perhaps he merely seized it. It is possible that there was a grey eminence beside him from the first; he was certainly joined very quickly by Giulio Genoino, a lawyer who had long before made himself the spokesman of the demands of 'the people' (in other words, the wealthier commoners), for parity with the nobles in municipal government.[23]

Just as it is impossible to say for certain who started the revolt, so it is difficult to give an exact account of what happened during those July days, despite the variety of sources, because these sources often contradict one another about the order of events. Yet the main sequence of this social drama is clear enough, and it is this sequence which will be studied here in the attempt to illuminate popular attitudes. It may be useful to divide the drama into four acts.

Act 1. Sunday 7 July was a feast of the Virgin Mary. There was a mock-battle in Piazza del Mercato – perhaps a rehearsal for the festival on the 16th – and there was also a dispute in the market over the distribution of the burden of the new fruit tax. Somehow or other the two happenings merged into one, whether or not this was planned in advance. The tax office and its records were burned, a proceeding so common in fiscal revolts from the Middle Ages onwards that it might reasonably be described as part of a ritual. There were equally predictable shouts of 'Long Live the King of Spain' and 'Death to Misrule' (*Muoia il Malgoverno*), the language to be expected whenever this particular scene was played. There were also shouts, more distinctively Neapolitan, perhaps, of 'Long Live God' and 'Long Live the Virgin of the Carmine'. It was at this point that Masaniello emerged as leader, carrying a tavern sign as a banner. 'In the twinkling of an eye, thousands and thousands of common people joined him'.[24] There was an attack on a flour store and a march on the palace of the viceroy by a crowd, some armed with sticks (perhaps the 'Arabs'), while others carried pikes with loaves on the points, a traditional gesture of ritualised aggression in protest against the price of bread. It was said at the time that 50,000 people took part in the march; the figure cannot of course be trusted, but it testifies to the impression made on the bystanders. There were demands for the abolition of the taxes on fruit and bread. The rebels won a bloodless victory, for the viceroy fled without offering resistance, leaving his palace to be sacked by the crowd. The mock-battle had certainly turned serious; a ritual of conflict had turned into a real riot. On the other hand, it might reasonably be argued that protest had so far taken a fairly light-hearted, festive form (in any typology of popular revolt, it might be useful to distinguish those which start in this way from those which do not). Since aggression was ritualised, it was kept under control (cf. Fox, 1977, and Marsh, 1978). Violence was largely symbolic. Popular action was neither blind nor furious.

Act II. The authorities – viceroy and bishop – now tried to restore order. The principal means adopted was that of religious rituals. The archbishop had the blessed sacrament exposed, together with the blood and the head of San Gennaro. The Dominicans, Franciscans, Carmelites, Jesuits and Theatines all came out in procession. At the viceroys's request, the prince of Bisignano, who had the reputation of being a friend of the people, appeared on Piazza del Mercato with a crucifix in his hand and spoke to the crowd from the pulpit of the Carmine, asking them to calm down, for the love of God and the Virgin. To readers more familiar with the Protestant world, this use of religious symbols such as the crucifix and the blessed sacrament as a means of crowd control may seem somewhat odd, but it was not at all unusual in Italy (as in Spain) at this time. In Naples in 1585, for instance, when the crowd began to loot houses, the Jesuits appeared with a crucifix, presumably because the normal reaction to that symbol would be to stop what one was doing and kneel down.[25] Again, in Palermo in 1647, a crowd went to burn the house of the Marchese del Flores, but were headed off by Carmelites carrying the sacrament. They set out for the house of the duke of La Montagna instead, but were intercepted by Theatines, again carrying the sacrament, and ringing bells to encourage reverence. The next day, crucifixes, relics and sacrament had again to be pressed into service to quell a riot.[26]

The people, for their part, believed that God and the saints and the Virgin of the Carmine were on their side. The crowd turned back the procession of the Jesuits, and an attempt was even made to capture a crucifix carried by the Dominicans.[27] Later in the revolt a crowd would succeed in capturing a silver image of St Anthony of Padua, saying that they had 'liberated' him from the Spaniards, who had, according to them, imprisoned him because he was Portuguese; a reference which is interesting because it reveals popular awareness of the Portuguese revolt against Philip IV.[28] One is reminded of the dispute which broke out in Naples in 1646 over the route which the relics of San Gennaro were to take in procession, a dispute which culminated in the archbishop's angry assertion that 'the relics were his, and the city had no part in them' (*le reliquie esser sue, e la città non aver parte in esse*).[29]

That the question, 'whose relics?' should have been such a topical and such a controversial one in Naples at this time may tell us something important about the mentality of both clergy and laity, upper classes and ordinary people. It was important to have the support of heavenly patrons (above, ch. 5). During the revolt, small children could be seen licking the floor of the church of the Carmine, in a traditional gesture of self-abasement still practised in South Italy by those who solicit supernatural help (Rossi, 1971, pp. 20, 92, 256–7, and p. 210 below).[30] Masaniello's proclamations carried the image of the Virgin of the Carmine. Coins struck by the rebels bore the image of San Gennaro. In the church of the Carmine, over a hundred witnesses (so we are told) shared a vision of San Gennaro holding a sword, presumably in defence of his people.[31] Thus the main happenings in the streets of Naples in 1647 had their reflections or counterparts in the supernatural world.

Act III. Another act in the social drama began when Masaniello mounted the stage on Piazza del Mercato (a literal stage, erected for the use of

popular entertainers), to call out the civic guard. It was at this point that
a more or less spontaneous riot was transformed into an organised revolt,
based no longer on a youth group or crowd but on the local militia, and
so involving respectable craftsmen and shopkeepers. The Florentine
envoy believed that there were now 150,000 people under arms, a quite
implausible number – in a population of some 300,000 – but a sign, like
other exaggerated figures, of the extent to which contemporaries were
impressed by the scale of the participation.[32] The militia was organised
on the basis of the twenty-nine wards (or *ottine*, as they were called in
Naples), and summoned by the ringing of the bells of the Carmine, San
Agostino (headquarters of the official representatives of the *popolo*), and
other churches.

According to some witnesses, this was no ordinary militia, or more
exactly, it included some extraordinary recruits. Women were reported
to have been seen marching under their own captains, ensigns and
sergeants (*capitanesse*, *alfieresse*, *sargentesse*), armed, according to some,
with spits and shovels, but according to others, with arquebuses and
halberds.[33] How seriously should we take the accounts of these 'Ama-
zons', as one contemporary called them? With at least one pinch of salt.
The work of Natalie Davis (1975) and of other historians in her wake
(such as Dekker, 1982, pp. 51–60) has taught us to be alert for signs of
female participation in popular revolts, and Naples (although, like the rest
of southern Italy, a stronghold of *machismo*), seems to have been no
exception in this respect. According to the Genoese envoy, 'many
women' had lobbied the viceroy about the new taxes a few days before
the revolt broke out, and women are also recorded to have burned down
the civic pawnshop, or Monte di Pietà.[34]

On the other hand, there are reasons for suspecting that the militia-
women may be a myth. The suggestion that they carried shovels and spits,
not implausible in itself, has overtones of the carnivalesque kitchen-battles
in Italian popular literature; so, for that matter, does the tavern sign
under which Masaniello is supposed to have rallied his men, and the
mountebanks' stage on which he mounted. These accounts would appear
to have been stylised, consciously or unconsciously, according to the
paradigm of the 'world turned upside down' (Cocchiara, 1963). It is also
possible that the halbardiers were men dressed as women; we are told of
a man who dressed in this way during the revolt.[35] But even this
testimony may reflect the upside-down paradigm. We can only approach
the revolt through contemporary perceptions of it, but we cannot afford
to forget that perceptions are influenced by cultural stereotypes.

What were the aims of the rebels at this stage? The best evidence is probably the 'hit list' of some sixty palaces on which attacks were planned. Their owners were leading collaborators with the Spanish administration (Cennamo and the Caraffa brothers, for instance), and leading financiers, such as Bartolomeo d'Aquino, Felice Basile and Geronimo da Letizia, who were heavily involved with the tax system.[36] Even hostile witnesses record that the sacking of these palaces was carried out in a relatively orderly manner. Religious images were spared and private looting was punished. What was found in the palaces was either destroyed or given to the poor. In other words, the attacks enacted a ritual, in the sense of stereotyped sequence of actions with a function which was primarily symbolic. The point of the operation seems to have been to make manifest a sense of exploitation, a sense that 'these goods are our blood' (*queste robbe sono il sangue nostro*).[37]

In this shift in the social basis of the revolt from festive society to the militia, and perhaps from the 'plebs' to the more respectable 'people', the necessary continuity was provided by the Virgin. The viceroy swore to an agreement with the people in the name of God and the Virgin of the Carmine. The failure of an attempt to assassinate Masaniello by shooting at him with an arquebus was seen as a miracle of the Virgin of the Carmine whose scapular he, like many Neapolitans, was wearing.

The attempted assassination also set off a more violent reaction, which reveals something about the mentality of the crowd. The would-be assassins, and the Caraffa brothers, were killed, and these killings were surrounded by rituals of popular justice reminiscent of the killing of Starace in 1585. The corpses were 'drawn' through the streets and pelted with rubbish. The severed heads were placed on pikes and taken round the city to the sound of drums (presumably the drums of the militia). One head was displayed with a crown of 'false gold' on it, and Masaniello insulted the head by pulling its moustache. Some corpses had their testicles cut off.[38] These rituals allowed the crowd to participate in the punishment of the guilty, but they also carried more precise messages.

The crown of false gold, for example, was probably intended as a symbol of treachery (falsity), and the placing of it on the traitor's head was an example of a degradation ceremony, or as the Russian literary critic Mikhail Bakhtin would have said, an 'uncrowning' (Bakhtin, 1965, p. 197; cf. H. Garfinkel, 1955–6). Such a crown was used in the official degradation of a priest-bandit in Rome in 1585 (Pastor, 1938–53, vol. 21, p. 77). In case onlookers were in doubt about the message of the ritual, it was confirmed in writing by placards bearing such inscriptions as

'Rebel against the Fatherland and Traitor to the Most Faithful People'. 'Traitor to the People' was still an unusual phrase (though it occurs in Shakespeare's *Coriolanus*, Act 3, scene iii), and so a revealing one. The idea that the actions as well as the words were designed to communicate precise messages is confirmed by an incident later in the revolt, when the head of an unpopular official, Cennamo, was displayed on Piazza del Mercato covered with pieces of melon rind and orange peel, at once an insult to the corpse – in the style of the Mannerist painter Arcimboldo – and a reminder that it was the fruit tax for which he had suffered.[39]

These rituals of degradation or desecration was accompanied by their converse, rituals of consecration. The revolt against the fruit tax was given secular as well as religious legitimation. It was justified in terms of the myth that Charles V had granted the Neapolitans a privilege exempting them from all taxes for ever. The crowd demanded to be shown the original document, parchment and seal.[40] Charles was turned into a popular hero as a result. His portrait, together with that of the reigning monarch Philip IV, was displayed in the street and treated with ostentatious reverence. This procedure of appeal by the opponents of a king's policy to an ancestor who was safely dead was, of course, quite common in early modern Europe. A myth of tax exemption was part of the ideological baggage of the rebels of Dauphiné in 1580, while the Norman rebels of 1639 appealed to Louis XII against Louis XIII (Le Roy Ladurie, 1979, p. 58; Foisil, 1970, p. 192). Such examples could easily be multiplied.

More unusual is the fact that Masaniello was also consecrated. 'A man sent from God', it was said, and some claimed to have seen a white dove circling his head.[41] Officially Captain-General of the People, he was treated 'like a king', according to one account, and acted 'with more than royal power' according to another, holding a dagger – or an arquebus – as if it were a sceptre and sitting on a kind of throne.[42] Having begun as the 'king' of a youth group, Masaniello now found himself really in command, in a situation with few early modern parallels (the closest analogy is perhaps Jan of Leiden in Münster in 1534). In conformity with his policy of avoiding confrontation, the viceroy encouraged or at least played along with Masaniello's metamorphosis, calling him 'my son' (*hijo mio*), giving him a horse and dressing him in cloth of silver, perhaps in the hope that power would turn his head and alienate his supporters. This brings us to the play's last act, the assassination.

Act IV. Whether Masaniello's head really was turned by power it is now impossible to say. That is certainly the message of the sources, but before accepting it we need to remind ourselves that all the contemporary accounts were written by members of the ruling class, some of whom were trying to justify the assassination, while they all expected a man of the people in Masaniello's position to behave in a peculiar way. What the sources record are stereotyped perceptions. It is claimed that the popular leader planned to erect a palace for himself on Piazza del Mercato, and also that he went mad, slashing at his followers with his sword, spouting nonsense and heresy from the pulpit of the Carmine, and finally dropping his trousers in public.[43] It was in the Carmine, on Wednesday 16 July, that the second attempt to assassinate Masaniello was made, by Michelangelo Ardizzone, keeper of the city's corn supplies, the baker Salvatore Cataneo and others, and this time the attempt met with success.[44]

Whether Masaniello went mad or not, whether or not his assassination was engineered by the viceroy, or by Genoino, are problems which, despite their intrinsic interest, should not concern us here. What is important for our purposes is the popular reaction to his death. This reaction went through two phases. In the first phase, there were shouts of 'death to the tyrant Masaniello!' while it was now the turn of his head to be carried round the city on the end of a pike, and of his body to be dragged through the streets by local children.[45] Like a carnival king, he had lasted no more than a few days. If he was not ritually killed, like one of Sir James Frazer's kings, as a sacrificial victim, to purify the community from their sins (Frazer, 1913, vol. 3, ch. 2), he was certainly given the full scapegoat treatment after his death.

At this point, however, the government was rash enough to reduce the size of the loaf to eighteen ounces. In Naples, as in other early modern cities, a loaf of bread did not normally fluctuate in price, but it fluctuated in weight instead and sometimes in quality as well. When the revolt began, the Neapolitan loaf was twenty-two or twenty-four ounces; it was then increased by the viceroy to thirty-two or thirty-three ounces. This thermometer of popular success recorded its highest reading (forty-two ounces), just before Masaniello's death.[46] The news of the reduction, by more than 50%, was followed, naturally enough, by a popular reaction in his favour. His body was carried round the city 'in triumph' to shouts of 'Viva Masaniello'. He was given a magnificent funeral with full military honours; standards lowered, arms reversed, drums muffled and over 6,000 people, so we are told, following the bier. 'He could not have received more honour', so the Venetian envoy declared, 'if it had been the king himself'.[47] The people, switching from one stereotyped response to another, now saw him as saint and martyr. Indeed, the archbishop even heard people referring to Masaniello as 'our father' and 'our redeemer'. His hair was torn out for relics. There were stories about his miracles. An unorthodox addition was made to the Litany; 'Saint Masaniello, pray for us' (*Sancte Masanelle, ora pro nobis*). It was even said that he would rise again. In short, Masaniello had already become a myth.[48]

As for the revolt, it did not come to an end till 1648. The viceroy's hope that calm would be re-established once Masaniello was eliminated turned out to be an illusion, as he soon admitted (Villari, 1985, p. 118). However, Della Porta's journal gives the impression that the revolt now disintegrated. On one occasion he records the march of the silk-weavers through the streets, demanding the prohibition of weaving in the countryside. On another day it was the turn of 300 armed students, protesting against increases in the price of doctorates. The lack of reference to larger groups with more general aims suggests that the unity of the July days had been lost.[49]

What, to sum up, were the functions of ritual in these ten days of revolt? They were essentially threefold. In the first place, there was the expressive function. Marching to the viceroy's palace with loaves of bread stuck on the end of pikes, or sacking the houses of financiers – in a disciplined way – communicated a clear message to the authorities. To enact traditional rituals of this type was to make the point that there were grievances, but also that the people, far from being carried away by blind fury, were very much under control.

In the second place, rituals had a legitimating function. The ritualisation of the lynchings turned them into executions. Dragging by the feet, crowning with false gold, and other marks of infamy were part of the apparatus of official justice, here imitated by popular justice (cf. ch. 8 above). The conspicuous reverence paid to the portraits of Charles V showed, and was surely designed to show, that it was not the crowd which was upsetting the order of things, but rather those who had levied an illegitimate tax. The appeal to the Virgin of the Carmine had a similar legitimating function. Curiously enough, the very phrase 'to legitimate' was used – 250 years before Max Weber – by one of the chroniclers of these events, noting, for example, that when the archbishop blessed Masaniello's sword, the Spaniards were shocked that 'he should have wished to legitimate the popular revolt' (*legittimare la mossa popolare*).[50]

In the third place, rituals had an organising function. Whether or not Masaniello or Genoino had planned the events of 7 July in advance, we may be sure that the crowd as a whole did not know what was about to take place. It has been pointed out that the coherence of crowd action depends on the 'shared expectations' which participants have of one another (Reddy, 1977, p. 82). How can people learn what others expect of them? If a crowd begins to take any kind of unrehearsed action, how does anyone know what to do next? A popular ritual is just what is needed in the circumstances, because it is a co-ordinated semi-spontaneous group action. Because it is familar, everyone knows what to do. In this sense crowd action, unrehearsed as it was, did have a script.

In other words, the rituals both expressed community cohesion and created it. However, to speak of 'community' takes us back to the problems of the Durkheimian approach mentioned at the outset and left in suspense. What is problematic about the notion of a moral community in early modern Naples emerges clearly from a recent controversy between the historians Rosario Villari and Giuseppe Galasso about the meaning of an incident discussed above, the lynching of Starace in 1585. Villari (1967, pp. 42–6), inspired by Le Roy Ladurie's analysis of the Carnival of Romans (in its original, 1966 version), discussed the lynching as an enactment of the popular desire to turn the world upside down. Galasso (1978, p. 91) retorted that the people of Naples, many of them recent immigrants uprooted from the countryside, cannot have possessed the common attitudes and values assumed by Villari.

The year 1647 presents us with a similar problem on a grander scale. The fragmentation of the revolt (as I see it, though Villari, 1985, denies this) after the death of Masaniello suggests that Galasso has a point; in this large city there were different occupational groups, such as students and silk-workers, whose interests and grievances had little in common. However, the first days of revolt were different. The sources which refer to those early days give an impression of genuinely collective action, held together by its close association with a particular quarter of the city. The Mercato–Lavinaro–Sellaria area was a community, even if the city of Naples was not. What made it a community was its dominance by one class, or at any rate one social group; in this sense both 'class' and 'community' interpretations of the revolt express important insights. Naples thus offers an illustration of what is wrong with the so-called 'uprooting theory of protest'. As in eighteenth-century Paris and London, so in seventeenth-century Naples, it does not seem to have been the uprooted who took the lead in revolt, but the settled inhabitants of particular quarters.[51] The Virgin of the Carmine was a powerful symbol of this sense of community.

The revolt of 1647 was not, of course, the only one in which the Virgin

Mary played a significant part. Indeed, it might be useful to think in terms of a 'Viva Maria' syndrome, the most famous example of it being the riots and risings in Tuscany and South Italy in the 1790s. In Arezzo and Livorno in 1796, for example, as Turi (1969) has shown, the Virgin helped to legitimate popular protest. As in the case of Naples in 1647, we find both the people and the authorities manipulating religious symbols for their own ends.

However, it would be misleading to end on a note of manipulation. The reactions of the Neapolitans to the Jesuit mission of 1651 as well as to the plague of 1656 show how seriously they took their religion (above, p. 11; below, p. 210). They looked to the Virgin Mary and to San Gennaro to protect them against unjust taxes as well as against plague. For their part the authorities did not, I think, use the crucifix and the blessed sacrament as the police use tear-gas today, merely as a device to disperse a crowd, or even simply to deny the legitimacy of popular protest. They were also trying to exorcise the devils which had got into the rioters; a conclusion which is suggested by the archbishop's letters to the pope stressing the role of the devil in the whole affair, and also by the solemn blessing of the city of Palermo after its parallel revolt had been suppressed.[52] (The blessed sacrament is not the normal vehicle for exorcism, but earlier instances of its use are recorded). Order had to be restored in the supernatural as well as in the natural world. In short, the authorities had recourse to ritual to placate God as well as the people. The viceroy offered a silver image to the Virgin of the Carmine, while the clergy who came out in procession on the first days of the revolt were said to have done so not only to calm the people but also 'to implore divine aid'.[53] In this social drama, all the actors were playing to two audiences, one in this world and one in the next.

A danger of the emphasis on ritual, necessary if we are to reconstruct popular attitudes, is to project an image of 1647 which is too archaic, a picture of 'primitive rebels' and nothing more. Perhaps it will serve as a corrective to the temptation to interpret 1647 in terms of 1789, a view encouraged by picturesque details like the heads stuck on pikes, and drums, and the figure of Masaniello portrayed wearing what looks like a cap of liberty; it is hardly surprising to learn that a play about Masaniello was indeed written – by a German – at an early stage in the French Revolution.[54] However, we need to remember that the ruling class did not participate in revolt in Naples in 1647 as it did in Paris in 1789. The tragedy of Masaniello, we may say with hindsight, is that he was a sansculotte leader without aristocratic or bourgeois support.

15
Rituals of healing in
early modern Italy

The aim of this chapter is to view sickness and health and especially attempts at cures in terms of perception and communication. The models for this investigation come from social anthropology. They include a famous essay on 'symbolic efficacity' by Claude Lévi-Strauss (1949); and monographs on healing rituals in Central Africa (Turner, 1968), Morocco (Crapanzano, 1973), and Sri Lanka (Kapferer, 1983). In Italy too, healing rituals have attracted the interest of scholars interested in the contemporary South. The celebrated Sicilian folklorist Giuseppe Pitrè (1896) collected a good deal of information; for an interpretation, it was necessary to wait for Ernesto De Martino, a major thinker who is still too little known outside Italy, and for his classic study of sufferers from the bite of the tarantula (1961). De Martino defies classification, and his book could equally well be described as anthropological, psychological, or sociological. The same might be said for the work of his followers, such as Rossi (1969), and Di Nola (1976).

In Italy as in other countries there has been a growth of interest in the history of medicine in recent years. An outstanding contribution has been made by Carlo Cipolla, a scholar whose interests range from guns to clocks, from ship to coinage, from demography to literacy (above, p. 124). In the 1970s he turned to the history of public health and the medical profession in Italy, more especially attempts to fight the plague, notably the disastrous and relatively well-documented plague of 1630 (Cipolla 1973, 1976, 1977, 1979). He has drawn attention to the relatively high proportions of professional physicians and surgeons practising in early modern Italy, and also to the relatively precocious development of a health bureaucracy with its accompanying forms, passes and certificates (above, p. 126). To complement this social history of medicine from above, more recent studies by younger scholars discuss unofficial as well as official healers in Pisa, Piedmont, Florence and elsewhere (Pesciatini, 1982; Naso, 1982; Park, 1985). And yet, despite the work of Carlo Ginzburg (1966) on cunning men and wise women, and his associates Piero Camporesi (1983) on the history of attitudes to the body, and

Giovanni Levi (1985) on the career of a seventeenth-century exorcist, there remains a gap between the social history and the social anthropology of sickness, health and medicine. There is no study of the cultural construction of illness in the case of Italy as there is, for example, for Japan (Ohnuki-Tierney, 1984). Although monographs are multiplying, it remains difficult to see the healing system as a whole. There is no general study of the ritual element in healing or the healing element in ritual.

It is with the last problem, that of ritual, that this essay is concerned. It will not deal, except in passing, with professional physicians. Some of their practices, from applying leeches to examining urine, might well be described as 'mere rituals' by anyone who doubts their efficacity, in the same way that sceptics describe some medical practices today (Illich, 1976), but this is a metaphorical usage. My concern here, as in earlier chapters, is with ritual as a sequence of actions designed to communicate (at one level with supernatural forces, at another with the sufferer), and that means concentrating on unofficial medical specialists, outside the guild of physicians. Whether or not these specialists used a term like 'ritual' (*ceremonie*), as the exorcists did, communicating with supernatural forces is what the sources suggest they were doing. These sources are as fragmentary, and as biassed, as sources for the history of popular culture – before about 1800, at least – usually are. Whether they consist of the deliberations of church councils, the descriptions of local customs by foreign travellers, the interrogations of suspect heretics by inquisitors, or the denunciations of fringe medicine by official practitioners, the sources generally express the attitudes, stereotypes and prejudices of the upper classes. However, unofficial healers were not infrequently able to read and write and some of their papers have survived, confiscated to be used as evidence against them. The picture which emerges has a good deal in common with the practices current in the South today (or at least as recently as the 1950s and 1960s), and something in common with contemporary Morocco, Zaïre, Nigeria, Sri Lanka, and other parts of the Third World.

One common feature is medical pluralism. If an ordinary man, woman or child fell ill in this period, they might have recourse to a considerable range of healers. For certain clearly-defined ailments, there was an appropriate unofficial or semi-official specialist such as the tooth-drawer (*cavadenti*) the bone-setter (*concia ossi*), the surgeon (*cerusico*) or barber, while women in labour called in the midwife (*comare* or *allevatrice*), who was also consulted in the case of sickness of mother or child after the birth.[1] Sufferers from snakebite could have recourse to the wandering *pauliani*, who claimed descent from St Paul, referring to his experience in Malta, when 'there came a viper out of the heat, and fastened on his hand... and he shook off the beast into the fire, and felt no harm' (Acts 28.3–5). The *pauliani* used and sold what they called 'Maltese earth', accompanied by herbs (such as juniper), and a healing formula.[2] Elsewhere in Italy there were snakebite specialists at work under other names (*serpari*, *sandomenicari*, *cirauli* and so on), but with similar techniques.[3]

Alternatively, a sufferer could have recourse to the saints directly. In 1541 the nun Caterina de'Ricci (later canonised) was 'cured of a serious pain in the stomach' by contact with 'certain holy relics'.[4] In Italy as elsewhere in Europe, some therapeutic saints were believed to specialise in particular ailments. Just as St Paul took charge of snakebite, sharing the responsibility with San Domenico of Sora (hence the name *sandomenicari*), so San Rocco and San Sebastiano specialised in the plague, St Antony Abbot in St Antony's fire, San Biagio in throats, Santa Lucia in eye problems, and Santa Margherita in difficult childbirths. Animals were not forgotten; to cure an ass, for example, the owner was supposed to pray to San Erasmo. Saints Cosimo and Damiano, who had been physicians in their earthly lives, continued in general practice. The Virgin Mary was a common recourse, whatever the trouble (Pitrè, 1896; cf. Rossi, 1969, 36f, 100f. 173f.). San Filippo and San Liberale will also make an appearance below.

The appeal to a saint involved not only the recital of a special prayer – some of them were printed in the form of broadsheets from the sixteenth century on – but the making and fulfillment of a vow. It was not uncommon to offer an image of the afflicted part of the body at the saint's shrine; a long-standing tradition in Italy, certainly prechristian and still alive today. In Castiglione's *Courtier* (Book 2, ch. 8), a story is told of a practical joke or *beffa* in which two travellers persuade a third that he has gone blind. His immediate reaction is to offer a pair of silver eyes to Our Lady of Loreto if she will restore his sight. Alternatively, one could leave a picture of the sufferer and the saint. Visiting Loreto in 1580, Montaigne remarked on the number of 'ex votos' there. He left one himself; the custom was not yet exclusively 'popular'. An English gentleman who was in Florence in 1594 describes the number of ex votos in the church of the Annunziata in particular: 'the walls are round about hung with Images of men and of many feet and Armes, some of wood, some of mettals, which were offered to our Lady upon vow, by those that

had recovered health of body'.[5] A number of painted ex votos of the
period still survive, at the sanctuary of the Madonna del Monte at Cesena,
for example (Novelli and Massaccesi, 1961).

However, a vow to a healing saint should not be reduced to the gift
of an object, central as this was. In the Castiglione story, the victim not
only offered silver eyes to Our Lady of Loreto, but 'to eat no meat on
Wednesday, or eggs on Friday, and to fast on bread and water every
Saturday' in her honour. He also promised to 'go naked' in pilgrimage
to her shrine. A pilgrimage was an important part of the process of appeal
to a saint. It was no ordinary journey to a particular shrine, it was a form
of ritual, which often involved mortifying the flesh, by going barefoot,
or climbing the steps to the sanctuary on one's knees, or licking the floor
(above, p. 199). Like many other rituals, pilgrimage can be seen as a kind
of drama, in which a series of acts have to be performed in sequence, and
the actor is in a 'liminoid' state, while in passage from one status to
another (van Gennep, 1908; Turner and Turner, 1978). The pilgrimage
to Rome in particular, a visit to the sacred centre involving a gradual
penetration into the holy of holies, has been described as a form of
initiation ritual (Labrot, 1978, p. 260). Another ritualised form of appeal
to the Virgin and the saints, organised from above this time, was the
procession, for example to beg for an end to a visitation of plague. In
Florence in December 1630, for example, there was a procession to the
cathedral with this intent, carrying the body of a local patron saint,
Antonino, while three years later the local miracle-working image of the
Virgin, Santa Maria Impruneta, was brought to Florence to prevent
plague breaking out once more.[6] In Venice, which was also struck by
plague in 1630, the Senate vowed to build a church to Our Lady in return
for deliverance. They kept their promise; Sta Maria della Salute is in fact
a gigantic ex voto. In Naples, when plague struck in 1656, it was said to
have been accompanied by signs from heaven. The image of St Francis
Xavier grew pale, while the blood of San Gennaro refused to liquefy. In
this case the people made the Stations of the Cross in a number of
churches

> in order to implore divine mercy...young girls walked barefoot,
> their feet bloody, with crowns of thorns on their heads, while the
> men had heavy stones hanging round their necks and beat
> themselves hard with whips. Others walked with heavy crosses on
> their shoulders and skulls in their hands, thick ropes round their
> waists, and long chains attached to their feet, their faces and clothes
> smeared with ash.

Processions with miraculous images followed.[7] A true theatre of penitence, along the lines of the one organised by the Jesuit mission a few years before (above, p. 11).

The therapeutic saint has been described by one historian of early modern Italy as a 'christian shaman' (Sallmann, 1979, p. 855). Strictly speaking, a shaman is a healer who has entered his or her profession in a particular way, and is able to make journeys in the spirit into the other world (Eliade, 1951). Without wishing to force the analogy between these two kinds of holy healer, it may be useful to bear it in mind when considering the power of Santa Margherita in particular. If a woman was having a difficult childbirth, a standard procedure was to recite the legend of Santa Margherita or to lay the book on the patient's stomach (above, p. 122). An interesting testimony to the power of the word; but why Santa Margherita? San Rocco was an obvious choice as a patron against the plague because he had looked after the plague-stricken while he was on earth. Santa Lucia was an acceptable eye specialist because she was martyred by having her eyes gouged out. Santa Margherita, who is not recorded as having given birth to any children, is more of a problem. However, a comparative approach does suggest a possible solution. In her legend, current in chap-book form in the sixteenth century, she was swallowed by a dragon but emerged safely, just as the baby is supposed to do. Identification with this saint perhaps helped concentrate the attention of the woman in labour on her own body, as Lévi-Strauss once suggested (1949), in an essay on 'the efficacity of the symbol', which is also concerned with difficult childbirths and with a legend which the shamans of the Cuna tribe (Indians of Panama) recite to ease the delivery. The active participation of the patient in this symbolic narrative apparently brings relief. 'The shaman provides the sick woman', the anthropologist concludes, 'with a language...it is the transition to this verbal expression...which induces the release of the physiological process'. In other words, it is because the ritual communicates with the patient that it helps her. If a legend of descent into the depths works as a 'talking cure' for the Cuna Indians, why should it not have been equally efficacious in sixteenth-century Italy?

The more obvious parallel, of course, is not with saints, but between shamans and those Italian healers who claimed supernatural powers, from the official exorcists to the unofficial cunning men and wise women, who dealt not only with illness but with other personal problems, from disappointment in love to the loss of valuables.

To take the exorcists first. Any sufferer might appeal to the Virgin and the saints, but the exorcist was called in only if the malady had supernatural causes. Lepida, a young lady in a sixteenth-century comedy, is ill, and her father wants to call in the physician. Her nurse, on the other hand, maintains that she is *ammaliata* – in other words, bewitched. 'Whenever women see an unusual illness', he grumbles, 'they think of witchcraft' (*credono che sieno malie*). But he calls in the exorcist all the same.[8] Friends and relatives of the patient would be quick to suspect the evil eye (*malocchio* or *jettatura*), especially if a young husband was suffering from impotence, or a young mother from the drying up of her milk. The sufferer might be described as *fatturato* (bewitched), or *spiritato* (possessed by spirits), or *oppressi da Demoni* (possessed by devils). Only in the case of Sardinia have I found any reference to possession by a saint; a church synod mentions practices reminiscent of Haiti, where worshippers are possessed by good spirits, or *loas* (Métraux, 1958) rather than of part of Europe.[9] Epilepsy was frequently perceived as demonic possession, but a variety of other ailments could also be diagnosed in these terms. The possessed might have recourse to a saint. In Sicily, for example, they went on 12 May to the church of San Filippo at Argira. A Dominican friar who was there in 1541 describes seeing and hearing over 200 women, all possessed by devils, shouting and screaming, speaking with tongues (Latin, Greek, and 'Saracen'), and throwing off their clothes 'shamelessly', a sure sign that they were outside themselves. In the presence of the relic, they trembled and groaned.[10]

The most common official cure, however, was a ritual of casting the devils out, performed by a priest (the laity, including 'devout women', could bless, but only the clergy could exorcise). The exorcist was able to drive out the evil, personified as evil spirits or demons, in a ritual in which (unlike the legend of Santa Margherita), the patients did not participate. Indeed, it included Latin formulae which they are unlikely to have understood. The exorcist read the prayers which the church had designated for the purpose (besides formal exorcisms, we are told that the Gospels and the Creed 'are of great virtue in expelling demons'), while making use of the sign of the cross, holy water, holy oil, and so on.[11] However, it was difficult, even for priests, to draw the line between official and unofficial exorcisms. After the Council of Trent it is not uncommon to find exorcists accused of 'superstition' by the Inquisition or the local bishop. Don Teofilo Zani, for example, not only exorcised a sick patient but administered healing herbs and unconsecrated hosts. When the patient died he found himself accused before the Inquisition of Modena in 1582, of having caused the man's death by occult means (O'Neil, 1984).

Don Giovan Battista Chiesa, of Santena in Piedmont, was summoned to account for himself in 1697 before the court of the archbishop of Turin because he had exorcised many people possessed by devils, not only by repeating the appropriate Latin formula but also by playing the violin and commanding the sufferers, as the trial records put it, 'to dance and skip in honour of St Antony and other saints' (Levi, 1985, p. 18).

It was hard to draw the line between official and unofficial, ecclesiastical and lay, or between 'legitimate' and 'superstitious' remedies (in the eyes of the 'church', which in this case means the upper clergy), but herbs, music, and unconsecrated hosts were part of the repertoire of the various kinds of unofficial lay healers already mentioned. So were texts, an important testimony to the power of the written word, whether they were perceived as 'prayers' or 'spells', written on paper, leaves or almonds, whether they were burned or hung from the patient's neck (above, p. 122).

We know a little, but not very much, about the rituals these healers employed. Take the *benandanti*, for example, discovered a few years ago by Carlo Ginzburg (1966). In addition to their nocturnal fights with witches, which aroused the interest of the Inquisition, some of these people, men and women, exercised the profession of healing. They worked their cures by means of salt and consecrated bread; certain herbs, notably garlic and fennel; certain gestures, such as the sign of the cross; and certain verbal formulae, which witnesses sometimes call 'spells' (*incanti*). One woman treated a patient with bones from a corpse and with an egg tied by a thread (Ginzburg, 1966, p. 64), but the rituals she employed are not clear. In the case of the *pauliani*, already mentioned, we know little more than that they made the sign of the cross over the sufferer from snakebite, saying 'Caro caruzet reparat sanum et manuel paraclitum'.[12] However, they are sometimes described as handling snakes, and this makes one think of the traditional association between snakes and healing (the rod of Ascepius, and so on), and of the long history of snake-handling cults, from ancient Greece to modern America, particularly the South, justified in the Christian world with reference to the biblical text (Mark 16.17), 'They shall take up serpents' (La Barre, 1962). Since rituals often re-enact important events, it is worth adding that the *pauliani* claimed that their snakes were descended from St Paul's snake, just as they were descended from St Paul, so that their healing was a kind of re-enactment, a sacred drama.

Some of the trials before the Inquisition of Venice inform us about healing rituals in a little more detail. Examples are the cases of two Greek women arrested in 1620 (Greeks formed a sizable minority of the

Venetian population). In the case of Serena, a witness who went to her after the doctors could do nothing about his illness (as if a wise woman was the last resort), declared that she made the sign of the cross on his breast and head and said some words he could not understand, while his mother added that Serena ground artichoke leaves and placed the paste on his stomach 'where the illness was', having made the sign of the cross and spoken a few words in Greek (which doubtless impressed the clients). In the case of Marietta, accused of healing a girl with holy water, holy oil, and words which, according to one witness, 'seemed Greek to me', we have the healer's own account of what she did. 'I say three Our Fathers and three Hail Marys and three Salve Reginas in praise of God, his Mother, the most holy Trinity and of San Liberal, who frees us from every illness.' She also makes the sign of the cross with oil on the patient while saying the 'Glory be to the Father...' The oil is not holy oil, 'but I call it holy, because it is of very great virtue against many illnesses'; it contains a powder of marjoram, rue and other herbs. She does not cure the bewitched. The accused was wise enough to guess what the Inquisition wanted to know and that they did not like the laity to make use of holy things without the mediation of the clergy. All the same, accused and witnesses together produce a fairly clear picture of the kind of ritual employed.[13]

So far, little has been said about music; but the priest of Santena with his violin was not as exceptional as he may have sounded. Rituals of healing from Haiti (Métraux, 1958), to Central Africa (Turner, 1968) to Sri Lanka (Kapferer, 1983), are generally accompanied by music, notably drumming and singing. Music encourages dissociation from everyday reality (Kapferer, 1983, p. 185), and helps put sufferers (or healers) into trance, which is often considered necessary for a cure. In the case of Italy, it is intriguing to find that the author of a treatise on the cure of the bewitched has the same name, Floriano Canale, as that of a canon of Brescia who was well known as an organist. Were they the same person, and did he find his music helpful in his cures?[14] We are on firmer ground, however, in the case of the *tarantati*, people who had been bitten by the tarantula spider. A speaker in Castiglione's *Courtier* (1528) remarks that 'in Apulia many musical instruments are used for those who are bitten by the tarantula' (Book 1, ch. 8), and this hearsay is confirmed from personal experience by a professional physician in a book published four years later.[15] The association between the illness and the music was so close in people's minds that a fifteenth-century description of fraudulent beggars includes those who pretend to have been bitten by the tarantula, 'shaking their heads, trembling at the knees, and often singing and dancing to the sound of music'.[16] However, the fullest descriptions come – as so often – from outsiders. The sharp-eyed Skippon is once again of service. 'In a nobleman's palace', he tells us, 'I saw a fellow who was bitten by a tarantula; he danced very antickly, with naked swords, to a tune played on an instrument.'[17] However, the fullest details come from another British traveller, the philosopher George Berkeley, who was in Apulia in 1717. Berkeley's medical interests are well known; and to judge by his journal, the tarantula took up a good deal of his attention. In Bari, he first records what appears to be hearsay: 'The number of the days of dancing not limited to three/different instruments of music for different patients/They see the Tarantula in the looking-glass which directs their motions.' Then comes personal observation of 'the Tarantato that we saw dancing in a circle', 'his cheeks hollow and eyes somewhat ghastly, the look of a feverish person';

> Staring now and then in the glass, taking a naked sword sometimes by the hilt and dancing in a circle the point to the Spectators and often very near particularly to myself who sate near the Glass, sometimes by the point, sometimes with the point stuck in his side but not hurting him, sometimes dancing before the musicians and making odd flourishes with the sword, all which seemed too regularly and discreetly managed for a madman.[18]

One might go further and say that what he witnessed was not so much a spontaneous reaction as a performance, the *tarantella*, something that had to be learned. I do not mean that it was fraudulent (as an earlier witness claimed it sometimes was in the Urbino area); the dance may well have been performed in a state of trance. I do mean that it was ritualised.

Music also figured in the performances of the best-known Italian healers of the period, the so-called 'charlatans'. It is time to bring these charlatans on stage. They did in fact operate from a stage, scaffold, or at the least a bench, whether the scene was Piazza San Marco in Venice, Piazza Navona in Rome (another favourite haunt of theirs), Bologna (Ginzburg and Ferrari, 1978), or a country fair, like that of Santa Maria Impruneta outside Florence, where their presence is recorded in an etching of 1620.[19] That is how they became known as 'mountebanks' (*monta 'inbanchi*). Charlatans were essentially people without medical degrees who sold medicines (and sometimes other commodities), in public, accompanying the sale with some kind of performance, in order to attract the attention of the spectators. This performance was largely verbal; the term *ciarlatano*, which came into regular use in the seventeenth century, and was pejorative from the start, is derived from the verb *ciarlare*, to speak eloquently, with overtones of blarney or spiel.[20] Individual charlatans achieved a considerable reputation in their own time; Marco Bragadin, for example, in the sixteenth century, who was best known as an alchemist, or Buonafede Vitali, (De Francesco, 1937), or 'Orvietan' (who practised in Paris) in the seventeenth, or Rosachio, whom Skippon visited in Venice to see his 'collection of rarities', including a salamander and a chameleon, which were doubtless properties of great value for his presentation of self.[21] Unlike their colleagues in France and England, they do not seem to have liked exotic names, perhaps because Italy exported rather than imported healers of this kind. One of the fullest descriptions of charlatans in full spate comes from the late sixteenth century. It portrays a double act on one corner of the piazza with two men telling stories, discussing, singing, losing their temper with each other, bursting out laughing, before coming to the point and making the sale. It is one more illustration of the continuing importance of oral culture in early modern Italy (above, p. 80). On another corner, our description continues, there is another double act with 'Burattino' and 'Gratiano', characters from the *commedia dell'arte*, but charlatans in disguise. Then there is 'Mastro Paolo da Arezzo... with a great long standard unfurled, on which you can see St Paul', accompanied by a tarantula, a viper and a crocodile. Someone is selling powder to prevent wind, someone else 'philosopher's oil', the quintessence for making oneself rich, memory ointment, or rat poison. Others are swallowing fire or pretending 'to cut someone's nose off with a cunning knife'.[22] An engraving of 1609 confirms the use by charlatans on Piazza San Marco of the masks of the *commedia dell'arte*, at least during Carnival.[23]

Another vivid description comes from the pen of an English visitor, not Skippon for once, but Thomas Coryate, who was himself a professional entertainer and had good reason to study the technique with some care. On Piazza San Marco, he explains,

> twice a day, that is, in the morning and in the afternoone, you may
> see five or six severall stages erected for them... After the whole
> rabble of them is gotten up to the stage, whereof some weare visards
> being disguised like fooles in a play... the musicke begins.
> sometimes vocall, sometimes instrumentall, and sometimes both
> together... after the musicke hath ceased, he [the leader] maketh
> an oration to the audience of halfe an houre long, or almost an
> houre. Wherein he doth most hyperbolically extoll the vertue of his

drugs and confections...After the chiefest Mountebankes first speech is ended, he delivereth out his commodities by little and little, the jester still playing his part, and the musitians singing and playing upon their instruments. The principal things that they sell are oyles, soveraigne waters, amorous songs printed, Apothecary drugs, and a Commonnweale of other trifles...I have observed marveilous strange matters done by some of these Mountebankes. For I saw one of them holde a viper in his hand, and play with his sting a quarter of an houre together, and yet receive no hurt; though another man should have beene presently stung to death with it. He made us all beleeve that the same viper was linealy descended from the generation of that viper that lept out of the fire upon St Pauls hand, in the Island of Melita now called Malta, and did him no hurt; and told us moreover that it would sting some, and not others. Also I have seene a Mountebanke hackle and gash his naked arm with a knife most pitifully to beholde, so that the blood hath streamed out in great abundance, and by and by he hath applied a certaine oyle unto it, wherewith he hath incontinent both stanched the blood, and so throughly healed the woundes and gashes, that when he hath afterward shewed us his arme again, we could not possibly perceive the least token of a gash.[24]

The natural philosopher Francesco Redi adds the detail that 'to show the power and value of their antidotes, the charlatans eat scorpions and the heads of vipers'.[25]

The parallel between the snakehandling activities of some of the charlatans, like Paolo d'Arezzo, and of the 'pauliani' is a striking one, to which we must return. However, I should also like to suggest that they adopted – and adapted – rituals from an older tradition, that of the shaman.

This brief account of the structure of the healing system in early modern Italy has emphasised its variety, its pluralism. From the patient's point of view this emphasis is probably appropriate, since court records not infrequently describe them as having gone to one kind of healer following another's lack of success. On the other hand, the modern term 'pluralism' risks misrepresenting the point of view of the healers, more particularly the more official healers; physicians and exorcists, who were quick to condemn the activities of their rivals. The system was not harmonious but racked by conflicts, which led in the course of time to change. Two conflicts in particular; in the first place, the physicians versus the clergy; in the second place, physicians and clergy versus the rest.

It is important to avoid describing these conflicts in anachronistic terms. Our modern distinctions (between rational and irrational, natural and supernatural, religious and superstitious), were in process of formation during the period; to apply them to the years before 1650, in particular, is to invite misunderstanding.

In the first place, there is the conflict over remedies for plague, which is central to the theme of this chapter, because it involves the question of the efficacity of ritual. The traditional clerical remedy, religious processions, evoked increasing opposition from physicians who were concerned to minimise the occasions for contagion (Cipolla, 1977, ch. 1). However, it would be wrong to view this conflict in the simple terms of faith versus reason or clergy versus laity. It was quite possible for clerics to be convinced by the argument from contagion without giving up their religious world-view, their therapeutic saints, their ex votos. In Naples in 1656, for example, the cardinal archbishop forbade public rituals of penitence (though as we have seen, they took place unofficially all the same).[26]

In the second place, there was the conflict involving the two official groups, clergy and physicians, on one side, and the unofficial healers on the other. Once again we have to avoid simplifying and modernising the issues at stake. What the clergy condemned in the activities of the cunning men and women was their 'superstition', but this term was not used in its modern sense. It did not refer to an uncritical belief in non-existent supernatural forces, but to attempts to reach supernatural beings by unofficial channels, which the Church was less and less prepared to tolerate after Luther's breach with Rome. The clergy, more particularly the upper clergy and the Dominican and Franciscan friars (from whose ranks the inquisitors were drawn), came to label these unofficial channels as 'witchcraft' (a form of heresy), and those who used them as 'witches'. The prayers of the cunning folk were perceived as spells, their use of the cross and the wafer (consecrated or unconsecrated) was interpreted as blasphemy. The theatrical self-presentations of the charlatans did not endear them to the clergy, some of whom (including Carlo Borromeo), thought that plays were 'the liturgy of the devil'. What the professional physicians, on the other hand, condemned in the activities of cunning men and women and charlatans was their administration of inefficacious and even fraudulent remedies. But their distinction was between the members of their own corporation (perceived as honest) and outsiders (perceived as untrustworthy), rather than between cures by natural and supernatural (or ritual) means.[27] It was in the period 1300–1650 that 'the physicians asserted themselves as a reputable and respected professional group' (Cipolla, 1976, p. 1), and this naturally involved distinguishing themselves more sharply than before from other healers. In Italy as in other parts of Europe, physicians were making increasing efforts to establish and legitimate a monopoly over medical resources and to marginalise their competitors (cf. García Ballester, 1976). The physicians made use of pejorative terms like 'charlatan', 'mountebank' and (in England) 'quack' to label (and libel) their competitors. (The suffering public turned the tables on them by applying the same terms to the professionals.) It was only after 1650 that Italian physicians began to take up the new mechanical philosophy, the ideas of Descartes and Gassendi in particular, and to doubt the efficacy of traditional healing rituals such as the music and dance cure for the *tarantati* (De Martino, 1961). As illnesses ceased to be perceived in terms of possession by spirits or devils, healing ceased to be a form of communication. However, the new attitudes affected only a minority of Italians. In the countryside, especially in the South, traditional healing rituals have survived until our own day. The separation between different kinds of healer is now cultural as well as social.

Despite the hostility of clergy and physicians, the sixteenth and seventeenth centuries saw the rise of the charlatans, as it is convenient to call the performers on Piazza San Marco, Piazza Navona, and elsewhere. From the later sixteenth century, references to them abound, particularly in Venice and Rome. This is unlikely to be coincidence; Venice and Rome were turning into cities which lived by catering to large numbers of visitors, to see the Carnival in the first case and the pope in the other (above, chs. 12–13). They were natural haunts for performers, whether rogues (ch. 6) or actors. The charlatans were probably a mixture of the two. They doubled as entertainers and healers and made one role serve the other, drawing a crowd and keeping them happy. This theatre of medicine was a form of advertising, a commercial for the medicine and its inventor. It was well suited to the conditions of a large city in a society which was becoming more and more commercialised. However, it should not be forgotten that the connexion between healing and dramatic performances is a traditional one. This is how shamans operate. Lévi-Strauss had a phrase for it; 'the efficacity of symbols'. Aristotle had a word for it; 'catharsis', the 'purging' of the passions through drama (this word for 'purification' had both religious and medical overtones). The snake-handling was a good stunt; but it was also, as we have seen, a tradition associated with the *pauliani*. Self-wounding was another stunt;

but it is also associated with shamans and their ecstasies. How much of a typical performance should be described as 'ritual' is not very clear; it was a stereotyped sequence of acts, but the efficacity (according to the charlatans themselves) lay not in these actions but in the pills and ointments. Unlike the wise women and cunning men, they ran a 'take away' business. The snakehandling ritual was traditional, but its meaning was not. The healer, a figure with religious powers, was turning into an entertainer, a salesman. More exactly, the 'general practitioner' characteristic of small communities in rural Italy (as of Turner's Ndembu or the Cuna Indians of Lévi-Strauss) now had to compete with a variety of specialists, from the charlatan to the professional physician with his medical degree. In short, the charlatans illustrate the process of cultural and social change in early modern Italy, and in particular the 'fit' between the growing opportunities to market medicine in large towns and certain local healing traditions. They were commercialised shamans.

IV

Conclusion

The earlier chapters of this book have tended to follow a pattern.
They have begun by the reconstruction of some kind of structure
or system; the system of papal rituals, the insult system, the
consumption system, and so on, and they have ended with a
discussion of change over time. The different accounts of change
and explanations of change in different sectors of Italian culture
have had more than a little in common, but no attempt has been
made so far to bring them together. Although the last chapter is
another case-study, it is more consistently concerned with the
explanation of change than its predecessors. It is also concerned
with Europe as a whole, a reminder that Italian developments were
not isolated. It deals with the form of communication that modern
readers are most likely to perceive as alien – ritual – and attempts
a historical explanation of that very perception.

16
The repudiation of ritual in early modern Europe

Conversation, like the Romish Religion, was so encumbered with Show and Ceremony, that it stood in need of a Reformation to retrench its Superfluities and restore it to its natural good Sense and Beauty.   (Addison)

It is often said that ritual has declined in modern societies, as a result of the rise of rationalism or technology or of the increasing value placed on individualism, privacy, spontaneity, authenticity and sincerity, 'the true voice of feeling' as Keats called it (cf. Trilling, 1972). The point is a sociological commonplace, or at least it was. Herbert Spencer, for example, argued that ritual was associated with what he called the 'millitant type of society' (whether tribal or feudal), and that it declined when this militant society was replaced by the industrial type. 'Observances' – as he called them – 'weaken as industrialism strengthens' (1876–85, vol. 3, pp. 218–19). A generation later, Max Weber associated ritual with magic and asserted that these forms of behaviour declined together in the modern 'disenchanted' rational world. More recently, the anthropologist Max Gluckman (1962) directed attention to the general decline in the 'ritualisation of social relations' (apart from odd survivals of tribal society in Oxford, Cambridge and elsewhere), while a similar point was made by the sociologist Edward Shils (1975). 'Decline' is an implicitly quantitative term, but Shils, at least, is prepared to argue that 'it is very probable that there are fewer ritual acts per capita practised nowadays than several centuries ago'.

This view, once sociological othodoxy, has come under increasing attack in recent years. It is now asserted, or assumed, that all societies are equally ritualised; they merely practice different rituals. If most people in industrial societies no longer go to church regularly or practice elaborate rituals of initiation, this does not mean that ritual has declined. All that has happened is that new types of ritual – political, sporting, musical, medical, academic and so on – have taken the place of the traditional ones (cf. Bocock, 1974; Lane, 1981). If we think that another society – Sweden, say, or Japan – is more highly ritualised than ours, that – so the argument goes – only reveals our own ethnocentrism. It is certainly difficult to be objective about such matters. A Dutch historian who knew the English well suggested, over fifty years ago, that it is they who 'go through life as though each of its moments were part of a prescribed and solemn ritual' (Renier, 1931, p. 167). Perhaps we simply notice our neighbour's rituals, while failing to be aware of our own. Lacking a scale for measuring ritual acts per capita, it might be prudent to suspend judgement. However, if historians shift their ground from ritual acts to attitudes to ritual, then they will have a story to tell which is just as dramatic as the old one told by Spencer and Weber, Gluckman and Shils.

According to Mary Douglas (1966, p. 34), 'Ritual has always been something of a bad word'. It would be more exact to say that – like rhetoric, with which it has not a little in common – ritual became a bad word in parts of western Europe in the course of the early modern period. From a comparative point of view, a striking feature of modern western culture is its dismissive attitude towards ritual. 'Mere ritual', we often say. 'Mere pageantry' wrote Gilbert Burnet in the seventeenth century about the public rituals of the Venetian Republic. 'But a ceremony', wrote Thomas Cranmer a century earlier, referring to the English coronation.[1] Many people besides the British Protestant clergy have associated ritual with the shadow rather than the substance, the letter rather than the spirit, the outer husk rather than the inner kernel. This feature of western culture is no less distinctive than the other features discussed by Max Weber in his famous contrasts between the West and the rest of the world, and it deserves some attention from historians.

It would of course be rash to assert that there have been no movements to reject ritual in Asia, say, or in the Americas. Examples to the contrary are not difficult to find. In ancient China, for example, the Taoist classic *The Way and its Power* describes 'rites' (*li*) as 'the mere husk of loyalty and promise-keeping', while the Realist or Legalist school was so called for attempting to replace ritual by law (Welch, 1957, p.31; Waley, 1939, pp. 158f). However, the ruling orthodoxy in China for 2,000 years was neither Taoism nor Legalism but Confucianism, and Confucius and his followers placed a very high value on ritual. In India, in the early nineteenth century, the Brahmin Ram Mohun Roy launched an attack on ritualism, in other words on the validity of ritual as a way to salvation. Despite his references to Hindu tradition, Roy was, however, influenced by modern western ideas (Bayly, 1981). The Peyote cult practised in this century by the Navaho has been described as a reaction against ritual, but this movement too was affected by Christianity (contrast Douglas, 1970, ch. 1, and Aberle, 1966). These brief references are no substitute for serious comparative study, but they do at least illustrate my contention that the struggle against ritual has been uniquely central to western culture. The struggle goes back a long way but the early modern period was, as I shall try to show, extremely important in the articulation and the development of the propensity to repudiate ritual.

There are of course awkward conceptual problems here. Modern writers on the subject define 'ritual' in different ways (Gluckman 1962, Leach 1968, Goody 1977, and so on). My own preference, throughout this book, has been to regard ritual as a form of communication by action which is public, stereotyped, and symbolic. However, what matters in this chapter is how early modern writers defined what they called 'caeremoniae', 'cultis', 'ritus' or their vernacular equivalents; and they did not agree either, as will be seen. The concept of the 'repudiation of ritual' is not theirs but mine and it is something of an umbrella term, covering a number of early modern attitudes which need to be distinguished, notably the rejection of certain claims traditionally made for ritual; the refusal to practice specific rituals; and the attempt to do without ritual altogether. However, distinctions such as these will emerge most naturally in the course of a historical account of this repudiation.

Criticisms of ritual go back a long way in the Judaeo-Christian tradition, to the prophets of the Old Testament. 'He that killeth an ox is as if he slew a man...he that burneth incense as if he blessed an idol' (Isaiah 66.3). In similar vein, Christ rebuked the Pharisees for taking ritual too seriously. St Paul's stress on interior religion led him to write that 'He is not a Jew which is one outwardly; neither is that circumcision which is outward in the flesh. But he is Jew which is one inwardly; and circumcision is that of the heart' (Romans 2.28–9). The stoics, Greek and Roman, criticised ritual (*eusebia*, *hierourgiai*, *nomoi*, *pietas*, etc.), as unnatural and as an obstacle to that tranquillity of mind which should be the wise man's goal. At best ritual was superfluous, one of those 'indifferent matters' (*adiaphora*), which had no influence on happiness one way or the other. Seneca and Plutarch suggest that it is the intention which counts, not the outward form. Plutarch glossed the terms *threskuein* (literally, to do like the Thracian women) as 'the celebration of extravagant and superstitious ceremonies' ('Life of Alexander'; cf. Babut, 1969, pp. 489f.). The stoic emperor Marcus Aurelius lived surrounded by ritual, but his 'Meditations' suggest that he made an effort not to take it seriously. The stoic and the christian traditions were fused in some of the fathers of the church. Augustine, for example, regarded the eucharist as no more than a commemoration ('sacramentum memoriae'), and declared that funeral rites were 'more of a solace for the living than an aid to the dead' (Rowell, 1977, p. 18), while John Chrysostom attacked exterior religion as 'Judaising'.

However, in the Middle Ages, ritual was taken much more seriously and given a much greater importance by the theologians as well as by the people. Hence the obvious point at which to begin an account of the repudiation of ritual is the early sixteenth century. The Reformation was, among other things, a great debate, unparalleled in scale and intensity, about the meaning of ritual, its functions, and its proper forms. The reformers condemned various traditional religious rituals as 'dumb', 'vain', 'idle', 'superfluous', 'outward' or 'carnal' (or their equivalents in the different vernaculars); as 'shows and shadows'; or, to use their favourite (if somewhat elusive) terms, as 'idolatry' or 'superstition'.

This condemnation of ritual was naturally associated with the critique of the traditional ritual specialists, the Catholic priesthood, and with the critique of 'works'. Luther's description of the traditional attitude to which he was opposed was that 'divine service was performed as a work whereby God's grace and salvation might be won'.[2] In this respect medieval Europeans resembled the Tikopia (Firth, 1940, vol. 1, p. 1). The repudiation of ritual was of course part of a general critique of exterior religion, of which the most famous exponent was Erasmus, who made John Chrysostom's term 'Judaising; his own.[3] Images were another exterior form repudiated by some reformers. Even language was suspect, at least if interpreted 'literally' rather than 'spiritually'. However, some of the most vigorous and eloquent criticisms of medieval religion focussed on ritual, like Milton's lament that 'all the inward acts of worship, issuing from the native strength of the soul, run out lavishly to the upper skin, and there harden into a crust of formality'.[4]

There was of course more than one issue under discussion in this great debate, and it may be useful to distinguish three in particular.

The first was the question of simplicity versus excess; whether the rituals of the medieval church were too elaborate, too distracting, too expensive or too obscure; and whether a change of ritual 'idiom' was necessary. The basic point was made with particular clarity by a seventeenth-century Scottish divine when he asserted that 'A true Church...keeps simplicity of ceremonies; and that 'outward glory and splendor...drawes away the minds of the people'.[5] Martin Bucer put forward the geographic thesis that 'The Greeks and other easterners, being of warmer temper, have relished an abundance of ceremonies.'[6] Cranmer, among others, put forward the historical thesis that 'the great excess and multitude' of ceremonies 'hath so increased in these latter days that the burden of them was intolerable'.[7] More precisely, the Centuriators of Magdeburg traced the gradual rise of the sign of the cross in baptism, and so on.[8]

How far to go in the return to simplicity was of course a divisive matter. Luther though it sufficient to purify the Mass from what he considered mercenary and clerical accretions, such as the Offertory and the Collect, and to translate the liturgy into the vernacular, so that the participants would understand 'what is spoken and performed'. 'In order to be gentle with tender consciences', his German Mass of 1526 retained the Introit, Kyrie, Gospel, Creed, and the blessing of the bread and wine.[9] Others were more radical, and objective not only to the sign of the cross at baptism, but also to kneeling to receive communion, using a ring in the marriage ceremony, and wearing surplices in chapel, and issue which led to sharp conflict in Cambridge in the 1560s, when the radicals threw their surplices off (Porter, 1958, p. 122). some, like the anabaptists, would have liked to do without ritual altogether.

The second issue was that of uniformity versus freedom. Luther, for example, argued that 'as far as possible we should observe the same rites and ceremonies' (*weyse und geberden*).[10] Others, however, complained that uniform ceremonies were an unnecessary burden, a 'heavy yoke', destructive of 'Christian liberty'.[11] A compromise between these two positions was possible, but such a compromise was in a sense the most radical (that is, untraditional) position of all. It was suggested by Erasmus, among others, when he wrote that 'too much has been made of rituals and vestments, but we might save, if we would, the useful part of such things'.[12] It was summed up by the humanist reformer Philip Melanchthon, at a time of negotiations for a religious peace in the Empire, in 1548, in his famous characterisation of ceremonies (in which he included Mass and the veneration of the saints), by the stoic term of 'adiaphora', things which do not matter (Maschreck, 1958, ch. 21).[13] In the same vein, a mid sixteenth-century English treatise gave a purely pragmatic, political justification for ceremonies, arguing that they were merely 'devised by such as are in authority, for a decent order, quietness and tranquillity'.[14] This view, formed under pressure of circumstances after the Reformation, was to be of great importance in the future. If we adopt Gluckman's distinction (1962) between ritual and ceremony in terms of the 'mystical notions' associated with the former, we can date the transition from one to the other to the early sixteenth century. We have reached the idea of 'mere' ceremony in the context of religion.

The third issue, and the one on which compromise was most difficult to achieve, was that of the efficacy of ritual. The reformers rejected claims for what might be called the 'material efficacy' of ritual, its power to effect changes in the physical world, its 'virtue' as contemporaries put it. They would have had no time for the healing rituals discussed above (ch. 15). They denied the power of the Mass and of exorcism to cure the sick as they denied that of the act of consecration to transmute the bread and wine. Some of them compared claims of this kind to the false claims made by magicians. Bucer described the Catholic view of transubstantiation as 'a more or less magical change' (*quasi magica...mutatio*), while the lively Calvinist controversialist Pierre Viret wrote of 'les enchantements des prestres; (cf. Thomas, 1971, pp. 41f).[15]

The reformers also rejected the medieval theory of the spiritual efficacy of religious rituals, their power to remit sins, for example, and the idea that they were vehicles of grace which was channelled through the ritual work 'automatically, without regard for the inner state of the recipient' (*ex opere operato sine bono motu utentis*). This was one of the main points of Erasmus's attack on 'Judaising'. 'Do you really think,' he wrote of baptism, 'that the ceremony of itself makes you a christian?...you have been sprinkled with holy water, but this accomplishes nothing unless you cleanse the inner filth of your soul' (Payne, 1970, ch. 9). Luther agreed. 'The sacraments are not fulfilled by the ritual', he wrote, 'but only when they are believed'. Calvin took a similar line, but stressed contract rather than faith. 'The whole virtue and efficacy of the sacraments depends, not on visible signs, but on God's promise.'

According to more radical reformers, notably Zwingli, the sacraments lacked spiritual as well as material efficacy. They were nothing but symbolic acts, mere tiruals, carried out simply as a reminder, as a commemoration (*Wiedergedächtnis*) of past events.[16] Tyndale defined ceremonies as 'signes that put men in remembrance'.[17] They might also be justified in terms of their psychological or social efficacy (as we would say), in terms of their effect on the participants, like the prayers at funerals, said (as the Presbyterians, following Augustine, argued at the Savoy conference in 1661), 'not for the benefit of the dead, but only for the instruction and comfort of the living' (Rowell, 1977, p. 91).

The reformers denounced traditional Catholic rituals not only as spiritually inefficacious but as harmful, as a means of mystification. Viret built one of his satirical dialogues around the extended metaphor of the

Catholic church as a vast apothecary's shop, and he described holy water, masses, and other *cérémonies papales*, as he called them, as so many druges (*drogues*), psychologically effective but harmful, an irrational means of persuasion. Catholicism, he seems to be suggesting, is the opium of the people.[18]

So far, only the opinions of the learned have been discussed. Since popular participation was an essential element in the spread of the Reformation, it is natural to ask whether ordinary people also rejected ritual at this time. As so often in the history of early modern popular culture, the evidence is ambiguous. Since texts emanating directly from ordinary people are usually lacking, we have to rely on the interpretation of behaviour (cf. ch. 14 above). Images, if rejected, can be smashed, but rituals can only be interrupted or parodied. The interruption may be directed against the celebrant rather than against what he is celebrating, while 'parody' (a word which prejudges the crucial issue) is highly ambiguous. The peasants of Languedoc in the fourteenth century imitated the elevation of the host, we are told, by holding up slices of turnip (Le Roy Ladurie, 1975, p. 230). The gesture may be a critique of the efficacy of the act of consecration, but we cannot be sure. A 'mock-baptism' or a 'mock-procession' may be a mockery of baptism or processions, but it may equally well be an example of the use of these ritual forms for the purpose of mocking something else. The historian may try to resolve these problems by turning to contemporary interpretations of parody, but even these are not necessarily infallible. Sometimes the Catholic clergy took lay parodies of sacred ritual in one sense, sometimes in the other. In 1538, for example, some young peasants from the Guadalajara region of Spain pulled up a wayside cross and organised a mock-procession, singing comic songs instead of the Litany. When the Inquisition heard about this incident, they treated it an nothing more serious than a youthful prank (Bennassar, 1979, p. 251). In 1655, on the other hand, a committee of doctors of theology at the Sorbonne condemned a local journeymens' initiation ritual (which involved the usual pouring of water over the head of the new recruit), as a mockery of the sacrament of baptism.[19] Which of them had got their hermeneutics right, the Spanish clergy or the French?

What is clear, amid this uncertainty, is that the great debate of the Reformation offers us a variety of learned and subtle indigenous interpretations of ritual. Many of these interpretations had a long history; indeed, it might be argued that the monolithic tradition of orthodoxy existed only in the minds of the reformers who were attacking it (as not infrequently happens in the history of traditions). One might take the example of the efficacy of ritual. In the eleventh century, heretics challenged the efficacy of the acts of baptism and consecration. Even orthodox theologians of the thirteenth and fourteenth centuries, such as Aquinas and Scotus, disagreed as to whether the sacraments were the 'causes' of grace or merely 'signs' However, the early sixteenth century remains the moment of an unusually radical and an unusually widespread critique of traditional claims for ritual, together with an effort to simplify it and even, in some cases, to do without it altogether.

All the same, the reformers quickly felt the need for substitutes for what they had abolished, and ritual, expelled at the door, came back in through the window. This was true even in the first stage, that of protest. Luther burning the pope's bull was performing a ritual (in my sense of the term if not in his), and so were the Cambridge men who threw off their surplices. Ritual was even more important in the second stage of the Reformation, which the communities of the faithful had to be held together. If ritual seemed 'empty' to reformers, the lack of ritual created an even bigger void. So Lutherans and Calvinists assembled for formal worship. Even Calvinist 'hedge-preaching' in the open air developed a stereotyped form, with a banner raised over the congregation and a distribution of bread and wine after the sermon (Crew, 1978, pp. 167f). Even the Anabaptists had their Lord's Supper and Quakers their meetings, not to mention recurrent symbolic acts such as 'going naked for a sign' (Bauman, 1983). Spontaneity easily congeals into ritual. *Communitas* (a relationship between individuals who burst through the confines of their ordinary social roles), cannot survive daily routine, 'and it is the fate of all spontaneous communitas in history to undergo what most people see as a "decline and fall" into structure and law' (Turner, 1969, p. 132). The major consequence of this long and intense debate over the form, functions and meanings of ritual seems to have been the unintended one of making western Europeans unusually self-conscious and articulate on the subject.

For the Protestants were not alone in giving attention to these questions. It is true that the Council of Trent concluded (in its twenty-second session), by reaffirming the doctrine of transubstantiation, and also the value of the invocation of saints and the use of vestments, candles, incense and so on, on the grounds that man is unable to meditate on divine things 'without exterior aids' (*sine adminiculis exterioribus*) However, there is evidence of an increasingly critical attitude within the church towards some traditional claims for ecclesiastical ritual. As the last chapter pointed out, Carlo Cipolla has drawn attention to the conflict in Italy over ritual as a defence against plague. Some churchmen still recommended the traditional processions, but some of the laity, on the other hand, had come to regard these rituals not only as inefficacious but as harmful as well, because they allowed the contagion to spread (Cipolla, 1977). In the fourteenth and fifteenth centuries, the commune of Florence was already divided 'between enforcement of hygienic regulations and recourse to processional solidarities; (Trexler, 1980, p. 363). However, in the seventeenth century there were even clergy, in France as in Italy, who discouraged processions in time of plague. One canon of Rheims remarked in 1668 that 'Since the procession took place, the contagion has become markedly worse, since God wishes to show men that he does not like irrational devotions [*les dévotions inconsidérées*], and that he should be approached in a prudent manner [*qu'il faut le prier avec sagesse*].' The belief in the material efficacity of ritual was declining.

The spread of this 'rationalist approach to ritual in the France of Louis XIV can be documented from a series of striking works published by Catholic priests, notably Jean-Baptiste Thiers, Claude de Vert and Pierre Lebrun. Thiers, a doctor of theology who chose to live the life of a country curé, is best known as the author of a scholarly treatise on what he called 'superstitions'. He tried to chip away at the encrustations of popular, unofficial beliefs and ceremonies which had accumulated around the theology and ritual of the church. For instance, he rejected the idea that hearing Mass cured the sick, or that a pregnant woman would not suffer during childbirth if she remained sitting during the Gospel a few days before. These were examples, to quote a favourite phrase of his, of 'un faux culte, un culte superflu, une vaine observance'.[20] He wanted a reduction in ritual, the removal of popular superfluities, though he had nothing against the official rituals of the Church.

Claude de Vert was a Benedictine who was asked by bishop Bossuet to reply to Calvinist attacks on the Mass, and chose arguments which he thought would appeal to recent converts from Calvinism. Hence he emphasised utilitarian or 'functionalist' explanations of ritual at the expense of what he called 'mystical and symbolic' ones. If candles are lit and placed on the altar, this is not, Vert declares, because Christ is the light of the world (as earlier commentators had asserted), but because the early christians needed light for the services they held at night. If we now see candles on the altar in daytime, this is simply because the times of services have changed. Symbolism is thus explained away, and a theory which we might describe in terms of functionalism and 'cultural lag' takes its place.[21]

Whether or not Vert's argument appealed to the Catholics newly converted from Calvinism, it certainly displeased some old ones, notably Pierre Lebrun. Lebrun was an oratorian and his work owes something to his two famous colleagues, the philosopher Nicole Malebranche and the philologist Richard Simon. His *Historire critique des pratiques supersitieuses*, published anonymously in 1702, is close to Malebranche in its concern with the question whether apparently supernatural phenomena, such as water-divining, are susceptible of naturalistic explanations However, the book pays homage to Simon not only in its title, which echoes his 'critical histories' of the Bible, but also, more important, in its historical method.

What Lebrun did was to criticise Vert for his love of conjecture and his love of system, which had led him into misinterpreting ritual by taking it too literally. Lebrun, on the contrary, read ritual as Simon read the Bible, with concern for the figures of speech. The true meaning of a ritual, according to Lebrun, is the one intended by its originator, and this meaning is often symbolic. This important, neglected contribution to hermeneutics put the meaning back into ritual, not by returning to the medieval writers rejected by Vert, who treated the symbols as inherent in the action, but by emphasising symbol-making at a human level. In other words, Lebrun abandoned traditional claims of ritual as decisively as his opponent.[22] There was also a group in the French church who wanted to simplify the liturgy. Some of the Jansenists would have agreed with the Protestant view (above, p. 226) that 'A true Church...keeps simplicity of ceremonies.' They criticised 'external piety' marked by 'foolish and courtly deference' (*inanibus et aulicis submissionibus*).[23]

So far this chapter has focussed on religious rituals. Secular rituals were also called into question on occasion. In this area there was no great debate, but there were sporadic discussions which seem to have followed the religious model, at least at first.

In Protestant Europe, for example, there are three well-known cases in which the critique of ritual was extended from the church to the university. At Wittenberg in the 1520s, Andreas Bodenstein von Karlstadt attacked academic rituals such as kneeling, banqueting and even the ward of degrees as vainglorious. Degrees disappeared from Wittenberg for a time, although they were brought back a few years later by Dr Luther (Sider, 1974, p. 177). At Cambridge in the 1650s, William Dell made similar points to Karlstadt, whether or not he knew of this precedent in his notorious attacks on academic dress and more generally on what he called 'outward and antichristian forms and follies'.[24] At the end of the seventeenth century, both at Leipzig and at the new university of Halle, the pietists made similar criticisms of outward academic forms (Hinrichs, 1971).

Traditional claims for royal rituals were also called into question, as were some of the rituals themselves. Erasmus expressed the radical view as forcefully here as in the case of exterior religion, describing court ceremonies as 'superstitious' and mocking the worship of the prince 'like some earthly god'.[25] Cranmer's rejection of the belief in the efficacy of the coronation rites followed the lines of the reformers' rejection of the efficacy of the sacraments – naturally enough, since coronation had sometimes been treated as an eighth sacrament. Cranmer objected in particular to the claims made for the virtue of the holy oil. 'The oil', he told Edward VI, 'is but a ceremony...If it be wanting, that king is yet a perfect monarch notwithstanding, and God's anointed, as if he were inoiled.' The 'solemn rites of coronation', he declared, are nothing but 'good admonitions' to the king.[26] Coke made a similar point in still stronger language in 1609, when he described the coronation as 'but a royal ornament' (quoted in Kantorowicz, 1957, p. 317). The practice of touching for the king's evil was also questioned. James I had doubts about performing this ritual, on good protestant grounds of unwillingness to pretend to divine powers. The House of Commons denounced this 'superstition' in 1647, while William III refused to take part in the ritual at all (Bloch, 1924, Book 2, ch. 6; Book 3, ch. 1).

There was also a critique of the ordinary rituals of everyday life. 'Salutation', wrote one British writer on good manners in 1607, 'is become so full of ceremonie and vanitie', that it needed to be reformed; 'those apish toies of bowing downe to everie mans show' were to be condemned.[27] Radical Protestants, notably the Quakers, went so far as to reject, in the name of sincerity and 'inwardness', the conventional modes of greeting, described by one of them in 1663 as the 'artificial, feigned and strained art of compliment, consisting in bundles of fopperies, fond ceremonies, foolish windings, turnings and crouchings with their bodies', while another declared that it was wrong for people 'to salute men in a complimentary way, by doffing their hats unto them and bowing before them, and giving them flattering titles'.[28]

In the Catholic world too one can find criticism of secular rituals on religious grounds. It may seem odd to cite Giovanni Della Casa in this connexion, since his famous conduct book, written in the early 1550s, may be described as a guide to the ritualisation of social relations. All the same, Della Casa does have critical remarks to make about 'ceremonie', as he calls them, denouncing them as 'insubstantial appearances' (*semb-ianti senza effetto*), vanities, superfluities, and even lies. His critique was in part a moral one, in the name of sincerity. 'We make a show', writes Della Casa with disgust, 'of honouring persons whom we do not respect at all but may even despise'. However, his particular objection is to the appropriation of religious forms for secular purposes, to kissing the hands of nobles, for example, as if they were the relics of a saint or the consecrated hands of a priest. It is his Counter-Reformation world view, his new sharp sense of the separation between the religious and the secular domains, which makes Della Casa into such a severe critic of lay rituals. Ceremonies are for church.[29]

In France, too, one finds critics of secular ritual. In 1609, two generations after Cranmer, A.Du Chesne argued that anointing makes no difference to the status of kings, and that it is simply a message to their subjects (*une declaration à leurs sujets*).[30] In the reign of Louis XIV, there were objections to some aspects of the cult of the king; the fact that courtiers stood facing him – with their backs to the altar – in the chapel at Versailles, or that lights burned before his statue on Place des Victoires.[31] To some, this smacked of blasphemy or 'political idolatry'. At much the same time, Pascal and La Rochefoucauld offered a more wide-ranging critique of ritual as simulation and mystification (*mystère* is their term). Like Goffman (1959), Pascal emphasises the importances of properties such as the robes and the palaces of magistrates, 'tout cet appareil auguste', as he calls it, as a means to overawe the spectators, while La Rochefoucauld puts more stress on what we would call 'body language'. 'La gravité est un mystère du corps inventé pour cacher les défauts de l'esprit'.[32]

With the last example we have reached the critique of secular rituals on secular grounds, in the tradition of the stoics. Stoic values had considerable appeal in early modern Europe. Erasmus, whose criticism of rituals has been noted more than once already, had considerable sympathy with stoicism. In France in the 1560s, Etienne de La Boétie was at once an admirer of the stoics and of republics and a critic of what he called the 'miracles' and 'mysteries' of the French kings. He described public rituals as 'drugs' to keep the people submissive, adapting Viret's phrase of the 1550s (above, p. 229) for use in a secular context.[33] Stoic and republican values were also central to a number of Italian social critics. The sixteenth-century Venetian patrician Alvise Cornaro, for example, declared that 'in our time adulation and ceremonies have eroded the sincerity of civic life' (*hanno tolti...a deprimere la sincerità del viver civile*).[34] In seventeenth-century Venice, there were attempts to organise meetings of intellectuals where participants would not be allowed to stand on ceremony, at the house of Andrea Morosini, for example, and in that of Gianfrancesco Loredan, of whom it was said that 'there was nothing he disliked more than to be treated ceremoniously and with deference' (*con ceremonie e ossequii*).[35] In Genoa, Andrea Spinola associated ritual with the absolute monarchies he disliked. The lack of ceremony in republican Switzerland, he wrote, is among their joys, and the recent increase of ceremony in his native Genoa he considered 'ridiculous' and inappropriate to the traditions of that republic.[36]

La Boétie's friend Montaigne was no republican and he gradually moved away from the stoic ideals of his youth, but in his essays he did offer a critique of ritual ('les loix cérémoinieuses de nostre civilité'), which does have a stoic ring to it. He described these customs as 'abject', 'servile', a form of 'prostitution' and as nothing but outward show, mere packaging. 'Nous ne sommes que cérémonie: la cérémonie nous importe, et laissons la substance des choses'.[37] Montaigne rarely expresses a simple attitude toward anything, but his critique of ritual looks very much like the negative side of his positive attempt to portray himself as sincerely as he could, part of the 'rise of sincerity' which Trilling (1972) dated to the later sixteenth century, or, to return to the contrast sketched elsewhere in this book, the gradual rise of the 'sincerity threshold' and the replacement of a 'theatre culture' or 'honour culture' by a 'sincerity culture' (above, p. 13). Montaign's disciple Charron also argued that the wise man should avoid 'captivity' to ceremony.[38]

It is of course extremely hard to say whether the ideas of Montaigne or Pascal or La Rochefoucauld were shared by many people in their own day. Better evidence of a trend towards the repudiation of ritual comes from casual phrases which express generally unspoken assumptions rather than self-conscious arguments. In 1469, for example, a Florentine patrician described a formal consultation held on the death of Piero de'Medici as 'a ceremony, which was considered an act of little weight (*una ceremonia, e stimasi atto di poco pondo*; quoted in Rubinstein, 1966, p. 174). In 1558, the writer Annibale Caro described some of his letters as purely formal and unimportant (*sono di cerimonie, che sono di poco momento*).[39] A friend of Michelangelo's reminded him that they spoke among themselves 'from the heart and not with the ceremonies of courtiers' (*di core et non per cerimonie cortigiane*).[40] In 1577, Philip II, who is generally seen as a man who took forms seriously, wrote that 'Now is not the time to discuss precedence or to waste time over trivial matters, when there are others of such great importance' (Lovett, 1977 p. 99), while Philip IV was once reproved for being ineffectual, a purely ceremonial king (es V. M. un Rey por ceremonia).[41] In Shakespeare, although 'rites' are taken seriously (and described as 'holy', 'fair' and 'noble'), the 'idol ceremony' is dismissed, not only by Timon of Athens (Act 1, scene 2) but also by Henry V (Act 4, scene 1). Spenser too expresses in his poetry his distrust of 'the outward shew of things', including 'pageants' (Giamatti, 1975).

It is not easy to show that there were changes over time in these more-or-less unspoken assumptions, but I have the impression that dismissive attitudes to ritual became more and more commonplace, particularly in the eighteenth century. From the standpoint of our own time, the old regime of twentieth-century Europe looks stiff, formal, highly ritualised, as if dancing a permanent minuet. However, people were more relaxed than they had been in the seventeenth century, or at any rate found formality more irksome. One famous expression of this attitude is Swift's criticism of the 'needless and endless way of multiplying ceremonies'. 'There is a pedantry in manners... I look upon fiddlers, dancing-masters, heralds, masters of the ceremonies etc. to be greater pedants than Lipsius or the elder Scaliger'.[42] Lord Chesterfield seems to have shared Swift's opinion, for he once remarked to Garter King of Arms, 'You foolish man, you don't know your own foolish business'.[43] In France, Montesquieu mocked the royal touch by imagining a Persian visitor surprised to find the king treated as a 'great magician'.[44] In Italy, Scipione Maffei's attack on duels and vengeance was in part an attack on ritual, denying that 'an insult has the force of a symbol' (ha forza di segno), while Gozzi, whom we have already encountered (p. 292) as an opponent of formal modes of address, argued that 'The simpler the ceremony, the closer to sincerity and virtue' and vice versa.[45] In the eyes of some social groups at least, identity was no longer linked as closely as it had been to institutional roles (Berger, 1970). It may be tempting to link this rejection of ritual to the so-called 'rise of the bourgeoisie', and their cultural warfare with the aristocracy, but it is important to realise that the criticisms of ritual were often made by nobles and sometimes even by monarchs.

Unlike Louis XIV, for instance, Louis XV seems to have found it a strain to live his life in public, and after the formal coucher du roi he would get up again and finish the day in his private rooms (Shennan, 1977). In England, court rituals were modified in line with George I's preference for simplicity (Beattie, 1967, pp. 258f.). In Vienna, Maria Teresa (according to a British visitor) 'abridged many of the irksome ceremonials formerly in use', and her successor showed 'total contempt of pomp and parade'.[46] The same witness recorded that a recent pope 'could not go through all the ostentatious parade which his station required, without reluctance and marks of disgust'.[47] Benedict XIII refused to occupy his grand apartments in the Vatican and scandalised the Congregation of Rites by appearing in public without an escort; Benedict XIV confessed to lacking 'gravity' and liked to entertain informally and to escape from public life in Rome to private life in Castel Gandolfo, and he refused to allow his friends to kiss his foot (Pastor, 1886, vol. 34, pp. 114f; vol. 35, pp. 32, vol. 38, 167, 181). There was a reaction against the elaboration of ritual characteristic of the sixteenth and seventeenth centuries. Like gardens, manners became more informal. There was at the very least a rhetoric of informality and not standing on ceremony to be discerned in France, England and Italy. There was a cult of spontaneity, most vividly expressed in the writings of Diderot and Rousseau. Diderot, for example, in his *Neveu de Rameau*, contrasted social roles with the real people playing them (Trilling, 1972, ch. 2). Rousseau, in his *Lettre à D'Alembert*, developed a critique of the rituals of social life as inauthentic; the Quaker position, but advocated on secular grounds (Sennett, 1977, pp. 115f). Modes of address and conventions of portraiture changed, at least among the upper classes in Italy, France and England (above, pp. 92, 165). Towards the end of the old regime, in 1775, Condorcet, Turgot and others discussed the expense of the coronation ritual, describing it as 'foolish', 'ridiculous' and 'a futile game' (quoted in Haueter, 1975, pp. 339f). The leaders of the French Revolution resembled Rousseau in their cult of sincerity and they regarded the enemies of the Republic as hypocrites who needed to be unmasked. However, like Anabaptists and Quakers before them, these anti-ritualists discovered the value of what Marat called the 'theatre of the state' and created a number of new festivals (Butwin, 1975; Ozouf, 1976).

The French Revolution revealed the dangers of demystifying a regime. The clock of ceremony was put back, to some extent at least, under Napoleon and after the restoration of the Bourbons. Although the ampulla containing the holy oil for the consecration of the kings of France had been solemnly smashed in 1793, the oil was preserved and the ampulla restored for the coronation of 1814 (Jackson, 1984, pp. 188–9). In the Church of England, the middle of the nineteenth century was a period of rising 'ritualism'. The period 1870–1914, so it has recently been argued, was one marked by the 'invention of tradition' (including rituals) partly as a way of legitimating new regimes, such as the Second Reich and the Third Republic (Hobsbawm and Ranger, 1983). However, the clock of consciousness cannot be put back. Even if many people still take rituals seriously – and it is possible that new media, television in particular, have been able to remystify authority – it remains true that a detached, indeed a dismissive attitude to 'mere' ritual has become firmly rooted in western culture.

Notes

1 The historical anthropology of early modern Italy

1 G. Pallavicino, *Inventione di scriver tute le cose accadute alli tempi suoi*, ed. E. Grendi (Genoa, 1975), p. 73.

2 These 'wetting sports', as he calls them, are discussed by R. Lassels, *A Voyage of Italy* (Paris, 1670), quoted in Shearman (1967), p. 130.

3 F. D'Andrea, *Ricordi*, ed. N. Cortese (Naples, 1923), pp. 216, 67.

4 A vivid description in N. Amelot de la Houssaie, *Histoire du gouvernement de Venise* (Paris, 1676), p. 17.

5 S. Paolucci, *Missioni de'padri della Compagnia di Giesù nel Regno di Napoli* (Naples, 1651), pp. 10f.

6 Pallavicino, *Inventione*, passim; F. Casoni, 'Costumi delli Genovesi', ACG, fondo Brignole Sale, ms. 110 E. 14, f. 7 verso.

7 Two fairly typical examples in ASR, TCG, Processi, 17th century, busta 517 (1659), ff. 430 *et seq.* and f. 1004.

8 ASR, TCG, Processi, 17th century, busta 140.

9 J. Addison, *Remarks on Several Parts of Italy* (1705; London, 1890), p. 378. There are some particularly flowery petitions, *c.* 1700, in ASV, Esecutori contra la Bestemmia, buste 1–2.

10 Some fifty Renaissance treatises on the subject are discussed in Bryson (1935).

2 The sources: outsiders and insiders

1 Sixty-odd accounts are listed in Schudt (1959), which makes no claim to be complete and certainly omits some Englishmen. The most perceptive study of foreign travellers is Venturi (1973); on the English, Stoye (1952) is to be recommended.

2 G. Baretti, *An Account of the Manners and Customs of Italy* (London, 1766).

3 T. Coryat, *Crudities* (1611; repr., 2 vols., Glasgow, 1905), vol. 2, p. 36.

4 R. Lassels, *The Voyage of Italy* (Paris, 1670), p. 124; G. Burnet, *Some Letters* (Amsterdam, 1686), p. 108; J. Addison, *Remarks on Several Parts of Italy* (1705; London, 1890), pp. 34f.

5 Coryat, *Crudities*, pp. 408, 399; J. Moore, *A View of Society and Manners in Italy* (3 vols., Dublin, 1781), Letter 50.

6 M. de Montaigne, *Journal de Voyage en Italie*, ed. M. Rat (Paris, 1955), pp. 68, 125–6.
7 P. Skippon, 'An Account of a Journey', in *A Collection of Voyages*, ed. A. and J. Churchill (6 vols., London, 1732), vol. 6, pp. 534, 589. Cf. Raven (1942), pp. 52f.
8 Pius II, *Commentarii* (Frankfurt, 1614). Written in the 1460s, the text was not published till 1584. A useful abridged translation is *Memoirs of a Renaissance Pope*, ed. L. C. Gabel (New York, 1962).
B. Cellini, *Vita*, ed. E. Camesasca (Milan, 1954). Written 1558–66, the text was not published till 1728. The Penguin translation by George Bull, *The Autobiography of Benvenuto Cellini* (Harmondsworth, 1956), is to be recommended.
G. Cardano, *De vita propria* (Paris, 1643). Written in 1575, the text was translated by J. Stoner as *The Book of My Life* (New York, 1930).
9 Pius II, *Commentarii*, p. 219. The reference is to Plutarch's life of Artaxerxes, Book 5, section 1.
10 Cellini, *Vita*, p. 159.
11 B. Castiglione, *Il Cortegiano* (1528), Book 2, sections 45 onwards. There are many modern editions and translations.
12 G. Della Casa, *Galateo* (1558; ed. D. Provenzal, Milan, 1950; trans. R. S. Pine-Coffin, Harmondsworth, 1958), ch. 3.
13 P. Belmonte, *Institutione della sposa* (Rome, 1587). On Barbara Spinola, ACG, fondo Brignole Sale, ms. 709.
14 ASR, TCG, Processi, 17th century, busta 50, ff. 883 *et seq.*

3 Classifying the people: the census as collective representation

1 I have incurred even more debts than usual in the course of preparing this chapter, which draws on earlier papers on the Florentine and Venetian censuses. My thanks to Natalie Davis, Rudolf Dekker, John Henderson, Martha Howell, Frederick Lane, Richard Mackenney, Lotte van de Pol, and Nicolai Rubinstein for their help.
2 *Anagrafi di tutto lo stato della serenissima Republica di Venezia* (5 vols., Venice, 1768).
3 ASF, 'Miscellanea Medici', 224; BNF, II.I.120
4 The samples taken were Via Pentolini (on which there was more information in the A-text), and Corso de'Tintori (on which it was the B-text which was fuller).
5 The Venetian envoy, Bartolomeo Comino, recorded this in a dispatch of 27 September 1591.
6 ASF, Strozziana, ser. 1, vol. 19; ASR, Camerale, Sanità 2, busta 4, fascio 12.

7 For Genoa, ASG, fondo B. Senarega, no. 1073; for Venice, Rapp (1976), ch. 3.

8 G. B. Tedaldi, 'Relazione sopra la città e il Capitanato di Pistoia', *Rivista Storica Italiana* 10 (1892). For Venice, see note 2 above.

9 ASF, Strozziana, ser. 1, vol. 24, f. 131 recto.

10 Campanella quoted in Bock (1974), p. 141n.

11 G. Franchi, *Poveri homini*, ed. G. Bertozzi (Rome, 1976), p. 331.

12 For the 1632 census I used the ms. in BNF, Magl. II.I.240; for Venice, see note 2 above.

13 On the numbers and classes of souls in 17th-century Rome, ASR Camerale II, Popolazione 7; cf. F. Cerasoli, 'Censimento della popolazione di Roma dall'anno 1600 al 1739', *Studi e documenti di storia e diritto* 12 (1891), 169–99.

14 The 17th-century censuses discussed here are in ASV, Provveditori della Sanità, 568–72.

15 N. Machiavelli, *Discorsi*, Book 1, ch. 55.

16 ASV, Dieci Savi alla Decima, condizioni de'decime, 1581, buste 143–72, and 1711, buste 267–82. On these documents see Canal (1908).

17 *Anagrafi* (note 2 above), vol. 1, p. iii.

18 G. B. Marino, 'donna che cuce'; B. Morando, 'bellissima filatrice di seta'; L. Tingoli, 'bella ricamatrice'; P. Zazzaroni, 'bella lavandaia'; Ciro di Pers, 'bella ricamatrice'; 'bella che cuce', 'bella dipanatrice'; A. Agostini, 'bella pollarola', 'bella sartora', 'bella ciarlatana'; G. Salomoni, 'bella astrologa'; G. F. Maia Materdona, 'bella libraia'. One is reminded of some late 16th-century paintings, notably the series made for the study of Francesco' de'Medici, Grand Duke of Tuscany.

19 ASV, Sant'Ufficio, Processi, vol. 75 (1620), the cases of Serena Greca and Marietta Greca.

20 If they had merely been sailor's widows, 'vedova' would have been the normal description: if boat-women, 'barcaiola'. It is always possible that they were the owners of craft operated by others. On the other hand, the Venetian navy was unusual in allowing wives on board, and in this milieu female 'seamen' might have appeared less abnormal.

21 L. Ghetti argued *c.* 1445 that 'according to natural reason' one man made five mouths 'between women, children and the old' (text quoted in Roscoe, 1796, appendix 6).
The same point was made in the 17th century; 'ordinarily one head makes five mouths' (ASF, Strozziana, sr. 1, vol. 24, f. 111 recto)

22 On Sansovino's guide, see p. 255 below. The Roman data are to be found in ASF, Strozziana, ser. 1, vol. 24, collected, according to the title page, by Luigi Strozzi in 1677.

4 The bishop's questions and the people's religion

1 S. Paolucci, *Missioni de'Padri della Compagnia de Giesù* (Naples, 1651), p. 29 Cf. Levi (1945).

2 A. Boschet, *Le parfait missionaire* (Paris, 1697), p. 96. A slightly more open-ended question was used in the valley of Niolo in Corsica by the missionaries of St Vincent de Paul in 1652: 'S'il y a un Dieu, ou s'il y en a plusieurs'; L. Abelly, *La vie de St Vincent de Paul* (Paris, 1664), vol. 2, p. 76.

3 Regino of Prum, *De synodalibus causis*, ed. F. G. A. Wasserschleben (Leipzig 1840), pp. 19–26.

4 Since this essay was first published, it has inspired one piece of research, Baratti (1981–2). My thanks to Adriano Prosperi, who supervised it, for bringing this thesis to my attention.

5 *Prime visite pastorali*, ed. R. Putelli (Mantua, 1934).

6 *Atti della Visita Pastorale del vescovo D. Bollani*, ed. P. Guerrini (3 vols., Brescia 1915–40). Cf. Cairns (1976), pp. 176–9.

7 *Aspetti della Controriforma a Firenze*, ed. A. D'Addario (Rome, 1972), p. 518.

8 *Atti della Visita apostolica di S. Carlo Borromeo in Bergamo*, ed. A. G. Roncalli (later pope John XXIII) (Florence, 1936–58), vol. 1, p. 401.

9 P. Fuschus, *De visitatione* (Rome, 1581), pp. 377–95; M. Timotheus, *Institutio visitandi ecclesias* (Venice, 1586), pp. 193–208; F. Ninguarda, *Manuale Visitatorum* (Venice, 1592), pp. 138–42.

10 The answers to even these questions were eliminated from the modern edition of the visitation: *Atti della visita pastorale di Feliciano Ninguarda*, ed. S. Monti (2 vols., Como, 1898). They are discussed in Baratti, part 2, ch. 2.

11 V. M. Orsini, 'Instruzioni', in G. Crispino, *Trattato della visita pastorale* (Rome, 1844), pp. 69–119. On him, see Pastor (1938–53), vol. 34, pp. 108f.

12 Crispino, pp. 22f, especially questions 37–9. On him, see De Rosa (1971), pp. 277f.

13 De Rosa, ch. 1.

14 *La visita pastorale di Ludovico Flangini*, ed. B. Bertoli and S. Tramontin (Rome, 1969).

15 *La visita pastorale di G. L. Pyrker*, ed. B. Bertoli and S. Tramontin (Rome, 1971).

16 *La visita pastorale di G. Grasser*, ed. L. Pesce (Rome, 1969).

17 *La visita pastorale di Federico Manfredini nella diocesi di Padova*, ed. M. Piva (Rome, 1971).

18 *Die Akten der Visitation des Bistums Münster aus der Zet Johanns von* Hoya, ed. W. E. Schwarz (Münster, 1913), p. 15.

19 Pérouas (1964); *T. Secker's Articles of Enquiry*, ed. H. A. L. Jukes (Oxford, 1957), pp. 4–5.

20 *Arti e tradizioni popolari*, ed. G. Tassoni (Bellinzona, 1973). Cf. Moravia (1970), pp. 187f.

5 How to be a Counter-Reformation saint

1 J. Moore, *A View of Society and Manners in Italy* (3 vols., Dublin 1781), letter 42.

2 Erasmus, *Enchiridion Militis Christiani*. The translation follows *The Essential Erasmus*, ed. J. P. Dolan (New York, 1964), p. 60.

3 Originally prefixed to his edition of Jerome's works, it has been reprinted in his *Opuscula*, ed. W. K. Ferguson (The Hague, 1933). On the Bollandists, see Delehaye (1959).

4 I follow the list compiled by G. Löw from the archives of the Congregation of Rites, and printed in his article 'Canonizzazione' in the *Enciclopedia Cattolica* (12 vols., Rome 1948–54). Slightly higher figures are given by other scholars, possibly as a result of adding unofficial saints.

5 A. Rocca, *De canonizatione sanctorum* (Rome, 1610), p. 5.

6 P. Lambertini, *De canonizatione* (Rome, 1766). Pastor (1938–53) is of course invaluable on the different popes. On Urban VIII, see vol. 29; on Benedict XIV, vol. 35.

7 Details in *Bibliotheca Sanctorum* (12 vols., Rome, 1961–70), s.v. 'Rocco'.

8 G. Gigli, *Diario romano*, ed. G. Ricciotti (Rome, 1958), p. 311.

9 P. Crasset, *Historie de l'eglise du Japon* (Paris, 1715).

10 V. Puccini, *Vita di M. M. Pazzi* (Florence, 1611), p. 1; S. Razzi, *Vita di santa Caterina de'Ricci* (1594; ed. G. M. di Agresti, Florence, 1965), pp. 133, 129.

11 G. B. Possevino, *Discorsi della vita di Carlo Borromeo* (Rome, 1591), p. 121; A. Valier, *Vita del beato Carlo Borromeo* (Milan, 1602), p. 53.

12 S. Di S. Silverio, *Vita di Andrea Corsini* (Florence, 1683), pp. 54f.

13 J. Addison, *Remarks on Several Parts of Italy* (1705: London, 1890 edn), p. 369.

14 G. Burnet, *Some Letters* (Amsterdam, 1686), p. 106; Montesquieu, 'Voyages en Europe', in his *Oeuvres complètes*, ed. D. Oster (Paris, 1964), p. 253, adding, 'Peu de fripons ont tant coûté à leur famille, que ce saint.' But some Italians made similar comments. In the 15th century the Roman lawyer Stefano Infessura recorded the canonisation of St Leopold by Innocent VIII, 'ex quo fertur recepisse ab imperatore summam 15m ducatorum' (*Diario*, ed. O. Tommasini, Rome, 1890, p. 177). Benedict XIV, no less, is the source for the story that the canonisation of François de Sales cost 32,000 Crowns (Delooz, 1969, p. 435).

6 Perceiving a counter-culture

1 The best and most accessible edition is in *Il libro dei vagabondi*, ed. P. Camporesi (Turin, 1973), pp. 351–4.

2 ibid., pp. 355–60.

3 Editions listed ibid., pp. 89–91; the text reprinted, pp. 93–165.

4 J. Callot, *Etchings*, ed. H. Daniel (New York, 1974).

5 M. Alemán de Alfarache, 1 (1599; Italian trans., Venice 1606), book 3, ch. 2. The Cervantes story was published in Spanish in 1613 and in Italian in 1626.

6 Reprinted in *Figures de la gueuserie*, ed. R. Chartier (Paris, 1982), 107–31.

7 Harman and Greene are reprinted in *Cony-Catchers and Bawdy Baskets*, ed. G. Salgādo (Harmondsworth, 1972), pp. 79–263.

8 T. Garzoni, *La piazza universale di tutte le professioni del mondo* (Venice, 1585), chs. 251–2, repr. Camporesi (see note 1 above), pp. 293–9.

9 I am grateful to Dr Charles Melville of the Faculty of Oriental Studies at Cambridge for sorting the Arabic out for me.

10 This was pointed out by Camporesi, who prints the Pini text in his anthology (pp. 3–77). It had never been published before.

11 Harman, ch. 11, in Salgādo, pp. 110–18.

12 B. Pullan, *Rich and Poor in Renaissance Venice* (Oxford, 1971), pp. 301f, using ASV, Provveditori alla Sanità, Notatorio, vols. 729–30. On London, Aydelotte (1913), p. 95.

13 'Technas, dolos, fraudes et machinas exhibet, ut caveas, non ut discas'; from the 'approbation' prefixed by a theologian, J. B. Magnavacca, to Barezzi's Italian translation of *Lazarillo de Tormes* (Venice, 1621).

14 *Il ballo delle zingare* (1614).

15 The texts have been printed five times. A. Massoni, 'Gli accatoni in Londra nel secolo xix e in Roma nel secolo xvi', *La Rassegna Italiana* (1882), pp. 20f, followed the Vatican copy; M. Löpelmann, in *Romanische Forschungen* 34 (1913), pp. 653–64, followed that of Berlin. Massoni's text was followed by Delumeau (1955–7, pp. 405f), and Löpelmann's by Camporesi (above, note 1), and also by Geremek (1980), pp. 205–12. Of these scholars, only Geremek expresses any doubts about the authenticity of the documents.

16 ASR, TCG, Processi, 1593, busta 262, ff. 630–757.

17 *Ricordi* (Venice, 1554 edition), no. 5.

18 B. Arditi, *diario di Firenze e di altre parti della Cristianità*, ed. R. Cantagalli (Florence, 1970), p. 126.

19 Montesquieu, *Oeuvres Complètes*, ed. D. Oster (Paris, 1964), p. 280; S. Sharp, *Letters from Italy in the Years 1765 and 6* (London, 1766), letter 24; T. Martyn, *The Gentleman's guide in his Tour through Italy* (London, 1787), p. 264.

7 Languages and anti-languages

1 This question is discussed at a more general level and at much greater length in my introduction to *The Social History of Language*, ed. P. Burke and R. Porter (Cambridge, 1986).

2 *Le prediche volgari di San Bernardino di Siena*, ed. L. Banchi (Siena, 1880–8). Preached in the main square of Siena in 1427, these sermons were taken down by a craftsman called Benedetto di Maestro Bartolomeo.

3 E. Masini, *Sacro Arsenale* (Bologna, 1665 edn), p. 157.

4 T. Rinuccini, *Usanze fiorentine del secolo xvii* (Florence, 1863).

5 Obvious examples are M. Bandello, *Novelliere* (1554), book 1, no. 3, book 2, no. 51 (of which the heroine is the courtesan Isabella de Luna), and book 4, no. 16; and A. F. Grazzini, *Le Cene* (written in the late 16th century but not published till the 18th), no. 4. The tradition is doubtless an old one: cf. Boccaccio, *Decamerone*, Day 6.

6 A. Rospigliosi, *Ricordi*, p. 3; A. Giuffredi, *Avvertimenti cristiani* (written *c.* 1585; ed. L. Natali, Palermo 1896), p. 84.

7 J. Moore, *A View of Society and Manners in Italy* (3 vols., Dublin, 1781), vol. 2, Letter 60.

8 M. Sanudo, *La città di Venetia*, ed. A. Caracciolo Aricò (Milan, 1980), pp. 205–6.

9 S. Guazzo, *La civil conversatione* (Venice, 1575), f. 40 recto. G. Politiano, *Del parlare e del tacere* (Milan, 1547) is disappointingly unspecific in its recommendations.

10 F. Barbaro, *De re uxoria* (*c.* 1450; I used the Paris, 1513 edition), Book 2, ch. 8.

11 V. Nofri, *Ginipedia overo avvertimenti civili per donna nobile* (Venice, 1631); cf. the treatises discussed in Casali (1982), 112f.

12 P. de Brantôme, *Les dames galantes* (written before 1614; ed. P. Pia, Paris, 1981, p. 237).

13 Quoted in Petrucci (1982), no. 178; the text was confiscated in a Roman prison in 1666. For clerical preoccupation with this form of magic, see G. Menghi, *Compendio dell'arte essorcistica* (Bologna, 1576), Book 3, ch. 11, and *Documenti etnografici e folkloristici nei sinodi diocesani italiani*, ed. C. Corrain and P. L. Zampini (Bologna, 1970), pp. 84, 201.

14 The nobleman or courtier is recommended to be a man of few words in D. Caraffa (d. 1487), *Instrutione del bon cortesano*, ed. E. Mayer (Rome, 1937), chs. 17–18, and in Saba da Castiglione, *Ricordi* (1549; Venice, 1554 edn), no. 42.

15 These examples from Sanudo, *Città*, 205f.

16 G. P. Lomazzo, *Rabisch dra Academigli dor Compa Zavargna* (1589; I used the Milan 1627 edition). Cf. Lynch (1966).

17 *Il libro dei vagabondi*, ed. P. Camporesi (Turin, 1973), pp. 183f, 189f, 203f.

18 Quoted by Vianello (1957), p. 69n. The fullest study of the subject I know is G. B. De Luca, *Discorso della stile legale* (Rome, 1697).

19 There seems to have been little research to date on these 'linguaggi settoriali' in Italy, but a beginning was made by Beccaria, 1969 (ch. 2), and Beccaria, 1973.

20 *Il tumulto dei Ciompi*, ed. G. Scaramella (Bologna, 1934), p. 14.

21 ACG, fondo Brignole Sale, 106B, ff. 11–12.

22 P. Adami, *Regole che s'osservano nelle schuole de'padri della Compagnia di Giesù nel loro collegio di Sta Lucia in Bologna*, ed. N. Fabrini (Rome, 1946), pp. 27, 32.

23 F. Moryson, *An Itinerary* (4 vols., Glasgow, 1907), vol. 1, p. 338; T. Coryate, *Crudities* (2 vols., Glasgow, 1905), vol. 2, p. 59; J. Ray, *Observations* (London, 1673), p. 393.

24 T. Boccalini, *La bilancia politica* (3 vols., Châtelaine 1678), vol. 1, p. 38. Boccalini died in 1613.

25 *Gazzetta Veneta* no. 17, 2 April 1760; P. Verri, 'Il Tu, Voi e Lei', in his *Opere varie*, ed. N. Valeri (Florence, 1947), 1, pp. 141–5; F. S. Quadrio, *Lettera intorno a'titoli d'onore* (Milan, 1751).

26 P. Aretino, *Sei Giornate*, ed. G. Aquilecchia (Bari, 1975), p. 82. Cf. Ross (1954), which launched the terms 'U' and 'non-U'.

27 G. B. Gelli, 'Ragionamento' (1551), in his *Opere*, ed. A. C. Alesina (Naples, 1970), pp. 495–522.

28 V. Borghini, *Scritti inediti or rari sulla lingua*, ed. J. R. Woodhouse (Bologna, 1971).

8 Insult and blasphemy

1 *Scrittura e popolo nella Roma barocca, 1585–1721*, ed. A. Petrucci (Rome, 1982), no. 78. It was thanks to the exhibition of which this is the catalogue that my attention was drawn to the material studied here.

2 ASR, TCG, Processi. There are 2 series, for the 16th and 17th centuries respectively, making something like 15,000 cases altogether. Cases of defamatory libel are indicated in the catalogue.

3 C. Baldi, *Delle mentite et offese di parole come possino accommodarsi* (Bologna, 1623).

4 ASR, TCG, Processi, 17th century, busta 580 bis (1666), f. 332 et seq; busta 581 (1666), f. 137 et seq.

5 G. Bonifacio, *L'arte de'cenni* (Vicenza, 1616), pp. 60, 79, 188, 229, 335. *Short Italian Dictionary* (Cambridge, 1923), s.v. 'ficha'.

6 M. Bandello, *Novelle*, Book 4, no. 16 (the author died in 1561). I have been unable to find this case in the records of the Tribunal of the Governor, but little before 1550 has survived.

7 J. Evelyn, *Diary*, ed. E. S. de Beer (5 vols., Oxford, 1955), vol. 2, p. 173. In Rome in 1606, a father complained of being insulted by his son, 'putting his finger in his mouth, a wicked and ugly gesture against a father who has treated him so well' (ASR, TCG, Processi, 17th century, busta 50, f. 885 verso).

8 Inscription on the church of St Clement, Rome, *c.* 1084, in *Le origini*, ed. A. Viscardi et al. (Milan-Naples, 1956), p. 510.

9 ASM, Notarile, busta 28,544 (M. Bossi), 7 March 1629.

10 G. Priuli, *I Diarii*, 2, ed. R. Cessi (Bologna, 1937), pp. 254, 394.

11 The literature on Pasquino is so far somewhat disappointing. For an anthology of his utterances with a historical introduction, see Silenzi (1932). Dr Anne Reynolds is preparing a more analytical study.

12 *La Venexiana*, ed. L. Zorzi (Turin, 1965); Ruzzante, *L'Anconitana*, ed. L. Zorzi (Turin, 1965); Ruzzante, *Due Dialoghi*, ed. L. Zorzi (Turin, 1968). The history of Italian swearing seems to have been neglected, although a student of Jean Delumeau's, Signora Piozza-Donati, is writing a thesis on the subject. On Italy today, see Averna (1977).

13 B. Cellini, *Vita*, ed. E. Camesasca (Milan, 1954), p. 71. A textual critic might add 'culo' or 'cazzo'.

14 P. Skippon, 'An Account of a Journey' in *A Collection of Voyages*, ed. A. and J. Churchill (6 vols., London, 1732), vol. 6, p. 520.

15 ASV, Esecutori contra la bestemmia, Processi, buste 1 and 2.

16 ASR, TCG, processi, 17th century, busta 69 (1608), f. 171 verso.

17 S. Maffei. *Della scienza chiamata cavalleresca* (second edn, Venice 1712).

18 *Documenti etnografici e folkloristici nei sinodi diocesani italiani*, ed. C. Corrain and P. L. Zampini (Bologna, 1970), p. 90.

19 ASR, TCG, Processi, 16th century, busta 278 (1594), f. 1243 et seq. This is presumably the only manuscript pasquinade of the period to survive, though many were preserved by being printed at the time.

20 ASR, TCG, Processi, 17th century, busta 442 bis (1651), f. 614 recto. G. Baretti, *An Account of the Manners and Customs of Italy* (London, 1766), p. 65.

21 ASR, TCG, Processi, 17th century, busta 114 (1613), f. 765 et seq., a nice example of verbal shuffling and blinding with science; cf. busta 167 (1620), f. 695.

22 ASR, TCG, Processi, 17th century, busta 69 (1608), f. 751.

23 ASR, TCG, Processi, 16th century, busta 108 (1565), f. 255 et seq.

24 My thanks to Rudolf Dekker of the Erasmus University Rotterdam and to Florike Egmond for providing me with a vocabulary of insult drawn from Dutch archives.

25 R. Cobb has an unpublished paper on insults in 18-century Paris; cf. D. Garrioch's chapter on the subject in P. Burke and R. Porter (eds.), *The Social History of Language* (forthcoming, Cambridge, 1987), and, on French Canada, Moogk (1979).

9 The uses of literacy

1 Villani mentions 8,000 to 10,000 'boys and girls' at reading-schools; 1,000 to 1,200 boys at arithmetic-schools; 550 to 600 boys at four grammar schools: *Cronica*, ed. F. Dragomanni (Florence, 1845), Book XI, ch. 92. His statement should not be taken to imply that boys and girls had equal access to primary education.

2 P. Morigi, *La nobiltà di Milano* (Milan, 1595), p. 299. G. B. Casale, carpenter who became one of the 'coadjutors' of these schools in 1563, tells us that he taught writing gratis ('Giornale': Milan, Biblioteca Ambrosiana, fondo Trotti, no. 413, ff. 7 verso, 10 recto).

3 See the life of the pope in Vespasiano da Bisticci, *Vite di uomini illustri*, ed. P. d'Ancona and E. Aeschlimann (Milan, 1951). On the shift from public to private reading, Chaytor (1945).

4 These distinctions can be found in sixteenth-century writing manuals such as G. A. Tagliente, *La vera arte de lo excellente scrivere* (Venice, 1536), and G. B. Palatino, *Libro nel quale s'insegna a scrivere ogni sorte lettere* (Rome, 1547).

5 The phrase comes from the pen of the merchant G. Rucellai in his *Zibaldone*, ed. A. Perosa (London, 1960). Cf. L. B. Alberti, *I libri della famiglia*, ed. R. Romano and A. Tenenti (Turin, 1969), p. 251.

6 A. Spinola, *Scritti scelti*, ed. C. Bitossi (Genoa, 1981), pp. 220, 228–9.

7 An early printed example of a textbook with commercial applications is P. Borgo, *De arithmetica* (Venice, 1484). Cf. G. A. Tagliente, *Luminario di arithmetica* (Venice, 1525), and D. Manzoni, *Quaderno doppio* (Venice, 1540), which have both been reprinted in facsimile (London, 1978).

8 F. Ghaligai, *Summa de arithmetica* (1521; new edition, Florence, 1548); H. Tagliente, *Tesoro universale* (Venice, c. 1530).

9 Paolo da Certaldo's 14th-century *Libro di buoni costumi*, ed. A. Schiaffini (Florence, 1945), no. 251.

10 A. M. degli Strozzi, *Lettere*, ed. C. Guasti (Florence, 1877).

11 A letter of 1540, quoted in Seneca (1959), p. 9.

12 Quoted in Luzio (1887), pp. 37f.

13 Quoted in Pieraccini (1924), pp. 204, 218.

14 Venice, Biblioteca Correr, Ms Donà 418, i, 5.

15 L. Landucci, *Diario fiorentino*, ed. J. del Badia (Florence, 1883).

16 G. Nadi, *Diario bolognese*, ed. C. Ricci and A. Bacchi (Bologna, 1886); B. Arditi, *Diario*, ed. R. Cantagallo (Florence, 1970).

17 G. Priuli, *I Diarii*, ed. A. Segre and R. Cessi (2 vols., Città di Castello and Bologna, 1912–37); G. Pallavicino, *Inventione di scriver tutte le cose accadute alli tempi suoi*, ed. E. Grendi (Genoa, 1975); G. B. Casale (above, note 2).

18 D. Velluti, *Cronaca*, ed. I. Del Lungo and G. Volpi (Florence, 1914).

19 See Velluti and also G. Morelli, *Ricordi*, ed. V. Branca (Florence, 1956), p. 81.

20 Rucellai (above, note 5), p. 2.

21 Paolo da Castaldo (above, note 9), nos. 136, 139.

22 G. da Sommaia, *Diario di un estudiante de Salamanca*, ed. G. Haley (Salamanca, 1977). Despite the modern title, the text is in Italian. Some interesting details are omitted from this printed version (the ms. is in Florence, BN).

23 R. Passegeri, *In artem notariae summule* (Venice, 1565).

24 *Documenti etnografici e folkloristici nei sinodi diocesani italiani*, ed. C. Corrain and P. L. Zampini (Bologna, 1970), pp. 36, 132, 147, 201, 282. Cf Millunzi (1900), from which the 'abracadabra' example comes, and O'Neil (1984). A good collection of magical recipes is to be found in ASV, Sant'Ufficio, busta 55 (1985), the case of Annibale da Perugia.

25 *Legenda et oratione di Santa Margherita* (Venice, *c*. 1550). The instructions for use are to be found on the title page.
26 ASV, Santo Officio, Processi, busta 55 (the case of Rinaldo Vio).
27 F. Moryson, *Itinerary* (4 vols., Glasgow 1907–8), vol. 1, p. 303.
28 Among the best-known treatises are G. B. Palatino, *Dalle Cifre* (1540; Eng. trans., Wormley 1970); G. B. Bellano, *Novi et singulari modi di cifrare* (Brescia, 1553); G. B. Della Porta, *De furtivis literarum notis* (Naples, 1563).
29 A useful selection in *Relazioni degli ambasciatori veneti al senato*, ed. A. Ventura (2 vols., Rome and Bari, 1980). The introduction discusses the history of the genre.
30 M. de Montaigne, *Journal de Voyage*, ed. M. Rat (Paris, 1955), p. 80; P. Skippon, 'An Account of a Journey' in *Collection of Voyages*, ed. A. and J. Churchill (6 vols., London, 1732), vol. 6, pp. 502, 549 etc.
31 P. Pantera, *L'armata navale* (1614), quotted by Cipolla (1969), p. 23.
32 P. Skippon, op. cit., p. 491.
33 A. M. degli Strozzi, *Lettere*, ed. C. Guasti (Florence, 1877), p. 540.
34 M. Sanudo, *I Diarii*, ed. F. Stefani et al. (58 vols., Venice 1879–1903), vol. 50. p. 500.
35 The testimony is that of a vagabond called Girolamo (above, p. 63), in *Libro dei vagabondi*, ed. P. Camporesi (Turin, 1973), p. 357.
36 Montesquieu, *Oeuvres*, ed. D. Oster (Paris, 1964), p. 278.
37 In Venice in 1711, a sea-captain named Angelo Boza declared nearly 1000 ducats' worth of property but signed his declaration with a cross. ASV, Dieci Savi alla Decima, Castello, no. 29.
38 ASR, TCG, Processi, 17th century, busta 18 (1602), f. 715 et seq.
39 ASV, Provveditori della Sanità, buste 568–72, and Venice, Biblioteca Correr, Ms Donà 351.
40 Strozzi, op. cit., p. 347; A. Spinola, *Scritti Scelti*, ed. C. Bitossi (Genoa, 1981), p. 276.

10 Conspicuous consumption

1 J. Soldani, *Delle lodi di Ferdinando Medici, Granduca di Toscana* (Florence, 1609), sig. Aiii verso.
2 F. D'Andrea, *Ricordi*, ed. N. Cortese (Naples, 1923), pp. 208, 219. D'Andrea wrote this advice to his nephews in 1696.
3 ASV, testamenti, will of Giovanni Bembo, procuratore di San Marco, 1617. This kind of phrasing recurs in Venetian patrician wills of the period.
4 D'Andrea, *Ricordi* (see note 2 above), p. 168.
5 F. Del Migliore, *Firenze Città Nobilissima* (Florence, 1684), p. 464.
6 J. Soldani, *Satire* (Florence, 1751 edn), p. 189.
7 'Genovese e Romano': Paris, BN, Mss. Ital. 751, f. 83 verso.
8 G. Botero, *Delle cause della grandezza delle città* (Venice, 1589), Book 2, ch. 10.
9 ASV, Aggregazioni, Polinaro, 1662.

10 ACG, fondo Brignole Sale, ms. 106B, s.v. 'Palazzo Publico'.

11 G. Gigli, *Diario romano* (*1608–70*), ed. G. Ricciotti (Rome, 1958), entry for 8 April 1655.

12 R. Lassels, *A Voyage of Italy* (Paris, 1670), p. 442.

13 J. Evelyn, *Diary*, ed. E. S. de Beer (6 vols., Oxford, 1955), vol. 2, pp. 174, 236, 471. Evelyn was in Italy in 1644–5.

14 G. Burnet, *Some Letters* (Amsterdam, 1686), pp. 178, 146.

15 H. Bavinck, *Wegzeiger* (Rome, 1625), in *Documenti sul barocco in Roma*, ed. J. A. F. Orbaan (Rome, 1920), p. iv, note.

16 G. Gualdo Priorato, *Relatione di Milano* (Milan, 1666), p. 131.

17 P. Skippon, 'An Account of a Journey' in *A Collection of Voyages*, ed. A. and J. Churchill (6 vols., London, 1732), vol. 6, pp. 567, 639.

18 G. Sandys, *A Relation of a Journey* (London, 1615), p. 259.

19 G. C. Capaccio, 'Napoli' (written *c.* 1607), *Archivio Storico per le Provincie Napolitane* 7 (1882), p. 534.

20 'Discorse contra carnevale' (written *c.* 1607) in *La commedia dell'arte e la società barocca*, ed. F. Taviani (Rome, 1970), especially p. 81.

21 G. Burnet, *Letters*, p. 185.

22 Soldani, *Satire*, pp. 104, 188–9.

23 'Rengo di Senatore' in *Paolo V e la Repubblica Veneziana*, ed. E. Cornet (Venice, 1859), p. 313.

24 A. Cutolo, 'Un diario inedito del doge Leonardo Donà', *Nuova Antologia* 1953, pp. 270–81.

25 A. Spinola, *Scritti scelti*, ed. C. Bitossi (Genoa, 1981), is a good introduction to the man and his ideas; but the remarks summarised above come from his unpublished reflections (cited above, note 9), s.v. 'Carozze', 'Essequie Private', 'Palazze Private', 'Parsimonia', 'Simie di Principi', 'Svizzeri', etc.

26 Gigli, *Diario romano* (see note 11 above), p. 323.

27 T. De Santis, *Storia del Tumulto di Napoli* (Leiden, 1652), p. 64.

28 B. Arditi, *Diario*, ed. R. Cantagalli (Florence, 1970), pp. 109, 217.

29 T. Rinuccini, *Le usanze fiorentine*, ed. P. Fanfani (Florence, 1863).

30 G. B. Agucchi, 'Passaggio del cardinale Pietro Aldobrandini nel Genovesato', *Giornale Ligustico* 4 (1877), p. 273; B. Paschetti, *Del conservare la sanità* (Genoa, 1602), p. 114.

31 T. Campanella, *De Monarchia Hispanica* (Amsterdam, 1640), ch. 14; G. C. Capaccio, 'Napoli' (see note 19 above), p. 534; and an anonymous report quoted in Villari (1967), pp. 165–6.

32 G. Lomellino, 'Relatione della Repubblica di Genova', in Genoa, ACG, ms. 120, p. 173.

33 G. Priuli, *Diarii*, ed. A. Segre and R. Cessi (3 vols., Città di Castello and Bologna, 1912–37), vol. 3, p. 50.

34 G. Cavalcanti, *Istorie fiorentine*, ed. G. di Pino (Milan, 1944), p. 25.

35 G. Lercari (?) *Le discordie e guerre civili dei Genovesi*, ed. A. Olivieri (Genoa, 1857), p. 17.

36 L. B. Alberti, *I libri della famiglia*, ed. R. Romano and A. Tenenti (Turin, 1969), pp. 195ff; G. Morelli, *Ricordi*, ed. V. Branca (Florence, 1956), p. 241.

37 ASV, Testamenti, Z. Contarini (500 masses, 1600); G. da Lezze (300 masses, 1642); D. Contarini (1,000 masses, 1674); N. Venier (1,000 masses, 1688); F. Corner (3,000 masses, 1706).

11 The presentation of self in the Renaissance portrait

1 This essay owes obvious debts to earlier general studies of Italian portraits, notably to Hill (1925), Pope-Hennessy (1966), and Castelnuovo (1973), as well as to monographs on individual painters, including Hope (1980), and Hirst (1981), who notes the wealth of evidence for 'a study still unwritten: the sociology of Renaissance portraiture' (p. 94n).

2 The remark by Titian is quoted in Hope (1980), p. 160; the description of Raphael, by Vernon Lee, *c.* 1898, is quoted in Ormond (1970), p. 53.

3 G. P. Lomazzo, *Trattato dell'arte della pittura* (1583; repr., ed. R. P. Ciardi, Florence, 1974), Book, 6, ch. 51.

4 F. Caraffa, 'Memorie', *Archivio Storico per le Provincie Napoletane* 5 (1880), pp. 242–61.

5 T. Boccalini, *La bilancia politica* (3 vols., Châtelaine 1678), vol. 1, p. 215.

6 G. Bonifacio, *L'arte de' cenni* (Vicenza, 1616), p. 78.

7 S. Guazzo, *La civil conversatione* (Venice, 1575), book 2, f. 43 recto.

8 G. B. Vico, *Scienza Nuova* (1744), paragraph 1027.

9 Some contemporaries disapproved; according to Bonifacio, *L'arte de cenni* (see note 6 above), 'Tenir le mani alla cintola, ò al fianco...è atto d'ocio e di pigritia' (p. 306).

10 G. Botero, *Ragione di stato* (Venice, 1589), Book 5, ch. 4.

11 Boccalini, *Bilancia*, p. 196.

12 B. Pelliciari, *Avvertimenti militari* (Modena, 1600), p. 5.

13 Lomazzo, *Trattato*, Book 6, ch. 51.

14 A. Spinola, 'Ricordi Politici', ACG, fondo Brignole Sale, ms. 106B, s.v. 'Simie di Principi'.

15 G. Paleotti, *Discorso intorno alle immagini sacre e profane*, (1582), Book 2, ch. 20.

16 ibid.

17 Aretino to Leoni (1545) in *Lettere sull'arte*, ed. E. Camesasca (3 vols., Milan, 1957–60), vol. 2, no. 237.

18 Lomazzo, *Trattato*, Book 6, ch. 51.

12 Sacred rulers, royal priests

1 N. Machiavelli, *Il principe* [written *c.* 1513], ch. 11. Of course one pope, Julius II, made war in person, and the early modern popes spent a considerable proportion of their revenue on military expenses; a record 62% in 1569, falling to 24% in 1657 and then rising again (Rietbergen, 1983), p. 203.

2 M. de Montaigne, *Journal*, ed. M. Rat (Paris, 1955), pp. 97–8. This section of the journal was written by Montaigne's secretary; hence the references to him in the third person.

3 C. Marcellus, *Sacrae Ceremoniae* (Venice, 1516), is a useful general account.

4 P. Skippon, 'An Account of a Journey' in *A Collection of Voyages*, ed. A. and J. Churchill (6 vols., London, 1732), vol. 6, p. 671.

5 C. Cartari, *La rosa d'oro* (Rome, 1681); A. Baldassari, *La rosa d'oro* (Venice, 1709). An example of a late medieval golden rose survives in the Cluny museum at Paris.

6 P. P. Vergerio, *Ceremonie della settimana santa* (Rome, 1552).

7 B. Bonfadino, *Le cerimonie che usano i sommi pontefici ad aprir la porta santa* (Rome, 1600); F. Sestini, *Il maestro di camera* (Bracciano, 1628), ch. 28.

8 See, for example, ASR, Camerale II, Ceremoniali, busta, 2, fasc. 2, which deals with the early 17th century.

9 P. Alaleone, 'Diario' in Orbaan (1910), pp. 21f.

10 Skippon, 'Journey', p. 684.

11 S. Infessura, *Diario*, ed. O. Tommasini (Rome, 1890), p. 66.

12 P. de Grassis, *Le due spedizioni militari di Giulio II*, ed. L. Frati (Bologna, 1886); *De ingressu summi pontificis Leonis X* (Florence, 1793); F. Toletano, *La triomphante intrata della S. di papa Paulo III in la nobile città di Piacenza* (no place, 1538).

13 ASR, Camerale II, Ceremoniali, busta 2, 'Memoriale della Ceremonie di Corte' (1685), pp. 1–4.

14 For a general account, see A. Rocca, *De canonizatione sanctorum* (Rome, 1610).

15 Skippon, 'Journey', p. 684.

16 There is a detailed account of Sixtus IV's funeral in J. Burchardus, *Liber notarum* (Rome, 1906), pp. 13f. On the 17th century, Martini (1970), pp. 189f, and the analysis, still unpublished, by Professor Olga Berendson.

17 A useful general account in F. Incoli, *Compendio* (Rome, 1667). Details on individual conclaves in Pastor. An unusual inside story of the 1458 conclave is presented in the memoirs of Pius II. Details on the 1667 conclave in the contemporary *Relatione delle cerimonie fatte dentro e fuori del conclave nell'elettione del sommo pontefice Clemente IX*. Papal coronations seem to have attracted less interest from historians of the early modern period than royal ones have done. Useful brief accounts can be found in Pastor, but are no substitute for monographs. I should like to thank Professor B. Schimmelpfennig for sending me his unpublished paper, 'Papstkrönungen in Avignon'.

18 Two occasions are described in detail in F. Albertonio, *Ragguaglio della cavalcata di nostro signore Gregorio XIV* (Rome, 1590); and in the anonymous *Relatione della solennissima cavalcata...nell'andare a pigliare il possesso* (Rome, 1655).

19 J. Moore, *A View of Society and Manners in Italy* (3 vols., Dublin 1781), vol. 1, letter 38.

20 J. Evelyn, *Diary*, ed. E. S. de Beer (5 vols., Oxford, 1955), vol. 2, p. 281.

21 G. Bonifacio, *L'arte dei cenni* (Vicenza, 1616), p. 216.

22 Vividly described in the anonymous account, cited above, of the inauguration of Clement VII.

23 Burchardus, *Liber notarum* (see note 16 above), P. de Grassis, 'Diarium' (covering the reigns of Julius II and Leo X) remains largely unpublished, but there are a number of copies of the manuscript. I consulted the one in Florence (BNF, ms. II III 144). On him, see Bishop (1892); I should like to thank Sir Richard Southern for drawing my attention to this underrated scholar. In the British Museum there are manuscript copies of the diaries of Burchardus, Martinelli, Firmano, Mucanzio and Alaleone (Add. mss., 8440–60).

24 Vivid examples in vol. 1, f. 156 verso and f. 249 recto.

25 Grassis, *Diarium*, 1, f. 114 recto.

26 Grassis, *Diarium*, 1, f. 417 recto.

27 Grassis, *Diarium*, 2, f. 52 recto.

28 Grassis, *Diarium*, 2, f. 40 *et seq.* There are significant discrepancies between this Roman view of what took place and the Venetian view reported in M. Sanudo, *Diarii*, ed. F. Stefani et al. (58 vols., Venice 1879–1903), vol. 10, pp. 9f.

29 P. de Grassis, *Il diario di Leone X* (Rome, 1884), p. xi. The work of Patrizi is reprinted and analysed in M. Dykmans, *L'oeuvre de Patrizi Piccolomini* (2 vols., Vatican City, 1980–2).

30 P. Alaleone, 'Diarium', B L, Add. mss. 8452, ff. 6 recto, 48 verso.

31 Reproduced in Incoli, *Compendio*. Similar Latin forms are still in use in the fellowship elections of some Cambridge colleges.

32 C. Du Molinet, *Historia summorum pontificum a Martino V ad Innocentium XI per eorum numismata* (Paris, 1679), a work which seems to have been inspired by the famous 'medallic histories' of Louis XIII and Louis XIV.

33 I should like to thank Ralph Giesey, Gábor Klaniczay and Peter Rietbergen for their helpful comments on the penultimate version of this paper.

13 Carnival of Venice

1 J. F. Reynard, *Carneval de Venise* (1699); M. Cuno, *Carneval von Venedig* (1723); R. Tickell, *The Carnival of Venice* (1781).

2 M. Misson, *Nouveau voyage d'Italie* (The Hague, 1691), pp. 182f. Misson was in Venice in 1688.

3 M. da Canal, *Les Estoires de Venise* (ed. A. Limentani, Florence, 1972), pp. 260f.

4 M. Sanudo, *Diarii* (ed. F. Stefani et al., 58 vols., Venice, 1879–1903), vol. 9, p. 516; vol. 17, p. 574.

5 A. Jouvin, *Le voyageur d'Europe* (Paris, 1972), p. 726; W. Bromley, *Remarks in the Grand Tour* (London, 1692), p. 89.

6 A. von Harff, *Pilgerfahrt*, ed. E. von Groote (Cologne, 1860), p. 52. F. Sansovino, *Venetia città nobilissima* (Venice, 1561).

7 P. Skippon, 'An Account of a Journey' in *A Collection of Voyages*, ed. A. and J. Churchill (6 vols., London, 1732), vol. 6, pp. 506f.

8 Sanudo, *Diarii*, 57, p. 548 and 49, p. 422.

9 Apart from written descriptions, there are good illustrations in G. Franco, *Habiti d'homini e donne* (Venice, 1610), and F. Bertelli, *Il carnevale italiano mascherato* (Venice, n.d., *c.* 1642).

10 Misson *Voyage*, p. 188.

11 Bromley, *Remarks*, p. 83; J. Evelyn, *Diary* (ed. E. S. de Beer, 5 vols., Oxford 1955), vol. 2, pp. 473f.

12 G. F. Busenello, 'Carneval', in Livingston (1913), p. 357.

13 W. Thomas, *The History of Italy* (1549; repr. Ithaca, 1961), p. 83.

14 ibid.

15 Evelyn, *Diary*, 2, pp. 473f.

16 F. Bertelli, *Il carnevale italiano mascherato* (Venice, n.d., *c.* 1642); Evelyn, *Diary*, 2, pp. 473f; Skippon, 'Journey', pp. 506f.

17 R. Dallington, *A Survey of Tuscany* (London, 1605), p. 65. Sir Robert Dallington was in Venice in 1596.

18 *Les voyages de M. Payen* (Paris, 1667), pp. 170f.

19 Bromley, *Remarks*, p. 83.

20 A. Calmo, *Opere*, ed. V. Rossi (Rome, 1888), pp. 438f.

21 R. Bellarmino, *Vita...quam ipsemet scripsit* (Louvain, 1753), p. 17. A vivid expression of moral objections to carnival is the anonymous *Discorso contro il carnevale* (Venice, 1607; repr. in *La commedia dell'arte e la società barocca*, ed. F. Taviani, Rome, 1970, pp. 70–81).

22 Sansovino, *Venetia*. 'Io la sento molto biasimar come debile e di poca importanza'.

23 W. Wey, *Itinerary* (London, 1857), p. 85 (a visit of 1458); S. Brasca, *Viaggio*, ed. A. L. M. Lepschy (Milan, 1966), pp. 49f (a visit of 1480); Harff, *Pilgerfahrt* (see note 6 above).

24 R. Torkington, *Pilgrimage* (London, 1883), p. 7.

25 F. Fabri, *Evagatorium*, ed. C. D. Hassler (Stuttgart, 1843), f. 31 recto, f. 211 recto; cf. Brasca, *Viaggio* (see note 23 above), p. 48, and Torkington, *Pilgrimage* (see note 24 above), p. 9. Lady Arundel witnessed the Wedding of the Sea in 1622. She brought back a gondola as a souvenir (Hervey, 1921, pp. 208, 277).

26 Franco, *Habiti*.

27 Skippon, 'Journey', p. 506.

28 Evelyn, *Diary*, p. 473; Payen, *Voyages*, p. 170.

29 Mission, *Voyage*, p. 184.

30 M. W. Montagu, *The Complete Letters*, ed. R. Habsband (3 vols., Oxford 1965–7), vol. 2, p. 177.

31 G. Burnet, *Some Letters* (Amsterdam, 1686), p. 149; M. W. Montagu, *Letters*, vol. 3, p. 235.

32 The pioneer was Sansovino, *Venetia*. A bibliographical study of this work would be as useful as it would be difficult (since subsequent editions appeared under other names, such as Bardi, Doglioni, Goldioni, Martinioni, Stringa, Zotti.) It was followed, *c.* 1700, by V. Coronelli, *Guida de'forestieri*, of which the 1744 edition calls itself the 38th, and by G. B. Albrizzi (?), *Il forestiere illuminato* (Venice, 1740).

33 T. Martyn, *The Gentleman's Guide in his Tour through Italy* (London, 1787), p. 373.

34 G. F. Coyer, *Voyages* (Paris, 1775), vol. 2, p. 18.

35 V. Coronelli, *Guida de 'forestieri* (Venice, 1744 edn), p. 32.

36 *Distinta relazione delle sontuose feste...nella città di Parma per celebrare le nozze di quel serenissimo principe* (*Venice*, 1690).

37 *Albrizzi, Forestiere*, Venice, 1792 edn, p. 464: 'oltre a certi funzioni simboliche di tagliare con un colpa la testa ad alcuni tori...'

14 The virgin of the Carmine and the revolt of Masaniello

1 J. Colerus, *Vie de Spinosa* (Brussels, 1731), p. 43, claims that the philosopher drew a portrait of himself dressed as Masaniello.

2 V. de'Medici's reports to Florence are printed in *Archivio storico italiano* ix (1846), pp. 348–53; A. Rosso's to Venice in *Archivio storico per le provincie napoletane* xxxiii (1952), pp. 167–235; O'Sauli's to Genoa in the same journal, xv (1890), pp. 355–87.

3 A. Filomarino to Rome, *Archivio storico italiano* ix (1846), pp. 379–93.

4 A. Giraffi, *Le rivolutioni di Napoli* (Venice, 1647), trans. J. Howell as *An Exact History of the Late Revolution in Naples* (2 vols., London 1650–2).

5 T. De Sanctis, *Storia del tumulto di Napoli* (Leiden, 1652; repr. Trieste, 1858), written by an officer of the Spanish army and dedicated to Philip IV; A. Nicolai, *Historia, o vero narrazione giornale dell'ultime rivolutioni della città e regno di Napoli* (Amsterdam, 1648), by a councillor of state to the duke of Lorraine, dedicated to Philip IV's son Don Juan; G. Tontoli, *Il Masaniello* (Naples, 1648), by a lawyer, dedicated to the same Don Juan; 'Nescipio Liponari', *Relatione delle rivolutioni populari di Napoli* (Padua, 1648).

6 G. Donzelli, *Partenope liberata* (Naples, 1647), dedicated to Henri Duc de Guise, a rare book of which I used the copy in Paris, B N; A. Della Porta,

'Giornale istorico di quanto più memorabile è accaduto nelle rivoluzioni di Napoli', Paris, BN, fonds italien, no. 299.

7　A. Mascardi, *Dell'arte historica trattati cinque* (Rome, 1636); *La congiura del Conte Gio. Luigi de'Fieschi* (Venice, 1629).

8　R. Della Torre, *Dissidentis Neapolis libri xvi* (Genoa, 1651).

9　As tragedy; Rosso, p. 185; Tontoli, p. 4. As tragi-comedy, Sauli p. 377; Liponari, p. 267; Tontoli, p. 5. Actual tragedies on the subject (to say nothing of later operas) were written by T. Asselijn (1668), and C. Weise (1683).

10　Filomarino, p. 381; Giraffi, p. 3.

11　Donzelli, title page; Della Porta, ff. 3 recto, 7 verso, 32 recto.

12　D. A. Parrino, *Teatro eroico e politico de'governi de'vicerè del regno di Napoli* (3 vols., Naples 1692–4).

13　T. Campanella, *La città del sole*, ed. B. Widmar (Milan, 1963), p. 47.

14　An early example is in Della Porta, f. 10 recto.

15　Buildings of six or seven storeys are mentioned in G. C. Capaccio, *Il forastiero* (Naples, 1634), p. 851, and represented in Coppola's painting of the surrender of the city in 1648.

16　T. Campanella, sonnet 'della plebe', in his *Poesie filosofiche*, ed. A.d'Ancona (Turin, 1854), pp. 79–80.

17　G. C. Capaccio, 'Descrizione di Napoli' (*c.* 1607), *Archivio storico per le provincie napoletane* vii (1882), p. 535.

18　A contemporary account is provided in T. Costo's addition to P. Collenuccio, *Compendio dell'istoria del regno di Napoli* (Venice, 1591), ff. 63–5.

19　Tontoli, pp. 4–5; Donzelli, p. 136.

20　Giraffi, p. 9; Rosso, pp. 178–80; Sauli, pp. 355–6.

21　Giraffi, pp. 7–8.

22　F. Capecelatro, *Diario dei tumulti del popolo napoletano*, ed. A. Granito (3 vols., Naples, 1850–4), i, pp. 15–16; Tontoli, p. 5; Donzelli, p. 7; Della Porta, f. 5 verso.

23　The importance of Genoino was emphasised as early as 13 July 1647 by Medici, p. 348.

24　Tontoli, p. 7.

25　Costo, f. 66 recto.

26　A. Pocili, *Delle rivolutioni della città di Palermo* (Verona, 1648), pp. 10–11, 16–17, 23.

27　Donzelli, p. 16; Della Porta, f. 11 verso; De Santis, p. 54.

28　Donzelli, p. 81; Della Porta, f. 41 recto; Santis, p. 59.

29　Della Porta, f. 2 recto.

30　Donzelli, pp. 90, 130; Liponari, p. 277.

31　Donzelli, p. 130; Liponari, p. 277.

32　Medici, p. 348.

33　Giraffi, p. 70; Donzelli, p. 39; Liponari, p. 55. These passages are so close to one another as to awaken suspicion.

34 Sauli, p. 355; Donzelli, p. 75.
35 Santis, p. 100.
36 Giraffi, p. 51.
37 Giraffi, p. 52. On the orderly nature of the destruction, Filomarino, p. 382; Sauli, p. 362; Tontoli, pp. 52–3.
38 Donzelli, pp. 33–5; Liponari, pp. 141–2; Santis, pp. 87–9; Tontoli, pp. 105–6.
39 Donzelli, p. 93; Liponari, p. 141; Santis, pp. 196–7.
40 Sauli, p. 358.
41 Sauli, p. 361.
42 Filomarino, p. 385; Tontoli, p. 47; Liponari, pp. 185, 255.
43 Nicolai, p. 86; Liponari, p. 270; Santis, pp. 113–4, 135.
44 Nicolai, p. 88; Liponari, p. 273; Santis, p. 138.
45 Rosso, p. 185; Giraffi, pp. 185–7; Liponari, p. 273; Santis, pp. 138–9.
46 Rosso, p. 185; Santis, p. 141.
47 Rosso, p. 185; Sauli, p. 380; Della Porta, f. 33 recto.
48 Filomarino, p. 385; Sauli, p. 380; Donzelli, p. 67; Tontoli, pp. 154–5.
49 Della Porta, ff. 38 verso, 40 verso.
50 Santis, p. 110; cf. p. 53.
51 Rudé (1959); Rudé (1971); Tilly (1974), p. 87.
52 Filomarino, pp. 383, 387; Pocili, p. 211.
53 Giraffi, p. 36.
54 J. F. E. Albrecht, *Masaniello von Neapel* (Berlin, 1789). Albrecht, a physician, also wrote novels and translated Rousseau.

15 Rituals of healing in early modern Italy

1 S. Mercurio, *La commare* (1604; I used the Venice, 1621 edn), part 3.
2 F. Ponzetti, *Libellus de venenis* (1521), Book 2, tract 1, ch. 5. Ponzetti was a physician who entered the Church and became a bishop; he claims to have acquired his information by questioning the healers themselves. Cf. De Martino (1961), pp. 106f, and Di Nola (1976), pp. 75f.
3 On the 'cirauli' of the valley of Noto in Sicily, N. Serpetro, *Il Mercato delle meraviglie della natura* (1658), quoted Camporesi (1978), p. 158.
4 S. Razzi, *Vita di santa Caterina de 'Ricci* (1594; ed. G. M. di Agresti, Florence, 1965), p. 121.
5 M. De Montaigne, *Journal de Voyage*, ed. M. Rat (Paris, 1955), pp. 142–3; F. Moryson, *An Itinerary* (4 vols., Glasgow, 1907), vol. 1, p. 324.
6 G. Baldinucci, 'Ricordi', ms. in Venice, Biblioteca Marciana, Ital. VI. 94 (= 5898), 5 December 1630, 21 May 1633.
7 A. Della Porta, 'Della peste di Napoli', ms. in Paris, BN, fonds italien, no. 299, ff. 139 recto, 145 verso.
8 G. Bargagli, *La Pellegrina* (première 1564), Act 1, scene 1.

9 Synod of Ales and Terralba, 1696: 'fingen, quel et tal Santo o Santa les viene a visitar, y que les entra dentro del cuerpo, y ablan en nombre del Santo'. C. Corrain and P. L. Zampini, *Documenti etnografici e folkloristici nei sinodi diocesani italiani* (Bologna, 1970), p. 286n.

10 T. Fazello, *Historia di Sicilia* (Venice, 1573), pp. 314f.

11 Details in G. Menghi, *Compendio dell'arte essorcistica* (Bologna, 1576). The book, the work of a famous Franciscan exorcist, went through a number of editions before the end of the century, in Italian and in Latin. Book 3, chapter 10, which describes how to do it, is extremely vague – no doubt on purpose. Cf. F. Canale, *Del modo di conoscer et sanare i maleficiati* (Milan, 1663).

12 Ponzetti, *Libellus de venenis* (see note 2 above).

13 ASV, Santo Ufficio, busta 5, cases of Serena Greca and Marietta Greca, 1620.

14 See above, note 10.

15 A. de Alessandro, *Genialium Dierum libri vi* (Paris, 1532), Book 2, ch. 17. The author lived for a time in the south of Italy.

16 T. Pini, 'Speculum Cerretanorum', in *Il libro dei vagabondi*, ed. P. Camporesi (Turin, 1793), p. 39. On Pini, see p. 68 above.

17 P. Skippon, 'An Account of a Journey' in *A Collection of Voyages*, ed. A. and J. Churchill (6 vols. London, 1732), vol. 6, p. 607. His visit to Italy was in 1663.

18 G. Berkeley, Journal, ms. in London, BL, Add. ms. 39,308, ff. 51–5. I should like to thank Ed Chaney for bringing this manuscript to my attention.

19 *Callot's Etchings*, ed. H. Daniel (New York, 1974), nos. 98–100. On Callot, above, p. 66.

20 As Camporesi (1973, p. cxiv) points out, the Latin term 'ciarlatanus' can be found as early as the 15th century, but the normal word was 'cerretanus'.

21 Skippon, 'Journey', pp. 517f.

22 T. Garzoni, *La piazza universale di tutte le professioni del mondo* (Venice, 1585), ch. 104.

23 G. Franco, *Habiti d'huomini et donne venetiane* (Venice, 1609).

24 T. Coryate, *Crudities* (2 vols., Glasgow, 1905), vol. 1, pp. 410–12. Coryate was in Venice in 1608.

25 F. Redi, *Esperienze naturali* (1671), ch. 12.

26 Della Porta, 'Peste', f. 145 verso.

27 S. Mercurii, *De gli errori popolari d'Italia* (Venice, 1603), Book 4, is a good summary of the physicians' case against charlatans.

16 The repudiation of ritual in early modern Europe

1 T. Cranmer, 'Speech at the Coronation of Edward VI', in *Thomas Cranmer*, ed. D. Duffield (Appleford, 1964), pp. 20–1; G. Burnet, *Some Letters* (Amsterdam, 1686), p. 143.

2 M. Luther, 'Von Ordnung Gottesdienst in der Gemeine' (1523), in his *Werke* (60 vols., Weimar 1883–1980), vol. 12, p. 35.

3 Erasmus published John Chrysostom's *Discourses against Judaising Christians* in 1527.

4 J. Milton, 'Of Reformation in England' (1641), in his *Areopagitica and other Prose Works*, ed. K. M. Burton (London, 1927), p. 56.

5 G. Gillespie, *A Dispute against the English-Popish Ceremonies obtruded upon the Church of Scotland* (no place, 1637), sig. B2, verso, and p. 19.

6 M. Bucer, *Loci communes* (English trans. Abingdon, 1972), p. 202.

7 T. Cranmer, 'Of Ceremonies', appendix to the Book of Common Prayer, 1549, in *The Two Liturgies*, ed. J. Ketley (Cambridge, 1844) pp. 155–7.

8 M. Flacius et al., *Centuriae Ecclesiasticae Historiae* (Basel, 1564–), 3rd Century, ch. 6.

9 M. Luther, *Werke*, (Weimar, 1883–, in progress), vol. 19, p. 72.

10 ibid.

11 Gillespie, *Dispute*, pp. 1, 7.

12 Erasmus, letter, 18 March 1528.

13 P. Melanchthon defined his position in a controversy with Flacius (the organiser of the 'Magdeburg Centuries') over the Leipzig Interim. See his *Opera*, 7, ed. C. G. Bretschneider (Halle, 1840), pp. 259f.

14 *The Rationale of Ceremonial*, ed. C. S. Cobb (London, 1910).

15 *Martin Bucer and the Book of Common Prayer*, ed. E. C. Whitaker (Great Wakering, 1974), pp. 56–7; P. Viret, *La necromancie papale* (Geneva, 1553), p. 28.

16 U. Zwingli, 'Auslegen und Gründe der Schlussreden' (1523), in his *Werke*, vol. 2, ed. E. Egli and G. Finsler (Leipzig, 1908), pp. 111f.

17 [W. Tyndale], *The Practyse of Prelates* ('Marborch', 1530), f. 64 recto.

18 P. Viret, *La physique papale* (no place, 1552).

19 *Collection des meilleurs dissertations*, ed. C. Leber (Paris, 1826), vol. 9, p. 472.

20 J. B. Thiers, *Traité des superstitions* (2 vols., Paris 1679–97), vol. 2, pp. 18, 147.

21 C. de Vert, *Explication simple, littérale et historique des cérémonies de l'Eglise* (4 vols., Paris 1706–13), esp. the preface. Vert's polemic with the Calvinists goes back to 1690. Cf. L. A. Bocquillot, *Traité historique de la liturgie sacrée* (Paris, 1701).

22 [P. Lebrun], *Histoire critique des pratiques superstitieuses* (no place, 1702), esp. preface and pp. 66f.

23 [A. Widenfeld] *Monita salutaria* (Ghent, 1673), pp. 9, 12.

24 W. Pell, *A Plain and Necessary Confutation* (London, 1654), fig. 23.

25 Erasmus, *De conscribendis epistolis* (ed. J. C. Margolin, Amsterdam, 1971, p. 294); *Opera* (ed. J. Leclerc, 10 vols., Leiden 1703–6), vol. 2, p. 773.

26 Cranmer, 'Speech', p. 21.

27 J. Cleland, *Heropaideia, or the institution of a young nobleman* (London, 1607), pp. 176–7. Cleland is among the writers discussed by Anna Bryson in an interesting thesis on 'civility' (D. Phil., Oxford, 1984).

28 Furly (London, 1663), p. 7; W. Caton, *The Moderate Enquirer Resolved* (London, 1671), p. 27.

29 G. Della Casa, *Galateo* (ed. D. Provenzal, Milan, 1950), chs. 14–17.

30 A. Du Chesne, *Les Antiquitez et recherches de la grandeur et majesté des roys de France* (Paris, 1609), Book 2, p. 416.

31 J. La Bruyère, 'de la cour' in his *Caractères* (1688; ed. G. Mongrédien, Paris 1960), esp. pp. 214–15;

32 B. Pascal, *Pensées*, ed. L. Lafuma (Paris, 1962, no. 44 (the traditional number is 82); La Rochefoucauld, *Maximes* (ed. F. C. Green, Cambridge 1946), no. 257.

33 E. La Boétie, *Oeuvres politiques*, ed. F. Hincker (Paris, 1971), pp. 65, 67, 68.

34 A. Cornaro, *Della vita sobria* (1558: Florence, 1946 edn, p. 39).

35 [F. Micanzio] *Vita del padre Paolo* (Leiden, 1646), p. 68. Micanzio, a servite friar close to Paolo Sarpi, and suspect of Calvinism, described worldly ceremony as 'cosa affettata e superflua, che stanca il cervello de'più perspicaci, e consuma vanamente tanto tempo in un mentir artificioso, e non significante per troppo significare' (ibid). He was equally dismissive of religious rituals: 'tutto va in cerimonie…Tutta la religione in cerimonia' (*Storici e politici veneti*, ed. G. Benzoni and T. Zanato, Milan–Naples 1982, pp. 844–5); A. Lupis, *Vita di G. F. Loredano* (Venice, 1663), p. 56.

36 A. Spinola, 'Ricordi Politici' in ACG, fondo Brignole Sale, ms. 106 B.11–12, sv. 'Cerimoniale'.

37 M. de Montaigne, *Essais*, Book 1, ch. 40 and Book 2, ch. 17; ed. M. Rat (3 vols., Paris, 1958), vol. 1, p. 284; vol. 2, p. 348.

38 P. Charron, *De la sagesse* (Bordeaux, 1601), Book 2, ch. 8.

39 A. Caro, *Lettere familiare*, ed. A. Greco (3 vols., Florence 1957–61), vol. 3, no. 528.

40 Beccadelli, quoted in Torbarina (1931), p. 49.

41 CODOIN 69 (Madrid, 1878), p. 76.

42 J. Swift, 'On Good Manners'. Cf. the satire on the British orders of chivalry in the 3rd chapter of Gulliver's voyage to Lilliput.

43 J. H. Jesse, *Memoirs of the Court of England* (3 vols., London, 1843), vol. 1, p. 353.

44 Montesquieu, *Lettres persanes* (1721; ed. G. Truc, Paris, 1946), letter 24.

45 S. Maffei, *Della scienza chiamata cavalleresca* (Venice, 1710), Book 1, ch. 3; G. Gozzi, *Gazzetta Veneta*, no. 17, 2 April 1760.

46 J. Moore, *A View of Society and Manners in France, Switzerland and Germany* (2 vols., London, 1779), vol. 2, letters 82, 86, 91.

47 J. Moore, *A View of Society and Manners in Italy* (3 vols., Dublin, 1781), vol. 2, letter 49.

Bibliography

Aberle, D. F., *The Peyote Religion among the Navaho* (Chicago, 1966)

Alatas, S. H., *The Myth of the Lazy Native* (London, 1977)

Allegra, L., 'Il parocco', *Storia d''italia, annali* 4 (Turin, 1981), 897–947

Allport, G. W., and Postman, L., The Basic Psychology of Rumour' (1945), repr. in *Mass Communications*, ed. W. Schramm (Urbana, 1960), pp. 141–55

Andrieux, M., *La vie quotidienne dans la Rome pontificale au 18e siècle* (Paris, 1962)

Ardener, S., 'Introduction' to *Perceiving Women*, ed S. Ardener (London, 1975)

Ariès, P., *Centuries of Childhood* (1960; English trans., London 1966)

Auerbach, E., *Mimesis* (1948; English trans., Princeton, 1954)

Averna, G., 'Italian and Venetian Profanity', *Maledicta* (1977)

Aydelotte, F., *Elizabethan Rogues and Vagabonds* (Oxford, 1913)

Babut, D., *Plutarque et le stoicisme* (Paris, 1969)

Bakhtin, M., *Rabelais and his World* (1965; English trans., Cambridge, Mass., 1968)

Baldo, V., *Alunni, maestri e scuole in Venezia alla fine del xvi secolo* (Como, 1977)

Baratti, D., *Bestemmiatori, superstiziosi...le domande sui laici nelle visite pastorali dei vescovi di como* (tesi di laurea, Bologna, 1981–2)

Barbagli, M., *Sotto lo stesso tetto: mutamenti della famiglia in Italia dal xv al xx secolo* (Bologna, 1984)

Barth, F., 'On the Study of Social Change', *American Anthropologist* 69 (1967), 661–9

Barthes, R., *Mythologies* (Paris, 1957)

Basso, K., 'To Give Up On Words' (1970), repr. in *Language and Social Context*, ed. P. P. Giglioli (Harmondsworth, 1972), ch. 4

'The Ethnography of Writing', in *Explorations in the Ethnography of Speaking*, ed. R. Bauman and J. Sherzer (Cambridge, 1974), ch. 20

Bataille, G., *La part maudite* (Paris, 1949)

Bauman, R., *Let Your Words Be Few: Symbolism of Speaking and Silence among Seventeenth-Century Quakers* (Cambridge, 1983)

Baxandall, M., *Painting and Experience in Renaissance Italy* (Oxford, 1972)

Bayly, C., 'Death Ritual in Hindu North India since 1600', in *Mirrors of Mortality*, ed. J. Whaley (London, 1981), ch. 7

Beattie, J. M., *The English Court in the Reign of George I* (London, 1967)

261

Bec, C., *Les marchands écrivains* (Paris and the Hague, 1967)

Beccaria, G. L., *Spagnolo e spagnoli in Italia: riflessi ispanici sulla linqua italiana del cinque- e del seicento* (Turin, 1969)

Beccaria, G. L., ed., *I linguaggi settoriali in Italia* (Milan, 1973)

Becker, H., *Outsiders* (New York, 1963)

Beltrami, *Storia della popolazione di Venezia* (Padua, 1954)

Benedict, R., *Patterns of Culture* (London, 1934)

Bennassar, B., *L'inquisition espagnole* (Paris, 1979)

Bercé, Y., *Histoire des Croquants* (Geneva, 1974)

Berger, P., 'on the Obsolescence of the Concept of Honour', *European Journal of Sociology* 9 (1970), 339–47

Bertelli, S., *Erudizione e storia in L. A. Muratori* (Naples, 1960)

  'L'egemonia linguistica come egemonia culturale', *Bibliothèque d'humanisme et Renaissance* (1976)

Bishop, E., 'Leaves from the Diary of a Papal Master of Ceremonies' (1897), repr. in his *Liturgica Historica* (Oxford, 1918), pp. 434–43

Bistort, G., *Il magistrato alle pompe nella Repubblica di Venezia* (Venice, 1912)

Bloch, M., *The Royal Touch* (1924; English trans., London, 1973)

Blok, A., 'Rams and Billy-Goats: a Key to the Mediterranean Code of Honour', *Man* 16 (1981), 427–40

Boas, F., *Kwakiutl Ethnography* (1897) ed. H. Codere (Chicago and London, 1966)

Bocock, K., *Ritual in Industrial Society* (London, 1974)

Bogucka, M., 'Les bourgeois et les investissements culturels. L'exemple de Gdańsk', *Revue historique* 259 (1978), 429–40

Boiteux, M., 'Carnaval annexé', *annales E.S.C.* 32 (1977), 356–77

Boltanski, L., 'La dénonciation', *Actes de la recherche en sciences sociales* 51 (1984), 3–40

Borsellino, N., *Gli anticlassicisti del '500* (Milan, 1973)

Bossy, J., 'The Mass as a Social Institution', *Past and Present* 100 (1983), 29–61

Bourdieu, 'The Sentiment of Honour in Kabyle Society' in *Honour and Shame*, ed. J. G. Peristiany (London, 1965), pp. 191–241

  La distinction: critique social du jugement (Paris, 1979)

Brandes, S. H., 'Like Wounded Stags: Male Sexual Ideology in an Andalusian Town' in Ortner and Whitehead, eds., Sexual Meanings (1981), ch. 6

Braudel, F., *The Mediterranean and the Mediterranean World in the age of Philip II* (1949; English trans., 2 vols., London, 1972–3)

Brizzi, G. P., *La formazione della classe dirigente nel '600–700* (Bologna 1976)

Brown, J. C., and Goodman, J., 'Women and industry in Florence', *Journal of Economic History* 40 (1980), 73–80

Brown, P., *The Cult of the Saints* (Chicago and London, 1981)

Brown, P., and Levinson, S., 'Universals in Language Usage: Politeness Phenomena' in *Questions and Politeness*, ed. E. W. Goody (Cambridge, 1978), pp. 56–289

Brown R., and Gilman, A., 'The Pronouns of Power and Solidarity' (1960), repr. in *Language and Social Context*, ed. P. P. Giglioli (Harmondsworth, 1972), ch. 12

Brunet, J., 'Le paysan et son langage', *Ville et campagne dans la littérature italienne de la Renaissance*, ed. Rochon, A., (Paris, 1976)

'Un "langage colakeutiquement profane", ou l'influence de l'Espagne sur la troisième personne de politesse italienne', in *Presence et influence dde l'Espagne dans la culture italienne de la Renaissance* (Paris, 1978), pp. 251–315

Bryson, F. R., *The Point of Honour in Sixteenth-Century Italy* (New York, 1935)

Buratti, A., et al., *La città rituale* (Milan, 1982)

Burckhardt, J., *Civilisation of the Renaissance in Italy* (1860; English trans., London, 1944)

Burke, P. *Venice and Amsterdam* (London, 1974)

Popular Culture in Early Modern Europe (London, 1978)

Butwin, J., 'The French Revolution as Theatrum Mundi', *Research Studies* 43 (1975), 141–51

Cairns, C., *Domenico Bollani* (Nieuwkoop, 1976)

Calvi, G., 'La peste fiorentina del 1630', *Quaderni storici* 56 (1984), 35–64

Camporesi, P., *Il corpo impassibile* (Milan, 1983)

Cancellieri, F., *Storia dei solenni possessi da Leone III a Pio VII* (Rome, 1802)

Canepa, A. M., 'From Degenerate Scoundrel to Noble Savage. The Italian Stereotype in Eighteenth-Century British Travel Literature', *English Miscellany* 22 (1971), 107–46

Cannadine, D., 'The British Monarchy and the Invention of Tradition', in *The Invention of Tradition*, ed. E. Hobsbawm and T. Ranger (Cambridge, 1983), pp. 101–64

Caro Lopez, C., 'Gli Auditori Nuovi e il dominio di terraferma in *Stato società e giustizia nella repubblica veneta*, ed. G. Cozzi (Rome, 1980), pp. 259–316

Casali, E., *Il villano dirozzato: cultura società e potere nell campagne romagnole della Controriforma* (Florence, 1982)

Castelnuovo, E., 'Il significato del ritratto pittorico nella società', *Storia d'Italia* 5 (Turin 1973), 1035–94

Cattaneo, E., 'Carnevale e Quaresima nell'età di San Carlo Borromeo', *Ambrosius* 34 (1958), 51–66

Caturegli, N., 'Le condizioni della chiesa di Pisa', *Bollettino storico pisano* 19 (1950), 19–24

Chartier, R., 'Les élites et les gueux', *Revue d'histoire moderne* 21 (1974), 376–88

Chastel, A., *The Sack of Rome* (Princeton, 1983)

Chaytor, H. J., *From Script to Print* (Cambridge, 1945)

Christian, W., *Local Religion in Sixteenth-Century Spain* (Princeton, 1981)

Ciampi, I., *Innocenzo X Pamphili e la sua corte* (Rome, 1878)

Cipolla, C. M., 'The Decline of Italy', *Economic History Review* 5 (1952–3), 178–87

  Literacy and Development in the West (Harmondsworth, 1969)

  'The Professions', *Journal of European Economic History* 2 (1983), 37–52

  Public Health and the Medical Profession in the Renaissance (*Cambridge*, 1976)

  Faith, Reason and the Plague (1977: English trans., Brighton 1979)

  'Economic Fluctuations, the Poor and Public Policy' in *Aspects of Poverty in Early Modern Europe*, ed. T. Ris (Florence, 1981), pp. 65–77

Clanchy, M. T., *From Memory to Written Record: England, 1066–1307* (London, 1979)

Clemente, F., *Il carnevale romano* (Rome, 1899)

Coates, W. A., 'The German Pidgin-Italian of the Sixteenth-Century Lanzich-enecchi', *Papers from the Fourth Annual Kansas Linguistics Conference* (1969), 66–74

Cocchiara, G., *Il linguaggio del gesto* (Turin, 1932)

  Il mondo alla rovescia (Turin, 1963)

Cochrane, E., *Florence in the Forgotten Centuries* (Chicago, 1973)

Codere, H., *Fighting with Property* (New York, 1950)

Cohen, A., 'Political Anthropology: the Analysis of the Symbolism of Power Relations', *Man* 4 (1969), 215–35

Cohen, S., *Folk Devils and Moral Panics* (London, 1972)

Cohn, N., *Europe's Inner Demons* (London, 1975)

Comparato, V. I., *Uffici e Società a Napoli* (Florence, 1974)

Coulton, G. G., *The Medieval Village* (Cambridge, 1925)

Cozzi, G., *Il doge Nicolò Contarini* (Venice and Rome, 1958)

Crapanzano, V., *The Hamadsha* (Berkeley, 1973)

Crew, P. M., *Calvinist Preaching and Iconoclasm in the Netherlands* (Cambridge, 1978)

Croce, B., 'I lazzari' (1985), repr. in his *Anecdotti* 3 (Bari, 1954), 198–211

  'Le cerimonie spagnuole in Italia', in his *La Spagna nella vita italiana durante la rinascenza* (Bari, 1917)

D'Amico, J. P., *Renaissance Humanism in Papal Rome* (Baltimore and London, 1983)

Davis, J. C., *The Decline of the Venetian Nobility as a Ruling Class* (Baltimore, 1962)

Davis, N. Z., 'The Rites of Violence', *Past and Present* 59 (1973), 51–91

  'Women on top' in her *Society and Culture in Early Modern France* (London, 1975), pp. 124–52

Dedieu, J. P., 'Christianisation en nouvelle castille', *Mélanges de la Casa de Velázquez* 15 (1979), 269–94

De Francesco, G., *Die Macht des Charlatans* (Base 1, 1937)

Dekker, R., *Holland in beroering* (Baarn, 1982)

Dekker, R., and Roodenburg, H., 'Humor in de zeventiende eeuw', *Tijdschrift voor sociale Geschiedenis* 10 (1984), 243–66

Delooz, P., 'Towards a Sociological Study of Canonized Sainthood in the Catholic Church' (1962), English trans. in *Saints and Their Cults*, ed. S. Wilson (Cambridge, 1983), ch. 6

Sociologie et canonisation (Liège, 1969)

Delumeau, J., *Vie économique et sociale de Rome dans la seconde moitié du 16e siècle* (2 vols., Paris 1957–9)

De Maio, R., 'L'ideale eroico nei processi di canonizzazione della controriforma', *Ricerche di storia sociale e religiosa* 2 (1972), 139–60

De Martino, E., *Terra di rimorso* (Milan, 1961)

De Mauro, T., *Storia linguistica dell'italia unita* (2nd edn., 1976)

De Rosa, G., *Vescovi, popola e magia nel sud* (Naples, 1971)

Derosas, R., 'Moralità e giustizia a Venezia nel '500–'600: gli esecutori contra la bestemmia', in *Stato, società e giustizia nella repubblica veneta* ed. G. Cozzi (Rome, 1980), pp. 431–528

Di Nola, A. M., *Gli aspetti magico-religiosi di una cultura subalterna italiana* (Milan, 1976)

Dolci, D., *Poverty in Sicily* (Harmondsworth, 1966)

Doria, G., *Uomini e terre di un borgo collinare* (Milan, 1968)

Le strade di Napoli (Milan and Naples, 1971)

Douglas, M., 'The Contempt of Ritual', *New Society* 31 March 1966, repr. in her *In the Active Voice* (London, 1982), pp. 34–8

Natural Symbols (London, 1970)

Douglas, M., and Isherwood, B., *The World of Goods* (London, 1978)

Driessen, H., 'Male Sociability and Rituals of Masculinity in Rural Andalusia', *Anthropology Quarterly* 56 (1983), 125–32

Dundes, A., Leach, J., and Ozkök, B., 'The Strategy of Turkish Boys' Verbal Dueling Rhymes' in *Directions in Sociolinguistics*, ed. J. J. Gumperz and D. Hymes New York, 1972), pp. 130–60

Dundes, A., and Falassi A., *La terra in piazza* (Berkeley and Los Angeles, 1975)

Durkheim, E., *Les formes élémentaires de la vie religieuse* (Paris, 1912; English trans., New York, 1961)

Edgerton, S., *Pictures and Punishment* (Ithaca, 1985)

Eggan, D., 'Hopi Dreams in Cultural Perspective' in *The Dream and Human Societies*, ed. G. E. von Grunebaum and R. Caillois (Berkeley, 1966), pp. 237–63

Eliade, M., *Shamanism* (1951; English trans., London 1964)

Le mythe de l'éternal retour (Paris, 1949)

Elias, N., *The Civilising Process* (1939; English trans., 2 vols., Oxford 1978–82)

The Court Society (1969; English trans., Oxford 1983)

Elliott, J. H., 'Revolts in the Spanish Monarchy', in *Preconditions of Revolution in Early Modern Europe*, ed. R. Forster and J. P. Greene (Baltimore and London, 1970)

Finlay, R., *Politics in Renaissance Venice* (London, 1980)

Firth, R., *The Work of the Gods in Tikopia* (2 vols., London, 1940)

Fishman, J., 'Who speaks What Language to Whom and When' (1965), repr. *Sociolinguistics*, ed. J. B. Pride and J. Holmes (Harmondsworth, 1972), ch. 1

Foisil, M., *La révolte des nu-pieds* (Paris, 1970)

Folena, G. F., 'Introduzione al veneziano "de là da mar"', *Bollettino dell'Atlante Linguistico Mediterraneo* 10–12 (1968–70), 331–76

Fortes, M., 'Inauguration Rituals', *Proceedings of the Royal Anthropological Society* (1966)

Foucault, *Madness and Civilisation* (1961; English trans., London, 1967)

Fox, R., 'The Inherent Rules of Violence', in *Social Rules and Social Behaviour*, ed. P. Collett (Oxford, 1977), pp. 132–49

Frake, C. O., 'How to Ask for a Drink in Subanun' (1964), repr. in *Language in Social Context*, ed. P. P. Giglioli (Harmondsworth, 1972), ch. 5

'How to Enter a Yakan House' (1975), repr. in his *Language and Cultural Description* (Stanford, 1980), pp. 214–30

Frazer, J., *The Golden Bough* (3rd edn., 12 vols., London, 1913)

Gaborieau, M., 'The Cult of the Saints among the Muslims of Nepal' (1978), English trans., in Wilson (1983), pp. 291–306

Gaeta, F., 'Alcune considerazioni sul mito di Venezia', *Bibliothèque d'humanisme et renaissance* 23 (1961), 58–75

Gaeta Bertalà, G., *Feste e apparati medicei* (Florence, 1969)

Galasso, G. *Intervista sulla storia di Napoli*, ed. P. Allum (Bari, 1978)

Galbraith, V. H. *Studies in the Public Records* (London, 1948)

The Making of Domesday Book (London, 1961)

Gambier, M., 'La donna e la giustizia penale veneziana nel xviii secolo' in *Stato società e giustizia nella repubblica veneta*, ed. G. Cozzi (Rome, 1980), pp. 529–75

García Ballester, L., *Medicina, ciencia, y minorías marginadas; los moriscos* (Granada, 1976)

Garfinkel, H., 'Conditions of Successful Degradation Ceremonies', *American Journal of Sociology* 61 (1955–6), 420–4

Geertz, C., *The Interpretation of Culture* (New York, 1973)

Negara (Princeton, 1980)

Gellner, E., *Saints of the Atlas* (London, 1969)

Gennep, van, A., *The Rites of Passage* (1908; English trans., London, 1960)

George, K., and George C. H., 'Sainthood and Social Status' (1953), repr. in *Class Status and Power*, ed. R. Bendix and S. M. Lipset (2nd edn., New York, 1967, pp. 394–410

Georgelin, J., *Venise au siècle des lumières* (The Hague, 1978)

Geremek, B., 'Renfermement des pauvres en Italie: xive-xvii siècles', *Mélanges Braudel*, 1 (Toulouse, 1973), 205–25

Geremek (ed.), *Truands et misérables dans l'Europe moderne (1350-1600)*, (Paris, 1980)

Giamatti, A. B., *Play of Double Senses* (Englewood Cliffs, 1975)

Giedion, S., *Space, Time and Architecture* (1941; 5th edn, Cambridge, Mass., 1967)

Gilsenan, M., 'Lying, Honor and Contradiction' in *Transaction and Meaning*, ed. B. Kapferer (Philadelphia, 1976), pp. 191–214

Ginzburg, C., *The Night Battles* (1966; English trans., London 1983)
The Cheese and the Worms (1975; English trans., London 1981)

Ginzburg C., and Ferrari, M., 'La colombara ha aperto gli occhi', *Quaderni Storici* 38 (1978), 631–9

Giuntella, V. E., 'Documenti sull'istruzione popolare in Roma durante il '700', *Studi Romani* 9 (1961), 553–60

Gluckman, M., ed., *Essays on the Ritual of Social Relations* (Manchester, 1962)

Goffman, E., 'On Face-Work' (1955), repr. in his *Interaction Ritual* (New York, 1967), ch. 1
The Presentation of Self in Everyday Life (New York, 1959)
'The Territories of the Self' (1971), repr. in his *Relations in Public* (London, 1971), ch. 2.

Goldthwaite, R., 'Schools and Teachers of Commercial Arithmetic in Renaissance Florence', *Journal of European Economic History* 1 (1972), 418–33
The Building of Renaissance Florence (Baltimore, 1980)

Gombrich, E. H., *Art and illusion* (London, 1960)

Goodich, M., 'A Profile of Thirteenth-Century Sainthood', *Comparative Studies in Society and History* 18 (1976), 429–37

Goody J., and Watt, I., 'The Consequences of Literacy', *Comparative Studies in Society and History* 5 (1962–3), 304–45

Goody, J., 'Restricted Literacy in Northern Ghana' in *Literacy in Traditional Societies*, ed. Goody (Cambridge, 1968), pp. 198–241
The Domestication of the Savage Mind (Cambridge, 1977)
'Against Ritual' in *Secular Ritual*, ed., S. F. Moore and B. G. Meyerhoff (Assen and Amsterdam, 1977), pp. 25–35

Gray, R. Q. *The Labour Aristocracy in Victorian Edinburgh* (Oxford, 1976)

Grayson, C., *A Renaissance Controversy, Latin or Italian?* (Oxford, 1960)

Greenblatt S. J., *Renaissance Self-Fashioning from More to Shakespeare* (Chicago and London, 1980)

Grendi, E., 'Profilo storico degli alberghi genovesi', *Mélanges de l'école française de Rome* 87 (1975), 241–302
'Pauperismo e Albergo dei Poveri nella Genova del '600', *Rivista storica italiana* 87 (1975), 621–56

Grendler, P., *The Roman Inquisition and the Venetian Press, 1540–1605* (Princeton, 1977)

Guglielminetti, M., *Memoria e scrittura* (Turin, 1977)

Hall, E. T., *The Silent Language* (New York, 1959)

Hall, R. A., *La questione della lingua* (New York, 1942)

Halliday, M. A. K., 'Antilanguages' (1976), repr. in his *Language as Social Semiotic* (London, 1978), ch. 9

Hallowell, A. I., 'The Role of Dreams in Ojibwa Culture' in *The Dream and Human Societies* (Berkeley, 1966)

Hannerz, U., *Exploring the City* (New York, 1980)

Hartog, F., *Le miroir d'Hérodote: essai sur la représentation de l'autre* (Paris, 1980)

Haskell, F., *Patrons and Painters* (London, 1963)

Haueter, A., *Die Krönungen der französischen Könige im Zeitalter des Absolutismus und in den Restauration* (Zürich, 1975)

Hay, D., *The Church in Italy in the Fifteenth Century* (Cambridge, 1977)

Heers, J., *Family Clans in the Middle Ages* (1974; English trans., Amsterdam, 1977)

Heinz, G., 'Realismus und Rhetorik im Werke des Bartolomeo Pasarotti', *Jahrbuch Kunsthistorisches Sammlung in Wien* 68 (1972), 153–69

Herlihy D., and Klapisch-Zuber, C., *Les toscans et leurs familles* (Paris, 1978)

Hervey, M. F. S., *Thomas Howard Earl of Arundel* (Cambridge, 1921)

Hill, G. F., 'Italian Portraiture of the Fifteenth Century', *Proceedings of the British Academy* (1925)

Hinrichs, C., *Preussentum und Pietismus* (Göttingen, 1971)

Hirst, M., *Sebastiano del Piombo* (London, 1981)

Hobsbawm E., and Ranger, T., eds., *The Invention of Tradition* (Cambridge, 1983)

Hofmann, R., *Die heroische Tugend* (Munich, 1933)

Hoggart, R., *The Uses of Literacy* (London, 1957)

Hope, C., *Titian* (London, 1980)

Howard, D., *Jacopo Sansovino* (New Haven and London, 1975)

Hyde, J. K., 'Some Uses of Literacy in Venice and Florence in the Thirteenth and Fourteenth Centuries', *Transactions of the Royal Historical Society* 29 (1979), 255–75

Hymes, D., 'Toward Ethnographies of Communication' (1964), repr. in *Language and Social Context*, ed. P. P. Giglioli (Harmondsworth, 1972), ch. 1

Illich, I., *Limits to Medicine* (London, 1976)

Ingram, M., 'Ridings, Rough Music and Mocking Rhymes in Early Modern England' in *Popular Culture in Seventeenth-Century England*, ed. B. Reay (London, 1985), ch. 5

Irvine, J. T., 'Strategies of Status Manipulation in the Wolof Greeting', in *Explorations in the Ethnography of Speaking*, ed. R. Bauman and J. Sherzer (Cambridge, 1974), pp. 167–89

Isaac, R., 'A Discourse on the Method', in his *Transformation of Virginia, 1740–1790* (Williamsburg, 1982)

Jackson, R. A., *Vive le roi!* (Chapel Hill and London, 1984)

Jakobson, R., 'Two Aspects of Language', repr. in his *Selected Writings*, 2 (The Hague and Paris, 1971), 239–59

Johansson, E., 'Literacy Studies in Sweden' (1973), repr. in *Literacy and Development in the West*, ed. H. Graff (Cambridge, 1981), ch. 8

Join-Lambert, M., 'La pratique religieuse dans le diocèse de Rouen sous Louis XIV' in *Annales de Normandie* 3 (1953), 247–54

Julia, D., 'La réforme post-tridentine en France', in *La società religiosa* (Naples, 1973), pp. 311–97

Jung-Inglessis E. M., 'La porta santa', *Studi Romani* 23 (1975), 473–85

Kantorowicz, E. H., *The King's Two Bodies* (Princeton, 1957)

Kapferer, B., 'Introduction', to *Transaction and Meaning*, ed. Kapferer (Philadelphia, 1976)

A Celebration of Demons (Bloomington, 1983)

Kemp, E., *Canonisation and Authority in the Western Church* (Oxford, 1948)

Klaniczay, G., 'Le culte des saints dans la Hongri médiévale', *Acta Historica* 29 (1983), 57–77

Klapisch-Zuber, C., 'Le chiavi fiorentine di Barbablu', *Quaderni Storici* 57 (1984), 765–92

'Compérage et clientélisme à Florence (1360–1520)', *Ricerche storiche* 15 (1985), 61–76

Women, Family and Ritual in Renaissance Italy (Chicago, 1985)

von Kraemer, E., *Le type du faux mendiant dans les littératures romanes* (Helsinki, 1944)

Kretschmayr, H., *Geschichte von Venedig*, 1 (Gotha, 1905)

La Barre, W., *They Shall Take Up Serpents* (Minneapolis, 1962)

Labov, W., 'Rules for Ritual Insults', in *Studies in Social Interaction*, ed. D. Sudnow (New York, 1972), pp. 120–68

Labrot, G., 'Le comportement collectif de l'aristocratie napolitaine du 16e au 18e siècle', *Revue Historique* 523 (1977), 45–71

Un instrument polémique: l'image de Rome au temps du schisme: 1534–1667 (Lille and Paris, 1978)

Baroni in città Naples, 1979)

Lane, C., *The Rites of Rulers* (Cambridge, 1981)

Larner, J., *Italy in the Age of Dante and Petrarch* (London, 1980)

Leach, E., 'Anthropological Aspects of Language: Animal Categories and Verbal Abuse' (1964), repr. in *Mythology*, ed. P. Maranda (Harmondsworth, 1972), ch 3

'Ritual' in *International Encyclopaedia of the Social Sciences*, ed. D. Sills (New York, 1968)

Culture and Communication (Cambridge, 1976)

Le Bras, G. *Etudes de sociologie religieuse* (2 vols., Paris 1955–6)

Lerner, D., *The Passing of Traditional Society* (Glencoe, 1958)

Le Roy Ladurie, E., *Montaillou* (1975; English trans., London, 1978)
Carnival (1979; English trans., London 1980)
Levi, G., *L'eredità immateriale* (Turin, 1985)
Levi Pisetzky, *Storia del costume in Italia* 3 (Milan, 1966)
Lévi-Strauss, C., 'Symbolic Efficacity' (1949), repr. in his *Structural Anthropology* (New York, 1963), ch. 10
'The Structural Study of Myth' (1955), repr. in his *Structural Anthropology* (New York, 1963), ch. 11
'The Story of Asdiwal' (1958), in *The Structural Study of Myth and Totemism*, ed. E. Leach (London, 1967), pp. 1–40
Löfgren, O., 'On the Anatomy of Culture', *Ethnologia Europea* 12 (1981), 26–46
Logan, O., *Culture and Society in Renaissance Venice* (London, 1972)
Lotz, W., 'Gli 883 cochi di Roma del 1594', *Studi offerti a Giovanni Incisa della Rocchetta* (Rome, 1973), pp. 247–66
Lovejoy A. and Boas, G., *Primitivism and Related Ideas in Antiquity* (Baltimore, 1935)
Lovett, A., *Philip II and Mateo Vázquez* (Geneva, 1977)
Löw, G., 'Canonizazzione' in *Enciclopedia Cattolica* (12 vols., Rome 1948–54)
Luzio, A., *I precettori d'Isabella d'Este* (Acona, 1887)
Lynch, J. B., 'Lomazzo and the Accademia della Valle di Bregno', *Art Bulletin* 48 (1966), 210–11
McArdle, F., *Altopascio: a Study in Tuscan Rural Society, 1587–1784* (Cambridge, 1978)
McCannell, *The Tourist* (London, 1976)
McIntosh, M., 'Changes in the Organisation of Thieving', in *Images of Deviance*, ed. S. Cohen (Harmondsworth, 1971), pp. 98–131
Mączak, A., *Zycie codzienne w podrozach* (Warsaw, 1978)
Magnuson, T., *Studies in Roman Quattrocento Architecture* (Stockholm, 1958)
Rome in the Age of Bernini (Stockholm, 1982)
Malanima, P., *I Riccardi di Firenze* (Florence, 1977)
Mâle, E., *L'art religieux après le Concile de Trente* (2nd edn, Paris 1951)
Mallett, M. E., and Hale, J. R., *The Military Organisation of a Renaissance State* (Cambridge, 1984)
Marcilhacy, C., *Le diocèse d'Orléans au milieu du 19e siècle* (Paris, 1964)
Marsh, P., *The Rules of Disorder* (London, 1978)
Martin, J. R., *The Ceiling Paintings for the Jesuit Church in Antwerp* (London and New York, 1968)
Maschreck, C. L., *Melanchthon: the Quiet Reformer* (New York and Nashville, 1958)
Masetto Zannini, G. L., *L'educazione femminile* (1980)
Mauss, M., *The Gift* (1923–4: English trans., London, 1954)
Mecklin, J., *The Passing of the Saint* (Chicago, 1941)

Melis, F., *Aspetti della vita economica medievale* (Siena, 1962)

Meller, P., 'Physiognomical Theory in Renaissance Heroic Portraits', in *Renaissance and Mannerism*, ed. I. M. Rubin (New York, 1963), 53–69

Merzario, R., *Il paese stretto: strategie matrimoniali nella diocesi di Como, secoli xvi–xviii* (Turin, 1981)

Métraux, A., *Voodoo in Haiti* (1958; English trans., London, 1959)

Migliorini, B., *Storia della lingua italiana* (Milan, 1960)

Millunzi, G., 'Un processo di stregoneria nel 1627', *Archivio storico siciliano* 25 (1900), 253–377

Mirollo, J. V., *Mannerism and Renaissance Poetry* (New Haven, 1984)

Mitchell, B., *Rome in the High Renaissance* (Norman, 1973)

Molmenti, P., *Storia di Venezia nella vita privata* (3 vols. Venice 1906–8)

Moravia, S., *La scienza dell'uomo nel '700* (Bari, 1970)

Morris, D., *Gestures* (London, 1979)

Mousnier, R., *Peasant Uprisings* (1967; English trans., London 1973)

Muir, E., *Civic Ritual in Renaissance Venice* (Princeton, 1981)

  'The Cannibals of Renaissance Italy', *Syraacuse Scholar* 5 (1984), 5–14

Murray, A., *Reason and Society in the Middle Ages* (Oxford, 1978)

Musi, A., *Finanze e politica nella Napoli del '600* (Naples, 1976)

Naso, I., *Medici e strutture sanitarie nella società tardo-medievale* (Milan, 1982)

Nicolet, C., *Le métier du citoyen* (Paris, 1976)

Niero, A., 'I santi padroni', in *Culto dei santi a Venezia*, ed. S. Tramontin (Venice, 1965), pp. 77–95

Novelli, L., and Masaccesi, M., *Ex voto del santuario della Maddona del Monte di Cesena* (Forli, 1961)

Oakley, F., 'Jacobean Political Theology', *Journal of the History of Ideas* 29 (1968), 323–46

Ohnuki-Tierney, E., *Illness and Culture in Contemporary Japan* (Cambridge, 1984)

O'Malley, J., *Praise and Blame in Renaissance Rome* (Durham. N.C., 1979)

O'Neil, M., Ecclesiastical and Superstitious Remedies in Sixteenth-Century Italy' in *Understanding Popular Culture*, ed. S. Kaplan (Berlin, 1984), ch. 4

Orbaan, J. F., *Sistine Rome* (Rome, 1910)

Orgel, S., *The Illusion of Power: Political Theatre in the English Renaissance* (Berkeley and Los Angeles, 1975)

Origo, I., *The Merchant of Prato* (1957): Harmondsworth, 1963)

Ormond, R., *Sargent* (London, 1970)

Ortalli, G., *La pittura infamante nei secoli xiii–xvi* (Rome, 1979)

Ortner, S. B., and Whitehead, H., eds., *Sexual Meanings: the Cultural Construction of Gender and Sexuality* (Cambridge, 1981)

Ozouf, M., *La fête révolutionnaire, 1789–99* (Paris, 1976)

Park, K., *Doctors and Medicine in Early Renaissance Florence* (Princeton, 1985)

Park, R. E., 'The City' (1916), repr. in his *Human Communities* (Glencoe, 1952) pp. 13–51

Parkin, F., *Class Inequality and Political Order* (London, 1971)

Partridge, L., and Starn, R., *A Renaissance Likeness: Art and Culture in Raphael's Julius II* (Berkeley 1980)

von Pastor, L., *History of the Popes* (1886; English trans., 6th edn. 40 vols., London 1938–53)

Payne, J. B., *Erasmus: his Theology of the Sacraments* (Richmond, Va, 1970)

Payne, S. L., *The Art of Asking Questions* (Princeton, 1951)

Pecchiai, P., 'Il secolo xvi, in *Riti, cermonie, feste e vita di popolo nella Roma dei papi* (ed. L. Fiorani et al., Bologna, 1970), pp. 123–73

Pérouas, L., *Le diocèse de La Rochelle de 1648 à 1724* (Paris, 1964)

Pesce, L., *Ludovico Barbo vescovo di Treviso* (2 vols., Padua 1969)

Pesciatini, D., 'Maestri, medici, cerusici nella communità rurali pisani' in *Scienze, credenze occulte, livelli di cultura*, ed. P. Zambelli (Florence, 1982)

Petraccone, C., *Napoli dal '500 al '800* (Naples, 1974)

Petrucci, A., 'La scrittura tra ideologia e rappresentazione' *Storia dell'arte italiana* 9 (Turin, 1980), 5–123

Scrittura e popolo nella Roma barocca (Rome, 1982)

Petrucci, A., ed., *Alfabetismo e cultura scritta* (special issue, *Quaderni storici*, 1978)

Pieraccini, G., *La stirpe dei Medici* (Florence, 1924)

Pillorget, R., *Les mouvements insurrectionnels de Provence* (Paris, 1975)

Pitrè, G., *La medicina popolare siciliana* (Palermo, 1986)

Pitt-Rivers, J., *The People of the Sierra* (London, 1954)

Polhemus, T., ed., *Social Aspects of the Human Body* (Harmondsworth, 1978)

Polišenský, U. V., *The Thirty Years' War* (English trans., London, 1971)

Politi, G., *Aristocrazia e potere politico nella Cremona di Filippo II* (Milan, 1976)

Pope-Hennessy, J., *The Portrait in the Renaissance* (Princeton, 1966)

Porter, H. C., *Reformation and Reaction in Tudor Cambridge* (Cambridge, 1958)

Portoghesi, P., *Roma barocca* (Rome, 1966)

Price, S., *Rituals and Power* (Cambridge, 1984)

Prinzivalli, V., *Gli anni santi* (Rome, 1899)

Prodi, P., *Il Cardinale Gabriele Paleotti*, vol. 2 (Bologna, 1967)

Il sovrano pontefice (Bologna, 1982)

Prosperi, A., *Tra evangelismo e Controriforma: G. M. Giberti* (Rome, 1969)

'Intellettuali e chiesa all'inizio dell'età moderna', *Storia d'Italia, Annali* 4 (1981), 161–252

Pullan, B., 'The Famine in Venice and the New Poor Law', *Studi Veneziani* 5–6 (1963–4), 141–94

Rich and Poor in Renaissance Venice (Oxford, 1971)

Quaife, G. R., *Wanton Wenches and Wayward Wives* (London, 1979)

Queller, D. E., *The Office of the Ambassador in the Middle Ages* (Princeton, 1967)

Rapp, R., *Industry and Economic Decline in Seventeenth-Century Venice* (Cambridge, Mass., 1976)

Raven, C. E., *John Ray* (Cambridge, 1942)

Reddy, W. M., 'The Textile Trade and the Language of the Crowd at Rouen, 1752–1871', *Past and Present* 74 (1977), 62–89

Renier, G. J., *The English: Are They Human?* (London, 1931)

Richlin, A., *The Garden of Priapus* (Cambridge, Mass., 1983)

Riederer-Grohs, *Florentinischen Feste des Spätbarock* (Munich, 1973)

Riesman, D., *The Lonely Crowd* (New York, 1950)

Rietbergen, P. J. A. N., *Pausen, Prelaten, Bureaucraten* (thesis, Nijmegen, 1983)

Romano, R., *Napoli dal Viceregno al Regno* (Turin, 1976)

de Roover, R., *The Rise and Decline of the Medici Bank* (2nd edn, New York, 1966)

Roscoe, W., *Lorenzo de'Medici called the Magnificent* (London, 1796)

Ross, A. S. C., 'Linguistic Class-Indicators in Prsent-Day English', *Neuphilologische Mitteilungen* 55(1954), 20–56

Rossi, A., *Le feste dei poveri* (Bari, 1969)

Rotondò, A., 'La censura ecclesiastica e la cultura', *Storia d'Italia* 5 (Turin, 1973), 1397–1492

Rotunda, D. P., *Motif-Index of the Italian Novella* (Bloomington, 1942)

Rowell, G., *The Liturgy of Christian Burial* (London, 1977)

Rubinstein, N., *The Government of Florence under the Medici* (Oxford, 1966)

Rudé, G., *The Crowd in the French Revolution* (Oxford, 1959)
 Hanoverian London (London, 1971)

Ruggiero, G., *Violence in Early Renaissance Venice* (New Brunswick, 1980)

Ruskin, J., *The Stones of Venice* (1851–3; 3 vols., London, 1886)

Sadoul, G., *Callot miroir de son temps* (Paris, 1969)

Sallmann, J. M., 'Il santo e le rappresentazioni di santità', *Quaderni Storici* 41 (1979), 584–602
 'Image et fonction du saint dans la région de Naples', *Mélanges de l'Ecole française de Rome* 91 (1979), 827–73
 'Il santo patrono cittadino nel '600', *Per la storia sociale e religiosa del Mezzogiorno*, ed. G. Galasso and C. Russo, 2 (Naples, 1982), 187–208
 'La sainteté mystique féminine à Naples au tournant des 16e et 17e siècles' in *Culto dei santi*, ed. S. Boesch Gajano and L. Sebastiani (Rome, 1984), pp. 683–701

Salmond, A., 'Rituals of Encounter among the Maori, in *Explorations in the Ethnography of Speaking*, ed. R. Bauman and J. Sherzer (Cambridge, 1974), pp. 192–212

Saxl, F., 'The Battle Scene without a Hero: Aniello Falcone and his Patrons', *Journal of the Warburg Institute* 3 (1939–40), 70–87

Schipa, M. A., 'La mente di Masaniello', *Archivio storico per le provincie napoletane* 9 (1913)

'La così detta rivoluzione di Masaniello', *Archivio storico per le provincie napoletane, new ser.*, 2–3 (1916–17)

Schofield, R. S., 'The Measurement of Literacy in Preindustrial England' in *Literacy in Traditional Societies*, ed. J. Goody (Cambridge, 1968), pp. 311–25

Schudt, L., *Italienreisen im 17. und 18. Jahrhundert* (Vienna and Munich, 1959)

Schulenburg, J. T., 'Sexism and the Celestial Gynaeceum', *Journal of Medieval History* 4 (1978), 117–33

Schutte, A. J., 'Printing, Piety and the People in Italy', *Archiv für reformationsgeschichte* 71 (1980), 5–19

Schwager, K., 'Kardinal Pietro Aldobrandinis villa', *Römisches Jahrbuch für Kunstgeschichte* 9–10 (1961–2)

Scribner S., and Cole, M., 'Unpackaging Literacy' in *Variation in Writing*, ed. M. F. Whiteman (Hillsdale, 1981), pp. 71–87

Segre, C., 'Edonismo linguistica nel '500' (1953), repr. in his *Lingua, stile e società* (Milan, 1963), pp. 355–82

Seneca, F., *Il doge Leonardo Donà* (Padua, 1959)

Sennett, R., *The Fall of Public Man* (Cambridge, 1977)

de'Seta, C., *Storia della città di Napoli* (Bari, 1973)

Sharpe, J. A., *Defamation and Sexual Slander in Early Modern England* (York, 1980)

Shearman, J., *Mannerism* (Harmondsworth, 1967)

Shennan, J. H., 'Louis XV: Public and Private Worlds' in *The Courts of Europe*, ed. A. G. Dickens (London, 1977)

Shils, E., 'Ritual and Crisis' in his *Center and Periphery* (Chicago and London, 1975), pp. 153–63

Sider, R. J., *Andreas Bodenstein von Karlstadt* (Leiden, 1974)

Silenzi, R., and Silenzi, F., eds., *Pasquino* (Milan, 1932)

Simeoni, L., 'Una vendetta signorile nel '400 e il pittore Franceso Benaglio', *Nuovo Archivio Veneto* 5 (1903), 252–8

Sorokin, P. A., *Altruistic Love* (Boston, 1950)

Spencer, H. *The Principles of Sociology* (4 vols., London, 1876–85)

Stone, L., *The Crisis of the Aristocracy, 1558–1641* (Oxford, 1965)

Stoye, J., *The English Traveller Abroad* (London, 1952)

Street, B. V., *Literacy in Theory and Practice* (Cambridge, 1984)

Summers, D., *Michelangelo and the Language of Art* (Princeton, 1981)

Szwed, J., 'The Ethnography of Literacy' in *Variation in Writing*, ed. M. F. Whiteman (Hillsdale, 1981), pp. 13–23

Tapié, V. L., *The Age of Grandeur* (1957; English trans., London, 1960)

Tas, E., *De vrouw in het economisch leven van Amsterdam tot 1700* (thesis, Amsterdam 1938)

Tazbir, J., 'Die gesellschaftlichen Funktionen des Kultus des heiligen Isidor des Pflügen in Polen', *Acta Poloniae Historica* 10 (1969), 120–37

Thomas, K. V., *Religion and the Decline of Magic* (London, 1971)
'The Place of Laughter in Tudor and Stuart England', *Times Literary Supplement*, 21 January 1977

Thompson, E. P., 'The Moral Economy of the English Crowd in the Eighteenth Century', *Past and Present* 50 (1971), 76–136
'Class Struggle without Class', *Journal of Social History*, 1978

Thompson, S., *Motif-Index of Folk Literature* (revised edn, 6 vols., Copenhagen, 1955–8)

Thurston, H., *The Holy Year of Jubilee* (St Louis, 1900)

Tilly, C., 'The Chaos of the Living City' in *An Urban World*, ed. C. Tilly (Boston, 1974)

Titone, V., *La società italiana sotto gli spagnuoli* (Palermo, 1978)

Toynbee, M. R., *St Louis of Toulouse and the Process of Canonisation* (London, 1929)

Trexler, R., *Public Life in Renaissance Florence* (New York, 1980)
'Correre la terra: collective insults in the late Middle Ages', *Mélanges de l'école française de Rome* 96 (1984), 845–902

Trilling, L., *Sincerity and Authenticity* (London, 1972)

Turi, V., *Viva Maria: la reazione alle reforme leopoldine, 1790–99* (Florence, 1969)

Turner, V., *Dramas Fields and Metaphors* (Ithaca, 1974)
The Drums of Affliction (Oxford, 1968)
The Forest of Symbols (Ithaca, 1967)
The Ritual Process (London, 1969)
Schism and Continuity in an African Society (Manchester, 1957)

Turner V., and Turner, E., *Image and Pilgrimage in Christian Culture* (Oxford, 1978)

Ullmann, W., *The Growth of Papal Government* (Cambridge, 1955)

Underdown, D., 'The Taming of the Scold' in *Order and Disorder in Early Modern England*, ed. A. Fletcher and J. Stevenson (Cambridge, 1985), ch. 4

Vauchez, A., *La sainteté en occident aux derniers siècles du moyen âge* (Rome, 1981)

Veblen, T., *Theory of the Leisure Class* (New York 1899)

Venturi, F., 'L' Italia fuori d'Italia', *Storia d'Italia* 3 1973), 987–1482

Veyne, P., 'L'obscénité et le "folklore" chez les romains', *l'Histoire* 46 (1982)

Vianello, N., 'Il veneziano, lingua del foro veneto', *Lingua Nostra* 18 (1957), 67–73

Villari, R., *La rivolta antispagnuola a Napoli* (Bari, 1967)
'Masaniello: Contemporary and Recent Interpretations', *Past and Present* 103 (1985)

Vitale, M., *La questione della lingua* (Milan, 1960)

Waley, A., *Three Ways of Thought in Ancient China* (London, 1939)

Warburg, A., 'Sandro Botticellis "Geburt der Venus" und "Frühling"' (1893, repr. in his *Gesammelte Schriften* (2 vols., Leipzig and Berlin,1932)

Weinstein D., and Bell, R. F., *Saints and Society* (Chicago, 1982)

Weise, G., *L'ideale eroico del Rinascimento* (Naples, 1961)

Weissman, R. F. E., *Ritual Brotherhood in Renaissance Florence* (New York, 1982)

Welch, H., *Taoism* (Boston, 1957)

West, M., *Children of the Sun* (London, 1957)

Whinnom, K., 'Lingua Franca: Historical Problems' in *Pidgin and Creole Linguistics*, ed. A. Valdman (Bloomington-London, 1977), pp. 295–310

Wiel, T., *I teatri musicali veneziani del '700* (Venice, 1897)

Wilks, M., *The Problem of Sovereignty in the Later Middle Ages* (Cambridge, 1963)

Williams, R., *The Country and the City* (London, 1973)

Wilson, S. ed., *Saints and Their Cults* (Cambridge, 1983)

Wirth, K. A., 'Imperator pedes papae deosculatur', *Festschrift H. Keller* (1963)

Wittkower, R., *Art and Architecture in Italy 1600–1750* (1958; 3rd edn, Harmondsworth, 1975)

Wood, M. W., 'Paltry Peddlars or Essential Merchants?', *Sixteenth-Century Journal* 12 (1981), 3–13

Wormald, P., 'The Uses of Literacy in Anglo-Saxon England', *Transactions of the Royal Historical Society* 27 (1977), 95–114

Worsthorne, S. T., *Venetian Opera in the Seventeenth Century* (Oxford, 1954)

Yinger, J. M., 'Contraculture and Subculture', *American Sociological Review* 1960), 625–35

Young, J., 'The Role of the Police as Amplifiers of Deviancy, Negotiators of Reality and Translators of Fantasy' in *Images of Deviance*, ed. S. Cohen (Harmondsworth, 1971), pp. 27–61

Zimmermann, T. C. P., 'Confession and Autobiography in the Renaissance', in *Renaissance Studies in Honor of Hans Baron*, ed. A. Molho and J. Tedeschi (Dekalb, 1971), pp. 121–40

Index

abacus schools, 114, 128
academic rituals, 232-3
accountants, 128
Addison, Joseph, traveller and journalist, 12,
    16, 17, 59, 102, 223
adiaphora, 225, 227
Aldobrandini, cardinal Pietro, 136
Alemán, Mateo, Spanish writer, 66-7, 70
Alexander VII, pope, 58, 136, 139, 176,
    179-80
Alexander VIII, pope, 58
ambassadors, rituals of receiving, 12, 171
amulets, 121-2
Anabaptists, 46, 230
Andrea, Francesco d', Neapolitan lawyer, 10,
    13, 134
animals, 32, 96-7, 158, 163, 184, 188-90
Anthony of Padua, St, 53, 199
Antony Abbot, St, 209
Anzani, Giovanni Angelo, bishop of Campagna
    and Satriano, 44, 47
archives, 113, 125, 127
Arcos, Duke of, Viceroy of Naples, 196
Aretino, Pietro, Italian writer, 93, 158, 165
Aristotle, Greek philosopher, 50, 134, 219
Auerbach, Erich, Germany literary critic, 193
Augustine, St, 226, 228

Bakhtin, Mikhail, Russian critic, 193, 201
Bali, 174
Bandello, Matteo, Lombard writer, 81
Barbaro, Daniele, Venetian patrician, 161
Barbo, Ludovico, bishop of Treviso, 42
Baretti, Giuseppe, Piedmontese man of letters,
    16, 87, 107
Bataille, Georges, French writer, 133
beards, 154-5
beggars, 34f, 63f
Bellarmine, Robert, Jesuit, 58, 187
Bellini, Giovanni, Venetian painter, 100, 153
Bembo, Pietro, cardinal, Venetian critic, 86,
    89, 155, 157
benandanti, 213
Benedict XIII, pope, 44, 58, 237
Benedict XIV, pope, 50, 58, 237
Benno, St, 49

Berkeley, George, Irish philosopher and
    traveller, 17, 215
Bernardino of Siena, St, 79
Bernini, Gian Lorenzo, Roman sculptor and
    architect, 139, 144, 180
Biagio [Blaise], Saint, 209
blasphemy, 45, 100f
Boas, Franz, German-American
    anthropologist, 132
Boccaccio, Giovanni, Tuscan writer, 89
Boccalini, Traiano, Italian satirist, 91, 127
Bollani, Domenico, bishop of Brescia, 42
bollettini, 126
books in portraits, 161
Borromeo' San Carlo, archbishop of Milan, 43,
    50-1, 55, 58-9, 123, 134, 141, 155, 187, 268
Botero, Giovanni, Italian political theorist, 135
Bourdieu, Pierre, French social theorist, 4,
    133
Braudel, Fernand, French historian, 145
bread, symbolism of, 198
Bronzino, Angelo, Italian painter, 153-4, 161,
    163
Bucer, Martin, German reformer, 226, 228
Burchardus, Johannes, papal master of
    ceremonies, 177f
Burckhardt, Jacob, Swiss historian, 19, 119
bureaucracy, 50, 124, 168
Burnet, Gilbert, Scottish traveller and bishop,
    16-17, 59, 138, 143, 189, 224
business, literacy in, 114

calligraphy, 128
Callot, Jacques, of Lorraine, artist, 66, 70
Calvin, Jean, French reformer, 228
Campanella, Tommaso, Italian philosopher,
    31, 146, 195
Canisius, Peter, St, 52
Caravaggio, Lombard artist, 66, 69, 107, 163
Cardano, Girolamo, physician and
    autobiographer, 19-20
Carmelites, 54, 199
Carnival, 181, 183-90
cartelli, 95, 196
Casa, Giovanni della, writer on manners, 21,
    80, 88, 233-4

21 3/2000

φ SINCE